GLOBAL OLYMPICS

HISTORICAL AND SOCIOLOGICAL STUDIES OF THE MODERN GAMES

RESEARCH IN THE SOCIOLOGY OF SPORT

Series Editor: Kevin Young

RESEARCH IN THE SOCIOLOGY OF SPORT   VOLUME 3

GLOBAL OLYMPICS

HISTORICAL AND SOCIOLOGICAL STUDIES OF THE MODERN GAMES

EDITED BY

KEVIN YOUNG

Department of Sociology, University of Calgary, Alberta, Canada

KEVIN B. WAMSLEY

School of Kinesiology, The University of Western Ontario, Ontario, Canada

ELSEVIER
JAI

Amsterdam – Boston – Heidelberg – London – New York – Oxford
Paris – San Diego – San Francisco – Singapore – Sydney – Tokyo

ELSEVIER B.V.
Radarweg 29
P.O. Box 211
1000 AE Amsterdam,
The Netherlands

ELSEVIER Inc.
525 B Street, Suite 1900
San Diego
CA 92101-4495
USA

ELSEVIER Ltd
The Boulevard, Langford
Lane, Kidlington
Oxford OX5 1GB
UK

ELSEVIER Ltd
84 Theobalds Road
London
WC1X 8RR
UK

First edition 2005

British Library Cataloguing in Publication Data
A catalogue record is available from the British Library.

ISBN-10: 0-7623-1181-9
ISBN-13: 978-0-7623-1181-1
ISSN: 1476-2854 (Series)

∞ The paper used in this publication meets the requirements of ANSI/NISO Z39.48-1992 (Permanence of Paper).
Printed in The Netherlands.

CONTENTS

PART II
THE OLYMPIC GAMES: CONTEMPORARY
ISSUES AND CONTROVERSIES

LIST OF CONTRIBUTORS

Michael Atkinson	Department of Sociology, McMaster University, Ontario, Canada
Douglas Booth	School of Education, University of Waikato, Hamilton, New Zealand
Douglas A. Brown	Faculty of Kinesiology, University of Calgary, Calgary, Alberta, Canada
Hart Cantelon	Department of Kinesiology and Physical Education, The University of Lethbridge, Alberta, Canada
Mark Dyreson	Departments of Kinesiology and History, Pennsylvania State University, PA, USA
Janice Forsyth	Faculty of Physical Education and Recreation Studies, The University of Manitoba, Winnipeg, Manitoba, Canada
John Hoberman	Department of Germanic Studies, The University of Texas at Austin, TX, USA
Barrie Houlihan	Institute of Sport and Leisure Policy, School of Sport and Exercise Sciences, Loughborough University, Leicestershire, UK
Bruce Kidd	Faculty of Physical Education and Health, University of Toronto, Ontario, Canada
Arnd Krüger	Institut für Sportwissenschaften, Georg-August-Universität Göttingen, Göttingen, Germany
Gertrud Pfister	University of Copenhagen, Denmark
Alan Tomlinson	Sport and Leisure Cultures, Chelsea School, University of Brighton, UK

ix

Cesar R. Torres   Department of Physical Education and Sport,
                         State University of New York at Brockport,
                         NY, USA

Kevin B. Wamsley   School of Kinesiology, The University of
                         Western Ontario, Ontario, Canada

Garry Whannel   Centre for International Media Analysis,
                         School of Media Art and Design, University of
                         Luton, UK

David Young   Department of Classics, University of Florida,
                         FL, USA

Kevin Young   Department of Sociology, University of
                         Calgary, Alberta, Canada

ACKNOWLEDGEMENTS

Global Olympics: Historical and Sociological Studies of the Modern Games is the third volume in the '*Research in the Sociology of Sport*' book series. We are enormously grateful to the contributors for being willing to share their research on the Olympics, past and present, and for their patience while the volume was being assembled. Sincere thanks to the staff at Elsevier Press, and to Ann Corney, in particular, for her encouragement and expert guidance throughout.

Introduction

COUBERTIN'S OLYMPIC GAMES: THE GREATEST SHOW ON EARTH

Kevin B. Wamsley and Kevin Young

Judged in terms of global participation, world media coverage, the construction and cost of elaborate facilities, billions of dollars in expenditures, environmental and community disruption, crises, scandals and political intrigue of various sorts, massive popular consumption, and the threat of terrorism, the Olympic Games may well be the most consistently compelling cultural phenomenon of modern times. Against a backdrop of nineteenth century industrialising nation-states engaged in assorted international cultural competitions, followed by twentieth century World Wars, the Cold War, numerous revolutions and, later, the expansive globalising of economies, the Games (both Winter and Summer) undulated through most of the twentieth century every four years, now alternating every two years. For spectators, politicians, patriots, corporations, and opportunists of all sorts, the Olympic Games became a focal point and where political, economic, and cultural interests intersected, where the hopes and accomplishments of modern sport were juxtaposed against the often imperialist, racist, and gendered imperatives of certain nations and international organisations. By the middle of the twentieth century, the International Olympic Committee (IOC) was, unequivocally, the most powerful sport organisation in the world, wielding influence on how people in more than 100 countries understood, organised, and played sport at a number of different levels (Wamsley, 2002).

Millions of dollars are spent by cities that bid for the rights to host a Summer or Winter Olympic Games and, quite literally, billions more are spent to host the festival itself. There are more than 200 countries that have National Olympic Committees, and the Olympic emblem of five interlocking rings may be the most recognised symbol in the world, along with other seemingly ubiquitous symbols such as that of the Red Cross, the United Nations, and corporate logos like the 'golden arches' of McDonald's or the

Nike 'swoosh' (Barney, Wenn, & Martyn, 2002). Successful participation at the Games has come to be viewed as so important that national governments have formed domestic and international policies around matters relating to the Olympics, establishing comprehensive sport programmes to improve the performances of teams and competing individuals. In addition to the contemporary significance of bidding for and hosting the Games, Olympic medals are widely coveted by nations and athletes for their symbolic and economic implications; so much so that athletes are willing to risk their reputations, their health, even their lives, to win. Concomitantly, nations have invested millions into performance-enhancement laboratories and child talent identification programmes, many of which, far from being viewed as ethical or humane, have elicited strong criticism for dubious motives and sometimes harmful practices (Hoberman, 1992; Ryan, 1995; Donnelly, 1997).

How did this once innocuous sporting competition attain a status of such magnitude and cultural significance? Many such socially pertinent questions animate the modern Olympic Games. Why do athletes take drugs?; why do corporations invest millions of dollars to become exclusive Olympic sponsors?; why are men and women treated differently in Olympic sport and the spin-off sport cultures it spawns?; why is the IOC plagued by scandal and corruption? The answers to these and similar questions rest in a long and often tawdry history that effectively emerged during the nineteenth century, leading to a popularly supported Olympic Games, where nations sought to position themselves among others economically, politically, and militarily throughout the twentieth, now into the twenty-first, century. Such questions and answers are addressed in depth in this volume.

Popular accounts typically credit the efforts of French aristocrat Baron Pierre de Coubertin in the modern 'rebirth' of the Olympics, and also typically invoke links to the religious 'Olympic' festivals of ancient Greece (Young, 1987). Once the Games established some measure of success in the modern era, de Coubertin himself took the bulk of the credit for their (re)introduction, even though he is known to have borrowed ideas from the work of others, capitalised on their organisational and fund-raising efforts, and ridden a growing tide of cultural interest in ancient Greece and in the establishment of a modern festival (Young, 1984). It cannot be denied, however, that de Coubertin tirelessly devoted the latter stages of his life to promoting the Olympic Games, securing their stability, fending off rival sport leaders and sport festivals, and ensuring that 'his' Games would become the most significant sporting competition among the nations of the modern world (Wamsley, 2002).

On a foundation of interest in amateur sport as a character-building and socially valuable exercise for boys and men, de Coubertin brought his observations of nation-state sport programmes and nineteenth century Olympic-like festivals and World's Fairs to bear at a Congress held at the Sorbonne at the University of Paris in 1894 (MacAloon, 1981). The Congress was scheduled to deal with international understandings of amateurism, but de Coubertin manipulated the programme to bring 'his' Olympic Games ideas to the forefront. Most influential on de Coubertin's plans for staging an international sport festival were the Olympic competitions organised by William Penny Brookes in England, juxtaposed against the competitive model and tourist appeal of the already popular World's Fairs and Expositions (Young, 1984). A nostalgic connection to ancient traditions and a profound sense of ownership and local support for the nineteenth century Olympic festivals in Greece contoured de Coubertin's plans, as he convinced European delegates and members of the Greek royal family that a new, internationally-based festival served the interests of all men concerned with sport as a worthy pursuit, both athletically and socially. Since it was popularly perceived as a training ground for instilling gentrified 'manly' values and promoting military preparedness among young men, there were few aristocratic delegates in favour of sport for women at this time. As such, from their modest beginnings and throughout the twentieth century, the Olympic Games remained a critical venue for the establishment and reproduction of gender differences (Wamsley, 2004). While there are undoubtedly more flagrant versions of gendered cultures and settings in the world of sport, and despite recent changes, it is clear that the Olympics have always operated as a site of male privilege. This trend endures, as may be seen today in, for example, the disproportionate number of Olympic events open to men (Coakley & Donnelly, 2004, pp. 226–227).

Due in large part to the political maneuvering, fundraising, and organisational efforts of Crown Prince Constantine of Greece, the first Olympic Games in 1896 were declared an unambiguous success (MacAloon, 1981). Thousands of spectators in a festive and beautified Athens, brandishing a new stadium and a proud sense of tradition, celebrated the first Games with athletes from 13 countries and ushered in a new era for modern sport. Eventually, de Coubertin's Games secured the interests of amateur sport leaders in all participating nations, promoting internationally regulated sport competitions as new symbols of cultural supremacy. Against the early wishes of the Greeks, who were principally responsible for the success of the first Games, de Coubertin, according to his own reckoning, insisted initially that the Games be ambulatory, gracing the great cities of the world every four years. Barney (1992, p. 93) reports that de Coubertin saw this as "...the original trinity chosen to emphasize the world character of the institution and establish it on a firm footing". De Coubertin confirmed this sentiment in a letter to the *New York Times*, April 30, 1896 (Müller, 2000, p. 363*)*, protesting the inference that the Games might be held permanently in Greece: "Nothing could be further from the truth. The Olympic Games will move about the globe as decided at the international congress held at the Sorbonne two years ago. The 1900 Games will be in Paris. In 1904, the committee will choose between New York, Berlin, and Stockholm".

However, the practical difficulties of organising various aspects of the Olympics, and the marshalling of interest, aid, and support, led to a direct reliance on the existing infrastructures of World's Fairs, where de Coubertin's Games became embedded in Paris in 1900, St. Louis in 1904, and London in 1908. Separate sporting events for men and women, increasing participation numbers, a growing interest by the world media, and a burgeoning nationalism evident in controversies and protests during and following competitions, represented the humble beginnings of de Coubertin's early twentieth century international festival.

At the same time, it was clear from the outset that the Games carried potential to crystallise and confirm broader social and political goals for participating countries. Already powerful sporting nations such as England and the United States used the events to assert their authority over rules and regulations, as well as matters of 'appropriate' social decorum, at a time when Olympic competitions were just beginning to resonate with political, cultural, and military undertones. As such, the early Olympic Games provided significant opportunities for nations to represent themselves outwardly to international audiences, as well as domestically, in myriad state-building exercises and social schemes (Dyreson, 1998; Senn, 1999).

Marking their 10-year anniversary in 1906, the Greeks celebrated a second successful modern Olympic Games, but de Coubertin exerted his authority over the fledgling enterprise and effectively removed any Greek proprietorship of the Games by rendering them 'unofficial' and unrelated to the record books of his 'Olympics' (Lennartz, 1996). Adhering to the by-then established four-year cycle, the nationalist controversies of 1908 in London and the residual organisational difficulties of the World's Fair Games, gave way to a rather successful event in Stockholm in 1912, securing a place for Sweden's Sigfrid Edström in de Coubertin's inner-circle of leading administrators (Wamsley & Schultz, 2000). Four years later, Berlin's place as host city was denied by the conflicts of World War I; yet, the interest in maintaining the Olympic competition cycle after a devastating

War signalled a promising place in twentieth century culture for de Coubertin's festival. The Belgians, in spite of the mass destruction wreaked by the War, offered to host the 1920 Games and utilised them as a focal point for national regeneration and rebuilding, themes which were repeated following World War II. Significant in these 1920 proceedings was Count Henri Baillet-Latour, the future IOC President (Goldstein, 1996). Baillet-Latour was named IOC President to replace the eminent de Coubertin at the IOC Congress in 1925. He faced many challenges during the prewar period, including matters related to women's participation, the Depression era Games of Los Angeles, and the Nazi Olympics of 1936.

The growing symbolic significance of the Games among nations, equating athletic victory with cultural and national progress in the early twentieth century, ensured that the Olympics would remain deeply politicised. In its first overtly post-war act, the IOC declined to send invitations to the so-called 'defeated' nations of World War I. For the allied nations, the post-war popularity of competitive sport for both men and women was evident in its use for projects of community boosterism and national identity construction. For example, real estate tycoons and Hollywood movie moguls had secured the 1932 Games for Los Angeles well in advance of the event, as early as 1923. And, during the 1920s, the IOC struggled to maintain control over the word 'Olympic' and to manage both women's participation and rival sporting events such as the Workers' Olympics.[1]

In 1925, de Coubertin, a consistent opponent of women's participation in the Games, and reluctant to stage a winter sport complement to its summer competition, stepped down as IOC President. Following his retirement, the International Amateur Athletics Federation, headed by Sigfrid Edström, negotiated the inclusion of women into Olympic track and field events, and all but dissolved the Women's Olympics as a rival event (Wamsley & Schultz, 2000).[2] During its 1925 session, the IOC declared the winter sport festival in Chamonix, France, held for 11 days during January 1924, to be the first Winter Olympics. Contrary to the views of some IOC members that a Winter Games might remove some of the lustre of the 'real' (i.e., Summer) Olympics, the new event engaged more people than ever in de Coubertin's project, as well, crucially, as creating new tourism opportunities for the alpine destinations of the world as potential Olympic hosts.

As Communist detractors had observed, the de Coubertin Olympics served the interests of class-structured societies through the doctrine of 'amateurism', thereby providing opportunities for predominantly middle- and upper-class sportsmen to participate in the Games. Further, a distinct gender order had prevailed in the competitions and ceremonies of the

Olympics from the outset, reinforcing the residual notion that sport was most suitably a pursuit for men. However, intense lobbying efforts by advocates of female participation in athletics secured a place for women in new events by 1928 (Wamsley & Schultz, 2000). Male fears of the (perceived) socially disruptive potential of female participation were reinforced by widespread misinterpretations of the women's 800 m event in Amsterdam. After observing several athletes in normal but serious states of fatigue during and after the race, in the meetings that followed, some IOC members threatened to expel women from subsequent Games. Edström had recognised that, in order to manage and control women's participation, they had to be included in the Games. Sport leaders from both the United States and Britain demanded that women remain on the programme. However, this IOC compromise led to a more open channelling of women into so-called 'feminine' sports such as gymnastics and figure skating, where traditional 'womanly' traits such as grace and flexibility could be showcased and celebrated at the Olympic level. It was not until the emergence of the mighty Soviet teams of the 1950s that other nations began to include full contingents of female competitors willing to challenge traditional gender markers (regarding qualities such as physical strength and power) that had prevailed for well over a century (Wamsley, 2002).

The increasing size of the Games inevitably raised concerns about costs, particularly during the 1930s, when many nations reeled from the effects of the Great Depression. How could Los Angeles concern itself with sport, the President of the United States declared, when there were more pressing matters at hand? President Hoover, as head of state, broke the Olympic tradition by refusing to officially open the Games. "It's a crazy thing", he remarked, "and it takes some gall to expect me to be a part of it" (Barney, 1996, p. 156). A simple retort might have been that Olympic leaders had always considered the Games as existing above politics, as more of a peaceful and uplifting human enterprise than a source of conflict or negativity. This sort of thinking permitted organisers, politicians, and sport leaders the leeway to infuse the Games with symbolic meanings that supposedly transcended the everyday political and economic, even military, realities of the world.

At no time was this clearer than during Berlin's preparations for the 1936 Winter and Summer Games. Initially opposed to the Olympics as a capitalist, bourgeois initiative, Chancellor Adolf Hitler eventually embraced the Games as a potent weapon of Nazi propaganda in a fashion chillingly, but brilliantly, demonstrated in Leni Reifenstahl's film, *Olympia* (Mandell, 1971; Kruger, 1998). By this point, the world already identified de Coubertin's

Olympics as an index of modernisation and cultural supremacy; in turn, Hitler positioned the festival as a declaration of German military prowess and a manifestation of Aryan supremacy in particular. Olympic leaders such as the Belgian IOC President Baillet-Latour claimed inherent value in the Berlin Olympics, and refused to move them, while future President, Avery Brundage of the USA, worked tirelessly to ensure the participation of the powerful American team and press entourage, in spite of the well-known atrocities being committed in Germany. In brief, the Berlin Olympics clearly showed that the Games could be manipulated by political forces for political reasons. Despite every sign to the contrary, in a stunning forecast of stereotypes that would come to pervade the contemporary world of sport, and absolving themselves of all responsibility for Hitler's machinations, Olympic leaders stubbornly explained that sport and politics should not and did not mix (Guttmann, 1992).

Similarly, the political potential of the modern Olympics was not lost upon the Cold War leaders of the post-World War II era. Indeed, with the exception of the programme to explore outer space, the Games became the most important global arena for the declaration of cultural supremacy and for the explication of national political statements at this time. Nations allocated unprecedented resources towards elite level sport, as participants, organisers, and spectators identified world record-breaking performances as direct indicators of national – and, implicitly, human – progress. So it was that the Olympic Games heralded the union of science and nationhood in a cultural arena. The Cold War era, fuelling the scientisation of human performance, also ushered in new levels of systematic performance enhancement through drugs and intensive, often-abusive, training techniques. The Cold War athlete trained full-time, pushed him/herself to new extremes, and carried the weight of entire social systems on his/her shoulders, personifying the successes and failures of Capitalism and Communism (Hoberman, 1992). As post-war allies jockeyed for military advantage in satellite countries and for rich, economic resources such as oil and gas reserves, these political tensions played out through a sequence of highly Olympic publicised boycotts.

World events such as the Suez Canal Crisis, the Soviet invasion of Hungary, and the lobbying efforts of the 'two Chinas' and 'two Germanies' plagued the presidency of Avery Brundage (1952–1972), the self-proclaimed watchdog of amateurism and guardian of Olympic ideals (Guttmann, 1984). Further, the entry of Black African nations into the Olympic movement and Soviet economic interests in Africa placed increasing pressure on the IOC to deal with the issue of racist Apartheid in South Africa. With the increasing symbolic significance of the Games, in concert with emerging satellite technology and the prevalence of television as the new mode of communication during the 1960s, the commercial exploitation of athletes and Olympic symbols presented by winter sports gnawed at the recalcitrant and aging Brundage, whose turgid leadership style many felt was outdated and out of touch. A typically insulated and reactive IOC, for example, could not foresee the burgeoning costs of hosting the Games, evident in Tokyo's billion dollar expenditures in 1964 (Barney et al., 2002), as a point of crisis for impoverished nations. Hence, its decision to distance itself from the social uprising and protest against such excessive expenditures in Mexico City in 1968, resulting in a horrific massacre, was hardly surprising (Paz, 1972). Once again, how could an organisation that claimed apolitical status accept responsibility for political problems, or for complicity in, such problems, when it perceived events as being only tangentially related to the Olympic Games?

By the 1960s and 1970s, the Olympic Games had become what de Coubertin had imagined – one of the most magnificent and celebrated cultural events in the world. Yet, only after the massacre of Israeli athletes and officials in Munich in 1972 did organising committees prepare extensively for breaches of security or acts of politically motivated violence occurring at the Games. And, only after the financially disastrous 1976 Montreal Olympics did the IOC seriously consider a modification in funding strategies. The sheer magnitude of these sorts of issues – the massacres of Mexico City and Munich, Apartheid and South Africa, the two Chinas, Montreal and its massive debt, the constant battles over notions of amateurism, and the significant United States-led boycott against Moscow in 1980 – left IOC President Killanin (1972–1980) in poor health. If one concedes that the turbulent terms of Presidents Brundage and Killanin enabled the Olympic Games to barely survive, then one must comparatively assert that the presidency of their Spanish successor, Juan Antonio Samaranch, brought the festival to new heights of commercial growth, including vast riches to the once impoverished IOC, and to new depths of scandal and corruption.

In spite of the athletic compromises forced by the Soviet-led boycott of Los Angeles, the 1984 Summer Games marked a new era in the commercialisation of the Olympics and a significant expansion in the extent to which countries willing to host the Games were willing to go that de Coubertin could never have imagined. The more than US$200 million profit that organiser Peter Ueberroth accrued remains, in part, responsible, some 20 years later, for the current levels of intensity that cities apply to their elaborate and costly bidding initiatives. Over the coming years, Samaranch's administration transformed the Olympic Games into a multi-billion dollar business, profiting immensely from the ensuing competitions for television broadcast rights, particularly in the United States, and through a new worldwide, exclusive corporate sponsorship arrangement – formerly The Olympic Program, now The Olympic Partners (TOP) (Barney et al., 2002). American television rights escalated from US$25 million in 1976 for the Montreal Summer Games, to US$309 million for the 1988 Winter Games in Calgary, to $2.2 billion for the Games to be held in Vancouver in 2010 and London in 2012. From these broadcasting agreements, organising committees received appreciable funds to support the building of facilities; yet, they continued to demand additional public monies to stage the Olympics, making the venues ever more elaborate and grandiose. Nations and cities became more desperate to host the Games, claiming that Olympic communities were 'world class', modern destinations with corporate advantages available to all citizens. Initially, de Coubertin had also used this line of argument but, in the early twentieth century, he sought to principally attach the Games to cities that boasted worldly traditions and established reputations. By the 1980s, this relationship had shifted again and the Games became as much about inventing 'new' traditions as confirming established ones (Wamsley, 2004).

The symbolic importance of the Games had prevailed throughout the post-World War II and Cold War eras. When symbolic value articulated with perceived economic potential early in Samaranch's term, the *value* of the Games reached new heights. As a private organisation, the IOC determined what cities might host the Games. Thus, the IOC membership gained significant power over nationalists and civic boosters alike. As a direct consequence, some IOC members created opportunities for personal profit through the bidding process, accepting lavish gifts in the form of money, trips, health care, tuition for their children, shopping sprees, and first-class entertainment and treatment from bidding cities (Booth, 1999). Although warnings had been issued as early as 1992, the scandal over gift-giving did not break until 1998, when it was discovered that the Salt Lake City organising committee had provided millions of dollars in gifts and services to secure the Winter Games of 2002. However, more than a decade of gift giving and bribery by many bidding cities was revealed through the rather embarrassing investigations that ensued. Ultimately, in late 2003, the Salt Lake City organisers were acquitted of criminal charges, citing the gift-giving 'culture' of the IOC, but troubling questions remain over the enormous power that the IOC continues to wield and enjoy in the modern world of sport.

At the level of the athletes themselves, the mid-century, Cold War emphasis on competition and winning, later translating into opportunities for profit, ushered in an era of systematic, full-time training, supported by scientific laboratories, state-run and medically prescribed drug programmes to improve performance. Ingesting substances such as alcohol and cocaine to improve performance had been common since the first Games in 1896, but the death of Danish cyclist Knud Jensen in 1960 led to limited drug testing in 1968 (Wilson & Derse, 2001).[3] Ultimately, from a policy perspective, the IOC was more interested in preserving the illusion of fair play, and placing more emphasis on verifying that men were not masquerading as women in the Games, than on fair and accountable drug testing per se. In 1968, the IOC subjected more than 600 female athletes to what it termed 'gender verification'. For more than a decade, however, weightlifters from Eastern bloc nations and from the United States had been engaged in drug-enhancement schemes (Fair, 1999). Mismanaged, even scandalous, drug-testing programmes of the 1970s and 1980s made a mockery of the IOC's claim to ethical and transparent standards in competitive sport. The highly publicised 1988 case of Canadian sprinter Ben Johnson (whose 100 m world 'record' was found to have been enhanced by anabolic steroids) resulted in improved drug-testing standards and forced a more serious commitment of IOC resources and interest. As a corollary to this, nations embarrassed by their 'cheating' athletes have felt obliged to also significantly step up their domestic anti-doping policies and to sponsor expensive investigations, such as the Canadian Dubin Inquiry that followed Ben Johnson's fall from grace in 1988. Even to the present day, however, the IOC has not assumed any responsibility for contributing to the conditions conducive to cheating, to the disproportional iconic status of gold medal winners, or to the nationalistic and often jingoistic fervour of competing nations, athletes, and fans. If anything, the historical evidence strongly suggests that the IOC has, indeed, profited from the long-celebrated exaggeration of the value of extreme human performance that provides the Games with much of its kudos in the first place.

It is clear that the phenomenon that we call the *Olympic Games* has a long and complicated history, enmeshed in broader epochal events in global politics and global change. The following chapters, written by some of the world's leading Olympic scholars, attempt to address some of the important historical and sociological issues pertinent to the emergence of the Games, as well as concerns of the present day. The first section (Part I) is dedicated to the history and development of the Olympics, attending to some of the myths of the revival of the Games and the work of Baron Pierre de Coubertin in establishing the premiere sporting festival of the twentieth century. The role of amateurism, the organisation of gender, and relations of race are explored, in addition to the place of the Games in Cold War politics and the development of emergent nationalisms in competing countries. Among other things, contributors examine how the IOC dealt with the existence of alternative and rival games and festivals, survived Hitler's Aryan spectacle in 1936, and some of the complexities of Apartheid and the political boycotts of the twentieth century. The second section of the volume (Part II) deals explicitly with sociological issues and controversies emerging from more than 100 years of Olympic experiences. The role of television and commercialisation, and its relationship to scandal and corruption in the IOC is examined by different authors, in addition to issues of performance enhancement, security and terrorism, and the role of Aboriginal peoples in Olympic ceremonies. We hope that the historical discussions and sociological case studies offered here will provoke further critical reflection on what has been called 'the greatest show on earth', and go some way in explaining how the Olympic Games and its guardians, the IOC, have inscribed their way so indelibly into the public consciousness in so many countries of the world.

NOTES

1. The Workers' Olympics emerged in opposition to de Coubertin's Games, permitting the entry of 'all comers', as opposed to Olympic amateurs, and focused on the internationalism of the event, as opposed to the nationalist lines of Coubertin's festival. The Workers' Olympics were held in Frankfurt in 1925, attracting 150,000 spectators. Workers' sport festivals reached their zenith during the 1920s and 1930s and, although such organisations still exist in the world today, they do not promote workers' culture and political education as they did in the past (Riordan, 1984; Kidd, 1989).

2. The Women's Olympics, first held in 1922, were organised in part to provide female athletes with the athletic opportunities denied them by de Coubertin's Games. The IOC and the International Amateur Athletics Federation (IAAF) rejected the inclusion of female competitors in athletics or track and field events at the Games of 1920 and 1924 but permitted limited participation in 1928. As part of the agreement, the name 'Women's Olympics' was changed to International Ladies Games, and the IAAF assumed full control over women's athletics.

3. Danish cyclist Knud Jensen and two teammates suffered heat stroke during the 100 km road race held in Rome in 1960. All athletes were found to have injected nicotinyl alcohol before the race. Jenson died and became the first high profile drug abuse case in the modern era. See Allan Ryan cited in Senn (1999, p. 120).

REFERENCES

Barney, R. K. (1992). Born from dilemma: America awakens to the modern Olympic Games, 1901–1903. *OLYMPIKA: The International Journal of Olympic Studies, I,* 92–135.

Barney, R. K. (1996). Resistance, persistence, providence: The 1932 Los Angeles Olympic Games in perspective. *Research Quarterly for Exercise and Sport, 67*(2), 148–160.

Barney, R. K., Wenn, S. R., & Martyn, S. G. (2002). *Selling the five rings: The International Olympic Committee and the rise of Olympic commercialism.* Salt Lake City: The University of Utah Press.

Booth, D. (1999). Gifts of corruption?: Ambiguities of obligation in the Olympic Movement. *OLYMPIKA: The International Journal of Olympic Studies, VIII,* 43–68.

Coakley, J., & Donnelly, P. (2004). *Sports in society: Issues and controversies.* Toronto: Mc Graw-Hill Ryerson.

Donnelly, P. (1997). Young athletes need child law protection. In: P. Donnelly (Ed.), *Taking sport seriously: Social issues in Canadian sport* (pp. 189–195). Toronto: Thompson.

Dyreson, M. (1998). *Making the American team: Sport, culture, and the Olympic experience.* Urbana and Chicago, IL: University of Illinois Press.

Fair, J. D. (1999). *Muscletown USA: Bob Hoffman and the manly culture of York Barbell.* University Park, PA: The Pennsylvania State University Press.

Goldstein, E. S. (1996). Henri de Baillet-Latour. In: J. E. Findling & K. D. Pelle (Eds), *Historical dictionary of the Olympic Movement* (pp. 357–361). Westport, CT: Greenwood Press.

Guttmann, A. (1984). *The games must go on: Avery Brundage and the Olympic Movement.* New York: Columbia University Press.

Guttmann, A. (1992). *The Olympics: A history of the modern Games.* Urbana and Chicago, IL: University of Illinois Press.

Hoberman, J. (1992). *Mortal engines: The science of performance and the dehumanization of sport.* New York and Toronto: Free Press.

Kidd, B. (1989). We must maintain a balance between propaganda and serious athletics: The Workers' Sport Movement in Canada, 1924–1936. In: M. Mott (Ed.), *Sports in Canada: Historical readings* (pp. 247–264). Toronto: Copp Clark Pitman.

Kruger, A. (1998). The ministry of popular enlightenment and propaganda and the Nazi Olympics of 1936. In: R. K. Barney, K. B. Wamsley, S. G. Martyn & G. H. MacDonald (Eds), *Global and cultural critique: Problematizing the Olympic Games* (pp. 33–48). London, ON: International Centre for Olympic Studies.

Lennartz, K. (1996). Athens 1906: The intercalated Games. In: J. E. Findling & K. D. Pelle (Eds), *Historical dictionary of the Olympic Movement* (pp. 26–34). Westport, CT: Greenwood Press.

MacAloon, J. (1981). *This great symbol: Pierre de Coubertin and the origins of the modern Olympic Games.* Chicago and London: The University of Chicago Press.

Mandell, R. D. (1971). *The Nazi Olympics.* New York: Macmillan.

Müller, N. (2000). *Pierre de Coubertin 1863–1937: Olympism, selected writings.* Lausanne: International Olympic Committee.

Paz, O. (1972). *The other Mexico: Critique of the pyramid.* New York: Grove Press.

Riordan, J. (1984). The Worker's Olympics. In: A. Tomlinson & G. Whannel (Eds), *Five ring circus: Money power and politics at the Olympic Games* (pp. 98–112). London: Pluto.

Ryan, J. (1995). *Little girls in pretty boxes: The making and breaking of elite gymnasts and figure skaters.* New York: Doubleday.

Senn, A. E. (1999). *Power, politics, and the Olympic Games: A history of the power brokers, events, and controversies that shaped the Games.* Champaign, IL: Human Kinetics.

Wamsley, K. B. (2002). The global sport monopoly: A synopsis of 20th century Olympic politics. *The International Journal, LVII*(3), 395–410.

Wamsley, K. B. (2004). Laying Olympism to rest. In: J. Bale & M. K. Christensen (Eds), *Post-Olympism? Questioning sport in the twenty-first century* (pp. 231–242). Oxford: Berg.

Wamsley, K. B., & Schultz, G. (2000). Rogues and bedfellows: The IOC and the incorporation of the FSFI. In: K. B. Wamsley, S. G. Martyn, G. H. MacDonald & R. K. Barney (Eds), *Bridging three centuries: Intellectual crossroads and the modern Olympic Movement* (pp. 113–118). London, ON: International Centre for Olympic Studies, University of Western Ontario.

Wilson, W., & Derse, E. (Eds) (2001). *Doping in elite sport: The politics of drugs in the Olympic Movement*. Champaign, IL: Human Kinetics.

Young, D. C. (1984). *The Olympic myth of Greek amateur athletics*. Chicago: Ares Publishers.

Young, D. C. (1987). The origins of the Modern Olympics: A new version. *The International Journal of the History of Sport, 4*, 271–300.

Part I

THE HISTORY AND DEVELOPMENT OF THE OLYMPIC GAMES

Chapter 1

FROM OLYMPIA 776 BC TO ATHENS 2004: THE ORIGIN AND AUTHENTICITY OF THE MODERN OLYMPIC GAMES

David Young

The Olympics! In ancient Greece, the very name conjured up notions of grandeur, excellence, and universal appeal, just as it does in our modern, globalised world. But both the ancient and the modern Games had remarkably humble origins. From a single, short foot race held at Olympia in 776 BC, the ancient contests greatly expanded in programme and importance. Even before the Golden Age of Classical Athens, the Olympics already exemplified the pinnacle of excellence and prestige, which was a focal point for all of the Greek culture. The Olympic Games[1] sustained that cultural significance and symbolic value of excellence throughout all of Greco-Roman antiquity for well over a thousand years. Although, in many ways, they are the same, our modern Olympics have important differences. The most significant difference, perhaps, is sheer magnitude; the Modern Olympics simply dwarf their ancient ancestor in size. In Athens, 2004, for example, more than 10,000 athletes from 200 countries competed in 300 events. By comparison, in the heyday of the ancient Olympics (the fifth century BC), there was a total of 14 events and perhaps 300 competitors.

The inaugural event of the ancient Games, was the 200 m dash, known as the *stade*, one length of the long, ancient stadium.[2] Somewhat indicative of

Global Olympics: Historical and Sociological Studies of the Modern Games
Research in the Sociology of Sport, Volume 3, 3–18
Copyright © 2005 by Elsevier Ltd.

the cultural significance of the Games, there are records of every 200 m victor, every 4 years, for a thousand years of Olympics. The second event of the games was the 400 m, the *diaulos*, or two lengths of the ancient track. Unlike in the modern era, when double victories in these running events are unusual, such an achievement was recorded at least a dozen times (Young, 2004, pp. 24–32).

The exact length of the distance race during the ancient Games – *dolichos* ('long one') – is not known, but is estimated as somewhere between 1 and 2 miles. Some 250 years after the Olympics began, a fourth and final running event was added. This was called the 'armed race', 400 m in length. The runners wore a helmet and carried a shield, yet were otherwise nude, as was the case with all Greek athletes in competition.

In addition to the foot races, three combative events were held – wrestling, boxing, and a brutal combination of the two, called *pancration*, or 'anything goes'. In wrestling, three of five 'falls' (requiring a knee or shoulder to touch the ground) earned the victory. The most renowned ancient athlete was Milo, Olympic wrestling champion for at least five Olympiads in the sixth century BC. Ancient boxing featured no rounds. The boxers simply hit one another until one of them could not continue. Since there were no weight divisions, all those of Olympic class were effectively 'heavyweights'. The bouts could be brutal, blood-splattering affairs. The third combat event, *pancration*, literally means 'all forms of power'. A fierce, no-holds-barred event, it combined boxing, wrestling, and street fighting, with almost no rules at all. Spectators in late antiquity especially favoured this event (Young, 2004, pp. 38–46).

There were merely three field events in antiquity – the discus, javelin, and long jump. They existed only as part of the five event all-around competition, the *pentathlon*; no separate winner of an individual event was recognised. Those three field events were joined with special competitions in the 200 m and wrestling for pentathletes only, and a single, overall winner was then declared. Unfortunately, the ancient sources do not explain precisely how that overall winner was determined (Young, 2004, pp. 32–37).

Unlike the Olympic Games of the modern era, there were no team games, and no ball games. Greeks participated in such activities, viewing them as rather trivial pursuits. They were not part of the Olympics or other athletic festivals. For the ancient Greeks, 'real' athletic competition pitted one athlete against all of the others, each trying to achieve what the others could not. Pindar, foremost among several poets who celebrated the ancient victors, wrote that the winning athlete is 'distinguished' – literally 'separated out' – from all of the others. The catch-phrase 'it is more important to take part than to win', is often invoked to emphasise ethical qualities with respect to the modern Olympics, and athletes sometimes express it with sincerity. But this sentiment did not apply to the ancient version at all.[3] On the contrary, there was neither second-place prize nor recognition; athletes either won or lost, and the latter was considered a disgrace (Pindar, *Olympian*, Vol. 8, pp. 65–73; *Pythian*, Vol. 8, pp. 81–87).

Despite these significant differences between the ancient and modern Games and in the remarkably different societies in which they were/are situated, the similarities in form outweigh them. Most notably, the modern Olympics also represent the pinnacle of athletic excellence, competition, and prestige. The ancient and the modern Games share the same dedication to the pursuit of excellence, and the same goals encouraged the maximum physical performance of individuals, valued at times in both eras. Both versions began modestly and developed and grew over many decades. And, most importantly, both were initiated by the Greeks *in Greece*.

It is commonly believed that the modern Games were the singular brainchild of a Frenchman, Baron Pierre de Coubertin. This version of the story has been celebrated for more than a century by the media, the International Olympic Committee (IOC) and, most forcefully, by Coubertin himself. Coubertin wrote that he was the first to promote this idea, situating himself as its instigator. In tribute to Coubertin, the IOC and the media still generally maintain this illusion, as do many people, including the Greeks, whose role in the story deserves closer historical attention.

Coubertin's version of the history of the modern Olympic Games insisted that the festival burst forth fully grown, fully supported, and already popular. He recalled the ancient Greek myth of Athena, born fully grown from Zeus's head, while anticipating his critics, who argued that the modern revival of the Games was a limited and tenuous enterprise. "La vérité est différente", Coubertin (1986, Vol. 2, p. 347) insisted – "The truth is different". However, the series of events which actually took place was significantly different from Coubertin's version. Indeed, the modern revival of the Games started on a limited scale, progressed slowly through the efforts of several dedicated proponents, and nearly failed many times. Coubertin explicitly denied this historical fact, in part to rationalise the significance of the Games in the modern era and also to assert his prominent role in their modern revival:

Vainly will later treachery strive to impose the notion of an uncertain creation whose stages followed one another timidly and haphazardly. The truth is different. Olympism was born this time fully armed, like Minerva! [Latin name of Athena] – with its programme complete and its geography entire; the whole planet would be its domain (1986, Vol. 2, p. 347).

The truth is very different. Modern Greece had held Olympic Games before Coubertin was even born, and the Olympic revival movement was decades old before he joined it. I stress here that I do *not* seek to discredit Coubertin. He probably rescued an almost moribund movement from eventual extinction. It is clear that Coubertin *was* important, and deserves a great deal of credit, but so do some other central contributors to the Olympic idea. There is compelling evidence that Coubertin would never have conceived the idea of a modern Olympic revival on his own (Young, 1996, pp. 74–86), and the Games' true origin holds especial importance for the meanings celebrated during the Olympics of 2004. Olympiad XXVIII, Athens 2004, marked not so much a revival of the ancient Greek Games as an authentic continuation of them. The modern Olympics are not 'Olympics' in name only. Besides all of the authentic similarities mentioned above, there is a legitimate, direct Greek line of descent, which can be traced all the way from the ancient Games and the simple stadium in Olympia, through Sydney and other cities of the world, to the modern Olympic stadium in Athens.

Despite Coubertin's comparing it to Athena's birth from the head of Zeus, and despite writing that, "As for me, I proclaim its paternity with raised voice" (Coubertin, 1896, p. 110), the revival idea was, in fact, the brainchild of a *Greek*. The seed of the modern Olympics was first planted on *Attic* soil by a modern *Greek* poet, inspired by the ancient deeds at Olympia. Like many Greek intellectuals of the early nineteenth century, Panagiotis Soutsos was expatriated while he was very young. After studies in Paris and Padua, he moved to Transylvania. When the Greeks won most of Southern Greece back from the Ottomans, Greece became an autonomous nation, after many years of foreign control. In 1832, the Greeks' allies imposed on them, as their king, a teenage prince from Bavaria. He became Otto I, King of the Hellenes. Soon after Otto arrived at Nafplion, the early capital of the new nation, the young poet Soutsos also moved to Nafplion. There he founded a newspaper, naming it *The Sun*.

In Nafplion, Soutsos also published poems, which he wrote to celebrate the birth of the new Greek nation. The centuries under Turkish rule had left Greece well behind modern, nineteenth century Europe. Greece had neither shared in Western Europe's Renaissance period, nor its Enlightenment. The infrastructure of Greece, its institutions, and its government were in disrepair. Like many Greeks after him, Soutsos felt the heavy burden of ancient Greek glory on his new nation. His poetry pointedly asks how modern Greece could gain the respect of the modern world and live up to its ancient reputation. Some Greeks wanted to emulate successful modern nations such as France, but Soutsos clearly saw that Greece could not suddenly advance to the top of the new world order. He decided that Greece should seek to restore its *ancient* glory instead, to re-establish the culture and institutions that had made ancient Greece great in the eyes of western cultures for centuries.

In an 1833 poem, Soutsos invoked the ghost of Plato gazing up from the underworld. He surveys his tattered native land in dismay, wonders aloud if he is really looking at Greece, and addresses the new nation: "Where are all your great theaters and marble statues?" Plato's ghost asks, "Where are your Olympic Games?"[4] Soutsos understood that the ancient Olympic Games had symbolised excellence and prestige, a focal point for all of Greek culture. He chose the Olympics here to represent the best features of ancient Greece, including theatres and art, a broad cultural view of what he suggested the ancient Games signified.

Once again, in Soutsos' next poem, the ghost of the ancient military hero, Leonidas, explicitly advises Greece to revive its Olympic Games. This idea of restoring the grandeur of antiquity by restoring the Olympics began to take root in Soutsos' own psyche. He boldly converted his poetic idea into a proposal. In 1835, he sent a lengthy memo to the government, proposing that Greece should revive the ancient Olympic Games as an emblem and part of its new independence.

Otto agreed on paper to a great national festival with contests in industry, agriculture, and ancient Greek athletic games but, in reality, he did nothing about it. In 1842, Soutsos put forward his proposal in print and in public, pleading to his king, "Let the ancient Olympic Games be revived in Athens". Soutsos implored the Greeks to restore the nation by resurrecting the glories of the past. In 1845, he delivered an enthusiastic speech to a crowd of thousands in Athens, again urging that the Olympics be revived. Indeed, for two decades Soutsos urged the Greeks to revive the ancient Games. It was not until 1856 that someone of considerable influence listened and responded.

Evangelis[5] Zappas, veteran of the Greek War of Independence, was born to Greek parents in southern Albania. After the war he expatriated to Romania, where he became one of the richest men in Eastern Europe, with vast land holdings and many other business enterprises. After learning of Soutsos' Olympic idea he, too, implored the Greek government in 1856 to revive the Olympics in Athens, and even offered to fund the entire project himself.

King Otto gave Zappas' Olympic proposal to his foreign minister, Alexandros Rangavis, who viewed athletics as a degenerative throwback to primitive eras and, as he correctly observed, people of the modern world did not participate in athletics. Indeed, modern forms of organised sport and athletics competitions did not emerge until the second half of the nineteenth century. When Zappas proposed an Olympic revival in 1856, there were no such athletics anywhere, unless one counts some cricket and rowing contests in England (Guttmann, 1978, p. 57). Consistent with the economic development policies of the day, Rangavis suggested to Zappas that agricultural and industrial contests be held instead.[6] The two men compromised and, in 1858, the first modern Olympiad was announced for Athens to be held the following year in 1859. There would be industrial Olympics and agricultural Olympics; but Zappas would also have his athletic Olympics, a revival of the Games of ancient Greece. On that he insisted, and then promised cash prizes for the winners. Within this context, a seemingly disconnected series of events began to unfold that ultimately gave shape to the Olympic idea.

The initiatives of Zappas, and the plans emerging in Athens, interested an English doctor, W. P. Brookes, who lived in the rural village of Wenlock. In the fall of 1858, Dr. Brookes discovered a small item in his local newspaper, reporting that the new Greek Olympics were to take place in 1859. It interested him so much that he clipped it out and pasted it in one of his scrapbooks, where it remains to this day. Brookes' meticulous records of all of his activities in the years to follow document this series of events – revealing how the modern Olympic movement emerged, drawing distinct historical connections from Soutsos' first poetic idea conceived in the nineteenth century to the grandiose festivities held in Athens in 2004.[7]

Brookes had already inaugurated a set of annual village games on a modest scale in England but, in July 1859, more than 2 months *before* the 1859 Athens Olympics took place, he sponsored the first of what he called the 'Annual Wenlock Olympic Games'. There was an expanded programme and a much more explicit Hellenic influence. Brookes wrote the British consul in Athens to find out more about the coming Athens Olympics. He sent the Greek organising committee £10 sterling as a prize for one of the victors. In other words, *before* the 1859 Olympiad, the Athens committee announced that, besides the drachma prize from Zappas, there would also be an extra prize from 'the Wenlock Olympic Committee of England'.

Zappas had given money to excavate the ancient Panathenaic stadium as a site for these Games, but the 1859 Olympics took place instead at the square now called 'Koumoundourou', on Pireus Street, just north of the Kerameikos. It was, at this time, located just outside of the main city. Zappas' and Brookes' cash prizes were indeed awarded, but the Games themselves were no great success. The programme was small and the athletes barely trained. In the flat city square, only the front row of the standing spectators could see the events, and those behind them pushed and shoved until police forced them back. In the featured distance race, the leading runner collapsed and died. Petros Velissariou of Smyrna then passed the fallen runner and won the race, along with Brookes' British pounds. The newspapers expressed the hope that the next Olympiad would be better, but such an Olympic follow-up was slow to come.

Otto was driven out of Greece in 1862, replaced by a Dane, who later became George the First. In 1865, Zappas died, leaving almost all of his immense fortune to Greece for the promotion and staging of the Olympics. He also left a rather baffling will. The will stipulated that Zappas was to be buried first at his estate in Romania. But, after one Olympiad, or 4 years, his body was to be removed from the grave, and severed at the neck. The main skeleton (including the bones below the neck) was to be reburied in his native village in Albania, but the head was to be sent to Athens and encased in the new Olympic building there. Zappas gave money for this building and assumed that it would be built within the 4-year span. But it was not built then, and the entire Soutsos–Zappas Olympic movement in Greece fell into a long hiatus.

During the 1860s, Brookes carried on the Olympic movement in England. When he learned the results of the 1859 Athens Olympiad, he sent a letter to Petros Velissariou, the man who had won his Wenlock prize. In it, he informed Velissariou that he had been elected the first Honorary Member of the Wenlock Olympic Society. Thus Velissariou, enrolled in 1860, was the first in the list of five Honorary Members. The last on the list, at the bottom of the same page, was Pierre de Coubertin, enrolled three decades later. Brookes sent his letter to Velissariou through N. Theocharis, head of the 1859 Greek Olympic Committee, to whom he also sent a separate letter of greetings. Velissariou and the Committee president both responded. Velissariou warmly thanked Brookes for the honorary Olympic membership. In his reply, Theocharis refers to Brookes' Olympic committee and his own Olympic Committee in Greece as "sister committees united by the same name and a common goal" (Young, 1996, pp. 27–29). In this sense, it is possible to speak of the existence of a version of an international Olympic movement as early as 1860.

This contact with Greece again spurred on Brookes, first to expand his local project to countywide Olympics, the Olympic Games of Shropshire County. He began to think in even grander terms – of National Olympic Games, which would draw athletes and spectators from all of Britain. Indeed, the first 'National Olympic Games' took place in 1866 in London. They were a great success, with many good athletes, including a young man named W. G. Grace, destined to become the most renowned cricketer the world has ever known. In London's large indoor arena, the Crystal Palace, site of the first World Exposition in 1851, 10,000 spectators looked on as Grace won the hurdles. But not everyone wished the Olympic movement success. In class-conscious England, it offended some upper-class men that Brookes' Olympics permitted everyone, even working-class men, to compete. Consequently, these self-styled aristocrats formed an elitist, counter-Olympic group called the Amateur Athletic Club, or AAC. The AAC formulated the first formal definition of an amateur athlete. It declared that working men, who were 'mechanics, artisans, or labourers' were *de facto* 'professionals'. They were, therefore, barred from all amateur contests, which were reserved for 'gentlemen'; that is, people who performed no labour for a living.

Members of the AAC generally boycotted Brookes' Olympics. A few competed in the London 1866 Games but, in later National Olympics, they generally abstained. They even published a rule that men who competed in contests 'with professionals' – that is, with working-class men in Brookes' Olympics – could not enter any contest sanctioned by the AAC. Since these elites *were* the power structure in Victorian England, they soon ran Brookes' Olympic movement aground. By 1869, they had forced him to abandon his project, for athletes wanting to compete elsewhere in England could not enter the National Olympic Games.

At the same time, in Greece, the government planned the next athletic competition. King George announced an end to the long hiatus, a renewed Zappas Olympics to be staged in 1870. For the Games of 1870, the organising committee acquired and excavated the ancient stadium in Athens. Luxurious marble seats that Zappas had paid for were not installed, but wooden bleachers accommodated 30,000 spectators who watched a successful competition. There were more events than in 1859, and the organisation was more thorough. Athletes from all points of the Greek world came to compete, from Crete to Constantinople. If they could not afford the trip or their uniforms, the committee met the costs, thus enabling everyone qualified to enter. The wrestling victor, for example, was an ordinary, manual labourer from Crete, and the 200 m winner was a butcher from Athens. With the exception of a few university professors, most observers judged the Games a success. These professors objected to the working-class victories in athletics. Wanting to emulate England's elite, they assumed control of the Greek Olympic committee. For the next Olympics in 1875, the committee simply excluded the working class. It declared *everyone* ineligible except university students – all socially *and* financially well heeled at this time. The

1875 Games were far inferior to the 1870 edition, with respect to participation and popularity. This time, the newspapers censured both the committee and the athletes. But the committee had lost all interest in athletics. No further Athens Olympics were announced until 1888.

In early 1888, the expensive Olympic Building, now called the 'Zappeion', was finally completed. The Olympic committee announced an Olympiad for autumn of 1888 to celebrate its opening. As discussed earlier, Zappas' head was duly transferred from Romania and encased in the new building. At this time, it seems, Zappas' body was divided, like Gaul, into three parts. His flesh stayed in Romania, as part of the bilingual inscription on his tombstone states. Another part reads, "Yours is not the only undying fame, Iphitos; from Zappas, too, Greece has Olympic Games."[8] Most of the skeleton was removed through a trap door (which is still visible) and reburied in southern Albania, where the epitaph, in Albanian, is still legible: "Here rest the bones of the philanthropist Evangelis Zappas". And in Athens, Zappas' head still lies encased inside a wall in the courtyard of the Zappeion, behind a plaque inscribed in ancient Greek. The 1888 committee announced that there would be athletic games in the stadium, but did nothing to organise any events or festivities. Consequently, the athletic contests of the 1888 Games were silently cancelled. It appeared that the now anti-athletic Greek Olympic committee had thwarted the revival of the Olympics.

In England, a combination of apathy and opposition to his British National Olympic Games hindered Brookes, who made several attempts to stage his games throughout the 1870s. In the 1880s, as Greece built the Zappeion, Brookes began a new tack. He proposed that *international* Olympic Games be held in – of all places – Athens, Greece. Although both Greek and English newspapers published word of his international revival idea, it fell on deaf ears. Brookes asked the Greek ambassador in London, John Gennadius, to help rally the Greek government behind his Athens plan. In the next decade, he wrote a dozen letters to Gennadius, but still nothing happened. At this point, Brookes turned to his other obsession – promoting physical education in his country's schools. At the same time, a young French nobleman and Anglophile, Baron Pierre de Coubertin, became obsessed with the same project in France. As a child, Coubertin had witnessed the defeat of the French at the hands of the Prussian army. Later in life, he blamed France's military losses on a lack of physical fitness. Coubertin travelled to many countries, including England, the United States, and Canada to research and observe their systems of physical education and sport. Excited about the Wenlock project, he began to quote

Brookes' writings in his own speeches. He also wrote Brookes asking if he could visit England to meet with him in person to discuss his vision of physical education.

Coubertin arrived in Wenlock in October, 1890, and Brookes held a special edition of his Wenlock Olympic Games in his honour. He also asked the Baron to plant a tree there, because Brookes believed that trees symbolised growth and expansion, and clearly hoped that his Olympic idea might grow and expand.[9] Brookes took Coubertin to his trophy room. There, Coubertin himself clearly wrote in 1890, Brookes showed him the victors' list from the 1859 Zappas Olympics – in printed English translation. Brookes provided for the Baron a precise account of the 1866 London Olympics. He showed him newspapers from 1881, reporting *Brookes'* proposals for starting international Olympic Games in Athens. Coubertin's recollections of these events became significant; he misrepresented the truth, claiming to have conceived the idea for the Games himself ensuring his place in history at the expense of W. P. Brookes and the nineteenth century Greeks. Several years later, Coubertin (1908) actually stated in print that there had *never been any* Zappas Olympics at all (p. 108), and pretended that he knew *nothing* of Brookes' own Olympic endeavours (p. 53).[10] Brookes' name does not appear in Coubertin (1932); in this respect, *le renovateur's* recollections were less than accurate or sincere.

Coubertin (1986) had already ridiculed the idea of modern Olympic Games when another Frenchman proposed it in 1888 (Vol. 1, p. 111). And, when he returned to Paris from Wenlock in 1890, he in effect belittled Brookes' idea of reviving the Olympic Games, writing that Brookes had "no need to invoke memories of (ancient) Greece" (1986, Vol. 2, p. 83). Yet, by 1892, he had entirely changed tack, making a public proposal for an Olympic revival, and maintaining that it was an *entirely novel idea, his idea alone*. Concurrently, there was action on other Olympic fronts. The Greeks had announced a revival of the Zappas series for 1892, but financial and political problems prevented it. Brookes still wrote in vain to Gennadius, because Coubertin had not told him of his own revival proposal that he planned to deliver in Paris. Indeed, by this stage, the Baron no longer responded to Brookes' letters.

What Coubertin *did* do was to plan an International Athletic Congress in Paris for June 1894, a meeting for sports leaders and enthusiasts. He was slow in sending out invitations, so that Europeans received no invitation until the month before the Congress. Brookes received one – a mere form letter – and wrote to Coubertin wishing him success in his Olympic enterprise. Brookes also sent a lengthy letter to the Prime Minister of Greece,

Charilaos Trikoupis, recalling his own earlier associations with the Zappas Olympics and the Zappas committee. The letter ended: "My friend Pierre de Coubertin, myself, and others are endeavoring to promote international Olympic festivals. I hope your King will patronize such Games". Rather ironically, Coubertin's later self-serving behaviour, Brookes considered himself and Coubertin as close associates and Olympic advocates.

Coubertin had originally named his 1894 Paris conference a 'Congress of Amateurs', expecting so controversial a topic to attract the greatest interest. Yet, by the time the delegates arrived at the Sorbonne to attend, it had been renamed the 'Congress to Revive the Olympic Games'. This event lasted several days. Delegates were wined, dined, and entertained in grand style, and the Baron held the delegates in his hands. When the sub-committee for Olympics met, no one opposed his proposals to form an international Olympic committee to 'revive' the ancient Games. He planned to host the first games in Paris in 1900, but somehow (the exact process remains unknown) the date was advanced by 4 years to 1896. Yet, the delegates did not at first vote for Athens as the 1896 site, selecting London instead. Strangely, the Anglophile Coubertin nominated Athens as a site, and insisted on it. When some delegates strongly opposed Athens, and it was clear that the London motion would pass, Coubertin had the whole question tabled (Young, 1996, pp. 100–102).

Thus, the choice of Athens for 1896 remains mostly a mystery, though the minutes reveal that Coubertin was unquestionably the first to nominate Athens. Earlier in that same June meeting, Demetrios Vikelas, a Greek intellectual who lived in Paris, had been elected President of that Olympic sub-committee, to his great surprise. He was a fascinating man of diverse talents, a novelist and historian who even translated Shakespeare and Racine into Greek. But he never before had a thing to do with athletics. At first, Vikelas did not support Coubertin's nomination of Greece, but later that same evening he changed his mind, and 4 days later, on the last day of the Congress, Vikelas himself made a second, more formal and far more successful, proposal for Athens' candidacy at a plenary session. In the meantime, he had communicated with Athens by telegram. Vikelas' Athens proposal was approved by acclamation. Vikelas was chosen the first President of the new International Olympic Committee (IOC), preceding Coubertin and all who followed, such as Brundage, Samaranch, and Rogge.

Although wholly inexperienced in athletic organisation, Vikelas was appropriate for the job. Coubertin became engaged to be married and also started to write a history book, thus losing much of his interest in the 1896

Games. Yet, in the fall of 1894, Coubertin and Vikelas made brief, separate trips to Athens. Each of them met strong opposition from the Greek government and from the Zappas Olympic committee, both of which said that they could not help and that Olympic Games were financially and practically unrealistic.

Vikelas returned in December, 1894. When Stephanos Dragoumis, Chair of the Zappas Olympic committee, emphatically told Vikelas "No", the Crown Prince of Greece, Constantine, offered to chair the organising committee. In early 1895, Vikelas and Constantine rallied other Greeks behind their efforts. Vikelas delivered speeches to labour union assemblies, and Constantine formed special sub-committees for each sport. In parliament, pro-Olympic Greeks invoked the tradition of the Zappas Games, and declared that these international Olympics would fulfil Zappas' dream. That argument won, the government changed hands, the Zappas committee stepped aside, and Athens began preparing enthusiastically for 1896. Vikelas, Constantine, and the other Greeks did almost all of the work. Coubertin remained absent from Athens, and contributed very little after the point of the Paris meeting.

The Athens organising committee somehow achieved amazing success. There were no previous international Olympiads to look to as models, and few communications from foreign teams or sportsmen. But, due in a large part to the efforts of Constantine, there *was* a great influx of goodwill and donations for the cause from Greeks both at home and abroad. Even peasants in the villages sent money to Athens. And Giorgos Averoff, an Egyptian Greek, paid to restore the ancient Panathenaic stadium, with magnificent marble seats. Unfortunately, Brookes did not live to see *his* Olympic dream fulfilled. He died just 3 months before the 1896 Games began, to join Soutsos and Zappas in Olympic oblivion, as Coubertin and history forgot all about them.

Against all odds and despite truly miserable weather, the 1896 Games were an astonishing success. The impressive stadium, one of the first in the modern world, overflowed with the largest crowd ever to witness a sporting event. Everyone observed virtually perfect decorum. Americans won most events in the stadium, and the Greeks applauded strongly, as they did for every winning athlete. But they yearned for a Greek victory in the stadium. Greek athletes were favoured to win both the discus and the shot put events but, in both cases, the best Greek athletes finished narrowly behind the American Robert Garrett Jr. Greatly disappointed, the Greeks nevertheless gave Garrett his applause. To the Greeks, it seemed almost as if the gods of Olympus had betrayed them.

All thoughts, all Greek hopes, now rested with the Marathon race, a completely new event, invented in the spirit of the running messenger tradition of the ancient world, and based primarily on the legend of Phidippides who ran from Marathon to Athens to bring word of victory at war. Before the race, there was great anticipation and excitement. Businessmen promised marvelous rewards to the winner – *if* he was Greek. As the afternoon of the race wore on, all other events in the stadium were finished except for the pole vault, which was suddenly interrupted by the entry of a runner. According to historical testimony, it seemed that the stadium had gone mad. "It's a Greek, it's a Greek", the crowd shouted in one voice. It was indeed a Greek, Spyros Louis, who entered the stadium first. Almost all eyewitnesses, including Coubertin, stated that it was one of the most memorable sights of their entire lives (Bijkerk & Young, 1999). All of Greece was euphoric for days afterwards. In short, it seemed as if the entire nation had suddenly been born again through the victory of this one young man. For a brief period, Soutsos' visions of national revitalisation had come to fruition.

These 1896 Olympic Games were so successful that almost everyone except Coubertin wanted Greece to become the permanent seat of all future Olympiads. But Greece itself fell into very hard times – the euphoria of the Games punctured by financial losses and military disasters. The Greeks could not oppose Coubertin's plans for 1900 in Paris. But the Paris 1900 Olympiad was a major disappointment for Coubertin and other Olympic enthusiasts. The French government refused to co-operate in their organisation, or permit the games to be called 'Olympics'. Athletes from around the world did compete sporadically on the outskirts of Paris but, since the Games were embedded in the Paris Exposition, an event celebrated for months, there were no crowds of sport spectators, and most athletes did not even know that they were competing in 'Olympics'. Following Coubertin's insistence on the great cities of the world hosting the Games, the next Olympiad was awarded to America, and ended up once again as an appendage to a World's Fair, this time The Louisiana Purchase Exposition of 1904 in St. Louis. The Games were not truly international; given the costs and distance of travel, few Europeans made the voyage and almost all of the athletes were North American. Coubertin, himself, did not attend. Although there was evidence of a certain awareness of the Coubertin Olympics, attendance was limited, organisation abysmal, and sometimes even perverse, as World's Fair officials organised a racist spectacle in the 'Aboriginal Days' events held during the Games, where 'savages' from Africa and the Americas were borrowed from the Fair's sideshows and made to compete in modern sports. Lacking knowledge and training they, thus, rather predictably demonstrated their supposed racial inferiority.

After two such fiascoes, the Olympics might well have died in the cradle, if Greece had not come to the aid of the faltering institution. There had been an IOC agreement, against Coubertin's wishes, that Athens would hold international Olympics in between the games that moved around the world, much as the Summer and Winter Games alternate now. In 1902, Greece was in no position to hold these 'in-between games'; but, in 1906, Athens hosted its second Olympic Games on the 10th anniversary of the first Games. Like the first, it was documented as a complete success, more grandiose, and hosting large numbers of spectators and athletes from many more nations. Most Olympic historians agree that, in 1906, Greece probably saved Coubertin's revival movement from early extinction (Young, 1996, p. 166). Indeed the following Olympics in 1908 held in London were marred by nationalist hostilities between the United States and Britain and a series of sport-related protests. When the highly successful Stockholm Games in 1912 seemed to assure a future for the movement, Greece was already planning for its 'in-between' Olympics of 1914. But, Coubertin and the IOC were forced to cancel the Games of 1916, scheduled for Berlin, due to World War I.

Consequently, the impressive Games of 1906, considered by some as the Games that saved the Olympics, were the last Olympics held in Greece before Olympiad XXVIII in 2004. Although the rest of the IOC at the time called 1906 an official IOC Olympiad, and even held an official meeting there, Coubertin declared it an unofficial event, and all of the record books refer to it as the 'unofficial Olympiad' (Lennartz, 2001). Efforts continue to reinstate these Olympics as 'official', but seemingly in deference to the wishes of Coubertin, current IOC President Rogge has rejected all such lobbying efforts (Bijkerk, 2003).

When one considers the majority of histories written about the revival of the Olympic Games, it is evident that certain myths have been consistently perpetuated. So credulous have Olympics enthusiasts been, that Coubertin's legacy has been significantly misrepresented. Historical evidence clearly demonstrates that Coubertin borrowed the ideas of others for his international festival and knowingly declined to give them appropriate recognition. Inspired by a distinct sense of connection to the ancient world, and conceived as a mechanism to rejuvenate a troubled nation, it was Soutsos' original proposal that set the chain of Olympic events in motion. Nor could it have succeeded without the financial support of Zappas and, later, the support of Vikelas and the organisational skill and untiring efforts of the

Crown Prince, Constantine. Without question, however, it was the Englishman W. P. Brookes who first conceived the idea for an international athletic festival. Coubertin's contribution lay in his successful establishment of such a festival, thus fulfilling the hopes and aspirations of his predecessors. So, the modern Games have not just one founder, but several. Undoubtedly, a modern sense of, and fascination with, the Olympic Games of ancient Greece inspired many to act for varied motives. Thus, the return of the Games to Greece in 2004, marked a 'coming home' not only to the point of their *ancient* origin, but as well to their *modern* birthplace.

NOTES

1. Because it is universal, I use the term 'Olympic Games' although it is actually a mistranslation of the Greek '*Olympiakoi agones*'. The error results from the intermediate Latin translation *Olympici ludi*. In Latin, *ludi* can connote sport and games – the first entry in Lewis and Short (1958) for the basic word *ludus* reads, "In general, a *play, game, diversion, pastime*". It is the ancestor of the English word 'ludicrous' (which originally meant 'playful'). The Romans never took Greek athletics seriously, but the Greeks did, and the word *agones* can never refer to 'sport' or 'games'. Rather, it means 'struggles' or 'contests', or even 'pains', the ancestor of our word 'agony'. Greeks used their word for 'play' (*paizein* – literally, 'to act like a child') when adults played music, board games, and even ball games, but never for any event in a Greek athletic festival, such as the Olympics.

2. Ancient stadiums varied in length from fewer than 180 m to approximately 210 m; that at Olympia was only 192.27 m, but the *stade* was clearly the equivalent of our 200 m sprint.

3. For the origin and history of this well-known saying, see Young (1994, 1998).

4. Full references and copious citations of all the rather arcane documents which I use in this chapter are given in Young (1996). Since many of them require an ability to read Greek and few are likely to be stored in libraries to which most readers have ready access, I forgo repeating them here, and refer interested readers to the documentation in my 1996 book.

5. Pronounced 'Evangélis', although the modern name is 'Evángelos'.

6. The original correspondence has been found and edited, with a German translation (Kivroglou, 1981). I thank the director of this unpublished thesis, Wolfgang Decker, for sending me a copy.

7. For details about this large, important collection of documents and their location see Young (1996, pp. 172–175).

8. Greek tradition attributed the founding of the ancient Olympics to a man named Iphitos.

9. This oak, just a tiny sapling in 1890, now towers high above the bystander's head.

10. Regarding the Zappas Games, Coubertin states that the "brothers Zappas" had left money for a memorial and convention centre, and "for physical exercises"

(he carefully avoids the word 'Olympics'); the occurrence of the latter, he claims, "had been held in abeyance" (*était restée en souffrance*). Coubertin refers to Brookes as "a doctor from another age" who held in his little village "popular sports" at a local festival "half ancient, half Middle-Ages". Of these "popular sports" he mentions none of the athletic events, but writes only of local farmers participating in "pig-sticking" (an event Brookes never held at Wenlock or anywhere else). The Baron avoids all mention of the word 'Olympics' and never mentions any of Brookes' more modern activities and aspirations, such as the National Olympic Games or his proposal for International Olympics – which he, himself, first heard about from Brookes directly (Young, 1996, pp. 77–78; Coubertin, 1897, pp. 63–65).

REFERENCES

Bijkerk, A. T. (2003). Message from the secretary-general. *Journal of Olympic History*, *11*(2), 4.
Bijkerk, A. T., & Young, D. C. (1999). That memorable first marathon. *Journal of Olympic History*, *7*(1), 5–24.
Coubertin, P. de (1896). Introduction. In: Sp. Lambros & N. G. Politis (Eds), *Olympic Games, 776 B.C.–1896 A.D.* (pp. 108–110), Athens: Beck.
Coubertin, P. de (1897). A typical Englishman: Dr. W. P. Brookes of Wenlock in Shropshire. *Review of Reviews*, *15*, 62–65.
Coubertin, P. de (1908). *Batailles de l'éducation physique: Une campagne de vingt-et-un ans. 1887–1908.* Paris: Librairie de l'Éducation Physique.
Coubertin, P. de (1932). *Olympic memoires* (no publisher listed (but Lausanne, 1972, International Olympic Committee [anonymous translation]); original French version, *Mémoires olympiques*, Lausanne (1932): Bureau international de pédagogie sportive).
Coubertin, P. de (1986). In: N. Müller (Ed.), *Textes choisis* (3 Vols). Zurich: Weidmann.
Guttmann, A. (1978). *From ritual to record*. New York: Columbia University Press.
Kivroglou, A. (1981). *Die Bemühungen von Ewangelos Sappas um die Wiedereinführung der Olympischen Spiele in Griechenland unter besonderer Berücksichtigung der Spiele von 1859.* Unpublished Diplomarbeit, Deutsche Sporthochschule, Köln.
Lennartz, K. (2001). The second international olympic games at Athens 1906. *Journal of Olympic History*, *10*(1), 10–27.
Lewis, C. T., & Short, C. (1958). *A Latin dictionary*. Oxford: Oxford University Press.
Young, D. C. (1994). 'It is more important to participate than to win'; Who said it first, Coubertin, Bishop Talbot, St. Paul, or Ovid? *OLYMPIKA: The International Journal of Olympic Studies*, *3*, 17–25.
Young, D. C. (1996). *The modern olympics: A struggle for revival*. Baltimore: Johns Hopkins University Press.
Young, D. C. (1998). More on the olympic maxim, 'It's more important … ': Its use in 1896 – and 1894 and 1908. *Journal of Olympic History*, *7*(3), 26–31.
Young, D. C. (2004). *A brief history of the olympic games*. Oxford: Blackwell Publishing.

Chapter 2

THE OLYMPIC GAMES EXPERIENCE: ORIGINS AND EARLY CHALLENGES

Douglas A. Brown

This chapter examines the Olympic Games experience from the perspective of cultural history. It offers a history of the Olympic Games that encourages readers to consider the ways in which people take *meaning* from this important international sporting event. In other words, it proposes a way of thinking about the range of experiences that the Olympic Games produce for athletes and spectators. Historical evidence and cultural theory support the argument that the modern Olympic Games have always represented a link between ideology and cultural forms and practices. The official ideological objectives of the Olympic Games and the cultural forms they assume have always shared a tenuous link. This thesis hinges on two underlying assertions. First, the Olympic Games owe their history principally to one man – Frenchman, Baron Pierre de Coubertin. With great energy, imagination, and single-mindedness, Coubertin ensured that the Games survived their initial period of growth. He founded the International Olympic Committee (IOC) in 1894 and convinced a small group of cosmopolitan men to support the introduction of Olympic Games in the modern era. For a number of reasons, his expectations and justifications for a modern Olympic Games continue to provide the dominant ideological underpinnings of the Games today. The first section of this chapter outlines several principles that informed Coubertin's vision for Olympic Games and international sport.

The second underlying assertion of this analysis draws on an anthropological interpretation of Coubertin's legacy. Theories of cultural performance

Global Olympics: Historical and Sociological Studies of the Modern Games
Research in the Sociology of Sport, Volume 3, 19–41

reveal that the Olympic Games were conceived as a hybrid event where invented rituals and ceremonies were integrated into the growing phenomenon of international sport competition. Through this combination of ritual, ceremonies, and sport, the Olympic Games were conceived as a festival that was intended to produce specific social experiences for athletes and observers (MacAloon, 1988). For anthropologists, festivals are very specific kinds of cultural performances, i.e., public activities that human beings produce to make sense of themselves and the societies to which they belong. Although Coubertin was not an anthropologist, his understanding of cultural performances and their social functions is evident in many of his writings on his international Olympic Games idea. The second section of this chapter describes the ideas and interventions that Coubertin used to produce an Olympic Games tradition – a modern sport festival – that united an international community of sportsmen who shared common values, co-operated in friendly competition, and symbolised peaceful internationalism (Müller, 2000, pp. 298–299).

The third section of this chapter develops from the following assertion: Olympic Games experiences have always been defined by a tension between the extraordinary quality associated with festivals and the mundane reality of modern sport. This section discusses this tension in the context of the *naturalisation* of the Olympic Games. Within a decade of the first Olympic Games in Athens, athletes, sport administrators, and even nation states began to see Olympic Games experiences as a logical extension of the practices of everyday life. Specifically, then, the final section discusses the improbable (if not flawed) notion of using modern sport as the basis for a festival intended to symbolise the harmony, balance, and peace of an international community. Very early in the history of the modern Olympic Games, international sporting success was highly valued by athletes, administrators, and even nations for a variety of social, economic, and political reasons. As a consequence, sporting success at the Olympic Games offers some very tangible and practical functions that extended from the necessity of everyday life. At the same time, however, this rendered the intended festival quality of the Olympic Games vulnerable to co-optation and corruption.

BARON PIERRE DE COUBERTIN

The founder of the modern Olympic Games was a complex man who chose an ambitious role for himself in a society that was rapidly changing. He established himself in the history of sport as the founder of one of the most prominent international events of the twentieth century. His ability to write himself into history was a reflection of his audacious and tenacious personality. Coubertin possessed a social and cultural sensibility that enabled him to create a specific type of event at a moment in time when the imaginations of modern sportsmen, statesmen, and entrepreneurs were receptive to grand ideas that harkened back to an ancient world (Boulongne, 1994, p. 42). He was an impresario of public theatre who knew how to trigger people's historical imaginations while serving their modern ambitions for sport, social reform, and international affairs. His idea of an Olympic Games for modern times brought social and cultural currency to a popular everyday pastime that was already entrenched in many sectors of nineteenth century European and North American society.

Pierre de Coubertin was born into an aristocratic French family on 1 January 1863. His father was Baron Charles Louis Frédy de Coubertin and his mother was Agathe Marie Marcelle Gigault de Crisenoy. As he grew up, Coubertin enjoyed the privileges of his social class. French historian, Georges Rioux, suggests that his love for sport and physical recreation was cultivated at the idyllic country estates of his parents, especially his mother's ancestral home in the Caux region of Normandy. Coubertin's education was traditional for boys of his class and religion; he attended College Saint-Ignace, a Jesuit-run school in Paris. This classical education contributed to his passion for history (Rioux, 2000, pp. 23–25). It is reflected in many of the values, beliefs, and decisions that he expressed later in his life. As a young man, Coubertin also made career choices that reflected his social class. His decision to promote educational reform is explained, in part, by the aristocratic ethic of *noblesse oblige* (MacAloon, 1981). He inherited this class-based benevolence towards the lower classes from his Catholic parents. At the same time, Coubertin's vocational choices reflected his ability to adapt to the political and social reality of his time. Unlike his monarchist parents, Coubertin embraced French Republicanism and was determined to invent a role for himself in the modern democratic industrial society. Also in keeping with his social class, Coubertin first chose to study law. As he grew disenchanted with this field of study, he was energised by the lectures he attended at the École Superieure des Sciences Politique.

The 1870s were a turbulent period, politically and socially, in France. France's defeat in the Franco-Prussian War and the violent civil uprising in the Paris Commune contributed to a climate of change. The École Superieure des Sciences Politique was a meeting ground for many of France's more progressive intellectuals and reformers. Socially conscious Frenchmen like Coubertin were reacting to, and critiquing, the very nature of French society and the institutions that shaped the daily lives of its citizens (Magraw, 2002). Existing systems of education and military training, they thought, were outdated and ineffective for the demands of the modern world. For politicians, intellectuals, and liberal members of the upper class, France's future and its international prestige were dependent on radical social reform. Late nineteenth century social reform movements tended to focus on urban working-class men. This sector of society was identified as the foundation of modern states. It was also perceived as a potential liability to French society. The ideal of France's Third Republic invoked a society where individuals lived independent, self-sufficient, economically produc-tive, and morally upstanding lives. To achieve this social ideal, individuals needed to discipline their minds and bodies (Magraw, 2002, pp. 98–104). The combination of social good with development of the mind and body appealed strongly to Coubertin's neo-Hellenic ideals.

Throughout the 1880s, Coubertin established himself as an authority on education in France, Europe, and North America. He fashioned himself as an activist for educational reform. The intellectual forces that shaped his vision of reform were diverse. He studied the work of Rabelais, Jean-Jacques Rousseau, John Locke, James Mills, and John Stuart Mill. More contemporary influences included Hippolyte Taine, Jules Simon, and Thomas Arnold (Boulongne, 1994, pp. 45–46). Coubertin was successful at making a name for himself among like-minded men of his era including the French Minister of Education, Jules Simon. Important and powerful men like Simon appreciated Coubertin's knowledge, enthusiasm, and spirit of volunteerism. As a consequence, the French government sent Coubertin on international fact-finding missions: one to England and Ireland in 1887, and one to Canada and the United States in 1889. From these expeditions, Coubertin published two books that hinted at the introduction of a modern Olympic Games. In particular, Coubertin's (1889) book *L'Education An-glaise en France* proposed that the English public school education, with its integration of athletic sports, provided the best model of education for modern French men. He was especially influenced by Dr. Thomas Arnold, the Headmaster of Rugby School, and indeed credited his vision for physical education to Dr. Arnold. Arnold encouraged student-run athletic games including Rugby's distinct style of football because he believed that these games taught 'manly behaviour' that was vital for young Christian men. Writers such as Thomas Hughes (*Tom Brown's School Days*) and Charles Kingsley were, however, responsible for bridging the notion of 'Muscular Christianity' with the practice of sport (Putney, 2001). Muscular

Christianity was a philosophy that promoted a very specific type of masculinity throughout the Victorian era. Through physically-active life-styles, which included sport, men were expected to embody a sense of duty, virtue, courage, self-discipline, and purity (Brown, 1987). Arnold suggested that student-governed athletic games and sports cultivated such moral and social qualities. Sport served at least two key functions: it trained bodies and developed leadership qualities that were much in need in Britain's powerful military forces. Knowledge of Arnold's leadership at Rugby School and the literary discourse espousing Muscular Christian manliness provided Coubertin with exactly the type of justification for promoting moral and social development through physical education and sport in France. Coubertin's infatuation with British sport culture and its potential for improving the lives of young men in France eventually led to even grander ideas of reforming the international 'society' through Olympic Games.

Coubertin's interest in educational reform was not the only factor that shaped his idea of modern Olympic Games. German historian Dietrich Quantz (1993) suggests that Coubertin's interest in international sport was shaped, at least in part, by his familiarity with the growing international peace movement of the late 1880s and 1890s. Quantz provides evidence that several men whom Coubertin invited to his 1894 Congress at the Sorbonne were active participants in the international peace movement. Coubertin was aware of the international peace movement and he developed a serious interest in it. All of this informed his methods of introducing and promoting the International Olympic Movement. In many ways, then, Coubertin's idea of a modern Olympic Games is closely bound to the discourse of international pacifism. He believed that a strong and co-operative international sporting community would contribute to a more peaceful and prosperous world order. Furthermore, he believed that such an international community needed to function independently of national state governments. As Quantz (1993, p. 15) remarked: "Coubertin did not imagine that international sport festivals would eliminate war between nation states; he did believe that they would foster cooperation and communication that might decrease the risk of war". In this sense, sport was a way of practising internationalism. However, Coubertin's ideas on internationalism and non-governmental participation in international activity are the most misunderstood and misrepresented dimensions of the IOC and the Olympic Games. The complete separation of international sport from nation state politics was an ideal of the IOC, but hardly a practical reality. Hoberman (1995, pp. 10–11) argues that Coubertin's Olympic Movement and the international peace movement were only two of many idealistic international

movements of the late 1800s. A number of different international movements grew out of wide-sweeping despair over the nature and pace of modernity in European society. Many of these international organisations
recognised the volatility of nation–state relationships and attempted to
introduce organisational structures that would diffuse this tension.

The culture of late nineteenth century internationalism is evident in many
of Coubertin's initiatives that promoted the Olympic Games and sport education. For example, from the early 1890s through 1925, Coubertin used
public meetings, or congresses, to rally support for his ideas. For international organisations, formal gatherings of international delegates represented more than simple administrative mechanisms; these congresses were
embodiments of *internationalism* itself. During his presidency (1896–1925),
Coubertin organised and choreographed thematic Olympic Congresses that
reasserted the idea that the IOC represented a true international movement
rather than simply a quadrennial sport competition. He did not simply talk
about internationalism – he practised it and worked to make it a reality
during Olympic Congresses (Müller, 1994).

International congresses were, in themselves, cultural expressions of modern internationalism. Coubertin was a master at exploiting this type of cultural practice. In June, 1894, he invited 78 delegates representing 37 sports
federations and 9 countries to a meeting in Paris. The meeting was held at the
Sorbonne University. The official agenda emphasised the objective of
resolving a number of issues concerning the distinction between amateur
and professional athletes. According to Coubertin, his purpose had always
been the creation of the IOC and the revival of Olympic Games. In *Olympic
Memories* (1979), Coubertin explained that the 1894 congress had been conceived as a means of launching the revival of the Olympic Games in modern
times. The congress was a success. When it concluded on June 23, Olympic
Games were planned for Athens in 1896. A wealthy Greek patriot, Demetrius
Vikelas, was appointed the first President of the IOC. This marked the
beginning of the administrative history of the modern Olympic Movement.

Following the first Olympic Games of the modern era in 1896, Coubertin
assumed the position of IOC President and retained it until 1925. During his
presidency, he used international congresses to expand the activities of the
Olympic Movement. The frequency and diversity of themes of the Olympic
congresses is evidence of Coubertin's passionate belief that 'grass roots'
sport and physical education were essential dimensions of the Olympic
Movement. They demonstrate how Coubertin worked methodically to
establish tangible links between the Olympic Games and everyday sport and
physical education reform. In his later years, after he retired from the IOC,

he must have grown skeptical that the IOC was operating as the leader of an actual sporting movement. His skepticism certainly would have been warranted. After his death in 1937, the IOC hosted no Olympic Congresses again until 1973. During his presidency, Coubertin ensured that Olympic Congresses were hosted at regular intervals and that they addressed a diversity of issues related to wider practices of sport and physical education. This is where Coubertin distinguished himself as the intellectual and philosophical leader of the international Olympic Movement. He did not envision the Olympic Games as an end in themselves. He argued that they ought to be the pinnacle of a social movement where experiencing the pleasure of everyday sport was a necessary and essential base. Throughout his life, he never lost sight of the fact that a difficult and tenuous balance between grass roots sport and elite international sport needed to be maintained. He recognised that the Olympic Games and elite athletes represented an extreme end that was often associated with the practices of everyday sport, and even acknowledged that the degree of specialisation and commitment to training that elite athletes demonstrated did not represent the type of balance that was essential for success in modern society (Coubertin, 1913).

At the same time, he tried to argue that Olympic athletes were fundamentally abstractions intended to motivate average men to incorporate physical activity into their lifestyles. From Coubertin's ideological perspective, sport needed to be practised in harmony with all of the other areas of life. He argued that moderation was a virtue – even in sport. It is far more difficult to achieve balance and harmony when some elements are practised excessively. At times, Coubertin revealed a degree of ambivalence towards the Olympic Games when he discussed the benefits of everyday sport. He recognised the contradiction that the Olympic Games posed for his ideas of 'Sport for All' and physical education. He seemed quite content to conserve the Olympic Games in the realm of the ideal, rather than the real. Olympic Games and Olympic athletes were intended to function as rarified symbols of athletic perfection. Like fine works of art, Coubertin believed that Olympic athletes were aesthetic objects – they were not necessarily practical. Rather, they were objects to contemplate and appreciate.

THE AESTHETIC IMPERATIVE OF THE OLYMPIC GAMES FESTIVAL

We tend to overlook Coubertin's efforts to resolve the paradoxical relationship between symbols of sporting excellence and the practice of everyday sport. In popular media discourses at the beginning of the twenty-first century, the Olympic Games spectacle has completely eclipsed the idea that the Olympic Movement is grounded in a philosophy of social reform. To some extent, Coubertin himself is at fault. Many of his early initiatives focused on the sensual embellishment of the Olympic Games. Indeed, his fastidiousness for creating the liturgy of symbols and traditions for the Olympic Games occupied much of his time (Hobsbawm, 1983; MacAloon, 1996; Slowikowski, 1991). For example, in 1906 he hosted a conference in Paris where artists, writers, and musicians were assembled to help him explore the aesthetic presentation of the Olympic Games and sport festivals in general (Brown, 1996b, 1999). The most tangible outcome of the conference was the introduction of fine art competitions to the Olympic Games programme. In 1912, the first Olympic Fine Art Competitions were contested in Stockholm. They remained a rather odd and ambiguous feature of the Olympic Games programme until 1948 when they were replaced with a cultural festival held in conjunction with the Games. Shortly after the 1906 conference, Coubertin recognised that the art competitions did not completely satisfy his aesthetic vision for modern sport. He wanted athletes and spectators to be united in a sensual experience that would invoke a shared appreciation of effort, excellence, and harmony. He referred to this sensual experience as *eurythmie*. It was an aesthetic imperative that Coubertin believed was essential in the process of cultivating young men with the taste, or appreciation, for sport participation. Eurythmie was an appreciation for the beauty for moving muscles. In this sense, it differed from the experience of fine art that was conceived as a visual or auditory experience.

In addition to the Olympic Games fine art competitions, Coubertin also took a more direct approach to demonstrate his aesthetic ideal for sport. In 1911, he co-ordinated an International Olympic Architecture Competition. Participants were asked to design a modern (secular) sanctuary for sport. Coubertin provided the architects with an essay in which he elaborated on his own vision of a modern Olympia. The competition was only a moderate success. Very few international submissions were received. In spite of this, the idea for the competition, his essay *Une Olympie Moderne* (1909) as well as the elaborately staged theatrical event at the competition's conclusion, represents the most vivid articulation of Coubertin's cultural theory for the experience of sport (Brown, 1996a). When examined within the context of the 1906 conference and a number of his publications between 1909 and 1912, the International Olympic Architecture Competition clarifies some of Coubertin's ideas about the paradox between Olympic Games and the practice of everyday sport. Ideally, he would have orchestrated Olympic

Games as intimate gatherings where the very best athletes who would compete among themselves and for themselves as well as a small audience whose own sport experiences would allow them to appreciate the athleticism displayed before them. Fundamentally, he hoped that the Olympic Games would produce a festival experience for the participants and spectators (Coubertin, 1967). Spectators would have their own deep knowledge of sport, a knowledge that they had cultivated through their own experiences in sport and physical activity in their daily lives. According to anthropological theory, Coubertin envisioned the Olympic Games as a festival: a cultural performance where athletic performers and observers shared common social and cultural experiences (MacAloon, 1984). He hoped that the Olympic Games would be a celebration within a community of international athletes. Within this model of interpretation, the festival was for athletes, not the global audience following the competition results.

Ironically, Coubertin promoted the festival ideal for the Olympic Games during an era when social, economic, and technological innovations brought about a significant change in the type of cultural performances that modern societies were producing. From the mid-nineteenth century onwards, massive urban spectacles were increasingly common. As a genre of culture performance, spectacles emphasise differences, rather than similarities, among participants. Spectacles privilege visual experience as opposed to movement experiences (MacAloon, 1984). Spectacle participants are clearly distinguished as performers or observers. The social function of spectacles is also markedly different than the social function of festivals. Where festivals emphasise the similarities and shared experiences of participants, spectacles magnify differences among participants. The design and scale of public spaces in modern Europe and North America contributed to the increase in public spectacles. Sport was drawn easily into the realm of spectacular modern entertainment (Brantlinger, 1990). Modern stadiums, theatres, and exhibitions helped institutionalise the spectacle genre of cultural performance as a common experience of the modern world. By the late 1800s, professional sport spectacles were commonplace throughout Europe and North America. Burlesque and cinema spectacles were also a thriving industry. Internationally, sport adapted easily to the spectacle genre. It was also highly marketable. From international expositions to pedestrian marathons, entrepreneurs and impresarios created sport spectacles for the explicit purpose of capturing profits in the entertainment industry. While entertainment sport succeeded as an industry, the sporting spectacles did not necessarily encourage more people to integrate sport and physical activity into their daily lives. Coubertin was fully aware that professional sport spectacles did not offer a model that would be useful for the Olympic Games.

While Coubertin was IOC President, he was aware that professional sport spectacles posed a serious threat to his Olympic Games ideal. At the same time, he recognised that the popularity of the Olympic Games themselves were a potential threat. As early as 1914, Coubertin expressed his concern that the Olympic Games were growing too large in scale. The Olympic Congress in Paris, 1914, proved to Coubertin that the scale and complexity of organising the Olympic Games was distracting the IOC and Congress delegates from the broader pedagogical motives of the Olympic Movement (Müller, 1994). In 1928, he made a direct reference to the impact of the spectacle phenomenon on the experience of modern sport:

> But one has to be in the company of athletes to sense their manly beauty. If one goes over to the spectators' benches, one notes an ever increasing lack of that same sporting spirit. More and more, modern crowds lack the chivalrous spirit that thrived in the middle ages among those attending tournaments and popular jousts... I would like it if we were to treat today's spectators like great children, walking among them with enormous cards to teach them how to appreciate a splendid athletic feat, and how out of place on such occasions are those outbursts of crude nationalism that give our era a semi-barbaric stench (Coubertin, 1928).

In effect, Coubertin was critical of the tendency of sporting audiences to participate as idle spectators who could not identify authentically with the athletic performances.

Coubertin's plan for presenting modern Olympic Games festivals was contingent on another theoretical consideration. He understood the experience of sport in very much the same way that he understood the experience of fine art. Although he never claimed that sport was art, he was adamant that sport participation could also be an *aesthetic* experience. Aesthetic experiences are those human moments when man-made beauty exposes profound insights into the human condition. Although beauty is generally associated with some form of sensual experience, aesthetic experiences merge sensation with intellectual and moral insight. For Coubertin, the Olympic Games were not merely beautiful events; they were intended to produce experiences that were aesthetic. As such, they were also conceived within a broader cultural context and demanded a specific knowledge of that context to be fully appreciated. Coubertin referred to this as *the taste* for sport.

He did not claim that appreciation for athletic sport was universal and beautiful across all social classes and in all communities. In his opinion, the true taste for sport extended from participation rather than mere observation. On the one hand, this was a very innovative theory and reflected a profoundly non-dualistic value of physical activity and sport. For Coubertin, the taste for sport could be nurtured in the body, its muscles, and its limbs. Participating in sport was the only way to achieve a refined taste for sport. It could not be acquired fully from books or spectating (Brown, 1999). On the other hand, Coubertin's theory of sport culture was an extension of the same modernist discourse that distinguished fine art from folk art, crafts, and other forms of popular culture. Fine art was the domain of true aesthetic experiences, where folk or popular art was the domain of simple sensual pleasure. This was a truly class-based version of aesthetics. Access and appreciation of fine art required the type of cultivation that was only available to the privileged classes. Access and appreciation of folk art, crafts, and popular culture did not require such refined taste. Like fine art, Coubertin suggested that a taste for sport would enhance the opportunity of the Olympic Games, exposing important truths about humankind and society. However, cultivation of this taste for sport was contingent on the opportunity to play specific types of sports in specific acceptable contexts. The type of sports and sporting contexts that Coubertin advocated were, for the most part, inaccessible to the working classes. Coubertin made no apologies for the inevitable class-based reality that provided the basis for his Olympic Games idea. A society divided along lines of economic wealth and inherited privilege was the reality of his era and his vision of the world that could not be dismissed. After all, for Coubertin, the elite nature of the Olympic Games and the experiences they gave its socially elite sportsmen was always intended to serve a social function in a paternalistic, or 'top-down', fashion. The social elite were expected to use their higher insights to benevolently guide the lower classes. Other types of sport and sport festivals could serve the lower social orders in other ways. In short, Coubertin assumed a practical and expedient approach to social reform through sport. By no means should his practical approach be interpreted as a complete disregard of sport's potential to providing healthier and happier lifestyles for lower-class men. Throughout his life, he always argued that it was the privileged classes' responsibility to initiate change 'from above'.

Coubertin's paternalism is evident in numerous articles that he passionately wrote on the sport of rowing (Brown, 1999); for him, rowing was the modern sport *par excellence* (Coubertin, 1986). It offered all of the essential qualities that made it a perfect Olympic sport as well as a perfect pastime for men of all classes. The physical demands of rowing provided a particular quality of experience that Coubertin promoted as the perfect expression of eurythmie. This aesthetic imperative could be experienced by a perfectly-trained athlete in a state-of-the-art racing shell with a sliding seat or a simple labourer or an office clerk pulling his way along in a row boat during his evenings or weekend. Movement of the body, the oars, the boat, and the water produced a perfect combination of harmony, balance, moderation, and precision. The activity was seen as a way for young men to embody these qualities. Under proper conditions, and with adequate training, rowers could experience eurythmie. As such, it was a sport with great aesthetic potential: a beautiful culmination of movement, power, control, and resistance. Importantly, as an aesthetic experience, Coubertin suggested that the eurythmie that rowing produced could give rowers profound insights into the human condition.

Coubertin's enthusiastic endorsement of rowing as the perfect modern sport also underscored his social realism. During Coubertin's lifetime, competitive rowing was primarily the domain of private 'prep' schools, universities, and exclusive sporting clubs. The social elite could afford to take advantage of new technology in expensive rowing shells with sliding seats, sophisticated oarlocks, and lightweight construction materials. Under these circumstances, rowing was undoubtedly a pastime for 'gentlemen'. In spite of the sport's social exclusivity, Coubertin suggested that men of modest social standing could also benefit from a derivative form of the sport. While they would not be able to experience the subtle perfection of fine watercrafts, men of modest social standing could still row in modified boats and with minimal technical expertise. Recognising the financial and time constraints of elite rowing, Coubertin explored ways of replicating the movement of rowing with modified rowboats and rowing machines. This practical, or realistic, approach to adapting sport was the basis of Coubertin's philosophy of 'making-do': *le philosophie du débrouillard* (Coubertin, 1909). Coubertin encouraged working-class men to approach life with this make-do philosophy. In terms of sport and physical activity, he hoped that working-class men would take responsibility for their own physical activity by making-do with the facilities, equipment, and time available to them.

Coubertin's vision of social reform through rowing, sport, and the Olympic Games is not without paradoxes and inconsistencies. For example, he recognised that elite, Olympic-level rowing, for all intents and purposes, produced a completely different type of motion and skills than the humble make-do type of rowing he promoted for lower-class men. Also, he was untroubled in assuming that the refined and precise movement of elite rowers was more aesthetically pleasing and ultimately more meaningful than the crude movement produced by working-class rowers. Furthermore, he suggested that working-class men would not gain any more benefit from exercising in the type of specialised racing crafts used by elite college oarsmen.

Similarly, he never suggested that upper-class men ought to satisfy themselves with basic rowboats. Coubertin was quite clear that one style of rowing was appropriate for the upper classes, while a different style of rowing was appropriate for the lower classes. This is where Coubertin's logic is problematic and sociologically deterministic. He seemed to suggest that men's bodies are somehow classed socially *for* sport rather than cultivated *by* sport. His theory of sport culture is innovative because it values the experience of muscles and joints. However, his theory of sport culture is troubling because he suggests that the potential for experiencing the body is determined by social class.

Between 1894 and 1925, Coubertin wrote prolifically on sport, physical education, art, culture, history, and his revival of the Olympic Games. When considered as an *oeuvre* (a comprehensive expression of Coubertin's vision for sport), we receive a clear picture of what the experience of the Olympic Games was claimed to be for athletes and spectators. Quite simply, Coubertin hoped that the Olympic Games would function as a sport festival. In spite of their international character, he argued that the Olympic Games could be an intimate communal gathering of sportsmen and spectators who experienced and understood the same qualities of sport. As a celebration among a community of elite sportsmen, the Olympic Games also constituted a symbol, or abstraction, of his aesthetic imperative of modern sport. The Olympic Games were a curious convergence of the real and the ideal. They were a real, rational, and logical conclusion for elite athletes. At the same time, they were an ideal, intended to reinforce the social value and aesthetic potential of everyday sport.

THE IMPROBABLE AND VULNERABLE IDEAL OF AN OLYMPIC GAMES FESTIVAL

From 1896 to the present, the cultural form of the Olympic Games has grown increasingly familiar to athletes and observers around the world (Morages et al., 2002). Its sport programme, ceremonies, symbols, and rituals have been refined and naturalised over time. We imagine that this common knowledge of the form of the Olympic Games is evidence of an international community that shares and celebrates common attitudes towards sport and its value to a peaceful and co-operative world. However, in many ways this naturalisation of the Olympic Games is stronger evidence of a global economic community bound together through trade and commerce

(Whitson & Macintosh, 2002). For most of the global population, the Olympic Games are a consumer experience. The vast sums of money that television networks pay for the right to broadcast the Olympic Games and the huge audiences that consume these broadcasts reveal a widening gap between the Olympic Games as a festival and the mediated television programming spectacle. The international sport festival ideal is frequently obscured by the reality of the global media spectacle that the Olympic Games generate. This distance between the ideal and the real makes it increasingly difficult to discuss Olympic Games experiences as something coherent and homogeneous. The meaning of the event itself seems impossible to comprehend given the overwhelming international economic significance of the Olympic Games. Whether considered singularly or collectively, the experiences of the Olympic athletes seem oddly irrelevant compared to the billions of dollars of economic activity that frame the Games. Indeed, the social and political management of the Olympic Games is so complex that the idea of producing a shared experience of community among a relatively small group of elite athletes seems ludicrous. It is important to question the value and integrity of this sporting enterprise as the connection between the Olympic Games festival ideal and the reality of Olympic Games consumer experiences grows increasingly difficult to comprehend.

Thus, I want to propose that the Olympic Games have always been challenged by this ambiguous tension between festival and everyday life. The ambiguity is evident at many levels. The festival ideal has been challenged by the very practical nature of sport itself. Early in the history of the modern Olympic Games, this event provided elite athletes with a very clear and specific sport-performance goal. Because of this, we can imagine that athletes have always had the potential to undermine the integrity of the festival quality of the Olympic Games by assuming a 'win at all cost' approach to their participation. This would effectively separate them from the festival ideal. Furthermore, we see specific examples from the history of the Olympic Games where individual athletes did not embrace the festival because the prospect of their own success superceded their desire to participate in a community celebration.

By definition, modern sport is institutional and hierarchical. In this context, the modern Olympic Games became a logical extension of the discourse of modern sport. As modern sport grew increasingly institutionalised in the late 1800s and early 1900s, distinctive, regularly occurring events like the Olympic Games brought further logic and continuity to sporting experiences. The distinctive quadrennial cycle of the Olympic Games invoked competitive peaks, even termination for many athletic careers. An Olympic

Games experience could signify an end point, terminus, or culmination of an athlete's competitive career. Ending an athletic career as an Olympic champion could add sufficient social justification for an athletic career. This practical function of the Olympic Games has always produced a tension between the communal celebration of the sporting festival ideal and the pursuit of individual objectives by competitive athletes.

The 4-year cycle added symbolic potency to the Olympic Games experience. In athletic careers, timing is especially crucial when defining one's place in history. Framing one's athletic career within an historical context is valuable, given the social paradox of modern sport in most western European capitalist countries: sport is a personal leisure pastime and socially unimportant until the success of a society's sportspeople is allowed to shape its collective identity. In countries like Canada and the United States, most Olympic sports garner very little public attention except during the Olympic Games. In spite of this obscurity, the elite athletes in these sports must train like professionals. Still, while demonstrating this commitment and single-mindedness, society interprets these serious pursuits as 'play'. Every four years, however, athletes in Olympic sports are given a chance to convert the cultural currency that they have accumulated in their sporting excellence into social currency. They do this by allowing their nations to attach their collective sense of well-being to their own athletic success. If they are successful, Olympic athletes' new social currency validates the time and resources consumed during all these years of play. The 4-year cycle of the Olympic Games creates a type of obstacle or barrier that makes this opportunity to exchange athletic currency for social currency even more precious. Very early in the history of the modern Olympic Games, this additional hurdle to success was accepted as a natural and logical mark of distinction among athletes, sport administrators, sport marketers, and the general public. Today, market-savvy athletes recognise the social currency of an Olympic Games experience. They see the Olympic Games as the only way to justify this prolonged and intense period of play. Indeed, some athletes argue that the opportunity to participate in the Olympic Games is a fundamental human right. Ending an international athletic career without an Olympic Games experience is often characterised by athletes, and the media, as an unnatural conclusion.

Athletes and spectators could not have known what to expect during the first three editions of the Olympic Games. In 1896, 1900, and 1904 athletes likely experienced the Olympic Games as a novelty, curiosity, and adventure. In view of the fact that Coubertin and Olympic Games hosts could not agree on the most fundamental organisational details of the festivals, we can hardly expect that athletes knew and anticipated particular types of experience. Issues such as the sport programme, selection of host cities, selection of athletes, duration of the festival, and even adherence to the 4-year cycle of the Games represented sources of confusion for administrators. At the first Olympic Games, some evidence suggests that the spirit of experimentation must have constituted part of the collective athletic experience. For example, a number of athletes elected to participate in events that were not necessarily their specialty. An American named Edwin Flack went to Athens to compete in the 'middle distance' events on the track but also opted into the marathon event – and even decided to play in the tennis tournament. Athletes representing different countries demonstrated a spirit of kinship by teaming up for the tennis tournament (Lennartz & Wassong, 1986, pp. 23–24). In Paris in 1900, the Olympic Games programme extended over such a long period of time (several months) that the temporal and spatial quality of the Olympic Games experience must have been lost on most athletes. Even as the sports were contested in Paris, uncertainty about the 'Olympic' status of specific events was unresolved. The Olympic Games in St. Louis, 1904, were also radically dissimilar to the first two events in Athens and Paris.

When did the Olympic Games experience become naturalised in modern sporting culture? When did they become a necessity rather than an opportunity? When did athletes and the general public begin to associate Olympic Games experiences with the definition of athletic success? Evidence from 1908 and 1912 suggests that the Olympic Games factored into national discourses on sport in European and North American countries. Certainly, the number of disputes between British and American athletes and officials in 1908 indicate that Olympic Games experiences were tied to matters of national prestige (Coates, 2004, pp. 53–55). In Canada, the Governor General encouraged different amateur sport associations to co-operate in the selection of the Canadian team heading to London in 1908 (Kidd, 1996, p. 34). Similarly, when planning the sport programme for the 1912 Olympic Games in Stockholm, strong national interests shaped a debate on sport officiating. During this period, the IOC grew increasingly aware of the need to ensure unbiased officiating in the Olympic Games. Coubertin perceived the 1912 Olympic Games as the culmination of his efforts to produce an aesthetically distinct and potent international sport festival. Paradoxically, while the IOC and Olympic Games hosts were discovering how to present the Olympic Games festival with all of its special and distinctive qualities, they were also attempting to ensure that the sport programme and sport officiating grew increasingly consistent by everyday standards.

The 1920s and 1930s were an historical era where distinct social groups and nations recognised that the Olympic Games offered a means of advancing specific social causes. By the 1920s, participating in the Olympic Games was the logical expectation for elite sportsmen in Europe and North America. For non-dominant groups, such as women, the Olympic Games did not offer such obvious or viable opportunities to test one's athletic talent. During this era, women launched a tactical campaign that eventually forced the IOC to include more events in the programme of the Olympic Games. Others groups outwardly rejected participation in the Games. A similar appropriation of the Olympic Games festival is evident in the history of workers' sport. In the 1920s and 1930s, athletes who were active in labour movements around the world participated in a massively successful series of Workers' Olympic Games (see Chapter 8; Krüger & Riordan, 1996, pp. vii–x). In many ways, the success of the Workers' Olympic Games validated the social and cultural significance of the Olympic Games. Unlike the feminist sport movement, the International Workers' Sport Movement (IWSM) did not seek inclusion in the Olympic Games and representation on the IOC. Members of the IWSM saw the IOC as a false leader of international sport. Olympic sport was *bourgeois* sport, not the sport of the *people*.

During this same era, the Olympic Games experience also entered international political discourse. Nation states recognised that success in international sport and, especially the Olympic Games, carried substantial diplomatic currency. As such, entire countries began to experience the Olympic Games. Historian Mark Dyreson (1998) demonstrates how Americans' collective identity represented an intersection of political identity and sporting identity that was influenced by the success of their athletes at the Olympic Games. Americans were among the first nations to reflect on the Olympic Games' experience and integrated in a popular construction of their collective national/republican identity. Non-European nations like Japan and China also interpreted participation in the Olympic Games as an assertion of their presence and legitimacy on the world stage. For China, in particular, the participation of one athlete, Liu Changchun, in the 1932 Olympic Games in Los Angeles was "seen as a great step in establishing a foothold in the community of modern nations" (Morris, 1999, p. 549). Japan began participating at the Olympic Games in 1912. Through the 1920s and 1930s, Japanese sport officials and politicians were successful at increasing the number and quality of the country's performances at the games. While athletic performance was certainly important to the Japanese, they also wanted to host the Olympic Games in Tokyo in 1940. The Olympic

Games experience was tied to their international political and economic identity as a nation. The Japanese claimed that hosting Olympic Games would put Tokyo and their country into the network of modern industrial nations (Guttmann & Thompson, 2001, pp. 126–127). These examples of national experiences tied to hosting and participating in Olympic Games extended far beyond the festival experience that Coubertin envisioned. Do they also represent corruption of the festival ideal, or are they merely banal extensions of it?

In the 1920s, Olympic idealism was tested in a variety of forms outside of the direct purview of the IOC. One man in particular drew upon the ideology of the Olympic Movement to initiate a trend towards Olympic-type continental sporting festivals. In the 1910s, American Elwood Brown saw international sport as a means of accelerating the modernisation of developing nations. Brown was a YMCA leader in the Philippines. The international activities of the YMCA provided an additional context to the activities of Coubertin and the IOC. Brown interpreted the Olympic Games as a viable means of accelerating the Americanisation of Asia. He created the Far Eastern Olympic Association as an adjunct to the International Olympic Movement. Brown suggested that the first Far Eastern Olympic Games (1913) demonstrated the positive impact that western sport had on the Americanisation of Asian culture (Dyreson, 1998, pp. 175–176). Elwood Brown's initiative introduced the IOC to the potential of regional Olympic-styled Games as a method of developing sport in non-European societies. At the time, it was a logical proposal considering that the sport programme of the Olympic Games hardly represented global sporting practices (Boulongne, 1994, pp. 168–171).

For the IOC, a central issue was defining how regional games would be perceived in relation to the Olympic Games. Would they function as developmental events giving athletes an opportunity to prepare for the ultimate international event, the Olympic Games? Would they end up competing against the Olympic Games – eclipsing and diluting the cultural impact of the Olympic Games? Would they become regional expressions of Olympism and signify the vibrancy of the Olympic Movement? Perhaps, they would become regional expressions of sporting values that could potentially undermine the universal ideal of Olympism. Opinions varied within the IOC. Once the debates were exhausted, regional games in parts of the world that were less Europeanised and Americanised were endorsed. Consequently, Far Eastern Games, South American and Latin American Games were awarded IOC patronage. African Games were certainly given some serious consideration but, ultimately, patronage was rejected.

Regional Games that extended from existing European sporting traditions were rejected. European Regional Games did not receive IOC patronage for political and economic reasons (Boulongne, 1994, pp. 205–206). Today, the IOC's patronage of regional games is more inclusive. Indeed, the IOC formally recognises five Continental Sport Organisations that co-ordinate and sponsor Regional and Continental Games.

The early history of IOC's patronage, or endorsement, tells us a great deal about the extent to which the Olympic Games experience was naturalised in sport discourses. While IOC patronage was initially a symbolic affiliation, the desire for this affiliation is evidence of the real and perceived social currency that the Olympic Games represented early in the history of the Olympic Movement. From 1894 to the present day, preserving the symbolic power of this social currency has been managed with heavy-handed authority by Coubertin and subsequent IOC Presidents and IOC executives. The function of IOC patronage extends well beyond the issue of recognising groups or regions of sportspeople who are socially disadvantaged.

CONCLUSION

Beyond the practical sport functions discussed here, the Olympic Games remain the subject of serious debate. The ideological rhetoric that Coubertin used to rationalise the Olympic Games in 1894 continues to frame the public discourse on the Olympic Games at the beginning of the twenty-first century. This ideological rhetoric has also been challenged by lived experiences at Olympic Games. From the very beginning, the symbolic function of the Olympic Games has been contested and corrupted. In other words, as a *culture performance*, the Olympic Games festival has never provided a perfect symbol of universal humanism. In spite of the efforts of Coubertin and subsequent IOC officials, conserving the symbolic potency of the Olympic Games has proven challenging, if not impossible. As a symbol, Olympic Games have magnified the fragility – if not impossibility – of utopian internationalism and universal humanism.

Examples of this vulnerability range from grotesque acts of violence against Olympic athletes to more subtle acts of cheating within the sporting events themselves. Regardless of the nature of these acts, all of them illustrate the ongoing tension between the Olympic Games *ideal* and the Olympic Games *reality*. When Palestinian terrorists invaded the Athletes Village at the 1972 Olympic Games in Munich, Germany, and abducted and murdered 11 Israeli team members, the symbolic quality of the festival experience was shattered. When American President Jimmy Carter orchestrated a western boycott of the 1980 Olympic Games in Moscow, the real and symbolic quality of the festival experience was eliminated for thousands of athletes from the US and other allied nations. The political boycotts of the 1960s, 1970s, and 1980s represent examples of how the Olympic Games often produce a negative (or inverted) symbol. The non-Olympic Games experiences of boycotting nations are real and symbolic evidence of the failure of peaceful international and universal humanism. When a pipe bomb exploded during an evening concert at the Olympic Plaza in Atlanta, 1996, the real and symbolic quality of harmonious peaceful internationalism was, once again, clearly compromised.

Athletes have also played a role in highlighting the vulnerability of the Olympic Games festival experience. Examples of cheats, foul play, and poor sportsmanship reveal how competitive sportsmen rarely constitute a perfect symbol of festival-like behaviour. The opportunity to succeed at sport, regardless of the context, regularly lures athletes away from the rules that make sport *sport*. Basing an entire festival on such a precarious cultural practice seems destined to failure. Cheating athletes are evident throughout the history of the modern Olympic Games. Apparently, French runners hitched rides on street trolleys during the marathon race in Paris, 1900. Unwittingly, Jim Thorpe broke the amateur code by playing professional baseball. By the standards of 1912, this was 'cheating' and Thorpe was stripped of his medals. In the past 30 years, hundreds of athletes have been caught in 'doping' scandals. When caught, they have been disqualified from the Olympic Games and stripped of their medals. No doubt, countless others have 'doped' and not been caught. Whether or not athletes are caught cheating, the Olympic Games festival experience, has been compromised. Cheats are not participating in the festival. Athletes may compete together, but their intentions, motives, and modes of competing vary greatly. When the cheats are exposed, the real and symbolic power of the Olympic Games festival is destroyed. Doping cheats clearly illustrate how athletes can participate in the same event (the same festival) without sharing the values and beliefs that are the basis of the entire festival.

While the real and symbolic potency of the Olympic Games festival has been considerably corrupted over the past century, something continues to survive and stimulate human curiosity and commitment to the experience of the Olympic Games. Perhaps a *real* Olympic Games festival experience has never really existed. More likely, the Olympic Games festival has always been experienced more intensely and authentically in our imaginations. This is a logical way of explaining how a nineteenth century European cultural performance can be experienced by a world of human beings who understand inherently the political, sociological, economic, and ideological plurality of this global community. Evidently, the longevity of the Olympic Games is not contingent on the experience of a perfect festival celebration or the perfect symbolic representation of an international festival.

We need to continue critiquing the Olympic Games experience. It is simply too costly and omnipresent in our culture to ignore. The Olympic Games festival is not a reality. It is an ideal that is imagined. Our ability to imagine and value the Olympic Games is bound to a human affinity for nostalgia. This chapter has examined the origins of the Olympic Games ideal. It proposed the historical and cultural context in which Pierre de Coubertin imagined the modern Olympic Games as a cultural performance that united an international community of sportsmen both functionally and symbolically. He imagined the Olympic Games as a festival experienced ephemerally as a participant and as a symbol of a festival that could be contemplated by the entire world.

The chapter has also demonstrated that the history of the modern Olympic Games must be allowed to evoke caution about the social expectations we may hold for this event in our postmodern times. This overview of the early history of Olympic Games experiences critiqued what they were claimed to be, and what we expect from them. According to an anthropological theory of festival and spectacle, athletic participants of the Olympic Games are the only true agents in this form of cultural performance. However, in our current postmodern era, defining participation and agency within a hyper-mediated (and cyber-mediated) global sporting event is far more challenging than Pierre de Coubertin could have ever imagined. We know that athletes and their performances are influenced by the media. We know that the media convert the sporting event into an entertainment product that is consumed by billions of television viewers around the world. We do not need to argue that the Olympic Games are essentially spectacle. However, we do need to try and understand how they may also retain some of the cultural integrity that they claim to possess.

REFERENCES

Boulongne, Y.-P. (1994). The Presidencies of Demetrius Vikelas (1894–1896) and Pierre de Coubertin (1896–1925). In: G. Raymond (Ed.), *The International Olympic Committee One Hundred Years: The ideas, the presidents, the achievements*. Lausanne: IOC.

Brantlinger, P. (1990). Mass media and culture in fin-de-siècle Europe. In: M. Teich & R. Porter (Eds), *Fin de Siècle and its legacy siècle* (pp. 98–114). Cambridge: Cambridge University Press.

Brown, D. (1987). Social Darwinism, private schooling and sport in Victorian and Edwardian Canada. In: A. Mangan (Ed.), *Pleasure, profit, proselytism: British culture and sport at home and abroad, 1700–1914* (pp. 215–230). London: Frank Cass.

Brown, D. A. (1996a). Revisiting the discourses of art, beauty and sport from the 1906 consultative conference for the arts, literature and sport. *OLYMPIKA: The International Journal of Olympic Studies, V*, 1–24.

Brown, D. A. (1996b). Olympic exploration of modernism, 1894–1920: Aesthetics, ideology and the spectacle. *Research Quarterly for Exercise and Sport, 67*(2), 121–135.

Brown, D. A. (1999). The sensual and intellectual pleasures of rowing: Pierre de Coubertin's ideal for modern sport. *Sport History Review, 30*(2), 95–118.

Coates, J. (2004). London 1908: The games of the fourth Olympiad. In: J. Findling & K. Pelle (Eds), *Encyclopedia of the modern Olympic movement* (pp. 51–56). Westport, CN and London: Greenwood Press.

Coubertin, P. de. (1889). *L'Education Anglaise en France*. Paris: Hachettte.

Coubertin, P. de. (1909). *La Philosophie du Débrouillard. Une Campagne de Vingt-et-un-ans (1887–1908)*. Paris: Librairie de l'Éducation Physique.

Coubertin, P. de. (1913). Une Campagne contre l'athlète specialize. *Revue Olympique*, (Juillet), 114.

Coubertin, P. de. (1928). The athletic spirit must dominate all other issues. In: N. Müller (Ed.), *Olympism: Selected readings* (p. 562). Lausanne: IOC. (Published originally in *La Revue Sportive Illustrée, 24*(3), 1928, 24.)

Coubertin, P. de. (1967). A modern Olympia. *The Olympic idea: Discourses and essays* (pp. 20–23). Stuttgart: Carl Diem Institute. (Originally published in French as a series in the *Revue Olympique* between 1909 and 1910.)

Coubertin, P. de (1986). La cure d'aviron. Pierre de Coubertin. *Textes Choisis* (p. 228). Tome III, Zurich: Weidmann. (Published originally in *Praxis, Revue Suisse d Medecine* 3 (Juillet) 1928, 1–2.)

Dyreson, M. (1998). *Making the American team: Sport, culture, and Olympic experience*. Urbana, IL and Chicago: University of Illinois Press.

Guttmann, A., & Thompson, L. (2001). *Japanese sport: A history*. Honolulu: University of Hawai'i Press.

Hoberman, J. (1995). Towards a theory of Olympic internationalism. *Journal of Sport History, 22*(1), 1–37.

Hobsbawm, E. (1983). Mass-producing traditions: Europe, 1870–1914. In: E. Hobsbawm & T. Ranger (Eds), *The invention of tradition* (pp. 263–307). Cambridge: Cambridge University Press.

Kidd, B. (1996). *The struggle for Canadian sport*. Toronto: University of Toronto Press.

Krüger, A., & Riordan, J. (Eds). (1996). *The story of worker sport*. Champaign, IL: Human Kinetics.

Lennartz, K., & Wassong, S. (1986). Athens 1896. In: J. Findling & K. Pelle (Eds), *Encyclopedia of the modern Olympic movement* (pp. 17–25). Westport, CN: Greenwood Press.

MacAloon, J. (1981). *This great symbol: Pierre de Coubertin and the origins of the modern Olympic Games*. Chicago: University of Chicago Press.

MacAloon, J. J. (1984). Olympic games and the theory of spectacle in modern societies. In: *Rite, drama, festival, spectacle: Rehearsals toward a theory of cultural performance* (pp. 241–280). Philadelphia: Institute for the Study of Human Issues (ISHI) Press.

MacAloon, J. (1996). On the structural origins of Olympic individuality. *Research Quarterly for Exercise and Sport, 67*(2), 136–147.

Magraw, R. (2002). *France 1800–1914: A social history.* London: Pearson.

Morages, M. de., Rivenburgh, N. K., & Larsen, J. F. (2002). Opening ceremony narratives. In: W. Adams & L. Gerlach (Eds), *The Olympic games: Ancient and modern Boston* (pp. 191–206). MA: Pearson Custom Publishing.

Morris, A. (1999). 'I Can Compete!' China in the Olympic Games, 1932 and 1936. *Journal of Sport History, 26*(3), 545–566.

Müller, N. (1994). *One hundred years of Olympic Congresses, 1894–1994.* Lausanne: IOC.

Müller, N. (2000). Coubertin's Olympism. In: N. Müller (Ed.), *Pierre de Coubertin, 1863–1937: Olympism Selected Writings* (pp. 33–48). Lausanne: International Olympic Committee.

Putney, C. (2001). *Manhood and sport in Protestant America, 1880–1920.* Cambridge, MA: Harvard University Press.

Quantz, D. R. (1993). Civic pacifism and sports-based intrenationalism: Framework for the founding of the international Olympic committee. *OLYMPIKA: The International Journal of Olympic Studies, II,* 1–23.

Rioux, G. (2000). Pierre de Coubertin's revelation. In: *Pierre de Coubertin, 1863–1937: Olympism, selected writings.* Lausanne: IOC.

Slowikowski, S. S. (1991). Burning desire: Nostalgia, ritual, and the sport festival flame ceremony. *Sociology of Sport Journal, 8,* 239–257.

Whitson, D., & Macintosh, D. (2002). The global circus: International sport, tourism, and the marketing of cities. In: W. Adams & L. Gerlach (Eds), *The Olympic Games: Ancient and modern* (pp. 241–252). Boston, MA: Pearson Custom Publishing.

Chapter 3

THE NAZI OLYMPICS OF 1936

Arnd Krüger

Commonly referred to as the 'Nazi Olympics' (Mandell, 1971; Krüger & Murray, 2003), the Olympic Games of 1936 changed the Olympic movement in magnitude and proportion. As the focal point of amateur sports, by the mid-1930s the Olympic Games had become a highly politicised international event which consistently made front-page headlines in the international press. With over 4,000 athletes representing 49 countries at the Berlin Games, participation was one-third larger than ever before. The gathering of 3.77 million spectators at the Olympic events was more than three times greater than at the preceding Summer Olympics in Los Angeles in 1932. At the opening ceremony of the Olympic Winter Games in Garmisch-Partenkirchen, there were more spectators than at all events of the Winter Games combined in Lake Placid in 1932.

German organisers ensured that their Games were technologically modern in every way. For instance, the Berlin Olympic stadium included the most up-to-date radio equipment, which transmitted the Games around the globe to a radio audience of more than 300 million. All-embracing, state-run propaganda machinery advertised the Games in Germany and abroad in 14 different languages. At the 1936 Games, many of the features that constitute modern sports were used for the first time, making the Games the grandest international media event the world had known to this point (Krüger, 2004).

In all likelihood, every sports fan would have been pleased about the extensive preparations, had the Games been held in the liberal German Weimar Republic (1919–1933). But, in 1933, Adolf Hitler and his fascist

Global Olympics: Historical and Sociological Studies of the Modern Games
Research in the Sociology of Sport, Volume 3, 43–57
Copyright © 2005 by Elsevier Ltd.

Nazi Party or NSDAP (National Socialist German Workers Party) came to power. When the site for the 1936 Games was transferred to Germany at the 29th Session of the International Olympic Committee (IOC) in Barcelona in 1931, the IOC had three German members: Theodor Lewald (1860–1947), Karl von Halt (1891–1964), and Duke Adolf Friedrich zu Mecklenburg (1873–1969). These men, along with the full-time General Secretary of the Organising Committee, Carl Diem (1882–1962), had assumed significant roles in the organisation of German sports for the previous 25 years or more. Lewald had been the highest-ranking German civil servant as Under-Secretary of State in the Home Office before he was elected President of the German Sports Federation (DRA) and President of the National Olympic Committee for Germany (NOC), IOC member, and member of the IOC Executive Board (1927–1937). Karl Halt, a 1912 Olympian whose personal bravery in World War I had seen him 'renamed' as Karl von Halt, was a banker, President of the German Track and Field Federation, and well-connected with the personalities of the international track elite. The Duke zu Mecklenburg, head administrator in the German African colonies prior to World War I, retained the European tradition of appointed nobility in sports. Diem had also been involved with national and international track and field on the administrative side. He had been the first full-time administrator in German sports as Secretary General of the 1916 Olympics, which had already been scheduled for Berlin. These Games had been cancelled because of World War I, but the plans remained in place. The experience of these men, their international prestige and standing, seemed to guarantee that the Berlin Games would continue the Olympic tradition of splendour, even though the economic hardships of the Depression had been worldwide (Krüger, 2003a).

During the Depression, the Nazi Party gained momentum in Germany. Essentially, it blamed the economic and political downfall of Germany on Jews and Communists (as leading Communists had been Jewish, both were part of a 'world conspiracy' in the view of the Nazis). The Nazis demanded a revision of the demoralising Treaty of Versailles which had concluded the German defeat in World War I and incorporated German de-militarisation, giving up border lands to Germany's neighbours and its colonies to Britain or France, and demanded restitution in the form of huge annual payments for the destruction Germany had caused in the 'Great War'.

In the field of physical education and sports, the Nazis did not have a clear-cut position. Before they came to power, they appeared to be anti-internationalist and racist. Bruno Malitz (1933, p. 42) published an official brochure of the Nazi Party in which he claimed:

> Sports and physical education are creating physical and spiritual values. The Jew is laying his hands at all things which create values, as he is destructive. So he tried to gain control of German sports for its decrement. The Jewish teaching destroys the vigour of the people. The Jewish sports leaders and those infected by the Jew, the pacifists, the Pan-Europeans have no more place in German sports. They are worse than cholera, tuberculosis, and syphilis...as these destroy only some Germans[;] the Jews, however, destroy Germany herself.

Similarly, on the occasion of the 1932 Olympics in Los Angeles, the official Nazi newspaper *Völkischer Beobachter* (August 19, 1932) commented:

> Negroes have no business at the Olympics. Today we witness that free white men have to compete with the unfree Negro. This is a debasement of the Olympic idea beyond comparison... The next Olympics will be held in Berlin in 1936. We hope that the responsible men know what will be their duty. The blacks have to be expelled. We demand it.

The IOC observed these discriminatory overtures and instructed its German members to resolve their domestic tensions. Von Halt volunteered to talk to Hitler; as both men had common friends, an introduction to the popular German Party leader was easily obtained. In a subsequent one hour interview, Hitler promised that if he were in power he would do his utmost to respect international obligations and be a 'good' host to all visitors to Germany. At that time, Hitler was an actively campaigning politician who was still heading the largest opposition party in the German parliament. When Hitler was appointed Chancellor by the German President von Hindenburg on January 30, 1933, the IOC was somewhat concerned but, on the whole, it was willing to accept the German political situation as long as the Games themselves were not impeded by the government.

A week before Hitler became the new German Chancellor, Theodore Lewald formed the Organising Committee (OC) for the Olympic Games as an independent non-profit organisation. On its Boards he did not include any prominent Nazis, recognising their ambiguities regarding international sports. Utilising his administrative abilities and professional connections, Lewald handled the formation, registration, and granting of non-profit status, etc., a procedure that would normally take 6 weeks, in a single day. A strict legalist, Lewald strategically situated the OC as independent from the NOC. This proved to be an effective strategy when, in the turmoil following the Nazi takeover, Lewald and Diem had to resign their posts in the NOC and the DRA – but they remained fundamental contributors to the OC.

Joseph Goebbels had only been Minister of the newly formed Ministry for Public Enlightenment and Propaganda for 5 days when he met with Lewald, who explained to him the propaganda potential of the Olympic Games. Lewald convinced Goebbels that the Olympics should have first priority in his new, but expanding, Ministry. Goebbels embraced Lewald's advice and counsel. This was surprising as neither Goebbels nor Hitler was known to be interested in sport. By contrast, their idol, the Italian fascist dictator, Benito Mussolini, was an acknowledged all-round athlete (Krüger, 1999a; Oelrich, 2003).

But Goebbels understood that having power was only part of the problem of seeking political success: one also had to win the hearts of the people. Sport was one way to achieve this, and eventually his Ministry instituted 11 sections dealing with sport (Teichler, 1976). In assuring Nazi hegemony, a 'culture of consent' (de Grazia, 1981) was reached to offset the more brutal, coercive elements of the regime. This included an extensive job programme to curb unemployment, a growing movie industry, cheap holidays, successful sports for national pride, and other forms of popular entertainment for the German people.

Following the Nazi-led boycott of Jewish businesses, the smashing of the windows of Jewish shops, and the burning of books of Jewish and liberal authors, an international boycott movement started to isolate Germany. One of the cultural targets of the boycott movement very soon became the Olympic Games of 1936, an opportunity of significant importance if the world was to reject Nazism and the brutality it displayed towards its Jewish citizens.

Not surprisingly, it was a Jewish newspaper that first raised the issue of a boycott in the US (Riess, 1998; Eisen, 1999). In April 1933, a *Baltimore Jewish Times* correspondent asked Avery Brundage, the President of the American Olympic Committee, about the American reaction to the German boycott of Jewish shops and the brutal pogroms after the Nazi takeover in Germany. The issue was raised again the following day by the *New York Times* (April 18, 1933, p. 18) with the headlines: '1936 Olympic Games may be cancelled due to Germany's Campaign against Jews'. According to Brundage, there were four possibilities: the Games could be transferred to a different country (both Rome and Tokyo were interested in staging the Games); they might be totally cancelled, as had been the case in 1916; or, the Games would take place in Berlin, but be boycotted by so many countries since Germany did not respect the Olympic spirit of racial, religious, and political tolerance, that the Games would have no propaganda value for the organiser – or Germany would abide strictly to Olympic rules.

THE VIENNA MEETING

The 31st annual IOC session took place in Vienna from 7 to 9 June 1933. This would have been the last reasonable chance to change the location of the Berlin Games (Hulme, 1990). But what were the viable options for the IOC? Rome? Italy was a fascist dictatorship; arguably less racist than Germany, it nonetheless served as a role model for the Nazis. Tokyo? Japan was already engaged in war and would not have served much better than Germany. Barcelona? The political instability of Spain was perceived to be anything but inviting. Besides, Lewald was on the Executive Board of the IOC while none of the competing cities had members in the six-person 'inner circle' of the Olympic sports governing body.

The IOC arranged a shrewd deal with its German members who were equally worried about the Nazis themselves and attempted to safeguard their own position: the IOC demanded that its members remain in charge of the organisation and that all Olympic rules would be strictly adhered to. When this was achieved, the American IOC-member General, Charles H. Sherrill, a former US Ambassador, demanded additionally that German Jews should not be excluded from the German team. This interference into the internal affairs of another country was unprecedented in IOC history. At a time of racial segregation, when competition between white and non-white athletes could not take place in the American South, when major US sports were still segregated, nobody had demanded that African-American athletes be given a fair chance to qualify for the 1904 or the 1932 Olympics in the United States. However, in this case, it was essential that Lewald secured such a statement on behalf of the German organisers to placate international critics.

In these respects, it seemed, all parties involved were contented; the American press celebrated its victory. The American IOC members were happy as they arrived home as victors in the battle, as they saw it, against Nazism. The German IOC members were pleased as they had defended 'their' Games; and, the Nazis were happy as they could host the Games in Germany. The declaration that had won the day for the Nazi Olympics was not even published by the state-controlled German press.

PREPARING FOR THE 1936 GAMES

Once the hosting of the Games seemed to be a practical certainty, the Nazi government stepped up its involvement. The meagre plans for the 1916 Olympics had been updated but remained basically unchanged; Hitler ensured that unlimited government funds were available. Instead of refurbishing an old stadium (seating 30,000), a new Olympic Stadium with a 100,000 spectator capacity was built in concrete covered by natural rock.

The new budget was 20 times the budget of that planned in the spring of 1933. Carl Diem tripled his personal salary as Secretary General for the Summer Olympics for the 3 years to follow.

However, the political situation in Germany became increasingly totalitarian. If one was not *with* the Nazis, one had little place to turn. The Nazis installed 'concentration camps', as the prison system was too limited to cope with political enemies. Only the churches provided venues for verbal resistance against Nazi brutality. The Nazis were strong advocates of Eugenics theory. While this form of 'social biology' was also practised in many other parts of the Western world, in Germany it was practised by new state law. To 'improve' the race, one had to encourage the racially 'best' by having many children, performing lots of exercise, marrying only those who were of 'good stock', and by preventing 'inferior' stock from procreating (Krüger, 1999b). By Nazi definition, such 'inferiors' included Jews, 'Gypsies', people who were 'feeble-minded', or had other hereditary 'diseases'. Since most forms of criminality and homosexuality were considered hereditary, many criminals and homosexuals were sterilised. It followed, then, that if one did not understand the benefits of the new government, one must therefore be 'feeble-minded' and, if approved by a racial tribunal, political opponents were faced with the threat of radical medical 'solutions' such as castration (Krüger, 1998).

In the summer of 1935, the Nazis cracked down on the social work of the churches. Church-related sports clubs were dissolved or placed under direct Nazi control. The anti-Semitism that had, to this point, been practised unsystematically was galvanised into state law. In the Nuremberg Racial Laws, 'Jewish' citizens were defined for the first time. By Jewish rites, if one was born by a Jewish mother and of Jewish faith, one was Jewish, regardless of who the father was. In such determinations, the Nazi racial 'law' was invoked over four generations. If, of one's 16 grand-grand-grand-parents, nine or more had been Jewish, one was considered Jewish; in the case of seven or less, one was not 'Jewish'. In the case of eight Jewish forefathers, one was a 'half-Jew', and one's present status was deliberated. If one was married to a Jew, one was considered Jewish; if one was married to an Aryan, one was considered to be non-Jewish. This range of definitions was applied irrespective of one's current religion, as Nazism was a racial, rather than a cultural, theory. These views and others like them raised an outcry from opponents in North America and beyond (Swanson, 2003).

However, preparations for the Berlin Games progressed. Germany's national teams held many international competitions, and there was no boycott of German sports in general; but the Olympics were still discussed by the international press, particularly as the US Olympic Committee (AOC) and the Amateur Athletic Union (AAU), the most powerful sporting body in the United States at the time, would not accept the German invitation at its 1934 meetings, and postponed the decision until December, 1935. Athletic 'powerhouses' such as Great Britain and France followed the American lead, while pro-Fascist countries like Italy and Austria, and neutral countries such as Sweden and Switzerland, had accepted the German invitation to the Olympics. The IOC approved the German plans for the Winter Olympics in Garmisch-Partenkirchen (at that time the host for the Summer Olympics had the right to propose the site for the Winter Games), and was pleased that its member, Karl Ritter von Halt, became the President of the OC for the Winter Games. By then, von Halt had joined the Nazi Party; Lewald also came under pressure as he was biologically a 'half-Jew' on his father's side.

BOYCOTT DISCUSSIONS

In the second half of 1935, discussions to boycott the Berlin Games gained momentum. This was, on the one hand, due to the Nuremberg Racial Laws, the prohibition and imprisonment of church men in Germany. On the other hand, however, it became obvious that the IOC would refuse to transfer the Games elsewhere.

Although Socialist and Communist sports organisations threatened an international boycott in most European countries, this was not taken very seriously, as they had always been against the Olympics and other forms of bourgeois sports (Krüger & Riordan, 1996). The main focus was on the US, as the American team had always placed first in the Olympics with the exception of 1912, and was considered neutral. In this respect, American opinion and participation mattered. American athletes had participated individually in German sports events during the Nazi years; however, the decision was not to be taken by the athletes but, rather, by the AAU and the AOC. Judge Jeremiah Mahoney, AAU President, was against participation, while Avery Brundage, AOC President, was in favour. American public opinion and the press were roughly divided (Krüger, 1972; Guttmann, 1998; Krüger, 2003b). Both sides published pamphlets, staged rallies, gave radio and newspaper interviews, and lobbied political representatives to take sides. Most of the public debate issues were outside the actual field of sports and dealt more with the question of having the most important international gathering, symbolising the search of the world's youth for peace, understanding, and equality, under the Nazi symbol of the Swastika, itself representing an entirely different set of values. Did participation in this meet mean at least tacit approval of the Nazi regime? Of the two American IOC members, one (Garland) argued for participation, while the other (Jahncke) favoured the boycott. Charles Sherrill had died (Krüger, 1978; Lucas, 1991). Comodore Jahncke, a former Navy administrator, wrote an open letter to his IOC colleague, Lewald, and IOC President, the Belgian Count, Baillet-Latour:

> Nor do I agree that it (US non-participation) will be catastrophic except, perhaps, to the prestige and self-esteem of the Nazi regime, if America does not participate in the games in Nazi Germany. On the contrary, from the point of view of the Olympics as an institution, it will be a calamity, in my opinion, if America does participate, for it now appears as if the Olympic idea can only be saved by the refusal of Americans and other peoples to have anything to do with the games if they are held in Germany. The whole world may see that America refuses to give even her silent approval of the manner in which Germany has dealt with her Jewish, her Catholic and her Protestant athletes (*American Hebrew* December 1935, p. 124).

The German Propaganda Minister and the sports authorities watched the bitter American fight closely from afar. When the Nuremberg Laws were finally applied to sport, the German authorities invited two prominent 'half-Jews' to compete for Germany. Helene Meyer, Olympic foil champion in 1928 and finalist in 1932, was studying in California and agreed to participate for Germany (she later won a silver medal in Berlin) and, Rudi Ball, a top ice hockey scorer for the German national team, who had been ousted from his Berlin club and continued to play semi-professional hockey in the first Italian League for Cortina. The international press did not, however, make any distinction between 'half Jew' and 'Jew', and the invitation of both athletes for the German team was seen as a symbol that the idea of fair play had won over Nazism.

The pro- and anti-boycott sides clashed, nevertheless, in a decisive showdown in New York in December 1935 (Wenn, 1989). But it was too late to ask for a transferral of the Games; the only question that remained was whether the American teams would go to Germany or not. The discussion followed along the lines of the aforementioned arguments.

At this time, Avery Brundage used two political tricks, which underlined his skill as a master strategist. Normally, the certification of an athlete for participation in the Olympics required three signatures – that of the athlete, that of the sports federation (here, the AAU), and that of the National Olympic Committee (here, the AOC). Brundage had secretly secured the agreement of Baillet-Latour that, under these extraordinary conditions, the signature of the AAU would not be necessary. Brundage described this to his friend and IOC member, Sigfrid Edström, as the "death knell for the AAU" (Krüger, 1976, 1978). By virtue of this secret agreement, a vote against participation and certification of the athletes by the AAU would have meant a reduction of its influence (Guttman, 1984).

Brundage's second trick was performed directly at the AAU convention. When he realised that he might still lose the final vote, he sought to stretch out the discussion through the night. By morning, he had secured several more eligible voters by telegram. With their help, he gained a final 58 1/4 vs. 55 3/4 victory. According to voting procedure, the AAU districts each had three votes (54 1/2 vs. 41 1/2 for non-participation), the past and present Presidents two votes (1 3/4 vs. 1/4 for going), and the associated sports bodies, many of which were brought in by Brundage over night – in a display of support never seen before – cast their ballot (one vote each) 15 vs. 1 in support of attending in Berlin. The next day, the AOC voted unanimously for participating in the Berlin Olympics.

Meanwhile, the German authorities closely monitored developments in the United States. American athletes had been very popular in Germany and non-participation would have been damaging to the prestige of the Olympic Games. However, the Berlin organising committee had already planned to host the Games, regardless of an American boycott, featuring German allies and neutral countries (Krüger, 1994). Indeed, over the years, Olympic Games have taken place in countries under extremely varied political conditions. The general and political issues of participation in the Nazi Olympics remain complicated. From hindsight, it might seem obvious that an early signal that the world would not tolerate Nazism might have made a difference. But, in 1935, the world wanted peace. 'Appeasement' was the catchword. There was also the naïve hope that Olympic Games might change things for the better in Germany (Lennartz, 1994).

In terms of the actual athletic contest, IOC members were enthusiastic about the preparation of the Games. The IOC conveniently overlooked the fact that its *Charter* demanded political independence of the OC – which was not the case in Germany. After a short discussion with the responsible Minister, Lewald signed a declaration that, internally, he would follow orders as he had eagerly accepted government subsidies, while towards the international sporting community he would maintain a sense of independence (Pfeiffer & Krüger, 1995).

All public relations activities were coordinated by the German Propaganda Minister. When Carl Diem 'invented' the Olympic torch relay to be run from Olympia to the site of the Summer Games, his plan had to be approved by the Minister. Without the approval of Propaganda Minister Goebbels, the currently popular Olympic torch relay ceremony may not have been inaugurated.

Germany had promised that German–Jewish athletes had a chance to qualify for the German team. A significant number of them took part in the pre-Olympic training camps. The IOC recognised that Germany did not plan to select Jewish athletes. General Sherrill was given an audience by Hitler on August 24, 1935, and was informed that Jews could not, and should not, represent Germany. The IOC accepted this tacitly as it had never been concerned as to how an athlete was selected to represent a country in the Olympics. As a country, Germany has always selected participants on the basis of previous athletic performances. The 'selector' in this case was the Reichssportführer von Tschammer. The only Jewish athlete (by German definition) who would have reasonably qualified was Gretel Bergmann (Krüger, 1999c; Meyer, 2000; Pfister, 2003) who equalled the German high jump record (an inch off the world record) at regional championships and was not nominated. However, the Reichssportführer preferred to have only two women in the high jump rather than the possible three to avoid having Germany represented by a 'Jew'. Jews, for von Tschammer, lacked the 'moral quality' to be included on the national track and field team. Bergmann was informed that she was not in sufficient physical condition, only after the American team had set sail for Germany.

THE 1936 WINTER OLYMPICS

In the Nazi heartland of Garmisch-Partenkirchen, the OC threatened people to remove anti-Jewish slogans during the Games. A part of the OC headquarters was erected on property confiscated from a local Jew (Schwarzmüller, 1995). The placards which declared Jews undesirable in a town or that a village prided itself in being 'cleaned of Jews', were also taken down in Munich and along the roads and train lines to Garmisch-Partenkirchen – but not yet in the rest of Germany.

For the 11 days of the Games (February 6–16, 1936), each Olympic team received carefully selected bilingual student helpers assigned the task of giving full reports on the 'attitudes' of the foreign teams. Spying was not difficult as the young Germans soon gained the confidence of the officials of the foreign teams (Krüger, 1972, p. 175f.). The 543,000 spectators (five times more than at any previous Games) were housed in the German ski resort and brought in by special trains from Munich. There was no special Olympic Village for the Winter Games to house the 755 athletes from

28 nations, more than ever before. All athletes and officials were privately housed. In this situation, it would have been quite difficult to supervise the foreigners had it not been for the student helpers. The latter were required to report back immediately and write lengthy reports, which went together with a systematic press review assembled by the foreign section of the Party – so that Berlin could learn from Garmisch-Partenkirchen.

As predicted, Norway won, by far, the most medals at the Winter Olympics; Germany finished in a distant second place, but improved seven places over its earlier performances in Lake Placid in 1932. The foreign teams were celebrated as much as the Germans, which was acknowledged by the international press, since far more German chauvinism had been expected. Some newspapers complained about the military 'character' of the Games, and the presence of so many persons in uniform worried athletes, officials, and press. Because of unpredictable snow conditions, the OC brought in 6,000 men from the Reichsarbeitsdienst, voluntary uniformed workers who had joined a para-military work service to avoid unemployment. These men were all soldiers. Ultimately, they were needed, as during the Games there was, at first, not enough snow, and later, too much. Most of the officials also arrived in uniform, so that when Hitler opened the Games he was one of the few senior officers dressed in civilian clothing (Krüger, 2003a).

While the friendly applause the French team had received in Garmisch-Partenkirchen served Hitler in the Reichstag to explain his peaceful intentions – the friendliness and non-military mindedness had to become more visible for the foreign guest to ensure a positive international reaction to the Berlin Olympics. In light of these plans, everyone was ordered by the Nazi Party to leave their uniforms at home for Berlin. A month later, Hitler violated the Treaty of Versailles and occupied the demilitarised Rhineland.

THE 1936 SUMMER OLYMPICS

The torch relay from Olympia to Berlin heightened public interest in the days prior to the Games, which were an almost complete 'sell-out'. The Berlin Olympics (August 1–16, 1936), still considered by many to be one of the greatest visual spectacles of modern times, will always be connected with the name of the Black American athlete, Jesse Owens, who won four Olympic Gold medals in track and field and, thus, seemed to indicate in the midst of Nazi Germany that the theories of Aryan supremacy did not hold true in one obvious respect (Baker, 1986). The Games are also remembered for Hitler opening the Olympics with the prescribed phrase, but not shaking

Owens' hand, which is generally considered to be an expression of Nazi hostility towards non-white athletes. In reality, the incident resulted from an attempt by the Germans to avoid difficulties with the IOC. After Hitler had invited the medal winners of the first three events into his VIP stand in the Olympic Stadium to congratulate them personally, commitments required that he leave the stadium in the evening. In this way, he could not attend the victory ceremony or receive the winners (including two African-Americans) of the last event of the day – the high jump. Hitler was told by the IOC that he should receive all athletes or none at all. To receive all would have been impossible, so he preferred to congratulate no more Olympic victors in public and, instead, he received all German medal winners in the VIP lounge inside the Grand Stand. Despite popular myths of Hitler snubbing Owens, this is the actual reason that he did not shake Owens' hand.

Germany won more medals than ever before in the Summer Olympics, placing ahead of the United States for the first time. This was the first and only time Germany won the medal count at the Summer Games and this, together with the considerable success of the organising committee, rendered the Games a huge success for the Nazis (Krüger, 1987). The Games provided unprecedented media attention for the Nazi regime. The German press interpreted this lavish attention as representing the people of the world paying homage to their leader.

During the Olympic Games, Germany initiated its involvement with troops in the Spanish Civil War on the side of the fascist, General Francisco Franco. The Nazi Party youth organization, 'Hitler Youth', was converted into the state youth organisation, meaning that if a person under 18 years of age wanted to take part in any extracurricular activity, it was only possible inside the Hitler Youth, thus assuring complete indoctrination outside the family. Sports clubs had to relinquish their youth sections, which also became part of the Hitler Youth.

Undoubtedly, the 1936 Berlin Olympic Games provided a political stepping stone for Hitler's advancement towards a devastating war. After the 8 months of relative liberty around the Games, the 'Jew-baiting' continued – the horrors of Auschwitz and the extermination of 6 million European Jews in the holocaust were soon to follow (Krüger, 1999c).

CONCLUSION

Pierre de Coubertin (1863–1937), the aging founder of the modern Olympic movement, who had publicly supported the Berlin Olympics in a radio message in 1935, was asked in a press interview after the 1936 Olympics what he thought of them. Coubertin responded to the interviewer: "What's the difference between propaganda for tourism – like in the Los Angeles Olympics of 1932 – or for a political regime? Most important is that the Olympic movement made a successful step forward" (Teichler, 1982; Krüger, 1999d, 2004, p. 37).

The rest of the IOC members were so impressed with the Nazi Olympics that, in 1939, after the German invasion of Czechoslovakia, they awarded the 1940 Winter Games to Garmisch-Partenkirchen. Admittedly, Sapporo, Oslo, and St. Moritz had, for varying reasons, declined the invitation to stage the Games, but the invitation to a country so obviously bent on aggressive war and xenophobic policies was made without a single objection (Krüger, 2003a).

For the Nazis, the view of the 1936 Olympics was evidently quite different from those on the outside. When Albrecht von Kessel testified at the Nuremberg Trials for war criminals in 1946, he remarked:

> In 1936 there was an episode which was very depressing for us as it seemed to be so symptomatic of the reaction of the foreign countries in relation to the Jewish question... I refer to the Olympic Games which were the biggest international triumph of the National Socialist regime... The International Olympic Committee had demanded as its condition to maintain the Olympic Games in Berlin that Germany gave up its discrimination against the German Jewish athletes... The Nazis did not keep their pledge. In the very last moment they excluded the German Jews (N. N., 1948, p. 6).

During the proceedings, trial Attorney, Dr. Becker, asked Kessel: "Is it true that this [the Olympic Games] was interpreted by the Nazis as a reinforcement of their position?" Kessel replied: "Oh yes. They said to themselves and also to us: you see, you can do anything, you just have to know how" (N. N., 1948, p. 6).

Nowhere is the image of the Nazi Olympics better encapsulated than in the classic cinematic record of the event, *Olympia,* by Leni Riefenstahl (McFee & Tomlinson, 1999). Riefenstahl presented 'perfect' sport in a 'perfect' setting. Sport supposedly celebrated in the tradition of the ancient Greeks. But, this was no longer the Greece of Athens, the cradle of democracy; it was the Greece of Sparta, driven by the most barbarous of ideologies and armed with the considerable might of modern technology (Krüger & Ramba, 1991).

REFERENCES

American Hebrew (selected editions, 1933 – 1936). *American Hebrew*.
Baker, W. J. (1986). *Jesse Owens. An American life*. New York: Free Press.

Eisen, G. (1999). Jews and sport: A century in retrospect. *Journal of Sport History, 26*(2), 225–239.

Grazia, V. de. (1981). *The culture of consent. Mass organization of leisure in fascist Italy.* Cambridge: Cambridge University Press.

Guttmann, A. (1984). *The Games must go on.* New York: Columbia University Press.

Guttmann, A. (1998). The Nazi Olympics and the American boycott controversy. In: P. Arnaud & J. Riordan (Eds), *Sport and international politics: The impact of fascism and communism on sport* (pp. 31–50). London: Spon.

Hulme, D. L., Jr. (1990). *The political Olympics: Moscow, Afghanistan, and the 1980 U.S. boycott.* New York: Praeger.

Krüger, A. (1972). *Die Olympischen Spiele 1936 und die Weltmeinung. Ihre außenpolitische Bedeutung unter besonderer Berücksichtigung der USA.* Berlin: Bartels & Wernitz.

Krüger, A. (1976). The Olympic Games–Berlin. In: H. Ueberhorst & P. Graham (Eds), *The modern Olympics* (pp. 168–181). Cornwall, NY: Leisure Press.

Krüger, A. (1978). Fair play for American athletes: A study in anti-semitism. *Canadian Journal of History of Sport and Physical Education, 9*(1), 42–57.

Krüger, A. (1987). Sieg Heil to the most glorious era of German sport: Continuity and change in the modern German sports movement. *International Journal of History of Sport, 4*(1), 5–20.

Krüger, A. (1994). Dann veranstalten wir eben rein deutsche Olympische Spiele. Die Olympischen Spiele 1936 als deutsches Nationalfest. In: H. Breuer & R. Naul (Eds), *Schwimmsport und Sportgeschichte. Zwischen Politik und Wissenschaft* (pp. 127–149). St. Augustin: Academia.

Krüger, A. (1998). A horse breeder's perspective: Scientific racism in Germany. 1870–1933. In: N. Finzsch & D. Schirmer (Eds), *Identity and intolerance. Nationalism, racism, and xenophobia in Germany and the United States* (pp. 371–396). Cambridge: Cambridge United Press.

Krüger, A. (1999a). Strength through joy. The culture of consent under fascism, Nazism and Francoism. In: J. Riordan & A. Krüger (Eds), *The international politics of sport in the 20th century* (pp. 67–89). London: Spon.

Krüger, A. (1999b). Breeding, rearing and preparing the Aryan Body: Creating the complete superman the Nazi way. *International Journal of History of Sport, 16*(2), 42–68.

Krüger, A. (1999c). Once the Olympics are through, we'll beat up the Jew. German Jewish Sport 1898–1938 and the anti-semitic discourse. *Journal of Sport History, 26*(2), 353–375.

Krüger, A. (1999d). The unfinished symphony. A history of the Olympic Games from Coubertin to Samaranch. In: J. Riordan & A. Krüger (Eds), *The international politics of sport in the 20th century* (pp. 3–27). London: Spon.

Krüger, A. (2003a). Germany: The propaganda machine. In: A. Krüger & W. Murray (Eds), *The Nazi Olympics. Sport, politics and appeasement in the 1930s* (pp. 17–43). Champaign, IL: Illinois University Press.

Krüger, A. (2003b). United States of America: The crucial battle. In: A. Krüger & W. Murray (Eds), *The Nazi Olympics. sport, politics and appeasement in the 1930s* (pp. 44–69). Champaign, IL: Illinois University Press.

Krüger, A. (2004). What's the difference between propaganda for tourism or for a political regime? Was the 1936 Olympics the first postmodern spectacle? In: J. Bale & M. C. Christensen (Eds), *Post-olympism? questioning sport in the twenty-first century* (pp. 33–49). Oxford: Berg.

Krüger, A., & Murray, W. (Eds) (2003). *The Nazi Olympics. Sport, politics and appeasement in the 1930s.* Champaign, IL: Illinois University Press.

Krüger, A., & Ramba, D. (1991). Sparta or Athens? The reception of Greek antiquity in Nazi Germany. In: R. Renson, M. Lämmer, J. Riordan & D. Chassiotis (Eds), *The Olympic Games through the ages: Greek antiquity and its impact on modern sport* (pp. 345–356). Athens: Hellenic Sports Research Institute.

Krüger, A., & Riordan, J. (Eds) (1996). *The story of worker sport.* Champaign, IL: Human Kinetics.

Lennartz, K. (1994). The Baillet-Latour Presidency (1925–1942). In: R. Gafner (Ed.), *The International Olympic Committee. One hundred years* (Vol. 1, pp., 211–293). Lausanne: IOC.

Lucas, J. A. (1991). Ernest Lee Jahncke. The expelling of an IOC member. *Stadion, 17*(1), 53–78.

McFee, G., & Tomlinson, A. (1999). Riefenstahl's Olympia: Ideology and aesthetics in the shaping of the aryan athletic body. *International Journal of History of Sport, 16*(2), 86–106.

Malitz, B. (1933). *Die Leibeserziehung in der nationalsozialistischen Idee.* München: Eher.

Mandell, R. D. (1971). *The Nazi Olympics.* New York: Columbia University Press.

Meyer, P. Y. (2000). *Jüdische Olympiasieger – Sport: Ein Sprungbrett für Minoritäten.* Kassel: Agon.

New York Times (selected articles 1933–1936). *New York Times.* New York.

N. N. (1948). Die Olympiade 1936 und die Juden: Aus den Nürnberger Akten. *Die Neue Demokratie im Bild, 3*(16), 6.

Oelrich, H. (2003). *Sportgeltung – Weltgeltung. Sport im Spannungsfeld der deutsch-italienischen Außenpolitik von 1918– 1945.* Münster: Lit.

Pfeiffer, R., & Krüger, A. (1995). Theodor Lewald: Eine Karriere im Dienste des Vaterlands oder die vergebliche Suche nach der jüdischen Identität eines Halbjuden. *Menora. Jahrbuch deutsch-jüdische Geschichte* (pp. 233–265). München: Piper.

Pfister, G. (2003). Gretel Bergmann – um den Olyympiasieg betrogen. In: A. R. Hofmann & M. Krüger (Eds), *Südwestdeutsche Turner in der Emigration* (pp. 189–202). Schorndorf: Hofmann.

Riess, S. A. (Ed.) (1998). *Sports and the American Jew.* Syracuse: Syracuse University Press.

Schwarzmüller, A. (1995). Juden sind hier nicht erwünscht. Aus der Geschichte der jüdischen Bürger in Garmisch- Partenkirchen von 1933–1945. *Mohr–Löwe–Raute. Beiträge aus der Geschichte des Landkreises Garmisch Partenkirchen, 1*(1), 184–232.

Swanson, R. A. (2003). Move the Olympics! Germany must be told!: Charles Clayton Morrison and the liberal protestant Christianity's support of the 1936 Olympic boycott effort. *OLYMPIKA: The International Journal of Olympic Studies, XII*, 39–50.

Teichler, H. J. (1976). Berlin 1936 – Ein Sieg der NS Propaganda? *Stadion, 2*(2), 265–306.

Teichler, H. J. (1982). Coubertin und das Dritte Reich. *Sportwissenschaft, 12*(1), 18–55.

Völkischer Beobachter (selected articles 1932–1936). *Völkischer Beobachter.*

Wenn, S. R. (1989). Hotel Commodore revisited: An analysis of the 1935 AAU convention. In: D. Morrow (Ed.), *Proceedings of the 6th Canadian symposium for the history of sport* (pp. 188–201). London, ON: The University of Western Ontario, Canada.

Chapter 4

THE COLD WAR GAMES

Cesar R. Torres and Mark Dyreson

In 1945, the 'new Germany', so cleverly advertised by Adolf Hitler and the Nazis at the 1936 Olympic Games, laid in ruins. Hitler's scheme for the construction of a colossal 450,000 stadium in Nürnberg as the permanent new home of a Nazi-controlled Aryan Olympic series had been consigned to the ash heap of history (Guttmann, 2002, p. 75). On the other side of the world, Japan, the nation whose leaders had hoped that hosting the 1940 Olympic Games would crown its rise to Pacific hegemony and global superpower status, had also been crushed by world war. Tokyo's grand plans for a massive Olympic complex had been incinerated, along with much of the rest of the Japanese capital (Collins, 2004). The Second World War also scuttled the 1940 and 1944 Olympic Games, threatening the future of one of the world's major international events.

Japan, Germany, and Italy, the totalitarian powers of the 1930s, which had used international sport as both martial propaganda and domestic jingoism were, in the 1940s, broken by total war. A new world order emerged from the Second World War's carnage, with neither the defeated Axis nor the traditional European nations at its head but, instead, the United States and the Soviet Union as rival leviathans contending for global dominion (Kennedy, 1987; Hobsbawm, 1996). The new superpowers quickly discovered that the Olympic Games provided a significant symbolic forum for measuring their enemies (Espy, 1979; Kanin, 1981; Hill, 1996; Senn, 1999; Guttmann, 2002). The United States has a long history of employing the Olympic Games to jockey for international advantage and stoke the fires of domestic nationalism. Indeed, the United States has legitimate claims to

Global Olympics: Historical and Sociological Studies of the Modern Games
Research in the Sociology of Sport, Volume 3, 59–82
Copyright © 2005 by Elsevier Ltd.

originating the custom of using the Olympic Games as an instrument of nationalism. Only Greece, which launched an ill-advised war against the Ottoman Turkish Empire fuelled by the intoxicating patriotism generated by its service as the host for the original modern Games, has used the Olympics as a national totem for as long as the United States (Kitroeff, 2004). The American press had been counting medals and ranking nations since the first modern Olympic Games at Athens in 1896. Americans quadrennially claimed that victory proved the superiority of their national culture while defeat was explained away as the result of foreign duplicity (Dyreson, 1998).

In stark contrast to the United States, the Soviet Union had not participated in the Olympic Games before the Second World War. Before the Russian Revolution, the old Tsarist regime sent a few athletes to the 1908 and 1912 Games but, after the Soviet seizure of power, Russia had neither been invited by the International Olympic Committee (IOC) nor shown any inclination to join the 'Olympic family' – a gathering the Soviets labelled during the inter-war years as a bourgeois cabal of capitalists who were sworn enemies of the Socialist revolution. If the lack of invitation or initiative was not enough, then the struggling Soviet economy and the lack of a national infrastructure for developing competitive international athletes convinced Soviet leaders that athletic combat with other nations would only lead to defeat and humiliation. When the Second World War ended, the Soviets emerged as the only counter to the significant global influence of the United States. To assure their new status as one of the two world superpowers, the Soviets began to play new roles in international affairs and, especially, to jump into the politically charged arenas of the Olympic Games. Soviet leaders began to craft a new Olympic strategy (Riordan, 1977; Edeleman, 1993).

The Cold War shaped the new Soviet Olympic policy, as it also shaped American Olympic designs. After defeating their common enemies, the wartime coalition led by the United States and the Soviet Union collapsed into a long and bitter conflict based in mutual antagonisms over security, influence, and power. This rift, which came to be known as the 'Cold War', began in the midst of the Second World War and lasted for five decades until the Soviet Union dramatically collapsed in the early 1990s. The Cold War dominated global politics for most of the second half of the twentieth century. It pitted the United States and the Soviet Union in a series of proxy wars, committed the two powers to an extravagant and destructive arms race, and required them to engage in constant competition for the hearts and minds of the rest of the world's nations. The Cold War sparked symbolic struggles for world supremacy between the Soviet Union and the United States in everything from chess to steel production to pop music. In such a climate, the Olympic Games, at the time the world's most popular athletic event, provided a particularly attractive stage for engaging in ritual battles for national supremacy (Saull, 2001; Harbutt, 2002; LaFeber, 2002; Keylor, 2003; McCauley, 2003; McMahon, 2003).

In the first half of the twentieth century, many nations had used the Olympic Games to tout their claims to an advanced global standing. Argentina mounted Olympic expeditions to prove that modern civilisation flourished on the Atlantic coast of South America (Torres, 2001, 2003). Finnish athletes chafed when they were required to run under the old Russian flag in 1912 and, during the 1920s, Finland's distance running phenoms ran to prove their nation's special character (Jorgensen, 1997). The Axis nations celebrated enthusiastically when Germany defeated the United States, Italy scored better than France, and Japan defeated Great Britain at the 1936 Olympic Games (Mandell, 1987). The very essence of the modern Olympic movement, which celebrated nationalism through the ritual display of team uniforms, national flags, parades, and the playing of national anthems to herald victory, made the modern Games a prime venue for nationalistic demonstrations. As one of the leading historians of nationalism in the modern era, Eric Hobsbawm (1992), asserted, the modern Olympic Games "unmistakably became occasions for competitive national self-assertion" (p. 43). The 'imagined communities', that many scholars consider as the central element of modern nationalism, sprang to life in the performances of national Olympic teams (Anderson, 1991; Cronin, 1999).

During the Cold War, the national tensions embedded in global sport increased markedly as United States' and Soviet Union leaders decided that Olympic stadiums were among the world's best forums for testing national prowess. In the chaos that followed the most calamitous war in human history, the Olympic Games were once again revived and slated for London. By the Olympic year of 1948, the Cold War was in full fury. The Soviets had seized much of Eastern Europe to provide a security buffer against the West. The United States had authorised the use of economic might and military force to 'contain' the Soviet threat. An arms race between the superpowers fuelled by nuclear weapons loomed. British Prime Minister, Winston Churchill's speeches about the fall of an 'iron curtain' heightened tensions, while the Berlin Blockade in a divided Germany signified the enormous divisions developing between the Eastern and Western blocs. Olympic sport seemed destined to become, in the prescient phrase of the Cold War's great novelist, George Orwell (1998), "war minus the shooting" (p. 442).

COLD WAR FRICTIONS AND THE PATTERNS OF
OLYMPIC POLITICS

Cold War nationalism soon emerged on several Olympic fronts, including IOC administrative practices. In the immediate aftermath of the Second World War, the IOC was very careful to grant Olympic hosting rights first and foremost to Allied nations that had suffered the brunt of combat against, or occupation by, Nazi Germany. Granting Olympic Games to Great Britain (the 1948 London Games) and Norway (the 1952 Oslo Winter Games) rewarded the victors. The war's losers, Austria, Germany, Italy, and Japan, were conspicuously excluded from all 1948 Olympic events. The ban on the Germans continued through the 1952 Winter Games in Oslo. The Summer Games of 1952 moved to the doorstep of the Soviet Union, when Helsinki, Finland, hosted the first modern Olympics to include Soviet athletes. The IOC did not grant the right to host the Olympic Games to the Eastern bloc until the 1980s when the Soviet Union (the 1980 Moscow Games) and Yugoslavia (the 1984 Sarajevo Winter Games) staged Olympic festivals. Increasingly during the Cold War, the IOC looked to globalise the Olympic movement by awarding Games to different parts of the world such as Australia (the 1956 Melbourne Games), Mexico (the 1968 Mexico City Games), and South Korea (the 1988 Seoul Games). As the Second World War receded into the past, the IOC also used host cities to welcome the former Axis 'villains' back into the fold of civilisation. First, Italy (the 1956 Cortina d'Ampezzo Winter Games and 1960 Rome Games), then Austria (the 1964 and 1976 Innsbruck Winter Games), then Japan (the 1964 Tokyo Games and 1972 Sapporo Winter Games) and, finally, Germany (the 1972 Munich Games) were presented to the world as redeemed and pacified members of the global community.

A variety of political conflicts affected not only the processes for selecting host sites but also the IOC's recognition of member nations. In 1894, the French aristocrat Pierre de Coubertin established the IOC; bourgeois European society was at its zenith. The IOC came to life when Europe did not merely dominate international affairs but also considered itself as the centre of Western civilisation. The IOC had historically promoted competitive sport and the ideologies that surrounded it as representative of the superiority of this Western culture (MacAloon, 1981; Guttmann, 1994). In spite of the complex tensions among the world's nations, many 'converted' to the Olympic idea that friendly and chivalrous international sport competitions bred mutual respect between rival nations and contributed to world peace. Evident in the resumption of the festival, not even two world wars could shatter this Olympian faith. The Cold War's alarmingly escalating arms race with its prospect for nuclear Armageddon convinced the IOC, long-dominated by liberal Western nations, that it could contribute to global harmony by including the Soviets and their new allies in the Olympic project. These efforts began under the leadership of IOC President, Sigfrid Edström (1942–1952), and his successor, Avery Brundage (1952–1972). Both the Swede, Edström, and the American, Brundage, had been staunch anti-Communists before the Second World War. Each came to understand after the War that for the Olympic Games to continue as an international force, the Soviets had to be included. Involving the Soviets guaranteed that Cold War politics would shape Olympic policies. The IOC confronted the same issues that divided international politics in the era, from mutual mistrust between the superpowers to old nations cloven in two by the conflicts between East and West, from the 'two Germanies' to the 'two Chinas', to the 'two Koreas' (Guttmann, 1984).

Old wounds from the Second World War and new rifts created by the Cold War shaped Olympic politics as the IOC announced the paramount importance of restoring Olympic competition in the post-war world. In 1945–1946, the IOC debated expelling IOC members from Germany and Italy who had ties to wartime regimes. While the IOC allowed some members with clear ties to Nazism and Fascism to remain in the Olympic 'family', it also barred Germany and Japan from competing in the first post-war Games, scheduled for 1948 (Hill, 1996; Senn, 1999; Guttmann, 2002).

These incongruities typified IOC policies throughout the second half of the twentieth century. The IOC's potentates granted the 1948 Olympic Games to London, an honour extended to a city that had earlier been awarded the war-cancelled 1944 Olympics as well as the capital of one of the leading Allied nations that had defeated the Axis powers. During the same period, the IOC extended tentative feelers towards the Soviet Union, exploring the possibility of incorporating the new superpower into the Olympic movement. Joseph Stalin and the Communist Party leadership had decided that the development of elite athletes to promote the Soviet system was a post-war necessity. However, Soviet officials understood that they were not ready to field a competitive team so quickly and declined to participate in the London Games (Riordan, 1977; Edeleman, 1993).

The 1948 London Olympics symbolised the revival of international sport in a world still devastated by the impact of the Second World War. Economically depressed Great Britain struggled mightily to host the Games. Limited resources made the London Games perhaps the most austere in modern Olympic history. The hosts could not even afford the expense of constructing an Olympic Village (Baker, 1996). So spartan were accommodations that an Argentine Olympian recalled that he and his teammates took turns serving as rest room 'doors' in his team's quarters (Diario Deportivo Olé, 2004). In spite of the war-damaged infrastructure, the struggling economy, and significant internal political opposition to the Games, London soldiered forward and prepared to host the world.

The Cold War also raised threats to the London Games. In the summer of 1948, a few weeks before the Games were set to commence, the Berlin Blockade raised Cold War tensions to new heights and threatened to substantially reduce the number of American spectators who British organisers hoped would buy tickets to the Games. In spite of financial trouble and political turmoil, the Games commenced. Contemporary observers judged them, in the main, a success. The Cold War tensions that soon enough raged through Olympic stadiums merely swirled about the London Games. North Americans and Western Europeans still dominated the athletic competitions and controlled the organisation of Olympic spectacles. The Soviets had not yet arrived in full force. That soon changed.

INCORPORATING THE COMMUNIST BLOC INTO THE OLYMPIC MOVEMENT

Although Soviet athletes failed to appear in London, Soviet observers flocked there, snapping pictures and taking notes at every venue. The announcement that Helsinki had won the right to host the 1952 Olympic Games spurred the Soviets to push forward their entry into the highest levels of international sport. As early as 1947, the Soviets had agreed to join the Olympic movement but only if the IOC acquiesced to several demands, including making Russian an official Olympic language, appointing a Soviet member to the IOC Executive Board, and expelling Spain, headed by the old Soviet enemy Francisco Franco, out of the Olympic 'family'. IOC members also worried that the state subsidies the Soviet Union provided to athletes would undermine amateur standards. After the London Games, the Soviets organised a National Olympic Committee (NOC) and applied for entry. At the IOC Congress in Vienna in 1951, the Soviets won admission. The IOC did not make Russian an Olympic language nor did it banish Spain, but it did submit on other issues. The Olympic bureaucrats even accepted Stalin-appointee Konstantin Andrianov to the IOC in violation of the IOC tradition that national governments were not permitted to select IOC members (Hill, 1996; Senn, 1999; Guttmann, 2002).

Soviet inclusion in the Olympic movement instantly juxtaposed Cold War politics and IOC issues. At the same IOC Congress during which the Soviets joined the Olympic movement, the IOC fully recognised the NOC of the new West German state constructed by the US, Britain, and France. Karl Ritter von Halt, a former member of the Nazi Party, led the controversial new contingent from the Federal Republic of Germany (FRG). The Soviets immediately demanded that the IOC recognise the NOC of its new East German client state, the German Democratic Republic (GDR). IOC leaders sought to broker a deal that would unite the two German nations as one Olympic team. Initial efforts at a unified team failed, and only the FRG was allowed to field a team for the 1952 Olympic Games in Helsinki. Not only two Germanies but two Chinas emerged from the Cold War. When the Chinese civil war ended with the establishment of a Communist state in mainland China, while the remnants of pro-western opposition fled to the island of Formosa (Taiwan), the IOC again faced the questions of whether the US-aligned nation in Formosa or the Soviet-aligned mainland nation represented the 'real' China. For the 1952 Olympic Games, the IOC rejected NOCs from both Chinas but allowed athletes from each country to compete. The Formosans boycotted while the mainland squad arrived 10 days after the Games began, too late for all but one member of the Chinese squad to join the competition (Hill, 1996; Senn, 1999; Guttmann, 2002).

The Soviet entry and the battles over the two Germanies and the two Chinas guaranteed that the 1952 Olympic Games would become a Cold War struggle. The looming confrontation of Soviet and US athletes consumed both nations. A telethon starring movie stars Bob Hope and Bing Crosby, the latter in his first appearance on television, raised money to send the US team to Finland. The Soviets decided to eschew Helsinki's Olympic village and stayed with Warsaw Pact allies in a separate compound (Hill, 1996; Senn, 1999; Guttmann, 2002).

The US media and fans expected their nation to once again dominate the various unofficial scoring systems and medal counts that the IOC failed to sanction but which had nevertheless dominated nationalistic discourse in previous Olympic arenas. The US quickly discovered that the Soviet Union was a more formidable athletic opponent than it had imagined. Close study of western sports programmes led the Soviets to concentrate their attention on the entire Olympic programme rather than just on track and field, swimming, and diving where the US had traditionally dominated. On the first day of competition, the Soviets erected a large scoreboard in the

Warsaw Pact compound to tally national standings. Using a '7-5-4-3-2-1 point system' to mitigate the US lead in gold medals, the Soviets established a large lead. Analysts in the US objected to the Soviet count, insisting that a '10-5-4-3-2-1 system', that gave more emphasis to gold medals, was more accurate. US journalists also dismissed Soviet successes in what they labelled as 'minor events' such as women's gymnastics. The IOC decried the point-counting, claiming that such systems were not, and had never been, officially sanctioned. No one paid much attention to the IOC's pronouncements. When the United States won a host of events in the last few days of the Helsinki Games, the Soviet tabulations suddenly disappeared. US journalists claimed victory for their nation in both points and medals. Soviet interpreters disagreed. In the final analysis, the US won 76 medals including 40 gold medals. The Soviet Union garnered 71 medals including 22 gold medals. Whether they won or finished a close second, the unexpectedly strong Soviet showing in Helsinki stunned the world (Hill, 1996; Senn, 1999; Guttmann, 2002).

Sparked perhaps by the Soviet–US confrontation and the re-admission of Germany, the 1952 Olympic Games featured a host of world's record performances. In the opinion of many observers, the heightened levels of competition and the sterling achievements confirmed that the Olympic Games had become the Cold War's centre stage. Some hoped that Olympic sport could do more than serve as surrogate combat for superpowers. Taking piety to the grail of Olympic peace to a new level, the *New York Times* (1952, 4 August) editorialised at the close of the Helsinki Olympics that "we welcome, rather than disparage, the good showing made by the representatives of the Soviet Union and the satellite countries". Citing the inspired performances of Czech distance running star Emil Zatopek, the editors then quickly stepped back from beneficent internationalism to boisterous nationalism. "We are glad that bad government has not destroyed good athletic performance", the *New York Times* (1952, 4 August) opined (p. 14). These sorts of responses typified US assessments of the Olympic battles with the Soviets throughout the Cold War.

Soviet Premier Joseph Stalin died in 1953, a year after his Olympic team had shocked the world with its athletic performances in Helsinki. For a moment, in the wake of Stalin's passing, a diminishing of Cold War tensions seemed a possibility. A new regime led by Nikita Khruschev began to 'de-Stalinise' the Soviet Empire and promised the possibility of 'peaceful co-existence' with the West. US President Dwight Eisenhower pitched arms-control schemes and vowed to de-escalate global conflicts. Beneath the diplomatic scouting missions and the more pacific rhetoric, however, the Cold

War became institutionalised. The Soviet Union and the United States had mutually exclusive ideologies and security concerns. The Cold War quickly permeated every aspect of global affairs as the East and West began their long crusades to win the sympathies on the 'non-aligned' nations of post-colonial Asia and Africa and to buttress the loyalties of traditionally aligned partners.

THE IOC'S COLD WAR INITIATIVES

From the Helsinki Games through the rest of the Cold War, the IOC took a strategically active role in the conflict. The Soviet entry into the IOC membership slowly but surely changed the composition of the organisation. What had been an exclusive fraternity headed by European and North American elites became more diversified as the Soviets insisted on the admission of client states and Third World nations that filled the Baron de Coubertin's old patrician club-house with members drawn from the same proletarian ranks of governmental bureaucrats who staffed the Soviet delegation. The Cold War quickly permeated internal IOC politics (Hill, 1996).

At the same time, the IOC, under the Avery Brundage regime, re-dedicated itself to proclaiming that the Olympic movement represented one of the few paths to international peace in a world consumed by fears of the cold logic of nuclear Armageddon embedded in strategic doctrines such as 'mutually assured destruction' (MAD). These efforts were surprising given the histories of both the IOC and its leadership. The IOC had, since its birth, touted the contributions of sport to human harmony without any real evidence that the Olympic Games had made the world's bloodiest century a whit less destructive. Brundage, a committed American Capitalist with impeccable anti-Communist credentials, seemed an unlikely candidate to make efforts to bridge the divides between West and East. Still, Brundage accommodated his views to new circumstances and began to speak admiringly of the 'Spartan' qualities of the Communist sports system. Even as *the* staunch defender of an elitist concept of amateurism, Brundage accepted the state-sponsored athletes of the Soviet Union and its satellites as no worse than the alumni-funded 'jocks' of the American inter-collegiate system and greatly preferable to the perfidious professionals who sometimes threatened to encroach on Olympian spaces (Guttmann, 1984).

The global public, enmeshed in the culture of fear that was a central by-product of the Cold War, easily forgave the myth-makers of the Olympic movement for the lack of a demonstrable causal link between the quadrennial international sports spectacles and world peace. The prophets of Olympism, during the Cold War, increasingly invoked the image of an Olympic truce, during which ancient Greeks had allegedly abstained from war and indulged in sport once every 4 years, as an example the modern world ought to emulate. In fact, the ancient truce sought not the abolition of combat between warring city-states but safe passage for Greek athletes and fans to and from Olympia. That trifling detail did not prevent the IOC's public relations promoters from touting the Olympic Games as a much-needed respite every 4 years from the interminable strife of the Cold War.

As the Winter and Summer Olympic Games of 1956 approached, the IOC provided evidence that perhaps it might be able to conjure the international goodwill that escaped other institutions when it knit divided Germany back together. After long negotiations, Brundage succeeded in doing for the Olympics what politicians and diplomats had no hope of achieving in the 'real world' when the IOC announced that East and West Germany would compete in the 1956 Games as a unified team. Brundage crowed that "we have obtained in the field of sport what politicians have failed to achieve so far" (Guttmann, 2002, p. 95). The symbolic re-unification of the German nation in one Olympic squad at least held out the dream of a different world order. The IOC, in typical fashion, presented the accomplishment as a victory of sport over politics. In fact, it represented a victory of Olympic politics over Cold War politics. Neither the leaders of the GDR nor the FRG were particularly happy with the combined Olympic team. The IOC triumph proved temporary. After debuting as 'one' Germany at the Cortina d'Ampezzo Winter Games in 1956, the union lasted through the 1964 Tokyo Games. By 1968, at Grenoble in the winter and Mexico City in the summer, the GDR and FRG competed as separate Germanies – 7 years after the erection of the Berlin Wall by the Soviets had re-inforced the harsh realities of that division.

The short-lived merger of East and West Germany into one Olympian entity highlighted the desires of IOC leaders to position the Games as a trans-national facilitator of peaceful intercourse during the Cold War era. Standing above the squabbling nations, the IOC sought to portray itself as a haven of human harmony in a world rent by ideological rifts. Two incidents from the 1956 Melbourne Games illustrated the IOC's increasingly conscious strategy. Australian organisers added a new ritual celebrating Olympism's power to transcend national difference to the traditional canon of Olympic practices. Instead of marching into the stadium for the closing ceremonies as national teams, as Olympic protocol had required in the past, Australian officials created a new finale in which the athletes of world gambolled onto the Melbourne Cricket Ground as a mass of participants without regard for nation or faction. The official report of the Melbourne Games marvelled that the new closing ceremony created "a prophetic image of a new future for mankind – the athletes of the world not now sharply divided" but linked in "a fiesta of friendship" (Organizing Committee of the XVI Olympiad, 1958, p. 26). The much ballyhooed romance between gold medalists from opposite sides of the 'iron curtain', Czech discus thrower Olga Fikotova and US hammer thrower Harold Connolly, provided the world press corps and public with a human interest story that blossomed, literally, as it turned out, into a marriage between East and West, which seemed to confirm the transcendent power of Olympism in a world terrified by the spectre of looming mushroom clouds (Connolly, 1968).

The 1956 Melbourne Games also illustrated that Cold War nationalism in Olympic arenas would not be confined to confrontations between East and West. Encouraged by the reforms flowing from the de-Stalinisation of Soviet communism after the long time dictator's demise, especially the promise of a variety of paths towards socialist utopias, restive Communist parties in Eastern Europe sought greater freedom from Soviet domination and pushed towards national independence. Uprisings arose in areas where Stalin had formerly ruled with an iron fist, first Poland and then Hungary. The October, 1956, revolution in Hungary installed a liberal Marxist reformer in power and forced the Soviet occupying forces out of the country. The Soviets responded by crushing the rebellion and re-imposing Moscow's control over its Hungarian satellite. The tragic revolution and bloody re-conquest took place only a month before the Melbourne Games debuted. The Netherlands and Spain withdrew from the Games to oppose Soviet actions. Several other nations threatened boycotts. Another conflict, the October 1956 Egypt–Israeli War, which provided a pretext for a joint British and French seizure of the Suez Canal from the Egyptians, sparked Egypt, Iraq, and Lebanon to withdraw from competition in Melbourne since Israel and its allies would be present in Australia. These events dealt serious blows to Brundage's efforts to construct a modern fable of the ancient Olympic truce (Hill, 1996; Senn, 1999; Guttmann, 2002).

The national conflicts spilled over into the Olympic competitions. While Australian crowds lustily cheered the Soviets in accordance with the new focus on transcendent internationalism, Hungarian and Soviet athletes engaged in an infamous, violent fracas in the Olympic pool during a water polo match. A brawl between the two teams led the Swedish referee to call off the match, which the Hungarians were leading, and to disqualify the Soviets. The picture of Hungarian water polo player Ervin Zador, with blood streaming from a gash over his eye, became one of the most enduring images of the Melbourne Games, symbolising for many the spirit of Hungarian defiance of aggressive Soviet domination. A large contingent of the Hungarian team defected in Australia rather than returning to their Soviet-controlled homeland. In the omnipresent tabulations of national standings, the Soviets clearly had a successful year in 1956, winning both the Winter and Summer Olympics under any scoring system. At Cortina d'Ampezzo, the Soviets earned 16 medals to defeat second place Austria. The Soviet triumphs included a stunning victory over Canada in ice hockey. In Melbourne, the Soviets clearly bettered the US medal total (Gordon, 1994).

The 1956 Olympic Games signalled that the Cold War and other international conflicts continued to challenge the Olympic movement both on and off the playing fields. During the next three decades, the IOC remained firmly committed to the complex task of offering the world a place free from politics. The escalating tensions of the Cold War during the late 1950s and 1960s, from spy planes, satellite launches, and space races, to the Cuban Missile Crisis, the Berlin Wall, and the Vietnam War, made the Olympian promise of universal harmony, however transitory and difficult to achieve, all the more intoxicating. Battles over teams for two Germanies, two Chinas, and two Koreas continued to challenge the IOC. Eastern and Western blocs developed rifts in the organisation. Soviet and US political desires to cultivate the hearts and minds of Africa, Asia, and Latin America, soon inserted the struggles of the crumbling colonial order over national liberation and international equity into the Cold War nexus. As the maelstrom of conflicts engulfed the Olympic movement, the IOC generally maintained a consistent, if unrealistic, posture that 'outside' political concerns had no place in the Olympic Games.

OLYMPIC SPECTACLES AND COLD WAR SQUABBLES DURING THE TUMULTUOUS 1960S AND 1970S

The 1960s began with the IOC still committed to expanding the politics of the Olympic truce to redress the crimes of history by welcoming the former Axis enemies back into the folds of competition. During this decade, Italy and Japan hosted the Games, and Germany won the right to host the 1972 Games. While IOC grants to host cities soothed older wounds, the contemporary animosities of Cold War grew more bitter on Olympic ski slopes and in Olympic stadiums. In 1960, the Soviets continued their domination of the medal count. On the home snow and ice of the California Sierras, the US turned in a surprisingly strong performance, including a first 'miracle on ice' in hockey where the US squad upset both the Soviets and the Canadians en route to victory. But the Soviet Union still easily won the most medals at Squaw Valley. In Rome, the USSR captured the mythical Olympic championship with the US placing a distant second. The US stumbled badly in track-and-field, the sport that American pundits had always considered the centrepiece of the Olympic spectacle. Embarrassing losses at the hands of the Soviets kindled a firestorm of speculation in the US about how to regain the Olympic crown. Democrats and Republicans both pushed for government funding of the US Olympic enterprise. In a 1963 *Parade Magazine* article demanding a national recommitment to the goal of winning the Olympic Games, liberal Democratic Senator, Hubert H. Humphrey of Minnesota railed that the US and the USSR were competing in "every level of life from spacemen to sprinters". The head of the conservative American Legion made the same pitch (Baker, 1988, p. 272).

In spite of domestic pressure, the US government did not authorise major subsidies to underwrite the American team. The domestic political hyperbole did, however, intensify the Cold War drama at the Olympic Games. The Soviets remained on top in three of the next four Winter Games, winning medals counts handily at Innsbruck in 1964, Sapporo in 1972, and Innsbruck again in 1976. Norway produced a narrow upset in Grenoble in 1968. Meanwhile, the US sank to the lower end of the winter competitions. In the summer spectacles, US teams improved dramatically, beating the Soviets by close margins in Tokyo in 1964 and Mexico City in 1968, before once again slipping behind the Russian juggernaut at Munich in 1972 and at Montreal in 1976. The final medal tally of the Montreal Games revealed another major surprise. The Soviet client-state in East Germany, the GDR, won 40 gold medals in Canada while the US managed only 34. After Montreal, many observers concluded that the Eastern bloc had decisively won the Olympic battlefield in the Cold War (Hill, 1996; Senn, 1999; Guttmann, 2002).

During the 1960s and 1970s, the Olympic Games mushroomed into supercharged showcases pitting the US and its allies against the USSR and its affiliates. The intense political currents swirling around Olympic spectacles made them unique in Cold War culture. Not only did the Olympic Games highlight superpower conflicts but they also offered a trans-national space that promised escape from Cold War perils. So successfully had the IOC marketed the Games as an agent of international understanding that the nebulous concepts of 'Olympism' developed a considerable global following. For the new 'mass medium' of the mid-twentieth century, television, the Olympic Games were irresistibly alluring. In one tidy package, broadcasters discovered all of the essential elements necessary to craft compelling visual stories for the world's consuming masses, especially sport, nationalism, and the promise of transcendence. Television seized on Olympic theatre in the 1960s and 1970s and transformed the Games into one of the world's most popular television events. The attention and the money that television brought made the Olympic Games centre stage for the electronic world's new global village (Roche, 2000; Barney, Wenn, & Martyn, 2002).

The conjunction of the Cold War, satellite television, and the IOC's efforts to bring evermore nations into the Olympic tent created new political dynamics in the international sport community of the 1960s and 1970s. As new money poured into IOC accounts from television contracts, rivalries developed between the centralised bureaucracy headed by Brundage, the National Olympic Committees, and the international federations (IFs) that shared control of Olympic sport. The IOC reached out in the 1960s and the 1970s through programmes such as the International Olympic Aid Commission to aid sports programmes in developing nations, especially in Africa and Asia. The more nations that the IOC could pack onto television screens for opening parades and closing ceremonies, the more vociferously the doyens of the Olympic movement could proclaim that their organisation contributed more to world peace than any other entity. While the IOC lost the unified German team and struggled mightily over the two Chinas and the two Koreas during this era, the sight of brand new nations from the post-colonial order making their global debut in Olympic stadiums provided new evidence of Olympic claims to transcendent universalism (Hill, 1996; Senn, 1999; Guttmann, 2002).

EMERGING NATIONALISMS AND RACIAL BOYCOTTS COMPLICATE THE COLD WAR GAMES

The entry of a flock of new polities into the Olympic family coincided with the expansion of the Cold War into the new areas of the developing world. Both the US and the USSR sought advantages and alliances in Africa, Asia, and Latin America. Both the US and the USSR had histories of supporting client-states in Olympic squabbles, as the skirmishes over the recognition of Germany, China, and Korea revealed. As the Olympic movement expanded, the superpowers and the smaller nations began to use the IOC in their political intrigues. Among the favoured tactics were threats of boycotts and demands for expulsion of various nations for various reasons. In 1963, at the IOC-sponsored Asian Games in Jakarta, the Indonesian hosts barred Israel and Taiwan from competition. India protested the expulsions to the IOC. Riots ensued, and the Indian IOC member in Jakarta for the Asian Games fled. The IOC responded by suspending Indonesia's NOC for politicising sport. Indonesian military strongman Achmed Sukarno, with support from Beijing and Moscow, riposted by creating the Games of the New Emerging Forces (GANEFO) to counter the IOC's 'bourgeois' control of world sport. The IOC threatened nations that participated in GANEFO with the suspension of offending athletes from any IOC-sponsored events. When Indonesia and North Korea appeared at the 1964 Tokyo Olympics with GANEFO veterans, the IOC declared them ineligible. Indonesia and North Korea then pulled their entire delegations from Olympic competition. The era of the Olympic boycott had officially begun (Hill, 1996; Senn, 1999; Guttmann, 2002).

More threatening than the rise of GANEFO loomed the spectre of South Africa's hard-line Apartheid regime. In the late 1950s, both the Norwegians and the Soviets demanded that South Africa respect the *Olympic Charter*, a constitution that prohibited racial discrimination. When an alternative South African NOC emerged in 1962, promising a multi-racial team to rival the existing South African NOC's commitment to Apartheid, the battle intensified. When the traditional South African Olympic lords refused to budge on the racial question, the IOC suspended South Africa from the Tokyo Games. Brundage and the IOC sought compromise and pushed the pro-Apartheid South African NOC to integrate. The new African members of the IOC protested vociferously and organised the Supreme Council for Sport in Africa (SCSA) to bar South Africa from all international sport. SCSA threatened to boycott the 1968 Olympic Games if South Africa fielded a team. The African nations found strong support from other countries in the Caribbean, in the Muslim world, and in the Communist bloc as well as more tepid encouragement from the West. At the Mexico City Games, the IOC again bowed to pressure and banned South Africa. In 1970, the IOC made the suspension permanent, barring South Africa until Apartheid in sport was dismantled (Lapchick, 1975; Nauright, 1997; Booth, 1998).

Other nations with racially exclusive policies also ran afoul of Olympic pressure. The Mexican government barred the Apartheid regime of Rhodesia from entering Mexico for the 1968 Games. Brundage was incensed by the unilateral action, particularly since, in his view, Rhodesia was not in violation of the *Olympic Charter* because it included a few non-white athletes on its team. With South Africa defeated, the SCSA turned its attention to Rhodesia and won a ban against the Rhodesian team for the 1972 Munich Games over the objections of Brundage and other IOC leaders (Hill, 1996; Senn, 1999; Guttmann, 2002).

The Soviets supported the new African and Asian nations in their struggles to expel regimes that they found abhorrent from the Olympic movement. But the Soviets had internal problems within the Communist bloc itself. After a short-lived 1968 revolution for greater freedom in Czechoslovakia, Soviet tanks crushed the uprising. The great Czech Olympic distance-running star, Emil Zatopek, resigned from the Communist Party over Soviet intervention. Norwegian IOC members demanded that the USSR and the GDR be punished by suspending them from participating in the Mexico City Games. Their protests fell on deaf ears. Battles between Czech and Soviet Olympians in Mexico City rivalled the hostilities between Soviets and Hungarians in Melbourne that had grown from an earlier Soviet repression of indigenous nationalism (Hill, 1996; Senn, 1999; Guttmann, 2002).

Political turmoil spread to Mexico and the United States. A few months before the Mexico City Games opened, the Mexican army slaughtered hundreds of student protesters in the centre of the nation's capital, projecting an international chill over the 1968 Olympic festivities. The US faced its own internal dissension in Mexico City over the legacies of the American version of Apartheid. Frustrated that the promises of the Civil Rights movement, which had begun to dismantle racial segregation in the US, had not reformed American society as quickly and thoroughly as many hoped, African-American athletes organised the Olympic Project on Human Rights. Some African-American athletes boycotted the 1968 Olympics, most notably basketball star, Lew Alcindor (later known as the National Basketball Association star Kareem Abdul-Jabbar). Others opted for symbolic protests at the Mexico City Games, including 'Cry for Freedom' gestures (referred to as 'Black Power salutes' by authorities) on the medal stands after victories in track events. The theatrical displays by African-American Olympians incensed the IOC's Brundage and focussed international attention on race relations in the United States. Cold War politics created public relations fiascos for both superpowers. Dissenters in both empires had discovered that they could use the Olympics to protest injustice in the same way that the Soviets and Americans used the Olympics to promote their societies as superior social arrangements (Wiggins, 1992; Bass, 2002; Hartmann, 2003).

In 1972, the Olympic Games returned to the homeland of the last of the old totalitarian aggressors of the Second World War. Thirty-six years earlier, Germany had hosted an Olympics in Berlin that was generally considered the most nationalistic of all the modern Games. West German organisers hoped that the 1972 Games would signal the emergence of a new Germany, this one a solid member of the liberal West. Nationalism roiled the Munich Games, but in a far different fashion than it had coursed through the 'Nazi' Olympics. East Germany competed at an Olympic Games for the first time under its own flag, with its own national uniforms, and its own national anthem – ironically debuting on West German soil. The GDR trounced the FRG in the athletic competitions (Mandell, 1991).

The Munich Games began as a classic Cold War struggle between East and West. The international press fixated on comparisons and contrasts between the Communist bloc and its rivals. Then, an entirely new strain of political factionalism seized the Olympic stage and turned the 1972 Games into a tragedy. Members of a radical Palestinian group known as 'Black September' slipped into the Olympic Village, killed two members of the Israeli delegation, and took nine others hostage. The terrorists demanded the release of 234 Palestinians held in Israel and of two German terrorists incarcerated in Germany. When German police and military units tried to liberate the hostages, after they had been moved from the Olympic Village to a nearby airport, all of the Israelis perished (Grousset, 1975; Reeve, 2000).

While the hostage negotiations had been underway, the Olympic programme was suspended. After the tragedy, Brundage and the IOC faced the issue of whether or not the Munich Games should continue. In a decision widely decried in the West, and widely disputed within the IOC, Brundage demanded that, after a brief memorial service, the Games would continue. Israeli leaders supported Brundage's position, arguing that cancelling the rest of the Munich Games would be tantamount to capitulating to terrorism (Hill, 1996; Senn, 1999; Guttmann, 2002). Family members thought otherwise.

THE ESCALATION OF COLD WAR BOYCOTTS AND THE THREAT OF OLYMPIC EXTINCTION

The Munich Massacre marked a heartbreaking new development in the nationalist struggles, which had always been a part of the modern Olympic Games. For the rest of the Cold War, the spectre of terrorism hung over

Olympic venues. During the same period, Olympic boycotts spiralled out of control. Brundage stepped down as IOC President in 1972. The organisation turned to a more conciliatory leader, long-time Irish IOC member Lord Killanin (Michael K. Morris). The amiable Killanin, however, did no better than the authoritarian Brundage in stemming the rising boycott tide (Killanin, 1983). As Montreal built its costly Olympic venues, the long fight over the two Chinas came to a head. During the 1970s, when a variety of international organisations began to consider adding the mainland People's Republic of China (PRC) and expelling the nationalist Republic of China (Taiwan), the Canadian government announced that it no longer recognised Taiwan. Taiwanese athletes were not permitted to enter the country for the Montreal Games. The IOC considered stripping Canada of the 1976 Games but, ultimately, surrendered to Canadian policy. Neither China competed in Montreal (Hill, 1996; Senn, 1999; Guttmann, 2002).

As the China situation ground to a conclusion, a new political storm clouded the horizon. South Africa had been effectively banned from much of international sport but New Zealand continued to play South African teams in rugby matches, incurring the wrath of other African nations. The SCSA demanded that the IOC remove New Zealand from the Olympic movement unless New Zealanders immediately ceased sporting relations with South Africans. New Zealand rejected the demand. Twenty-eight African nations boycotted the 1976 Games after the IOC refused to exile New Zealand (Hill, 1996; Senn, 1999; Guttmann, 2002).

The Olympic boycott tradition was just beginning. When the Communist bloc failed to join the African boycotters, another political fissure opened. The Soviets had just won the right to become the first Communist nation to host the Olympic Games and did not want to risk IOC displeasure. Anticipating a huge Cold War drama, the Soviets struck a lucrative deal with a US television corporation to broadcast the 1980 Moscow Games. Ironically, the 1980 Winter Games were scheduled for the other side of the Iron Curtain, Lake Placid, New York. The selection of Moscow ignited controversy in the West. Some groups began to urge a boycott of the Moscow Games as a protest for harsh Soviet repressions against dissidents and crackdowns against Jewish immigration to Israel. But the boycott calls did not become serious until 1979 when the Soviet Union sent its military into Afghanistan to quell an uprising against Kabul's pro-Soviet regime. In the absence of any other viable alternatives to deter the Soviet incursion, US President Jimmy Carter announced in January of 1980 that, unless the Soviets withdrew from Afghanistan, the US would not compete in Moscow (Hazan, 1982; Hoberman, 1986; Hulme, 1990).

The US Congress quickly endorsed Carter's stance. US government officials pushed to move or cancel the Moscow Olympics. The stunning upset a few weeks later by the US ice hockey team over the favoured Soviet team, en route to an improbable American gold medal at the Lake Placid Winter Games, intensified the hostilities. The IOC rebuffed US pressure to relocate or suspend the Moscow Games and urged the United States Olympic Committee (USOC) to defy government policy. While Carter and US Congress did not hold the power to force the USOC to endorse the boycott, Olympic bureaucrats surrendered to the politicians – over the strident objections of many American athletes (Hill, 1996; Senn, 1999; Guttmann, 2002).

US public opinion supported Carter and he moved to globalise the boycott. The British government endorsed the American plan but the British NOC refused to accede and British athletes competed in Moscow. Carter had more success convincing Islamic nations to boycott, since the Muslim world was incensed over the Soviet occupation of Afghanistan. Ironically, Israel joined the Islamic world in withdrawing from the Moscow Games. So, too, did Canada, Japan, Kenya, and West Germany. The People's Republic of China, engulfed in its own dispute with the Soviet Union, also pulled out. Eventually, 62 nations boycotted the Moscow Olympics, while 81 nations competed. American television cancelled its coverage of the 1980 Games (Hazan, 1982; Hoberman, 1986; Hulme, 1990).

With the US and many allies absent from the competitions, the East convincingly beat the West in the medal count, reinforcing the growing perception that Communists had won the Olympic battle in the Cold War. The IOC hoped that the boycott frenzy would end during the next Olympiad. Since the 1984 Games were scheduled for Los Angeles, those hopes appeared unfounded. East and West united once again through the Olympic pageantry at the 1984 Sarajevo Winter Games. The USSR and the GDR once again dominated the re-vitalised competitions. The harmony did not extend to the Summer Games. The fall-out from the US-led boycott of the Moscow Games tarnished the 1984 Los Angeles Olympics when, just a few months before the start of festivities, the Soviet Union announced its withdrawal. Sixteen Communist-bloc nations joined the Soviets in their retaliatory boycott. The People's Republic of China and Romania competed in California, as did 138 other nations – the most that had ever competed in an Olympic Games. Clearly, the US won the 'nation count' in the boycott war (Reich, 1986; Shaikin, 1988).

With its strongest rivals boycotting the Los Angeles Games, the US dominated the sporting contests in front of partisan crowds bedecked in national colours and chanting patriotic slogans. The media, both foreign and domestic, commented on the intensely jingoistic atmosphere at Los Angeles but also generally judged the 1984 Games a financial and an athletic success. US President, Ronald Reagan, revelled in the nationalistic fervour kindled by the 1984 Olympics, invoking the Los Angeles Games as symbolic of a new "springtime of hope for America" in his re-election stump speeches. Reagan, ever the ardent Cold Warrior, equated the Olympic flame to the Statue of Liberty's beacon as emblems of American virtue brightening the dark shadows cast by the Soviet 'evil empire' (Reagan, 1984, p. A12).

In the aftermath of Los Angeles, it seemed that the Olympic Games had reached the limit of their Cold War utility. Two successive boycotts prevented the struggle for symbolic supremacy in Olympic arenas between Soviet and US athletes. Instead, both nations led coalitions against Olympic sport. The IOC had lost control of Olympic politics. The Cold War seemed to have finally subverted the Olympic Games into a mere appendage in the interminable propaganda skirmishes between the East and West. US television mogul, Ted Turner, moved into the breach, inaugurating a new 'Goodwill Games' that he suggested would supplant the Olympics by guaranteeing the participation of both the US and the Soviet Union. Mixing commercial and ideological motives, Turner managed to stage Goodwill Games in Moscow in 1986 and in Seattle in 1990 (Senn, 1999; Guttmann, 2002).

Chastened defenders of the Olympic movement, reeling from more than a decade of boycotts as well as Turner's clever scheme to steal the Olympic market niche, entertained the possibility of a radical change to the basic structure of the modern Games in order to alleviate the political morass into which the IOC had wandered. The idea that the Olympic Games be located in one permanent, politically neutral site, such as Greece or Switzerland, received serious consideration (Kitroeff, 2004).

The IOC, instead, rendered a decision that seemed to guarantee the rage of Cold War enmity, when it selected a site for the 1988 Olympic Games that literally stood at the epicentre of the Cold War – Seoul, South Korea. Korea had been divided into a Communist North and US-aligned South since the 1950–1953 War that had marked the expansion of the Cold War to Asia. More than three decades later, North and South Korea were still technically at war. The two Koreas possessed two of the world's largest armies, regularly threatened to conquer one another, and hostilely faced off across the heavily militarised 38th parallel that marked their border. Recognition of the two Koreas had long been a thorny problem for the IOC. Many observers wondered if the IOC could possibly have made a worse choice. In fact, the IOC, led by a newly installed president, Juan Antonio Samaranch of Spain, did not really have other viable alternatives. Faced with a seemingly insurmountable challenge, Samaranch began a series of negotiations that political scientist Christopher Hill argues ultimately saved the Olympic Games from the Cold War (Hill, 1996).

Preparations for the Seoul Games were delayed when North Korea demanded that half of all the events be staged on its soil. Another round of boycotts appeared inevitable. Samaranch worked towards a compromise. He dangled the right to host archery and table tennis – extremely popular sports in East Asia – in front of North Korea. He also promised the North Koreans a share of cycling and soccer. South Korea objected vociferously to the proposal. When North Korea rebuffed the offer, the South Koreans gained control of the entire Olympic operation. North Korea then demanded its Communist allies to join in a boycott of the Seoul Games. In an earlier phase of the Cold War, such a ploy would almost certainly have worked. In the late 1980s, however, the global political situation had changed. The Soviet Union, under the West-leaning policies of *glasnost* and *perestroika*, crafted by Premier Mikhail Gorbachev, ignored the North Korean call and eagerly rejoined Olympic competition in Seoul. North Korea's old patron, the People's Republic of China, also preferred the lure of Olympic gold to ideological purity. Only Cuba, Nicaragua, and Ethiopia stayed away from Seoul in solidarity with the North Korean boycott (Hill, 1996; Senn, 1999; Guttmann, 2002).

THE END OF THE COLD WAR AND THE CONTINUATION OF OLYMPIC NATIONALISM

In 1988, at the Calgary Winter Games and the Seoul Summer Games, the Soviet Union and East Germany once again won more medals than any other nations for what turned out to be the last time. Unbeknownst to the competitors, commentators, and spectators, the Calgary and Seoul Games were the final Cold War Olympics. Four years later, at the Albertville Winter Games and the Barcelona Olympic Games, Germany once again competed as a unified team, while the former Soviet Union competed as a collection of Olympic squads representing newly independent republics and a strange amalgam that the IOC dubbed the 'Unified Team' of the 'Commonwealth of Independent States'. This time, the united Germany was a political reality and not just a clever IOC arrangement. The 'Balkanised' former Soviet teams were also a political reality. The 1989 collapse of the

Berlin Wall and the re-unification of Germany marked the beginning of a rapid disintegration of the Soviet empire. In 1991, the USSR imploded. The Cold War ended and the age of Olympic boycotts evaporated (Hill, 1996; Senn, 1999; Guttmann, 2002).

Albertville and Barcelona signified the dawn of a new epoch in world and Olympic history (Lucas, 1992; Hargreaves, 2002). Confused US television commentators attempted to identify all of the new nations that dotted opening parades in 1992, a testimony to the uncertainties of new global realties. Historian Allen Guttmann (1992) has asserted that "with the end of the cold war, political controversy seems much less likely to destroy the Olympic movement" (p. 171). While that optimistic interpretation remains to be seen, the end of the Cold War, just as its beginning, fundamentally changed the politics of the Olympic movement. It did not, however, diminish the power of nationalism in Olympic sport, as another decade of chauvinistic scuffles has demonstrated. Olympic teams continue to embody nations. Paradoxically, they simultaneously threaten to destroy the Olympic movement, guarantee passionate public devotion to its spectacles, and provide its ultimate *raison d'étre*. The prospect of war minus the shooting, as George Orwell termed it, remains one of the central attractions of the modern Olympic Games.

REFERENCES

Anderson, B. (1991). *Imagined communities: Reflections on the origin and spread of nationalism.* London: Verso.

Baker, N. (1996). Sports and national prestige: The case of Britain, 1945–1948. *Sporting Traditions, 12*(2), 81–97.

Baker, W. (1988). *Sports in the western world.* Urbana, IL: University of Illinois Press.

Barney, R., Wenn, S., & Martyn, S. (2002). *Selling the five rings: The international Olympic committee and the rise of Olympic commercialism.* Salt Lake City: University of Utah Press.

Bass, A. (2002). *Not the triumph but the struggle: The 1968 Olympics and the making of the black athlete.* Minneapolis: University of Minnesota Press.

Booth, D. (1998). *The race game: Sport and politics in South Africa.* London: Frank Cass.

Collins, S. (2004). Tokyo/Helsinki, 1940. In: J. Findling & K. Pelle (Eds), *Encyclopedia of the modern Olympic movement* (pp. 115–123). Westport, CN: Greenwood Press.

Connolly, O. (1968). *The rings of destiny.* New York: David McKay.

Cronin, M. (1999). *Sport and nationalism in Ireland: Gaelic games, soccer and Irish identity since 1884.* Dublin: Four Courts.

Diario Deportivo Olé [Buenos Aires]. (2004). *Diario Deportivo Olé,* 18 January.

Dyreson, M. (1998). *Making the American team: Sport, culture, and the Olympic experience.* Urbana, IL: University of Illinois Press.

Edeleman, R. (1993). *Serious fun: A history of spectator sports in the USSR*. New York: Oxford University Press.

Espy, R. (1979). *The politics of the Olympic games*. Berkeley, CA: University of California Press.

Gordon, H. (1994). *Australia at the Olympic Games*. St. Lucia, QLD: University of Queensland Press.

Grousset, S. (1975). *The blood of Israel*. New York: William Morrow.

Guttmann, A. (1984). *The games must go on: Avery Brundage and the Olympic movement*. Urbana, IL: University of Illinois Press.

Guttmann, A. (1992). *The Olympics: A history of the modern games*. Urbana, IL: University of Illinois Press.

Guttmann, A. (1994). *Games and empires: Modern sport and cultural imperialism*. New York: Columbia University Press.

Guttmann, A. (2002). *The Olympics. A history of the modern games* (2nd ed.). Urbana, IL: University of Illinois Press.

Harbutt, F. (2002). *The cold war era*. Malden, MA: Blackwell.

Hargreaves, J. (2002). *Freedom for Catalonia: Catalan nationalism, Spanish identity, and the Barcelona Olympic games*. Cambridge: Cambridge University Press.

Hartmann, D. (2003). *Race, culture, and the revolt of the black athlete: The 1968 Olympic protests and their aftermath*. Chicago: University of Chicago Press.

Hazan, B. (1982). *Olympic sports and propaganda games: Moscow 1980*. New Brunswick, NJ: Transaction Books.

Hill, C. (1996). *Olympic politics* (2nd ed.). Manchester: Manchester University Press.

Hoberman, J. (1986). *The Olympic crisis: Sport, politics, and the moral order*. New Rochelle, NY: Caratzas.

Hobsbawm, E. J. (1992). *Nations and nationalism since 1780: Programme, myth, reality* (2nd ed.). Cambridge: Cambridge University Press.

Hobsbawm, E. J. (1996). *The age of extremes. A history of the world, 1914–1991*. New York: Vintage Books.

Hulme, D. (1990). *The political Olympics: Moscow, Afghanistan, and the 1980 U.S. boycott*. New York: Praeger.

Jorgensen, P. (1997). From Balck to Nurmi: The Olympic movement of the Nordic nations. *The International Journal of the History of Sport, 14*(3), 66–99.

Kanin, D. (1981). *A political history of the Olympic games*. Boulder, CO: Westview Press.

Kennedy, P. (1987). *The rise and fall of the great powers. Economic change and military conflict from 1500 to 2000*. New York: Random House.

Keylor, W. (2003). *A world of nations: The international order since 1945*. New York: Oxford University Press.

Killanin, L. (1983). *My Olympic years*. New York: William Morrow.

Kitroeff, A. (2004). *Wrestling with the ancients: Modern Greek identity and the Olympics*. New York: Greekworks.com

LaFeber, W. (2002). *America, Russia, and the Cold War, 1945–2000* (9th ed.). Boston: McGraw-Hill.

Lapchick, R. (1975). *The politics of race and international sport: The case of South Africa*. Westport, CN: Greenwood.

Lucas, J. (1992). *The future of the Olympic games*. Champaign, IL: Human Kinetics.

MacAloon, J. (1981). *This great symbol: Pierre de Coubertin and the origins of the modern Olympic games*. Chicago: University of Chicago Press.

Mandell, R. (1987). *The Nazi Olympics* (2nd ed.). Urbana, IL: University of Illinois Press.

Mandell, R. (1991). *The Olympics of 1972: An Olympic diary*. Chapel Hill, NC: University of North Carolina Press.

McCauley, M. (2003). *The origins of the Cold War: 1941–1949* (3rd ed.). London: Pearson/ Longman.

McMahon, R. (2003). *The Cold War: A very short introduction*. New York: Oxford University Press.

Nauright, J. (1997). *Sport, culture, and identities in South Africa*. London: Leicester University Press.

Organizing Committee of the XVI Olympiad. (1958). *The Official report of the organizing committee for the games of the XVI Olympiad: Melbourne, 1956*. Melbourne: WM Houston.

Orwell, G. (1998). The sporting spirit. In: P. Davidson (Ed.), *The complete works of George Orwell* (Vol. 17, pp. 440–443). London: Secker & Warburg.

Reagan, R. (1984). Transcript of Regan's speech accepting GOP nomination. *The New York Times*, 24 August.

Reeve, S. (2000). *One day in September: The full story of the 1972 Munich Olympics Massacre and the Israeli revenge operation "Wrath of God"*. New York: Arcade.

Reich, K. (1986). *Making it happen: Peter Ueberroth and the 1984 Olympics*. Santa Barbara, CA: Capra.

Riordan, J. (1977). *Sport in Soviet society: Development of sport and physical education in Russia and the USSR*. Cambridge: University of Cambridge Press.

Roche, M. (2000). *Mega-events and modernity: Olympics and Expos in the growth of global culture*. London: Routledge.

Saull, R. (2001). *Rethinking theory and history in the Cold War: The state, military power, and social revolution*. London: Frank Cass.

Senn, A. (1999). *Power, politics, and the Olympic games*. Champaign, IL: Human Kinetics.

Shaikin, B. (1988). *Sport and politics: The Olympic games and Los Angeles*. New York: Praeger.

The New York Times. (1952). Olympic victories. *The New York Times*, 4 August.

Torres, C. (2001). Tribulations and achievements: The early history of Olympism in Argentina. *The International Journal of the History of Sport, 18*(3), 59–92.

Torres, C. (2003). "If we had our Argentine team here!" Football and the 1924 Argentine Olympic Team. *Journal of Sport History, 30*(1), 413–428.

Wiggins, D. (1992). "The year of awakening": Black Athletes, Racial Unrest and the Civil Rights Movement of 1968. *International Journal of the History of Sport, 9*(2), 188–208.

Chapter 5

AMATEURISM, HIGH-PERFORMANCE SPORT, AND THE OLYMPICS

Hart Cantelon

What more can be written on the topic of amateurism and sport? After all, there are more than 12,000 websites on the topic that can be easily accessed through the Internet. The International Olympic Committee (IOC) (1984) no longer uses the designation *amateur* for athletes who compete in its high-profile Olympic Games; and, the media frenzy that surrounds the professional sport entertainment business situates the Games in a much more favourable light than was the case in earlier times of debate and tension between notions of amateurism and professionalism.

While there are countless discussions about amateurism and sport, there is less written that specifically addresses the concept of 'amateurism' within the limits and possibilities presented by social structures and the historical legacies emanating from social structures. Too often, *relative* concepts such as amateurism are elevated to the status of universal truths. In other words, amateurism is reified into something that exists outside of particular social and historical circumstances. Amateurism is a free-floating concept that every person, regardless of class, gender, race, age, wealth, national origin, in fact any social category, can understand and, if so desired, aspire to. Moreover, there is often the implication, in the way the term is used, that it transcends history. It is implied, for instance, that competition in ancient Greece attracted athletes with a zest for competition in a context similar to

Global Olympics: Historical and Sociological Studies of the Modern Games
Research in the Sociology of Sport, Volume 3, 83–101

contemporary high-performance sport. Not only is such idealism misguided, it has led to participatory exclusion and the justification for undeserved social, political, and economic privilege.

A selected reading of relevant scholarship leads one to conclude that the concept 'amateurism' is highly dependent upon social/historical factors that contoured the amateur/professional debates in different time periods. Further, persons in positions of authority and influence were able to maintain notions of amateurism that contradicted the lived experiences of the majority of participants involved in high-performance sport. Important watershed events/persons 'ground' these debates, including the following:

- The de Coubertin vision of Hellenic-based Olympism
- The Brundage evangelism towards amateurism
- Soviet sport and the Stakhanovite Olympian
- Samaranch's notions of a 'Dream Team' and a 'media-friendly' Olympics.

Before beginning this historical journey, it is important to operationalise some terms that, like amateurism, have a relative connotation. The notion of 'high performance' refers to sport that is organised in such a way that only the most skilled and/or dedicated choose (or are selected) to participate. Therefore, high-performance athletes may be engaged in elite minor league competition in the local community, at the Olympic Games, or at the professional level. In other words, high-performance sport is not for athletes or people for whom sport is a hobby, a pastime, or a spontaneous competitive occurrence. As Huizinga (1970) might suggest, we are interested in those for whom sport is not *play* per se but, rather, serious and committed competition. It is such persons who aspire to achieve the Olympic motto of 'faster, higher, and stronger' whatever the standard might be, and for whom questions of amateur/professional are negotiated in the structured activity of organised competition.

It is also important to briefly explain the concept of 'relative connotation'. In her book, *Inside Language*, Vivian Cook (1997) provides an excellent example of relatively based connotations. Cook prefaces her discussion with the important observation that language is much more than mere words representing things. Words also impart meaning to things – how they are viewed and interpreted within a culture. Cook then illustrates this complexity with the example of the objective phenomenon of colour. She notes that, since colours are part of the physical make-up of the natural world (they set wavelength, determine reflective character, luminosity, etc.), the empirical details concerning colour are consistent across cultures. Logically, it would follow that, regardless of the language that identifies a colour, there also should be consistency in the range of words that describe colour. Of course, this is not the case. Different languages have different meanings attached to objective colour. The world is not seen in a uniform way; it contains important subtleties of a *relative* nature. Debates surrounding the binary opposition between amateur/professional are similarly relatively based. Ola Agevall (1999, p. 5) clarifies the notion of binary pairs: "It is common that concepts are born in pairs, partly defining each other by their opposition. It might well happen that one of the two concepts survives, whereas its twin falls into oblivion". In the context of these binary opposites and relative notions of what it means to be an athlete, this chapter explains the amateur/professional relationship in sport within the historical and structural contours that informed these debates, relating the conscious effort on the part of the leaders of the Olympic movement to relegate professionalism to purgatory.

THE DE COUBERTIN VISION OF GENTLEMANLY PARTICIPATION

Much has been written about Pierre de Coubertin and 'his' vision of an international sports festival (MacAloon, 1981; Brown, 1997). Nonetheless, there are several observations that deserve emphasis. On the 70th anniversary (1964) of the founding of the IOC, then President, Avery Brundage, wrote of Coubertin:

> It is not yet generally understood that the revival of the Olympic Games is only the first phase of Coubertin's program. The Games were to arouse the interest of Governments, of educators, and of the public in establishing national programs of physical training and competitive sport, which would assist in the tasks of eradicating social injustice, of combating the growing materialism of our times, and of correcting the features of the growing industrialism and urban living that are destructive to health and morals. In addition, by extending the ancient Greek ideal, which was strictly national, to all countries, they were to create and develop international amity and good will (Brundage, 1964).

While all of this may be true under particular circumstances, it ignores or marginalises other critical questions such as the following:

- Who exactly were these national representatives recruited to administer the revitalised Olympic Games (questions of gender and class being paramount here)?
- In the establishment of national programmes of physical training and competitive sport, it is well documented, albeit exaggerated, that de

Coubertin was enamoured of the educational philosophy of Thomas Arnold and the game structure at English public schools. Did the Baron envisage national programmes based predominately on social class lines (McIntosh, 1968)?

• Was the eradication of the perceived social injustice meant to address that encountered by the bourgeoisie, or did it include the grave inequities endured by an emerging proletarian workforce (Marx & Engels, 1998)?

• Exactly whose moral code did Brundage have in mind when he addressed the question of a code being under siege?

• Does it necessarily follow that if athletes compete against one another, amity and good will be the end result (Goodhart & Chataway, 1968; Orwell, 1958)?

• Do any of these observations presume the inclusion of women?

My intent here is to sensitise the reader to certain undeniable facts as opposed to providing concrete answers to these questions. De Coubertin's Olympic vision was grounded in his personal life experiences, and in a world in which women, for instance, were mostly absent from public life. While he championed the creation and delivery of state-funded education, he also presumed a paternalistic curriculum meant to inject middle-class morality into the working-class educational experience (MacAloon, 1981). Further, his nationalistic-based Olympics collided with the internationalism associated with worker sport (cf. Krüger & Riordan, 1996). In short, de Coubertin's everyday life experience was, as it is for every person, a fusion of language, knowledge, ideology, and culture, embodied as 'the personal' and through this linkage, suggesting individual interpretations as to how life ought to be lived.

Clearly, de Coubertin was not involved in some well-conceived conspiracy, nor did his vision of Olympism exclude worthwhile and laudable goals. What his vision of international sport implied, however, was an idea whose basis grew out of an extremely privileged life experience. It is from such life circumstances that the concept of the gentlemanly amateur sportsman also came to represent the Olympic competitor. In fairness to him, de Coubertin lobbied long and hard at the 1894 Sorbonne Congress (on amateurism) to have the assembled participants reject the class rigidity of the British definition of 'amateur', established in 1878 (Allison, 2001; MacAloon, 1981).

However, it is also important to remember that conflicting and/or oppositional views of the world make problematic any message that implies universality. If the Olympic vision generally, and the type of competitor it was meant to attract, was to have any chance of success, it had to make sense to others, most of whom would have shared similar life experiences as

Coubertin. Some, of course, did not. The American James Edward Sullivan, founder of the US Amateur Athletic Union and Director of the St. Louis Olympics, for instance, was continually a thorn in the side of the Baron (Lucas, 1977). While Sullivan, no doubt, would have agreed in principle with Coubertin's concept of amateurism, he also thought amateur athletes should be less interested in gentlemanly camaraderie and more intent on winning competitions that they entered.

Tensions such as those between Sullivan and Coubertin are important for several reasons. First, they reinforce the importance of ideological vigilance in promoting a particular view of sport but ensuring that it is imbued with enough flexibility that dissenting positions can be accommodated without destroying the integrity of the dominant idea (see Gramsci's notion of 'hegemony' in Boggs, 1976). Thus, while Sullivan and Coubertin disagreed over the intensity with which athletes might engage in competition, both prohibited professional athletes from competing in the Olympic Games. Both were firm in their assertions that there was a direct connection between the competitive ethos of ancient Greece and the revived Olympics of Coubertin, an ethos that professional athletes could not share. Second, the differences between the two IOC members demonstrate the *relativity* associated with a concept propagated as universal and acknowledged as such. For example, in word and action, it became clear to female athletes that the Coubertin Olympic Games were a 'boy's club' (though this club did not include *all* boys) and, despite the most staunch commitment to amateurism that these female athletes might have held, they were not fully welcomed as high-performance athletes until 1960 and, even today, retain token status at the administrative level (Buchanan & Mallon, 1995). A third observation involves a more subtle process – the importance of enlisting others to propagandise the legitimacy of a particular vision. Coubertin cultivated an idealistic vision he called *Olympism* (Cantelon & McDermott, 2001). It was imperative that others be persuaded that the vision was an authentic one worth pursuing; in this regard, the Baron was enormously successful.

Many years later, Coubertin argued that his 'amateur' plan was to see Olympism realised through an international sports festival (in the form of an Olympic Games). For him, this did not mean the creation of something new. Rather, the vision was built on the revival of a sports festival steeped in the history of ancient Greece. This connection cannot be over-stated – it has endured to the present day. For example, even as the 2004 Summer Olympics were about to begin, one could read statements like, "Passport to Athens: More than 2700 years after their mythic birth, the Olympic Games return to their ancestral home. And Greece is ready" (*Bell 2004 Summer*

Olympics Viewer's Guide, 2004, p. 4). The implications were clear. The 2004 'media-friendly' mega-event had ancestral connections to an ancient festival based at Olympia. Often blurred are the radically different social conditions under which each event took place, and the limits and possibilities that come to light through these diametrically different social conditions (Bouchard, 2004).

It is notable that Coubertin's vision of amateurism and the ancient–modern Games connection took root in the context of consistent interpretations of ancient Greek society made by reputable scholars of Classics. Academics such as Norman Gardiner (1967), H.A. Harris (1964, 1972), Henry Roxborough (1960), and Jan Parandowski (1939) produced influential works that took a particular Victorian notion of sports participation (focusing on the gentleman amateur) and carefully reconstituted it as an ancient Greek ideal of the true 'spirit' of sport (Lucas, 1992; *Royal Bank of Canada, Monthly Letter*, 1978). Tragically, so the argument went, this ancient Greek amateur ideal was ultimately spoiled by Roman professionalism, loosely described as blatant commercialisation (in Rome and its Gladitorial Games), cheating and 'gamesmanship' tolerated by corrupt political officials, and the concentration of event specialisation by paid professionals.

This theme was reiterated so often, and with such scholarly certitude that it was a short step to conclude that professionalism was to blame fully for the demise of the ancient Olympic Games and, if the mistakes of history were to be avoided, the Coubertin Olympics had to adopt an uncompromising 'amateur-only' policy. At the same time, however, the blatantly discriminatory class-based nature of amateurism went unaddressed. Rather, amateurism was glorified as a universal ethical ideal, a symbol of the true spirit of sport (Allison, 2001). Inevitably, the good–evil duality between amateurism and professionalism became an Olympic 'given'. Professionalism was to be avoided at all costs by the 'true' Olympic athlete.

More sophisticated arguments such as that of Lincoln Allison (2001) suggest that the play spirit can and does include the professional sports performer. Cynics might declare that this is no more than a weakly veiled justification for the presence of professional athletes in the contemporary Games. Regardless, what must always be acknowledged is the fact that, historically speaking, the ideology of amateurism effectively excluded women and most working-class men from amateur sport. Even if the patriarchal basis of amateurism could be overcome, domestic labour responsibilities and social expectations about female full-time parenting excluded women. As Dunning and Sheard (1979) have ably demonstrated in their discussion of the development of Rugby Football, the working classes found it almost impossible to compete in sport on a regular basis without some form of remuneration for missed work (i.e., 'broken-time' payments). As recently as 1992–1993, the amateur code of Rugby Union declared: "The game is an amateur game. No one is allowed to seek or receive payment or other material reward for taking part in the game" (Allison, 2001, p. 173). Such rigidity left commercialised professional sports as the logical alternative for working-class men intent on playing i.e., with a thirst for the spirit of play.

The presumed connection between the 'true spirit' of play and amateurism is significant. Consider, for instance, the very real national sense of disappointment that emerges when contemporary 'amateur' athletes are caught cheating, such as when they test positive for performance-enhancing drugs. Many Canadians were profoundly upset when, having won the 100 m sprint final and beaten his arch-rival, American Carl Lewis, Ben Johnson subsequently tested positive for steroids at the 1988 Seoul Olympic Games. The Greeks experienced similar frustration at the 2004 Athens Games with the premature exit of the Greek sprinting heroes Kostas Kenteris and Katerina Thanou who withdrew upon being admitted to hospital, following a mysterious motorcycle crash, after failing to appear for a drug test. Chief Justice Charles Dubin (1990) who chaired the Canadian government's Royal Commission after the Seoul debacle was clearly bewildered by the testimonials of track and field's Charlie Francis (Johnson's coach) and members of the Canadian weight-lifting establishment. In his summation of the 86 volumes of testimony, the Chief Justice spoke of a 'moral crisis' in Canadian sport (p. 502) in reference to the assumed loss of the universal play spirit from international sport.

One may applaud Baron Pierre de Coubertin for bringing to fruition his vision of an international sports festival, but one must also realise that his vision grew out of his personal life experience, as well as the misplaced conviction that athletics in ancient Greece and a 20th century sporting experience for gentlemanly amateurs were somehow connected. However, this commitment to the amateur ideal did not end with de Coubertin. In particular, it was Avery Brundage, IOC President from 1952 to 1972, who will best be remembered for his rabid denouncement of professional sport and the evangelical fervour with which he championed an 'amateur-only' Olympic Games.

AVERY BRUNDAGE AND RABID AMATEURISM

Without question, it was the fourth IOC President who especially fanned the coals of amateurism. As Lord Killanin, IOC President from 1972 to 1980, remarked, Coubertin was not opposed to modest recompense for athletes. Avery Brundage, on the other hand, insisted on 'Simon pure' competitors (Killanin, 1983). Brundage's uncompromising 'separate from life' stance for the Olympic Games is well-documented (Guttmann, 1984). It was Brundage who, following the Palestinian Liberation Organization's hostage-taking and assassination of Israeli athletes in Munich (1972), insisted that "the Games must go on" – a reference to his insistence that Olympic sport must not be exploited for ulterior purposes. It was also Brundage who refused to reconsider the case of Jim Thorpe, stripped of the gold medals won at the 1912 Stockholm Games for playing summer baseball for which the First Nations athlete received modest remuneration. Thorpe was not an amateur. He had accepted payment for play. It was Brundage who lauded Carl Diem and his organisation of the 1936 Berlin Olympic Games, while ignoring the plight of German Jews under the Nazi regime, a position he later adopted towards Blacks in Apartheid South Africa (Cantelon & McDermott, 2001; Hoch, 1972; Mandell, 1971). And, it was Avery Brundage who did more than his share to elevate Pierre de Coubertin to near-sainthood via the adoption of a particular interpretation of the de Coubertin vision.

Tellingly, it was also Avery Brundage who insisted on a rigid notion of amateurism that contradicted the rationalising work world of post-World War II high-performance sport (Beamish & Borowy, 1988). Like contemporary drug-enhanced athletes, many Olympic competitors during the Brundage presidency were compelled to lie about remuneration received in order to retain their amateur status (Strenk, 1988); and yet these modest payments were/are often critical to maintain a high-performance training regime. It is reputed that Brundage disdainfully dismissed professional athletes as 'trained monkeys'; team sports were always under suspicion as harbingers of closet professionals, and Brundage openly loathed the Winter Olympics for the same reason. Through a seemingly tireless career of speeches, memos to IOC members, and personal 'watch-dogging' tirades, Brundage evangelised his interpretation of the Coubertin vision, one that the Baron "did not revive...for the journalist, the cinema or the counting house" (Brundage, 1957a, p. 1). Paradoxically, evidence (Killanin, 1983) shows that de Coubertin was far less concerned about the upper-class patronage supporting Olympic competitors such as Spiridon Loues, the Greek marathon winner in 1896, or modest broken-time payment for athletes than Brundage chose to admit (MacAloon, 1981). Avery Brundage would not tolerate such a travesty; he believed in his destiny as the self-appointed prophet of the 'authentic' Coubertin vision (Cantelon & McDermott, 2001).

Brundage was appointed to the IOC in 1936 and has been referred to as "one of the keenest advocates of the Olympic ideal until his death in 1975" (IOC, 1984, p. 25). In fact, the IOC declared him to be one of the 20th century's top sports administrators (*Olympic Review*, 1999). In 1952, Brundage attained an important personal goal when he was elected President of the IOC. Killanin described his predecessor as a man of "rock-like conservatism; [with a] determination to hold on to the reins of power; [an] archetypal old-fashioned American Republican, full of strong prejudices and a spirit of tough independence" (Killanin, 1983, p. 59). These aspects of Brundage's personality were instrumental in keeping alive a version of amateurism becoming, over the course of the 20th century, increasingly redundant through the structural changes in organised sport and the personal commitment to high performance by athlete and coach alike (Brohm, 1978; Rigauer, 1981; Strenk, 1988).

Elsewhere, Killanin described Brundage as "a man with absolute ideals who would not deviate from them" (Quick, 1987, p. 43) and, on at least one occasion, the former lost his temper and called the former IOC President a fascist (Killanin, 1983, p. 61). But it is again important to understand that absolutism has its basis in historical and social determinants. The limits and possibilities made possible through Brundage's life circumstances led him to appropriate, as his rightful legacy, the role of 'true' interpreter of the Coubertin vision. He pledged his undivided attention to guard and protect at any cost what he interpreted as the 19th century ideals of Olympism (Pariente, 1989). In truth, the term 'Olympism' did not appear until well into the 20th century. *Inter alia* was his dogmatic belief in the separation of the Olympics from the political and social realities of the world. This was clearly evident in 1954 when, as President of the IOC, Brundage wrote a confidential circular letter to IOC members. In it, the President was adamant that the IOC had to *select* members to its Olympic family, for only the chosen were able to "be free from obligations or ties of any kind" (Brundage, 1954, p. 4). Brundage was singly interested in recruiting those who thought as he did about the Olympic movement and the athletes who should be allowed to participate in the Olympic Games. In addition to the statement that Brundage wrote about de Coubertin at the 62nd Session of the IOC in Tokyo in 1964, in the same speech, Brundage unashamedly declared that: "The amateur code, coming to us from antiquity, contributed to and strengthened by the noblest aspirations of great men of each generation, embraces the highest moral laws. No philosophy, no religion, preaches loftier sentiments".

As true disciples are expected to demonstrate, Brundage insisted upon a serious commitment to his brand of amateurism (Brundage, 1954). Such an unequivocal position eventually placed Brundage and the IOC in a position of conflict with the changing world of high-performance sport and the growing international appeal of the Olympic Games (Andrianov & Romanov, 1962). What Brundage may have suspected, but which he seemed helpless to harness, was the particular brand of amateurism that, at the 1952 Helsinki Olympic Games, marched out of Eastern Europe, specifically from the Soviet Union. But, before exploring the erosion that the Soviet-style worker-athlete brought to Brundage's concept of amateurism, it is important to briefly trace the concept from Coubertin through Brundage to the Soviet Olympian.

EXCURSUS: THE HISTORICAL JOURNEY OF THE AMATEUR IDEAL

MacAloon (1981) argues that de Coubertin was less intent on the cultivation of a movement of social elites than he was on the cultivation of morally upstanding (read middle-class morality) participants. Again, the Baron's view on such matters must be situated in the sporting atmosphere of his day. Coubertin's Olympic Games were not the popular media event that they were eventually to become. Women athletes, prohibited from full participation in the early years of the Games, simply formed a rival association – the Fédération Sportive Feminine Internationale (FSFI) – which sponsored 'Women's Olympics' in 1922 (Paris) and 1926 (Göteborg) (Buchanan & Mallon, 1995). Similarly, the Workers' Olympiads were considerably more popular than were the rival Olympic Games (Krüger & Riordan, 1996; Kidd, 1979). The 1931 Workers' Olympics in Vienna, for example, attracted 100,000 worker-athletes from 26 countries, with more than a quarter of a million spectators enjoying the competition (Krüger & Riordan, 1996, p. vii). Obviously, de Coubertin had to exercise a degree of tolerance and restraint as regards strident amateurism that his successors did not. The FSFI was short-lived. The Spanish Civil War disrupted and effectively led to the cancellation of the Third Workers' Olympiad and, by 1936, the Red Sport International (RSI) and Social Democratic Workers' Sport movement were irrevocably locked in an acrimonious struggle that split the movement (Wheeler, 1978). Consequently, when Avery Brundage became President of the IOC in 1952, the world of international sport had changed considerably. It was in the year 1952 that the Soviet Union turned its political back on the RSI and, with its eastern European satellite states in tow, entered its athletes in 'bourgeois' Olympic competition. Brundage's Olympic Games had become *the* primary sports festival for non-professional athletes. And so, Brundage's vision of amateurism could be (and was) much more inflexible than that tolerated by Coubertin. In fact, it shared with the early British code, a rigidity that, if exercised to the letter, would totally eliminate all but the privileged social elite from participation. Brundage's concept of amateurism is worth citing verbatim, for it demonstrates just how out-of-step was the IOC President from the world of international sport he wished to lead. In a confidential letter to IOC members on May 20, 1957, Brundage (1957b) stipulates:

The following are not eligible for Olympic competitions:

- Those who have participated for money, for merchandise prizes easily converted into money or, without permission of their governing body, for prizes exceeding $40.00 in value.
- Those who have been paid for training or coaching others.
- Those who have capitalised in any fashion on their athletic prowess.
- Those who have accepted gifts, rewards, or special inducements of any kind because of their athletic fame.
- Those who have accepted reimbursement in excess of the actual outlay for expenses.
- Those who have accepted payment for broken time.
- Those who have decided to become professional athletes and are participating to enhance their commercial value.
- Those who make a business of sport.
- Those who have neglected their usual vocation or employment continuously for more than a reasonable time (30 days in any one year) in training or competing in sport.
- Those who have been subsidised directly or indirectly because of their athletic ability by anyone, their Government, their school or college, or their employer.

Brundage's vision of amateurism simply did not fit with the circumstances of a post-World War II world. Two major allies in the defeat of the Nazis, the United States and the Soviet Union, were quickly to become hardened Cold War enemies, with the division of Europe into two political blocs. Given that both the USSR and the USA had access to nuclear weapons and with visions of Nagasaki and Hiroshima branded in the public consciousness, international sport became the preferred instrument for demonstrating political, economic, and cultural superiority. In this connection, authors Philip Goodhart and Christopher Chataway (1968) referred to sports as a 'War Without Weapons' (Lucas, 1992; Orwell, 1958).

In many ways, the Cold War centred upon the competition between two rival economic systems, market economy Capitalism, and the planned economy of state Socialism. Any evidence of the superiority of either of these diametrically opposed systems was used as a lightning rod in the aggressive recruitment of non-aligned allies in Africa, India, and Latin America. Sporting prowess was consistently used to demonstrate the superiority of one 'super-power' over another. Such economic and political differences also included vastly different interpretations of concepts such as democracy and amateurism.

There were further aspects of the post-War world that also underlined how Brundage-style amateurism was out-of-step with rapidly changing social conditions. In a war-torn world, weary of the death and destruction caused by global conflict, the presumed harmony offered by sports competition served to emphasise the increasing importance of international sport (Downing, 1999). With the spreading popularity of international competition such as the FIFA World Cup, the International Sports Federations gained far more authority and influence in relation to the IOC than in the early years of the Olympic Games. Whereas Brundage could dictate his will on the international sports community, relatively unimpeded, with only a few exceptions in the International Federations (IFs), his successors had to cooperate fully with the politically powerful leaders such as football's João Havelange and athletics' Primo Nebiolo.

The restructuring of a military industrial economy into that of peace-time production also had a dramatic impact upon sport at this time. The spread of demand induction among consumers fed a thirst for commodities absent or in scarce supply because of war-time rationing. This included the rapid expansion of commercial television and a desire for entertainment programming that fanned a growing acceptance and infatuation with the professional sports industry. "Television has made it a new game" was the claim of television sports producers (Cantelon & Gruneau, 1988; Talamini & Page, 1973) and, for the athlete, there was the developing promise that athletic talent could precipitate financial success.

Under the constant vigilance of an autocratic President and, if so inclined, the Olympic athlete had to seek financial remuneration in alternative and often deceitful ways. 'Under-the-table' payments (often called 'boot money' because of the ubiquitous envelope found in one's shoe) and excessive appearance fees became rampant. Travel expenses were padded and, by the 1968 Olympic Games in Mexico, the rivalry between the two Dassler brothers (of the Puma and Adidas shoe companies) had rendered Brundage's understanding of amateurism farcical make-believe (Hill, 1992). The scientisation of the physical education discipline also had its impact (Demers, 1988). Sporting technology and the knowledge of the body as a 'sporting machine' rapidly rationalised the way athletes trained. Sport became, as Jean Marie Brohm suggested in his scathing critique of sport, 'a prison of measured time' (1978). The German sociologist, Bero Rigauer (1981), spoke of two work worlds, the factory and the sports club – one which exhausts, and the other which exhausts even further. The consequence was that post-war high-performance sport quickly became important for political reasons. The skilled performer learned that money could be made at sport, and increasingly it was approached in a work-like fashion. This approach to sports training and competition owes much to the ethos and organisation of high-performance sport in the Soviet Union.

Arguably, the Soviet approach to sport was the catalyst in the collapse of the amateurism facade so diligently defended by Avery Brundage. While the IOC President was paranoid in his distrust of Communism, he worked tirelessly to ensure that the Soviet Union would be admitted to the Olympic movement (Guttmann, 1984, p. 134). With the inclusion of the USSR in the Olympic 'family' at the 1952 Helsinki Games, the new sibling confronted the older family members with a different type of amateur competitor.

THE SOVIET SPORTING STAKHANOVITE

In the early 1930s, a young Donetz coalminer named Alexei Stakhanov was reputed to have extracted 16 times as much coal as had been the normal shift standard. It was not accomplished with exceptional physical effort but simply through a reorganisation of the extraction process. Stakhanov's feat was rapidly duplicated in other Soviet industries and the efficient innovators were thus labelled 'Stakhanovites'. Stakhanovites were technically trained and committed to precision and accuracy in their work. They counted not only the minutes of work, but also the seconds, as Stalin is reputed to have said (Stalin, 1954). In a worker state like the Soviet Union, it was a logical step to introduce Stakhanovite principles into sport as well (Cantelon, 1979). This rationalised work process partially explains the fact that, by 1939, Soviet athletes held 44 unofficial world records in sports such as weight lifting, athletics, and speed skating.

The industrial and sporting Stakhanovites shared a similar dilemma, however. The Soviet Union was not affiliated to any major sporting federations until after 1946 and, therefore, records set by its athletes remained unofficial. Similarly, for the industrial workers: "The Soviets learned...that socialist citizens cannot cheer industrial Stakhanovites in stadiums and that there are no international festivals for steel workers" (Mandell, 1976, p. 262). By joining the International Olympic movement, the Soviet leaders assumed a reputable platform from which to promote the superiority of the Socialist path. Soviet records set in ratified international competition had to be recognised and the political leaders could lay claim to the opportunities that Socialism provided for athletes to develop. Most significantly, however, the expected Soviet superiority could be won in the relatively 'safe' environment of international sport, a venue that included its superpower rival, the United States of America.

It has already been noted that the USA, from at least the Olympic tenure of James Sullivan, had entered Olympic competition to win, which happened regularly until 1952. This pattern changed, however, at the Helsinki Games. The Soviet sport leaders arrived in Helsinki with a very different view of how sport should be approached. Their athletes had been trained in a sports system based upon 1936 Stakhanovite principles – a preoccupation with technique, efficiency, rational training, and performance. Moreover, as 'worker-athletes' in a 'worker state', Soviet athletes were provided with the resources needed to continually surpass performance records in all sports. And, frustratingly for the Western superpower rivals (particularly the USA), these full-time athletic workers did so as 'amateurs' for there was no such thing as professional sport in a worker state (Washburn, 1977). This, then, is a graphic example of the collision course that occurred because of *relative connotation*. In the Soviet Union, because of its vastly different structural fabric, concepts such as democracy and amateurism took on entirely different meanings than those in the Western nation states. The Soviet worker-athletes trained full-time for their sports but without most of the economic rewards afforded professional athletes elsewhere. There were 'perks' like better housing and preferential queuing for scarce commodities, but there were also obligatory responsibilities to the planned economy. Perhaps it was semantics, but the Soviet sports officials could truthfully reassure Avery Brundage that their athletes were indeed *amateur*, for implicit in the IOC President's understanding of the term was the professional athlete from the United States.

The Socialist worker state and its widely different concept of welfare provision ensured that those with ability were able to compete, regardless of economics, class, ethnicity, or gender. At the same time, the way in which the worker state athlete trained (following the protocol of Stakhanovism) compelled other states to follow suit, if they wanted to be able to compete with Eastern Europe (Gilbert, 1980). Some states embraced the Soviet model enthusiastically, others reluctantly (Cantelon 1981), but the end result was the same. International sport became a rational work world with 'amateur' competitors training year-round in their sports. Many athletes from the non-Socialist countries, who expected to compete with their state amateur rivals at the Olympic Games, reverted to the shadowy underbelly of so-called 'shamateurism' to escape the rigidity of Brundage-driven amateurism. The pressure of competing systems was mounting, and an anecdotal story involving the Canadian high jumper, Debbie Brill, provides a clue to the eventual outcome. Whether it is true or not is less relevant than the circumstances under which it is told. Supposedly, when filling out her income tax for the Canadian government some time after the 1976 Montreal Olympic Games, Brill listed her profession as 'high jumper'. In the 1950s and 1960s, such audacity would have been shocking; at the start of the 21st century, the declaration of an athlete that her sport is her profession is simply a taken-for-granted feature of modern life.

JUAN ANTONIO SAMARANCH, DREAM TEAMS, AND THE IDEA OF OPEN GAMES

Lord Killanin (1983) was President of the IOC from 1972 to 1980 and had been an IOC Vice-President since 1966. It is clear from reading his biography, *My Olympic Years* (1983), that Killanin and Brundage did not see eye-to-eye on the issue of amateurism. It is also clear that Killanin did much to pave the way for the radical changes in the Olympic movement that are generally credited to Juan Antonio Samaranch, who succeeded the Irish Lord as IOC President.

Killanin recalls that, in 1971, Avery Brundage delegated the three IOC Vice-Presidents (Jean de Beaumont, France; Herman van Karnebeek, Holland; and Killanin, Ireland) to meet with representatives of the International Sports Federations on matters of mutual concern (1983, pp. 79–88). In hindsight, Brundage no doubt regretted his selection of the committee members, for all three were far more open to flexible interpretations of the concept of amateurism than was the President. Also, the Vice-Presidents carried out their duties in a manner that Brundage had not anticipated. Rather than meeting with the IFs as a group, one-on-one meetings were conducted. It was clear to the sub-committee that there were widely different interpretations of the amateur code in effect, that each IF had unique problems in the administration of sport, and that some organisations such as the world body of Association Football (FIFA) and athletics (IAAF) were emerging as extremely powerful international organisations unto themselves. The outcome of these meetings was dramatic. At its 1974 meetings, the IOC adopted a new eligibility code, which gave increased authority to the IFs in the selection of Olympic competitors. Article 26 (Eligibility Code) now stated that:

To be eligible to participate in the Olympic Games a competitor must:

- Observe and abide by the rules of the IOC and, in addition, the rules of his or her IF as approved by the IOC, even if the Federation's rules are more strict than those of the IOC.
- Not receive any financial rewards and material benefits in connection with his or her sports participation except as permitted in the bye-laws to this rule (Killanin, 1983, p. 82).

Thus, the door to flexible interpretations of amateurism had been forced open and it was not long before broken-time payments (subsidies), athletic scholarships, and open state support such as Canada's carded athlete programme (Cantelon, 2003; Kidd, 1988), had replaced clandestine under-the-table appearance fee payments. Clearly, the 1970s had become an era in which high jumpers (and others) could openly declare that their sport was also their chosen profession.

Implicit in the 1980 election of Juan Antonio Samaranch as IOC President was the fact that the IOC would further disassociate itself from the rigidity of Avery Brundage. The diminutive Spaniard had extensive experience both as a political bureaucrat and a business entrepreneur (Lucas, 1992). At the 1981 Baden-Baden conference, IOC delegates were encouraged by the new President to raise all major issues that were pertinent to the Olympic Games and to make "suggestions of a progressive nature" (Lucas, 1992, p. 150). Generally speaking, all of the major issues could be grouped under the category of economic commodification: these included the negotiation of television contracts for the global coverage of the Games, the marketing of exclusive rights of sponsorship (The TOP programme – Gruneau & Cantelon, 1988), athlete training and competition support, and the problem of maintaining fair competition in the context of the growing presence of performance-enhancing drugs.

Under Samaranch's presidency, the Olympic Games quickly became a televised mega-event. The 1984 Los Angeles Games model of Peter Ueberroth ("a private Olympics without government subsidies" – Callaghan, cited in Gruneau & Cantelon, 1988, p. 356) became the preferred template for Games organisation. Significantly, Samaranch openly negotiated with professional sports associations for the presence of National Basketball Association (NBA) professionals at the 1992 Barcelona Summer Games, and the National Hockey League professionals at the 1998 Nagano Winter Games. The American NBA 'Dream Team' that coasted to a gold medal in the basketball competition was a graphic and dramatic end to an amateur-only Olympic Games. The contemporary Games, Christopher R. Hill categorically states, is one in which "amateurism is more or less a dead issue" (Hill, 1992, p. 240). Or is it? In *Amateurism in Sport* (2001), Lincoln Allison argues that amateurism has more to do with the *spirit* in which competition is entered than whether or not one is *paid* for participation. Without question, it is critical to understand the notion of 'amateur' as a *relative* concept and in relation to the specificity of historical and social conditions in which it was/is being defined. The forms, understandings, and implications of amateurism for sport in the 21st century remain to be seen.

REFERENCES

Agevall, O. (1999). *A science of unique events: Max Weber's methodology of the cultural sciences.* Uppsala: Uppsala University Press.

Allison, L. (2001). *Amateurism in sport: An analysis and a defence.* London, Portland, OR: Frank Cass.

Andrianov, K., & Romanov, A. (1962). *Some proposals on modification of the Olympic Games Charter.* Agenda of the Moscow Session, IOC Archives. Lausanne: Olympic Studies Centre.

Beamish, R., & Borowy, J. (1988). *What do you do for a living? I'm an athlete.* Kingston, ON: Sports Research Group.

Bell 2004 Summer Olympics Viewer's Guide. (2004). *Summer Olympics viewer's guide.* Bell Canada in conjunction with Time Inc. Custom Publishing.

Boggs, C. (1976). *Gramsci's Marxism.* London: Pluto Press.

Bouchard, G. (2004). *Olympics viewed differently by ancient Greeks.* Express News. www.ualberta.ca August 13.

Brohm, J. M. (1978). *Sport: A prison of measured time.* London: Ink Links.

Brown, D. (1997). *Theories of beauty and modern sport: Pierre de Coubertin's aesthetic imperative for the modern Olympic movement, 1894–1914.* Unpublished Doctoral Thesis. University of Western Ontario, London, ON, Canada.

Brundage, A. (1954). *Confidential circular letter to members of the IOC – 30 January. Avery Brundage collection.* Lausanne: Olympic Studies Centre.

Brundage, A. (1957a). *Confidential circular letter to members of the IOC – 2 May. Avery Brundage collection.* Lausanne: Olympic Studies Centre.

Brundage, A. (1957b). *Confidential circular letter to members of the IOC – 20 May. Avery Brundage collection.* Lausanne: Olympic Studies Centre.

Brundage, A. (1964). Baron Pierre de Coubertin. Message sent by Avery Brundage, President of the IOC. August. Cited at www.ioa.leeds.ac.uk

Buchanan, I., & Mallon, B. (1995). *Historical Dictionary of the Olympic Movement (Religions, Philosophies, and Movements, Serial No. 7)*. Langham, MD: Scarecrow Press.

Cantelon, H. (1979). *Stakhanovism and sport in the Soviet Union*. Kingston, ON: Working Papers in the Sociological Study of Sport, 2(2).

Cantelon, H. (1981). Ideal-typical models of sport: The USSR and the Canadian adaptation. *Proceedings of the national association for physical education in higher education*. Champaign, IL: Human Kinetics.

Cantelon, H. (2003). Canadian sport and politics. In: J. Crossman (Ed.), *Canadian sport sociology*. Toronto: Nelson Publishing.

Cantelon, H., & Gruneau, R. (1988). The production of sport for television. In: J. Harvey & H. Cantelon (Eds), *Not just a game: Essays in Canadian sport sociology* (pp. 194–197). Ottawa: University of Ottawa Press.

Cantelon, H., & McDermott, L. (2001). Charisma and the rational-legal organization: A case study of the Avery Brundage–Reginald Honey correspondence leading up to the South African expulsion from the International Olympic movement. *OLYMPIKA: The International Journal of Olympic Studies, X*, 33–58.

Cook, V. (1997). *Inside language*. Oxford: Hodder Arnold Publishers.

Demers, P. (1988). University training of physical educators. In: J. Harvey & H. Cantelon (Eds), *Not just a game: Essays in Canadian sport sociology* (pp. 159–172). Ottawa: University of Ottawa Press.

Downing, D. (1999). *Passovotchka: Moscow Dynamo in Britain, 1945*. London: Bloomsbury.

Dubin, C. L. (1990). *Commission of inquiry into the use of drugs and banned practices intended to increase athletic performance*. Ottawa: Canadian Government Publishing Centre.

Dunning, E., & Sheard, K. (1979). *Barbarians, gentlemen and players: A sociological study of the development of Rugby Football*. Oxford: Martin Robertson.

Gardiner, N. (1967). *Athletics of the ancient world*. Oxford: The Clarendon Press.

Gilbert, D. (1980). *The miracle machine*. New York: Coward, McCann & Geoghegan, Inc.

Goodhart, P., & Chataway, C. (1968). *War without weapons: The rise of mass sport in the twentieth century – And its effect on men and nations*. London: W.H. Allen.

Gruneau, R., & Cantelon, H. (1988). Capitalism, commercialism, and the Olympics. In: J. Segrave & D. Chu (Eds), *The Olympic Games in transition*. Champaign, IL: Human Kinetics.

Guttmann, A. (1984). *The games must go on: Avery Brundage and the Olympic movement*. New York: Columbia University Press.

Harris, H. A. (1964). *Greek athletes and athletics*. London: Hutchinson of London.

Harris, H. A. (1972). *Sport in Greece and Rome*. London, Southampton: Thames & Hudson.

Hill, C. (1992). *Olympic politics*. Manchester, New York: Manchester University Press.

Hoch, P. (1972). *Rip off the big game: The exploitation of sports by the power elite*. Garden City, New York: Doubleday & Company, Inc.

Huizinga, J. (1970). *Homo Ludens*. London: Granada Publishing Ltd. (Paladin).

International Olympic Committee (IOC). (1984). *The Olympic movement*. Lausanne: International Olympic Committee.

Kidd, B. (1979). The popular front and the 1936 Olympics. Paper presented at the 4th Canadian symposium on the history of sport and physical education. University of British Columbia, June 24.

Kidd, B. (1988). The elite athlete. In: J. Harvey & H. Cantelon (Eds), *Not just a game: Essays in Canadian sport sociology* (pp. 287–308). Ottawa: University of Ottawa Press.

Killanin, L. J. (1983). *My Olympic years*. London: Secker & Warburg.
Krüger, A., & Riordan, J. (Eds) (1996). *The story of worker sport*. Champaign, IL: Human Kinetics.
Lucas, J. (1977). Early Olympic antagonists: Pierre de Coubertin versus James E. Sullivan. *Stadion, III*(2), 258–272.
Lucas, J. (1992). *Future of the Olympic Games*. Champaign, IL: Human Kinetics.
MacAloon, J. (1981). *This great symbol: Pierre de Coubertin and the origins of the modern Olympic Games*. Chicago, London: The University of Chicago Press.
Mandell, R. (1971). *The Nazi Olympics*. New York: The Macmillan Company.
Mandell, R. (1976). The invention of the sports record. *Stadion, II*(2), 250–264.
Marx, K., & Engles, F. (1998). *The communist manifesto: A modern edition*. London, New York: Verso.
McIntosh, P. (1968). *Physical education in England since 1800. Revised and enlarged edition*. London: G. Bell & Sons Ltd.
Olympic Review. (1999). Best leaders of the century. *December, XXVI*(30), 8–9.
Orwell, G. (1958). In: G. Blott (Ed.), *The sporting spirit/selected writings*. London: Heinemann Educational Books, Ltd.
Parandowski, J. (1939). *The Olympic discus*. London: Minerva Publishing Co. Ltd.
Pariente, R. (1989). On the threshold of the XXIst century. *Olympic Message, 23*, 21–29.
Quick, S. (1987). *Black knight checks white king: The conflict between African bloc nations and Avery Brundage during the 1960s*. Unpublished Master's Thesis, The University of Western Ontario, London, ON, Canada.
Rigauer, B. (1981). *Sport and work. Translated by Allen Guttmann*. New York: Columbia University Press.
Roxborough, H. (1960). *Olympic hero: A tale of the 8th Greek Games*. Toronto: Ryerson Press.
Royal Bank of Canada. (1978). Sports in the World Today. *Monthly Letter, 59*(10), October.
Stalin, J. (1954). *Problems of Leninism*. Moscow: Foreign Languages Publishing House.
Strenk, A. (1988). Amateurism: The myth and the reality. In: J. Segrave & D. Chu (Eds), *The Olympic Games in transition*. Champaign, IL: Human Kinetics.
Talamini, J., & Page, C. (1973). *Sport and society: An anthology*. Boston, NY: Little, Brown.
Washburn, J. (1977). Censored statues used to develop the USSR sport complex for international competition. *Amateur Sports Act: Hearings before the Committee on Commerce, Science, and Transportation*, Serial No. 95-53, October 18 and 19. United States Senate. Washington: US Government Printing Office.
Wheeler, R. (1978). Organized sport and organized labour: The workers' sports movement. *Journal of Contemporary History, 13*, 191–210.

Chapter 6

OLYMPIC MEN AND WOMEN: THE POLITICS OF GENDER IN THE MODERN GAMES

Kevin B. Wamsley and Gertrud Pfister

In 1896, 245 men and no women competed in Pierre de Coubertin's Olympic Games in Athens, Greece, overseen by 15 male members of the International Olympic Committee (IOC) (Mallon & Widland, 1998). For decades, the founder of the Olympic Games, Pierre de Coubertin, unambiguously advocated that the festival be organised to celebrate the athletic accomplishments of men, and his IOC only reluctantly accepted the participation of sporting women after much conflict and forced concessions (Wamsley & Schultz, 2000). One hundred and eight years later, in 2004, 6,452 men and 4,412 women participated in the Summer Olympics in Athens overseen by 112 male and 12 female members of the IOC (2005, http://multimedia.olympic.org/pdf/en_report_955.pdf). In the twenty-first century, the IOC (2004) explicitly advertises itself as an organisation devoted to the promotion of equity in sport: "The IOC...considers sport to be an important means of communication and emancipation, which can contribute to developing the physical and psychological well-being. Through sport women and young girls can become aware of their role in society" (http://multimedia.olympic.org/pdf/en_report_846.pdf:1). However, the historical evidence suggests that the Olympic Games have a long history of inequities and, moreover, a foundation of basic meanings about sport predicated on gender differences and distinctions (Pfister, 2000).

Global Olympics: Historical and Sociological Studies of the Modern Games
Research in the Sociology of Sport, Volume 3, 103–125
Copyright © 2005 by Elsevier Ltd.

The distributive evidence identifying the early Olympics as a male enterprise, and the Cold War as a catalyst in promoting women's participation in
sport, is unequivocal (Pfister, 1987; Wamsley, 2002). However, the Olympic
Games *have* created opportunities for female athletes. But, with few female
IOC members and low percentages of women in positions of administrative
authority among the International Sport Federations (IFs) and National
Olympic Committees (NOCs), women do not play a significant role in the
decision-making processes governing international sport. Thus, it follows
that, historically speaking, women have not participated equally in the
production of cultural meanings attached to the Games, a fact not lost upon
the billions of spectators who have viewed the Olympics in some form since
their inception in the late nineteenth century.

The cultural meanings attached to sport as celebrated and promoted
through the Olympics, and the relative access to opportunities and rewards,
have been remarkably different for men and women. Behavioural and appearance standards always existed for men and women but, generally, the focal
point of interest in male athletics has always been performance while, for
women, personal appearance has mattered more. Official reports, the press,
and national and international sport leaders have always positioned men as the
most important participants in the Games. Even challenges to these gender
polarities, mounted by the athletic feminists of the 1920s and 1930s, were
qualified, reshaped, and absorbed within the gender hierarchies of international sport. Women eventually came to be accepted as Olympic athletes but,
for decades, only under certain terms. Olympic culture, fostered by IOC and IF
leadership, effectively channelled women into 'feminine appropriate' sports
and, later, forced sex testing or 'gender verification' to sustain traditional gender distinctions within sport and to limit the influence of women's participation
upon the world of sport. These strategies continue to be applied even today.

The Olympic Games have served to sustain a form of cultural hegemony
(Williams, 1977), broadly ensuring the authority of men over women with
respect to defining, shaping, and controlling the parameters of sport. This
was achieved by its organisation, historically influencing, through various
media, how sport was consumed and understood by spectators, and in
the course of restricting access to rewards, both symbolic and material
(Bourdieu, 1978), and participation. As the most pervasive cultural spectacle
of the twentieth century (Wamsley, 2002), the Olympic Games have played
a significant role in the organisation of gender relations, in part by encouraging the celebration of specific brands of masculinity and femininity.
Hierarchies of masculinity or degrees of 'maleness' have also been created,
negotiated, and sustained through Olympic sport. However, the reproduction

of a gender order has neither been static nor final. In fact, an important corollary to the gendering of the Olympic Games has been opportunity for the transformation of social processes through sport (White & Young, 1999, p. xvii), made possible by the sheer scale, popularity, and ubiquity of Olympic 'culture' and the capacities of individuals to act within these environments. As much as men and women competed throughout the twentieth century, restricted by the gendered boundaries of sport and broader social structures, including the dehumanising forces of Cold War sport (Hoberman, 1992), the Olympic Games also created opportunities for the empowerment of both male and female participants.

GENDER RELATIONS IN EARLY SPORT

Sport in the late nineteenth century became a significant public venue to position social meanings about men and women, maleness and femaleness. In many countries, men assumed primary positions of authority in matters relating to the economy, politics, religion, the professions, and the order of the family. During the industrialising processes and the formation of political–legal complexes in nation-states, forms of culture, and sport in particular, reinforced the public authority of men, sustaining and reinforcing the binary opposites of the sex categories, male and female, which served to order societies. Through various applications of Social Darwinism, privileging the Caucasian male, similar to the social categories created to distinguish racial hierarchies, societies embraced a paradigm of opposites for female and male attributes, which people generally accepted as biological 'facts', including strength, intelligence, emotional stability, and rationality, among others (Morrow & Wamsley, 2005). Institutions of religion, science, medicine, and education perpetuated and naturalised these traits. As such, people experienced gender orders through daily experiences at work, home, and at play. The military and social class-based foundations of modern sport, thus, endorsed the Victorian notion that men and women should/did inhabit separate spheres and in very different ways.

We examine the social construction of these spheres as they relate to the emergence of de Coubertin's Olympic Games. Within the context of major sporting institutions, Thomson's (2002, p. 115) reflections about sport represent a salient analytical point of departure for considering the gender order produced within and by the Olympics. She analyses sport as:

> ...a key site for creating ideologies of male dominance, where images, beliefs and practices of masculine power and superiority are continually replayed and reproduced. The

potency of messages about male power relies upon maintaining beliefs in distinct differences between genders, which is assisted by producing images of male physical
strength and muscularity, alongside those that denigrate femininity, women and their
sporting activities.

When considering beliefs, practices, and images invoked for organising and
promoting the Olympics, we do not deny the biological connections to gender (Hall, 1990) and do not conceive of the gender order as a 'finished
product'. Rather, we analyse the gender order as a dynamic process (Messner
& Sabo, 1990, p. 12) within the Games and the emergent gender ideologies
celebrated through the Olympics (Fasting, 2004) by its sport leaders, organisers, the media, spectators, and participants. We examine the early foundations of the gender order as the Olympic Games emerged, and briefly raise
questions about the later twentieth century relations of gender emanating
from these early distinctions. In these respects, we examine how and why men
and women have historically experienced the Olympic Games differently.

DE COUBERTIN'S ATHLETES

Throughout his lifetime, Pierre de Coubertin wrote extensively about sport,
physical training, and the value of the Olympic Games, in relation to morality, education, peace, religion, and art (Müller, 2000). Although much of
de Coubertin's writing addresses the power of sport to shape peaceful societies and develop 'whole' people, without question, his earliest inspirations
for the advancement of physical education programmes and sport competitions were militarily based. De Coubertin's early life experiences, social
inspirations and aspirations, and his travels around the world to examine
systems of physical education are well-documented (MacAloon, 1981;
Guttmann, 1992; Senn, 1999; Wassong, 2002). As a young man, de
Coubertin was deeply concerned about France's position among nations.
He perceived that his country's ill fortune was directly attributable to inferior physicalities in French men and boys, and to a distinct lack of physical
training and physical education:

> In these years, Coubertin was haunted by memories of the Franco-Prussian War. He
> attributed the defeat not to the arrogance of Napoleon III, who fancied himself to have
> inherited the military skills of his uncle, but rather to the physical inferiority of the
> average French youth (Guttmann, 1992, p. 8).

Large-scale physical activity movements in the forming nations of the
eighteenth and nineteenth centuries were, in the first instance, related to the

military. In response to defeat at the hands of Napoleon during the early nineteenth century, the Germans engaged in a mass movement of political activism and national regeneration through widespread gymnastics exercises. Other countries responded similarly. The captains of industry for imperialist Britain learned how to be tough, aggressive, and leading men in the public schools through violent, but rule-bound, organised sports (Mangan, 1981). Physical training and educational institutions in the United States and Canada adopted fragments of European gymnastics training and sports and games (Morrow & Wamsley, 2005). Aware of these varied applications of sport, de Coubertin searched for, what he perceived to be, the best model.

De Coubertin thus travelled to England, Germany, Sweden, the United States, and Canada, noting each nation's approach to the physical training of men and boys. At the personal level, late nineteenth century organised sporting relations were matters of symbolic exchange (Bourdieu, 1978), contextualised by complex codes of broader social behaviours, relating to social class, the labour process, and masculinity. The hierarchical relationships that men experienced with other men through organised sport were just as significant as the distinctions created to distance them from women and femininity. Generally, organised sport, clubs, and competitions in forming nation-states encouraged certain brands of masculinity, which were founded upon such things as hierarchy, leadership, and deference to rules and authoritative structures as well as middle class-based notions of honour which rationalised the physical application of the body to certain rule-bound tasks and contests (Wamsley, 1999). As noted in his early writing, de Coubertin saw the most value in the physical training of English men and boys to augment their leadership abilities in serving the nation. England's success at establishing an 'Empire', he suggested (Müller, 2000, p. 286), was due to instilling *masculine* character among youth through education: "The reason for England's expansion, its prodigious progress over the past forty years, is none other than its children's love for the 'fortifying exercises of the gymnasium, the manly games, the outdoor sports that give health and life'". De Coubertin also marvelled at what he referred to as the "disciplinary frenzy" of the Germans who had established a Turner movement which had been politically inspired by Friedrich Jahn, who fought for a nation state, human rights, and a constitution. At the same time, he viewed Ling's Swedish gymnastics as 'effeminate' or better suited for the old and the sick (Müller, 2000, p. 293).

De Coubertin wrote extensively about the necessity for men to receive a 'proper' education, to have the freedom to think, to learn, and to act 'responsibly'. He endorsed a class-based version of sport, based upon principles of 'Muscular Christianity', where sport was governed by codes of masculine honour to be "ranked equally with the fear of God" (Müller, 2000, p. 115). Writing in 1887, he argued that, "to put solid fists to use in God's service is a condition for serving him well". However, even after de Coubertin had relinquished his quest to promote physical education in the schools of France, and had begun to see the value of W.P. Brookes' idea for international Games (see Chapter 1), he continued to recommend sport in the service of the nation and for instilling appropriate masculine traits in the next generation of leaders. Without such training, he feared, the social opposite as conceived within contemporary hierarchies of masculinity – the effeminate or cowardly non-athlete – would prevail. His fear in this connection was made clear in his 1892 proclamation that "whoever learns not to shrink from a football scrimmage will not retreat from the mouth of a Prussian cannon" (Nye, 1993, p. 220). In his view, maleness was a matter of education being connected to one's sense of national purpose and to self-development. "In both youth and man", he argued (Müller, 2000, p. 177), "there exists a fighting instinct which is not only excusable but normal, and which can only be appeased by affording it some outlet. That is why a boy's education is not complete without some contact with 'combat sports'". For de Coubertin, an idealised masculinity consisted of a balance in mind and body developed in the service of the nation – the *raison d'etre* of his Olympic Games:

> Of course, it is absolutely noble and beautiful to engage in manly exercises with the intention of defending one's country better and fulfilling one's duties as a citizen better. But there is another thing that is more perfectly human, if one dare speak in such terms. That is to seek in athletics a marvel[l]ous solidification of the human machine, a delicate balance of mind and body, the joy of a fresher and more intense life, the harmony of the faculties, calm and happy strength. Athletics can best serve the interests of a nation and enrich its destiny when viewed in this light (Müller, 2000, p. 534).

Conversely, it seemed to be self evident and natural that women's destiny was to serve the nation in different bodily capacities. Their participation in sport during the nineteenth century was extremely limited. Victorian era ideologies of the body, buttressed by medical and scientific discourse and religious doctrine, perpetuated a biologically deterministic approach to assessing and labelling the physical abilities and disabilities of men and women. In short, commonly held assumptions asserted: that men were inherently strong and women were weak; that men of social standing should participate in sport; and, that women should not exercise at all. Scientific theories, specifically anthropological, medical, and psychological, of women's supposed weakness and susceptibility to reproductive damage and emotional distress as a result of physical over-exertion framed professional and popular conceptions of the appropriate social roles of women. This was certainly true for matters of sport and exercise (Hall, 2002; Vertinsky, 1994; Pfister, 1990; Lenskyj, 1986; Whorton, 1982). Further, as physical strength and ability represented men's contribution to the nation, so was maternity positioned within the rubric of national service for women (Mangan, 1989). However, during the late nineteenth century, due in part to a gradual relaxation of some strict medical and social attitudes, women in some countries began to participate in sport and exercise, established sporting clubs, and others sought entry into men's clubs and competitions (Hall, 2002). At the turn of the twentieth century, it became fashionable for female elites to exercise in private. Publicly visible exertion, overt physical strain, and sweating, however, remained appropriate for men only.

Generally, sport clubs and competitions occurring at national and international levels with increasing frequency towards the turn of the century, endorsed and promoted the display of physical masculinities through athletic events, while implicitly reproducing the social opposite – passive femininity via spectatorship at such events (Wamsley, 1999). In the creation of such a distinction, athleticism was positioned as an exclusively male preserve; it followed, then, that if women participated in sport or similarly physically challenging events, this distinction would become blurred. To sustain such distinctions, indeed the prevalent Victorian gender orders in which sport was an active contributor, signs and symbols had to be protected. Such was the social, scientific, and educational environment which contextualised the opinions of de Coubertin and his contemporaries, with respect to the participation of women in sport and exercise. Sport had deep class-based connotations, intermingled with gender-based assumptions and practices, which informed the decision-making and organisational parameters of nascent 'international' sport when the IOC was being established.

An affinity for classical Greek culture, both intellectual and physical, typified de Coubertin's generation of aristocratic and influential peers, in part rendering them amenable to the recasting of the ancient games motif in modern Athens in 1896. Modern interpretations of the ancient education of Athenian males underscored de Coubertin's juxtaposition of athletics, education, morality, and the artful beauty of the sporting body and, consistent with Social Darwinism and the logic of industrial capitalism, rationalised the notion that defeating others in competition was a natural, if not valuable, masculine trait. Against a background of more pronounced contexts of political, military, and economic competitiveness, typical of international relations between nations of the day, spectacles such as World's Fairs confirmed that competitions in cultural events also denoted national strength and character for nations. For de Coubertin, success in direct competition with others demonstrated personal worth, implying that the physical domination of others had significant social value for men. Sport, he wrote, "creates an atmosphere of absolute frankness" (Müller, 2000, p. 275). In other words, through sport, men learned their place in the socio-physical hierarchy. The basis of competitive sport was physical domination, beating one's opponent. The basis of Coubertin's Olympic Games was/is physical domination, defeating others. A physically powerful, active female body employed in the service of dominating others, held no cache within, and in fact contradicted, this paradigm of human 'development' by threatening the myth of the weaker sex and thus, the balance of the gender order. However, some women challenged the exclusivity of physical competition and, ironically, de Coubertin's Olympics came to provide an increasingly significant beacon for sporting women in the early twentieth century.

ORGANISING GENDER

No women participated in the first modern Olympics in Athens in 1896, although evidence suggests that two Greek women completed the marathon distance race outside of the stadium venue. The Greek organising committee did not recognise Melpomene and Stamatia Rovithi as official competitors or as competitors in any capacity (Mallon & Widland, 1998, p. 14; Lennartz, 1994), but these women demonstrated that the outright rejection of female athletes was a purely cultural, as opposed to biological, restriction. The responsibility for the athletic programme, including all events, rested with each organising committee, and not the IOC, for the first five Olympic Games. Consequently, in spite of the overtures presented by de Coubertin, women participated in various 'unofficial' events at the Olympic Games. These events in early Games included archery, tennis, skating, 'fancy diving', and, by 1912, swimming, but did not encroach upon the competitions considered more physically strenuous such as shot-putting, sprinting, distance running, or tug-of-war. As discussed in other sections of this book, the early Olympics inspired controversies over the issues of amateurism, race, nationalism, even substance abuse; but international sport, new as it was, also brought forward issues related to the gendered body and the sexual overtones of its public display.

Dyreson (1998, p. 98) argues that, for the United States, the Olympic Games of the early 1900s served to build an American sporting republic, which featured men of appropriate skill and social standing. The early Games, he suggests, featured men of "world-beating prowess" who invigorated the new, politically motivated, American sense of civilisation. Always implied was that men had to be of the 'right' sort. As reflected in *New York Times* reports of the Games, and guided by the new science of anthropometry, people had a distinct sense of an 'appropriate' body type for male athletes, even in the early twentieth century when sport was a relatively new phenomenon. For example, when athletes gathered to depart for the Interim Games of 1906 in Athens, a reporter for the *New York Times* (Sunday, April 8, 1906, p. 14) lamented:

> ...the most striking characteristic was the absence of the 'athletic physique'. There was none of that remarkable development that one is accustomed to associate with athletic skill. Neither were the men of the slender, agile, clean-limbed type one pictures for a sprinter. They were, with two or three exceptions, rather under-sized in stature, quick, wiry, and nervous, absolutely unlike any world's champion one can call to mind...Big Josh Mitchell, with his massive chest and shoulders, like the circus strong man, looked painfully out of place in such a lot.

In hierarchies of sporting masculinity, size mattered. American shot-putter, Ralph Rose, was consistently celebrated in the press, over several Olympiads, for his size and strength. Affectionately nicknamed the Western Hercules, Rose stood six-foot-four and weighed 275 lb before he departed for Stockholm in 1912 (*New York Times*, 1912, Wednesday, June 12, p. 11). Reporting Olympic successes in Sweden, the *Times* author gushed over the appearance of the other American men: "a finer lot of men was probably never got together. The average height is nearly six feet, and not even the Swedish gymnasts are more symmetrically built". Along with stature and personal character, race, too, was woven into gender hierarchies, for some nations. A reporter for the (*New York Times*, 1912, Sunday, August 25, p. 10) assured Americans that the Olympic Games were evidence: "that our race is not losing stamina ... [that] young men were of a high type, intelligent, strong, and fearless"; [were evidence] "as to just how long it takes to make a real American"; and "we have not as yet crossed the danger line in immigration"; and [are] "still assimilating those whom we receive". As Dyreson (1998) points out, the Olympic Games offered opportunities for people to tell stories about themselves, to project national identity both inwardly and to other nations, and to reaffirm commonly held notions about gender, race, and social class.

ATHLETIC FEMINISTS

By 1912, although encouraged that the Olympics had grown, de Coubertin and the IOC were concerned about the administration and control of the athletic programme by host organising committees. Consequently, the IOC, in collaboration with the IFs, assumed authority over what events would be held at the Olympics. De Coubertin's careful selection of IOC members ensured his command over Olympic-related issues and prevented hostile take-overs from rival sport leaders (Lucas, 1977) and organisations seeking to 'capture', or at least influence, 'his' Olympics (Wamsley & Schultz, 2000). Within this organisational structure, de Coubertin steered the Olympics in directions he thought appropriate. Vehemently defending the gender polarities of the Victorian era, he opposed the participation of women in his Olympics, from their outset until his death in 1937 (Hargreaves, 1994). His often-cited remarks demonstrated a strong disapproval, even offence, towards female athletes, while solidifying the position of men as the rightful beneficiaries of all Olympic opportunities. Often articulating the close connection between art and the male sporting body in his writing, he referred to women's participation in sport as "the most unaesthetic sight human eyes could contemplate" (Simri, 1979, pp. 12–13). "A woman's glory", he argued moreover (Spears, 1972, p. 63), "rightfully came through the number and quality of children she produced, and that where sports were concerned, her greatest accomplishment was to encourage her sons to excel rather than to seek records for herself".

De Coubertin (1912) frequently asserted his stance publicly to sport leaders, reaffirming his intentions for the Olympics: "…the Olympic Games represents the solid period of manifestation of male sports based on internationalism, on loyalty as a means, on art as a background, and the applause of women as a recompense" (p. 109). IOC members generally supported de Coubertin's position and were careful not to challenge his leadership. Sigfrid Edström, IOC member for Sweden, for example, negotiated with the Baron to establish the International Amateur Athletics Federation IAAF (1914) as a supportive organisation, which conceded the Olympic competition as a world championship. Recognising that athletics or 'track and field' was the marquis event at the Olympics, de Coubertin would not have tolerated a rival organisation, and future IOC President Edström well understood his appointed position on the IOC (Wamsley & Schultz, 2000). De Coubertin and the newly formed IAAF (1914) presented formidable administrative barriers to the growing numbers of women who wished to compete in Olympic track and field competitions.

Failed lobbying attempts to secure women's track and field on the Olympic programme of 1920 in Antwerp led to the formation of the Fédération Sportive Féminine Internationale (FSFI) in 1921. Political activist and athletic feminist, Alice Milliat of France, led a relentless lobbying effort to place women on the athletics programme of de Coubertin's Olympics (see Chapter 8; Leigh & Bonin, 1977; Simri, 1979; Hargreaves, 1994; Wamsley & Schultz, 2000). The IOC refused applications for the 1920 Olympics and, through the IAAF, for 1924. Edström did not support women's participation, but he clearly understood the growing significance of the popular Women's Olympics (Paris, 1922; Götheborg, 1926; Prague, 1930; London, 1934) and the increasing numbers of women participating in athletics events in many countries of the world, following World War I (Wamsley & Schultz, 2000). Although eventually successful, Milliat's negotiations with Edström incurred some costs. Indeed, Milliat had gone to some lengths in her career to ensure the control of women's sport by women but, in exchange for participation in what had become the most important international sporting event by the 1920s, she effectively ensured the IOC's control over women's international sport by agreeing to abrogate the use of the word 'Olympic' in the Women's Games and, more significantly, she was forced to cede all authority for women's athletics to the IAAF (Wamsley & Schultz, 2000). From 1932 to the present, the IOC and IFs determined which events would be held for women at the Olympics.

Edström and de Coubertin's successor, Count Henri Baillet-Latour, granted only five events to female track and field athletes, a decision which led to the boycott of these Games at Amsterdam in 1928 by the British women's team that had demanded a full programme of events. For the first time in history, women participated in events at the Olympics considered to be traditionally masculine, but not without incident. The already sceptical members of the IOC became, at first, embarrassed, and then, infuriated at what they perceived to be a horrific catastrophe in the women's 800 metres event. Fully aware of the normal conditions of fatigue experienced by male runners in this event, IOC members were appalled that female athletes should experience the same symptoms. In spite of several members of the field breaking world records in the event, some women – those who evidently had not trained for that distance – collapsed on the track in various states of exhaustion. Members of the IOC, President Baillet-Latour in particular, argued for the complete expulsion of women from the Olympic Games. "Exclusion of women's events entirely from the Games" appeared on the IOC Session agenda in Lausanne in 1929 (Wamsley & Schultz, 2000, p. 170). After many meetings between 1928 and 1931, considerable politicking by Edström and American Gustavus Kirby, and a threatened boycott of its own Olympics in 1932 by the US men's track and field team, the IOC eventually voted to permit women's athletics to remain on the programme, albeit in a limited capacity and under close scrutiny. Athletic feminists had won a victory for women's participation in the Games but had lost the right to control their own destinies in track and field. They had ceded in these rights the power to shape the parameters of women's sport, and did not win the rights to representation on the IOC or IFs. Even with respect to participation, female athletes competing in the Olympics in the early years of the century, the 1920s, and the 1930s were treated quite differently by sport leaders at national and international levels, as well as by the press.

THE OLYMPIC GAMES AND THE BODY: VOYEURS, MOVIE STARS, AND NAZI SUPERMEN

The Victorian era endorsed a modest, conservative, and class-based sense of fashion, even with respect to sport clothing. For men, the more strenuous sports necessitated allowances for the exposure of skin. Club and institutional sport promoted the widespread adoption of uniforms, and specialised equipment positioned the athlete in a unique fashion context (Pfister, 1992). For Victorian women, elites who chose to engage in 'gentle' sports, or those who dared to ride bicycles, sport encouraged opportunities for dress reform, heralded by the appearance of the split skirt and bloomers for cycling (Cahn, 1994; McCrone, 1988; Cunnington, 1970). For most fashionable women, however, the restrictive corset, voluminous layers of clothing, and dress shoes prevented any sort of physical freedom through movement – sport for these women was simply beyond the immediate imagination. But the performance principle of the Olympic Games, embraced by all participating nations, promoted new ways of thinking about bodies and, thereby, undercut some of the moral strictures placed upon fashion and upon bodies in general. People coveted athletic victories, and change occurred. Athletes adopted new techniques to improve athletic performances, such as Kraenzlein's revolutionary hurdling (Howell & Howell, 1996, p. 15), distance runners consumed concoctions of drugs and alcohol to increase their chances of victory at the Games (see Chapter 13), and athletes began to consider how sport clothing could enhance or diminish speed and agility (Schweinbenz, 2001). The 1912 women's singles tennis champion, Marguerite Broquedis of France, for example, discarded the long-sleeved blouse typical of all of her opponents for a shorter version, exposing her arms. Tennis star Suzanne Lenglen competed in a short skirt, permitted because of her young age, and she later became known in the media for her flamboyant style of dress (Bandy, 2001). At the pool, race and diving officials closely monitored the bathing costumes worn by swimmers, as clearly prescribed in the rules for the Stockholm Olympics. Female Olympic swimmers wore tighter, un-layered, and cropped outfits, far less cumbersome than common beach attire for the era (Schweinbenz, 2001, pp. 92–94).

The athletic uniforms worn in the Olympics Games offered opportunities for spectators to view male and female bodies, relatively exposed, at a time when residual Victorian social values still prevailed. Reporters from the *New York Times* (1900, 1908, 1912) noted the admiring female spectators, attractive and well-dressed, in Paris (Sunday, July 15, p. 4), in London (Sunday, July 26, p. C2), and in Stockholm (Sunday, July 7, p. 2). By 1912, however, the tone of the reports appeared to be shifting. A story printed across the wire (*New York Times*, Friday, July 12, p. 2; *Toronto Star*, Monday, July 15, p. 10; *Montreal Gazette*, 1912, Friday, July 12; *Manitoba Free Press*, 1912, Friday, July 12, p. 6) represented more visceral images of the Olympic athletes, male and female:

> The wrestling continues slowly. The assemblage of picked giants of Europe, who in scantiest tights and with sun-browned limbs bang each other about on platforms all day under a blazing sun, furnishes a picturesque side show. The swimming draws fashionable array to the waterside nightly, the most popular feature being the women who do high diving and play polo in tightly fitting garments.

Physical emancipation was a potential effect of Olympics, but broader social and cultural pressures came to bear on this venue, in addition to the internal pressures of dress conformity and behaviour regulation applied by the IOC, IFs, and a growing number of NOCs and Amateur Athletic Unions.

In the post-World War I era, more women participated in sport, albeit with restrictions and specific competitions. Men's sport, Olympic in particular, became more closely intertwined with twentieth century notions of progress, featuring a general focus on breaking records as a measure of human advancement and national pride. The 1920s brought increased newspaper coverage for sport, presaging the later process of athlete commodification in international sport, at the 1920 Olympics the press heralded the American sprinter, Charley Paddock, as the "World's Fastest Man" (Carlson & Fogarty, 1987, p. 13), an invocation that remains significant today. The Olympic Games had celebrated the performance principle since their inauguration in 1896, emphasising the exemplary masculinities of successful athletes – this is why the Games appealed to nations and sport leaders from the outset. However, in the decades to follow, Olympic performances took on increasing significance among nations. Within the

116 KEVIN B. WAMSLEY AND GERTRUD PFISTER

context of this growing sense of sportive nationalism, and the changing sport landscape, gender orders shifted, in part as a response to the growing number of female athletes who participated in traditionally male events or demonstrated speed, strength, or aggression. Newspaper reporters focused explicitly on the physical appearance, beauty, grace of the female athletes or spectators – any qualities deemed to be appropriately feminine – endorsing traditional gender orders for the reading public.

A media or administrative focus on the feminine characteristics of women athletes drew attention away from what were considered to be the masculine traits of the day – musculature, power, and speed. It focused attention away from the contradictions imposed by the presence of athletic females. While the Olympic Games provided emancipatory opportunities for female athletes and the women who admired them, new pressures emerged in the form of compulsory heterosexuality, extensive and overt attention towards physical beauty, and the rule-bound assurance of appropriate behaviour, accomplished vaguely but effectively through the doctrine of amateurism. Sporting culture recognised and endorsed the physical form and character development of male athletes, as well, but performance for men was always highlighted in the first instance. These pressures served to diminish the accomplishments of female athletes throughout this era. They sustained the position of male athletes at the pinnacle of sporting performance and absorbed any challenges to masculine hegemony. Women could participate in some events at the Olympic Games, provided that the events and the women were appropriately feminine. The Olympic motto, *Citius, Altius, Fortius*, adopted in 1920, was to be reserved for men. Further, all IOC members, officials, referees, and coaches, of course, were men.

At the opening of the Games in Antwerp, a (*New York Times*, 1920, Sunday, August 15, p. 19) reporter marvelled at the arrival of female gymnasts and swimmers: "the group of flaxen-haired Danes, in their light blue gymnasium bloomers, was the most picturesque in the field". The press provided feminising nicknames to the successful female Olympians of the 1920s and 1930s. For some sports, such as gymnastics, this sexualisation continues to the present day. Beautiful female athletes in general became 'belles' and 'nymphs', swimmers became 'mermaids', 'queens', or 'wax dolls'; later gymnasts became 'pixies' and 'sprites' and, by the 1970s, it became common for television commentators and newspaper reporters to proclaim a 'darling' of specific Olympic Games (Schweinbenz & Wamsley, 2001).

The child athletes, Aileen Riggen, 14-year-old diving champion of 1920, and multiple Olympic medallist and world figure skating champion, Sonja

Henie, attracted much press and spectator interest, as did the fashion exploits of tennis players Suzanne Lenglen and Helen Wills (Schweinbenz, 2001). These female tennis players had altered women's fashion in their sport to the extent that the *New York Times* (1924, Monday, June 16, p. 16) announced that the Olympic Games had doomed the corset to "share the fate of the hoop skirt and bustle". Track and field athletes faced added pressures from critics, beyond those faced by the 'more feminine' swimmers, fencers, and tennis players, since the medical community had always suspected the emotionally destabilising influence of exercise strain. In these events, it was particularly crucial for the press to focus upon an athletic 'beauty'. High jumper, Ethel Catherwood of Canada, provided relief to those who feared the arrival of female athletics to the Olympic programme. The press nicknamed Catherwood the 'Saskatoon Lily' for her beauty and her smile and she became *the* female athletic icon, the "beauty of the Olympics" (Schweinbenz, 2001, p. 136). The long-held social and scientific assumption that sport was dangerous for women became replaced by the notion and social stigma that sport *masculinised* women. As such, reporters felt compelled to alert their readership to the feminine qualities and heterosexuality of internationally successful athletes; otherwise, a nation could not fully capitalise on the opportunities to celebrate Olympic victories as national victories. Maxwell Stiles, reporter for the *Examiner* (cited in Roxborough, 1963, p. 86), covered the opening ceremonies in 1932:

> The Canadian girls are undoubtedly the prettiest and most wholesome looking group of girls who have arrived for the competition. They constitute a denial of the general idea that a woman athlete must be built like a baby grand piano and have a face like a hatchet. Their ages range from 16–21, and they are here to show the world that Canada has some splendid young women who are good-looking and who know how to conduct themselves.

The response by the IOC to the spirited debates over women's participation was to implicitly encourage female athletes to participate in appropriately feminine sports on the Olympic programme. During the remainder of Baillet-Latour's Presidency, through Sigfrid Edström's brief reign, and the long term of Avery Brundage as IOC President (1952–1972), women were channelled into 'feminised' sports such as gymnastics and figure skating, which had emerged as two spectator favourites by the 1970s (Wamsley, 2000). Cahn (1994) argues that women's Olympic swimming had become nothing short of a beauty pageant by the 1930s. Outside of the pool, the press attended to the graceful bodies and feminine curves of female swimmers and the muscular bodies of the men. And Olympic athletes began to actively trade on these images. The Hollywood movie industry, which emerged concurrently with the sport celebrity iconography of the Olympic Games, sought athletes to play starring roles in feature films. American Olympic swimmers Johnny Weismuller and Clarence (Buster) Crabbe, and decathlete Glen Morris, played the role of 'Tarzan' in Hollywood films, and swimmer Eleanor Holm, under contract with Warner Brothers, also performed in professional aquatic shows (Carlson & Fogarty, 1987). Holder of seven world records (Pieroth, 1996), Holm assured her fans that swimming did not make her 'mannish': "It's great fun to swim and a great thrill to compete in the Olympics, but the moment I find my swimming is making me athletic looking, giving me big, bulky muscles, making me look like an Amazon rather than a woman, I'll toss it to one side" (Guttmann, 1991, p. 145).

The symbolic potential of athletic bodies, images, and success had been evident to Hollywood producers, as they had long been utilised by the administrative promoters of the American sporting republic (Dyreson, 1998, p. 207) to bridge gaps between intellectual and popular culture. By the 1930s, the Olympic Games had been the most important sporting event in the world for some time, and rival events had fallen by the wayside. Minister of Propaganda in Germany, Joseph Goebbels, recognised the promotional value of the Games and soon convinced the new Chancellor, Adolf Hitler, that the Berlin Olympics presented tremendous opportunities to demonstrate the superiority of the German Empire (see Chapter 3). In the extensive preparations that followed, the National Socialists widely invoked collective memories of the war hero in Germany, emphasising the physically fit soldier as the exemplary male (Mangan, 1999; Kruger, 1999; Hoberman, 1999; Pfister, 2004). The Olympic poster for the Berlin Olympics featured a conquering, victorious male athlete with 'Nordic' features rising over the Brandenburg gate, the symbol for Berlin and victory over the French in 1813. The ideological properties of Hitler's Olympic architecture denoted the central place of Aryan men as evident in the giant 'superhuman' statues which confronted the spectators at the stadium. In the cultural programme of the Games, Carl Diem's 'Festival of Youth' reinforced prevalent gender hierarchies which emphasised the central place of German heroes, men who played and competed, fought bravely, died, and were mourned by women (Alkemeyer, 1994). The marginal, maternal role of women in National Socialism was also evident in Leni Reifenstahl's introduction to the film *Olympia*, which juxtaposed the muscular, athletic properties of ancient and modern nude men, and portrayed the more traditionally feminine qualities of women. The Berlin Olympics, more extensively and effectively than any other to date, promoted nationalist symbolism through venue and ceremony alike. However, in the post-World War II, Cold War era, particularly after the arrival of the Soviet Union in 1952, the Games became one of the primary cultural venues of the world to depict symbolic struggles between competing political ideologies of the world's new 'superpowers', the Soviet Union and the United States.

GENDER HIERARCHIES IN THE COLD WAR PERIOD

Despite the implicit emphasis on feminised sport in the Olympic Games, Cold War tension and competition dramatically increased the participation of female athletes in many events, even those traditionally reserved for men. Western nations responded quickly to the entry of the massive Soviet men's and women's teams, in the early 1950s, to remain competitive in the medals race. The increasing national significance of gold medal victories brought widespread performance-enhancing drug use in both East and West (see Chapter 13). However, the fear of masculinisation impeded women's sport in Western countries, whereas in Eastern bloc nations, women trained like men. The identification of athletes in a broader spectrum of sports, full-time training aided by sport science, which included extensive weight lifting programmes, altered the physiological make-up of Olympic bodies. The gender polarities, long sustained through competitive sport, became blurred as female athletes generally became bigger and stronger, and competed in events such as shot put and discus, which IOC leaders had publicly denounced as recently as the early 1930s (Wamsley, 2000). The debates between IOC President Avery Brundage and his contemporaries about the appearances of female athletes were newly framed by suspicions of the genetic make-up of Communist Olympians. Brundage had launched complaints about 'inappropriately sized' female athletes as early as 1936 but, by the 1960s, he often criticised Eastern Bloc athletes as looking 'unfeminine' and 'mannish' (Wamsley, 2004b). Yet, the IOC turned its back on male athletes such as the weight lifters who ingested steroids to enhance their training programmes – muscle mass was appropriate, even desired for some Olympic sports, but not for women.

The blurring of gender distinctions that had been preserved through sport for more than a century created widespread fears that men were masquerading as women. These Cold War-inspired fears led to degrading procedures of sex testing or gender verification for women who, in the early years of testing, had to display their genitalia to doctors to obtain official eligibility for the Olympics (Ritchie, 2003). Sport leaders did not grow suspicious of training techniques, substance abuse, chronic injuries and over-training, record-breaking male athletes, or appropriately feminine competitors. Nor did they envision that the channelling of women into feminised sports would create a contingent of child athletes in the sports of gymnastics, figure skating, and diving. By 1972, with the astonishing gymnastics routines of Olga Korbut in Munich, followed by Nadia Commenici in Montreal, the gymnastics community departed completely from the woman athlete, in favour of children. The Olympic motto (*Swifter, Higher, Stronger*) had been operationalised through the 'quantitative' sports – those that could be measured in time, distance, and weight. The twentieth century races to break records in myriad human achievements accelerated in symbolic importance during the Cold War period. The cultural venue – most popular, most watched, most coveted – became the Olympic Games, as athletic victories became national victories, political victories of Communism over Capitalism, and vice versa. The markers of these achievements, the points of fascination for spectators and training indices for sports programmes, became world and Olympic records, which visibly demonstrated the twentieth century notion of human progress to increasingly massive audiences via satellite television (Wamsley, 2004a).

Breaking world records became the pinnacle of achievement naturalised through the quantitative sports. For the judged, artistic, or 'qualitative' sports such as gymnastics, figure skating, and diving, human progress, thus conceived, was not fully represented. Consistent with the logic of performance and secondarily to sustain popularity, to generate excitement, the parameters of these sports shifted considerably in the early 1970s. The Federations, coaches, judges and athletes, through concerted efforts gradually increased the risk and difficulties of moves and routines, a strategy that ensured similar trajectories to the quantitative sports and a market share of the interest in Olympic events. Athletes broke no records, but single somersaults became doubles, then triples; single twists became doubles, then triples; tumbling routines featured elaborate combinations; skating routines included double, triple, and eventually quadruple jumps. The Codes of Points for each qualitative sport gradually changed and older movements and movement sequences were downgraded. According to biomechanical principles, female athletes with more compact, lighter body types performed these skills more easily. For women, the strength to body weight ratio was greater at younger ages and child athletes began performing at the Olympics during the 1970s. Complicated compulsory routines and highly complex individualised routines necessitated years of training, so that talent identification programmes enlisted very young children into gymnasia in all of the best competitive nations (Wamsley, 2000). Further, the social corollary to the feminising of women athletes in the twentieth century had always been significant attention to bodily appearance and beauty. In sports where body size and weight increasingly mattered for performance, in response to comments from international judges, coaches enforced standards of thinness and often diet restrictions upon their athletes (Ryan, 1995). Body image issues and eating disorders, whose relationship to the feminising process in Olympic sport has not been adequately examined in the literature, became serious problems for these sports.

CONCLUSION

Gender relations in the Olympics and the phenomenon of the gender order in the Olympic Games are clearly complex, and require a substantive depth that is well beyond the limitations of any single chapter such as this. We have attempted to discuss some of the historical conditions under which the Olympic Games emerged that have contributed to the creation and reproduction of specific gender orders and hierarchical relations of gender. Greater attention has been allotted to the early decades of the Games, establishing a foundation of gender relations on which the Cold War Games and current Olympics rest. There are many important theoretical and substantive issues that have not been raised here: the feminisation of some of the qualitative men's sports in Olympic culture; the gendering of pain and injury among Olympic athletes; the selling of Olympic female bodies to photo spreads and calendars to raise money for sports programmes to name but a few. In many respects, it is impossible to do justice to the many challenges and issues faced by male and female athletes over the past century.

Principally, Pierre de Coubertin and the IOC created the Olympic Games to celebrate the accomplishments of *men*. Had the IOC not relied on host organising committees to provide the early Games with a solid, cyclical footing, women probably would not have participated until after World War I. For men, the hierarchies of masculinity epitomised in the celebration of the Games had distinct military and nationalist overtones from the beginning. As in other forms of institutionalised sport, these relations drew meaning from the gender polarities established in societies more broadly, but effectively reproduced such distinctions in part because sport was a saleable commodity, susceptible to invocations of nationalism, localism, and patriotism, and was marketable as spectacle entertainment. How these relations shifted as the Games became more popular was, in the main, commensurate with the relatively insular gatekeepers of the festival, the IOC, and like-minded international sport leaders.

Male sport leaders accommodated the challenges of athletic feminists because, ultimately, it was better to control and reshape women's sport in acceptable terms than to permit it to develop as a rival institution. The international sporting complex of the early twentieth century, governed by an exclusive IOC, International Federations, NOCs, and Amateur Athletic Unions set clear boundaries for the behaviour, dress, appearance, and performance of Olympic athletes. The IOC and its sporting network established the parameters of competition in all respects as it saw fit. While it permitted political entities to capture the Games for their own purposes of promotion and propaganda, it also capitalised on the immense popularity that such political affinities and opportunities delivered. The Olympic Games rode tides of popularity through political opportunism, and its guardians permitted the invocation of their festival as the pinnacle of human physical achievement, on the backs of its athletes, without assuming *any* responsibility for the human problems it had created, tolerated, and endorsed. That men and women experienced the Olympic Games quite differently is not surprising – the IOC, sport culture more broadly, and the men who dominated both, would have had it no other way.

REFERENCES

Alkemeyer, T. (1994). Vom Wettstreit der Nationen zum Kampf der Völker. Aneignung und Umdeutung der "olympischen Idee" im deutschen Faschismus. *Der Olympismus Pierre de Coubertins und die Olym- pischen Spiele von 1936 in Berlin*. Berlin: Freie Universität, Diss. phil.

Bandy, S. (2001). Lenglen, Suzanne. In: K. Christensen, A. Guttmann & G. Pfister (Eds), *International Encyclopedia of women and sports* (pp. 657–658). New York, NY: Macmillan.

Bourdieu, P. (1978). Sport and social class. *Social Science Information, 17*, 819–840.

Cahn, S. K. (1994). *Coming on strong: Gender and sexuality in twentieth-century women's sport*. Cambridge, MA: Harvard University Press.

Carlson, L. H., & Fogarty, J. J. (1987). *Tales of gold*. Chicago: Contemporary Books.

Cunnington, D. W. (1970). *Handbook of English costume in the 19th century*. Boston, MA: Plays Inc.

de Coubertin, P. (1912). Sports and the feminine Aux Jeux Olympique. *Revue Olympique*, January, p. 109.

Dyreson, M. (1998). *Making the American team: Sport, culture, and the Olympic experience*. Urbana, IL: Univerisity of Illinois Press.

Fasting, K. (2004). The gendering of the winter Olympic Games. In: L. Gerlach (Ed.), *The winter Olympics: From Chamonix to Salt Lake City* (pp. 87–109). Salt Lake City, UT: University of Utah Press.

Guttmann, A. (1991). *Women's sports: A history*. New York: Columbia University Press.

Guttmann, A. (1992). *The Olympics: A history of the modern games*. Urbana, IL: University of Illinois Press.

Hall, M. A. (1990). How should we theorize gender in the context of sport? In: M. A. Messner & D. F. Sabo (Eds), *Sport, men, and the gender order: Critical feminist perspectives* (pp. 223–240). Champaign, IL: Human Kinetics.

Hall, M. A. (2002). *The girl and the game: A history of women's sport in Canada*. Peterborough, ON: Broadview Press.

Hargreaves, J. (1994). *Sporting females: Critical issues in the history and sociology of women's sports*. London: Routledge.

Hoberman, J. (1992). *Mortal engines: The science of performance and the dehumanization of sport*. New York: Free Press.

Hoberman, J. (1999). Primacy of performance: Superman not superathlete. *International Journal of the History of Sport, 16*(2), 69–85.

Howell, R. A., & Howell, M. L. (1996). Paris 1900. In: J. E. Findling & K. D. Pelle (Eds), *Historical dictionary of the Olympic movement* (pp. 12–17). Westport, CT: Greenwood Press.

International Olympic Committee (IOC). (2004). Women in the Olympic movement. http://multimedia.olympic.org/pdf/en_report_846.pdf. Accessed 20 July 2005.

International Olympic Committee (IOC). (2005). IOC members facts and figures. http://multimedia.olympic.org/pdf/en_report_955.pdf. Accessed 20 July 2005.

Kruger, A. (1999). Breeding, bearing and preparing the Aryan body: Creating supermen the Nazi way. *International Journal of the History of Sport, 16*(2), 42–68.

Leigh, M., & Bonin, T. (1977). The pioneering role of Alice Milliat and the FSFI in establishing international track and field competition for women. *Journal of Sport History, 4*(1), 72–83.

Lennartz, K. (1994). Two women ran the Marathon in 1896. *Citius, Altius, Fortius. The ISOH Journal, 2*(1), 19–20.

Lenskyj, H. (1986). *Out of bounds: Women, sport, and sexuality*. Toronto: Women's Press.

Lucas, J. A. (1977). Early Olympic antagonists: Pierre de Coubertin versus James L. Sullivan. *Stadion, 3*(2), 258–272.

MacAloon, J. J. (1981). *This great symbol: Pierre de Coubertin and the origins of the modern Olympic Games*. Chicago, IL: University of Chicago Press.

Mallon, B., & Widland, T. (1998). *The 1896 Olympic Games: Results for all competitors in all events, with commentary*. Jefferson, NC: McFarland and Co.

Mangan, J. A. (1981). *Athleticism in the Victorian and Edwardian public school: The emergence and consolidation of an educational ideology*. New York: Cambridge University Press.

Mangan, J. A. (1989). The social construction of Victorian femininity: Emancipation, education, and exercise. *International Journal of the History of Sport, 6*(1), 1–7.

Mangan, J. A. (1999). Blond, strong and pure: 'Proto-Fascism', male bodies and political tradition. *International Journal of the History of Sport, 16*(2), 107–127.

Manitoba Free Press. (1912). Friday July 12.

McCrone, K. E. (1988). *Playing the game: Sport and the physical emancipation of English women, 1870–1914*. Lexington, KY: The University Press of Kentucky.

Messner, M. A., & Sabo, D. F. (1990). Introduction: Toward a critical feminist reappraisal of sport, men, and the gender order. In: M. A. Messner & D. F. Sabo (Eds), *Sport, men, and the gender order: Critical feminist perspectives* (pp. 1–16). Champaign, IL: Human Kinetics.

Montreal Gazette. (1912). Friday July 12.

Morrow, D., & Wamsley, K. B. (2005). *Sport in Canada: A history*. Don Mills, ON: Oxford University Press.

Müller, N. (2000). *Pierre de Coubertin 1863–1937. Olympism: Selected writings*. Lausanne: International Olympic Committee.

New York Times. (1900). Sunday July 15.

New York Times. (1906). Sunday April 8.

New York Times. (1908). Sunday July 26.

New York Times. (1912). Wednesday June 12.

New York Times. (1912). Sunday July 7.

New York Times. (1912). Friday July 12.

New York Times. (1912). Sunday August 25.

New York Times. (1920). Sunday August 15.

New York Times. (1924). Monday June 16.

Nye, R. A. (1993). *Masculinity and male codes of honor in modern France*. New York: Oxford University Press.

Pfister, G. (1987). Women in the Olympics (1952–1980): An analysis of German newspapers (beauty awards vs. gold medals). Paper presented to the Olympic Movement and Mass Media Conference, Calgary, Canada.

Pfister, G. (1990). The medical discourse on female physical culture in Germany in the 19th and early 20th centuries. *Journal of Sport History*, *17*, 183–199.

Pfister, G. (1992). Vom turnrock zum bodystocking - Zur entwicklung der frauenturn und sportkleidung. In: T. Kefeld (Ed.), *Sportswear* (pp. 45–55). Krefeld: van Acken.

Pfister, G. (2000). Women and the Olympic Games. In: B. Drinkwater (Ed.), *Women in sport* (pp. 3–19). Malden, MA: Blackwell.

Pfister, G. (2004). Gender, sport, und massenmedien. In: C. Kugelmann, G. Pfister & C. Zipprich (Eds), *Geschlechterforschung im Sport. Diffenz und/oder Gleichheit* (pp. 59–88). Hamburg: Czwalina.

Pieroth, D. (1996). *Their day in the Sun: Women of the 1932 Olympics*. Seattle, WA: University of Washington Press.

Ritchie, I. (2003). Sex tested, gender verified: Controlling female sexuality in the age of containment. *Sport History Review*, *34*(1), 80–98.

Roxborough, H. (1963). *Canada at the Olympic Games*. Toronto, ON: Ryerson.

Ryan, J. (1995). *Little girls in pretty boxes: The making and breaking of elite gymnasts and figure skaters*. New York: Warner.

Schweinbenz, A. (2001). *All dressed up and nowhere to run: Women's uniforms and clothing in the Olympic Games from 1900 to 1932*. Master's Thesis. London, ON: The University of Western Ontario.

Schweinbenz, A., & Wamsley, K. B. (2001). Lilies, pixies, and mermaids, and sweethearts: The feminization of Olympic female athletes in the popular media. Paper presented to the International Society for Comparative Sport and Physical Education, Windsor, ON.

Senn, A. E. (1999). *Power, politics, and the Olympic Games*. Champaign, IL: Human Kinetics.

Simri, U. (1979). *Women at the Olympic Games.* Wingate Monograph Series, 7, Netanya, Israel: Wingate Institute for Physical Education and Sport.

Spears, B. (1972). Women in the Olympics: An unresolved problem. In: P. Graham & H. Ueberhorst (Eds), *The modern Olympics.* Cornwall, NY: Leisure Press.

Thomson, S. M. (2002). Sport, gender, feminism. In: J. Maguire & K. Young (Eds), *Theory, sport, & society* (pp. 105–128). Oxford: Elsevier.

Toronto Star. Monday, July 15, p. 10.

Vertinsky, P. A. (1994). *The eternally wounded woman: Women, doctors, and exercise in the late nineteenth century.* Manchester, UK: Manchester University Press.

Wamsley, K. B. (1999). The public importance of men and the importance of public men: Sport and masculinities in nineteenth-century Canada. In: P. White & K. Young (Eds), *Sport and gender in Canada* (pp. 24–39). Don Mills, ON: Oxford University Press.

Wamsley, K. B. (2000). The organization of gender in the modern Olympic Games. Keynote address presented at the Singapore Olympic Academy, Singapore.

Wamsley, K. B. (2002). The global sport monopoly: A synopsis of 20th century Olympic politics. *International Journal, LVII*(3), 395–410.

Wamsley, K. B. (2004a). Laying Olympism to rest. In: J. Bale & M. K. Christenson (Eds), *Post-Olympism? Questioning sport in the twenty-first century* (pp. 231–242). Oxford: Berg.

Wamsley, K. B. (2004b). Womanizing Olympic athletes: Policy and practice during the Avery Brundage era. Paper presented to the Second Roundtable on Olympic sport. Waterloo, ON: Wilfrid Laurier University.

Wamsley, K. B., & Schultz, G. (2000). Rogues and bedfellows: The IOC and the incorporation of the FSFI. In: K. B. Wamsley, S. G. Martyn, G. H. MacDonald & R. K. Barney (Eds), *Bridging three centuries: Intellectual crossroads and the modern Olympic movement* (pp. 113–118). London, ON: International Centre for Olympic Studies.

Wassong, S. (2002). *Pierre de Coubertin's American studies and their importance for the analysis of his early educational campaign.* Würzburg: Ergon.

White, P., & Young, K. (Eds) (1999). *Sport and gender in Canada.* Don Mills, ON: Oxford University Press.

Whorton, J. C. (1982). Athlete's heart: The medical debate over athleticism, 1870–1920. *Journal of Sport History, 9*(1), 30–52.

Williams, R. (1977). *Marxism and literature.* Oxford: Oxford University Press.

Chapter 7

INTERNATIONAL POLITICS AND OLYMPIC GOVERNANCE

Barrie Houlihan

A quarter of a century ago, David Kanin (1980, p. 3) wrote "Sport is a political process based on play, game, and posture. If the activity is not serious, neither can be the positions, political or otherwise, of the national players". It is hard to imagine similar words being written today, particularly about the Olympic Games. International sport and especially Olympic sport is woven into the fabric of most domestic political systems in the form of Ministers and departments of state for sport, often substantial public funding of elite sport, and occasional debates in parliaments and senates about the achievements (or failures) of elite athletes at Olympic Games. Furthermore, the increasing willingness of governments to humble themselves before the International Olympic Committee (IOC) through lavish hospitality and the strategic deployment of Presidents, Prime Ministers, royalty, film stars, and supermodels is a reflection of the value that is now placed on international sport. It is not just the recognition of the Olympic Games as a valuable political prize or the acknowledgement that the IOC and, in particular, its President are significant political actors that indicates the current international political significance of Olympic sport. It is also the extent to which the Olympic movement is itself a political issue, for example, concerning its leadership on matters such as doping and its own governance arrangements. This chapter will explore not only the international politics that surround the Olympic Games as a major political

Global Olympics: Historical and Sociological Studies of the Modern Games
Research in the Sociology of Sport, Volume 3, 127–142
Copyright © 2005 by Elsevier Ltd.

resource, but also the controversy that surrounds the governance of what is arguably *the* dominant global sports body today.

Before exploring the international politics of the Olympics, it is important to consider the main reasons for the rise in the political significance of the Olympic Games and Olympic movement. The first reason is the growth of the Olympic Games as a media event. From being a side-show in most broadcasting companies' schedules, the Games are now, thanks partly to live broadcasting, the dramatisation of ideological and nationalist rivalries by the media, and the increasingly elaborate staging of the event, watched by huge audiences. Two-thirds of adults in developed countries were estimated to have regularly watched the 1984 Los Angeles Games (Real, 1986), while the Athens 2004 broadcast reached 3.9 billion viewers in 220 countries and territories (IOC, 2004, p. 77). The Olympic Games is therefore a publicity opportunity without rival. Second, the Olympic Games can rival the United Nations in terms of its global scope. The 2004 Athens Games was attended by 201 countries, and the 2002 Salt Lake City Games attracted participants from 77 countries. Third, the Olympic Games and international sport in general provide governments as well as other political actors, such as human rights and environmental groups, with a high visibility, low cost and, from the point of view of governments, low risk opportunity for diplomacy. Boycotts and protests can be organised in the knowledge that they will receive global media coverage, but at little cost and generally with little likelihood of damaging retaliation.

The final reason for the rise in the political significance of the Olympic Games concerns the explicitly political character of the *Olympic Charter*. Unlike most international federations, which might make some general statement about the positive value of sport, their primary rationale is not to effect political change but to organise sporting events. In contrast, successive Olympic Presidents have confirmed the political objectives contained in the *Charter* and are happy to refer to themselves as leading the Olympic *movement*. The *Charter* is full of statements that reflect the political ambitions of that movement: "Olympism is a philosophy of life...the goal of the Olympic movement is to contribute to building a peaceful and better world" (IOC, 1991, p. 7). However, at the same time as expressing support for the values and mission of the Olympic movement, Olympic Presidents have also argued that politics should be kept out of sport. Unaware of, or at least unconcerned by, the irony of their actions, both Avery Brundage and Juan Antonio Samaranch protested against attempts by other international policy actors, such as the anti-Apartheid movement, to use the Olympic movement to further their political objectives while at the same time actively involving the Olympic movement in the major issues associated with South Africa and the Cold War. Overall, the leaders of the Olympic movement have never been reluctant to engage in international politics and the IOC has generally benefited from being courted by major international political interests.

INTERNATIONAL POLITICS AND THE OLYMPIC MOVEMENT

The Promotion of Ideology

The IOC and its President, the Olympic Games, and the Olympic movement are variously influential policy decision-makers to be courted, resources to be fought over, opportunities to be exploited, and symbols to be defined. Perhaps most notably, the Olympic Games and the Olympic movement generally are seen as a particularly valuable resource in the promotion of, and challenge to, particular ideological positions. For example, US President George W. Bush used the opportunity of the 2002 Salt Lake City Winter Games to promote US nationalism and express his defiance in the face of international terrorism (Atkinson & Young, 2003). Rather than follow Olympic protocol and say "I declare open the Games of Salt Lake City...", President Bush proclaimed "On behalf of a proud, determined and grateful nation I declare ... " (*Guardian*, 15 February 2002). He also took ample opportunity to be photographed with members of the US team while NBC, the US host broadcaster, reminded American viewers that the two skiers from Iran were part of the 'axis of evil' referred to by the President; and 72 million Americans tuned in to watch the opening ceremony. Given the widely broadcast attacks on New York and Washington 5 months earlier, it was not surprising that the Salt Lake City Winter Olympic Games were rife with expressions of American nationalism.

Twenty-three years earlier, in 1979, the United States called for an international boycott of the 1980 Games scheduled for Moscow. Prompted in part by the Soviet Union's invasion of Afghanistan and President Carter's search for a high profile, but non-military response, the US government placed severe pressure on the US Olympic Committee (USOC) to withdraw its athletes. Threats were made to withdraw the tax benefits enjoyed by the USOC, to renegotiate the generous lease on the government-owned USOC headquarters and training facilities in Colorado Springs, and to use the

International Emergency Economic Powers Act to prevent athletes from attending (Guttmann, 1992; Hill, 1996). The US government also puts pressure on its allies to join the boycott, many of which, including Canada, West Germany, and Japan, acquiesced, resulting in a situation where many of the most strident critics of the use of boycotts by Communist countries were now exploiting the Olympic Games for ideological purposes. The Moscow Games, despite being undoubtedly diminished by the absence of many of the leading Capitalist countries, were still deemed a success by the Soviet authorities who saw the Games as an opportunity to showcase their organisational capacity and the achievements of the Communist system through the attention of a largely uncritical international sports media. Not surprisingly, the Olympic Games scheduled for Los Angeles in 1984 were also disrupted by a retaliatory boycott by the Soviet Union and 16 of its allies. Nonetheless, the 1984 Games also fulfilled an important ideological function on behalf of Capitalism as the first Games to be organised with only minimal public subsidy and the first to generate a surplus, even though the surplus was substantially due to the fact that very few new facilities had to be constructed.

Apart from the ideological confrontation between Communism and Capitalism that dominated the Games of the 1980s, the Olympic Games have always been exploited as a resource for the promotion of nationalist ideology. Indeed, it may be argued that the structure of the Olympic movement and Olympic Games provide ideal opportunities for the expression of nationalism, which should be no surprise, given that the modern Olympics were revived at the high point of modern European nationalism (Caldwell, 1982). Since the 1904 Games, the IOC has defined participation in the Games in terms of nations rather than individual athletes. For example, Germany, Austria, and Bulgaria, among others, were excluded from the 1920 and 1924 Games and Hungary's admission to the Olympic movement was delayed because these countries were on the 'losing side' in the First World War. In 1936, the smooth management of the Berlin Games was more important to the Olympic movement than the exclusion of Jews from the German national team. Similarly, in 1960, the participation of South Africa was considered more important than the exclusion of Black athletes from its Olympic squad.

Not only is nationalism deeply embedded in the fabric of the Olympic movement and the IOC, it is the defining narrative of the Games themselves: the opening parade of athletes in national groups (rather than by sport, for example); the wearing of national team colours on their kit (rather than Olympic colours); and the playing of national anthems and the raising of national flags at medal ceremonies (as opposed to an Olympic anthem and the Olympic flag). The formal acknowledgement and encouragement of nationalism is complemented by the informal trappings of nationalism that individual teams have, on occasion, brought to the Games such as: the practice of US medal gold winners posing with their hands on their hearts in salute during the playing of the US national anthem; the German medal winners at the 1936 Games who gave the Nazi salute; and, the current fashion for almost all winners in track events to drape their national flags over their shoulders before they embark on their lap of honour. Attempts over the years to reduce the nationalist trappings of the Games have been stoutly resisted. In the 1960s, Avery Brundage, President of the IOC, proposed the discontinuation of the practice of playing national anthems and the flying of national flags – but without success. Of particular interest is that some of the most vigorous opponents to his proposals were the IOC members from the 'internationalist' Communist bloc (Guttmann, 1984).

It is unlikely that there will be any diminution in the strength of the association between nationalism and the Olympics. Indeed, it can be argued that there is a symbiotic relationship between the Games and nationalism. Just as the ideological confrontation between Capitalism and Communism gave the Olympic Games added media value so, too, does the series of often-exaggerated, current national rivalries. It can, therefore, be argued that the Olympic Games depend upon the 'social' adrenalin of nationalism.

Diplomatic Recognition, Distance, and Isolation

The Olympic movement and the Olympic Games have consistently proven to be popular and highly effective means of seeking diplomatic recognition and de-recognition, as well as indicating the desire for closer or more distant contact with other countries. With respect to recognition, there are many examples including disputes involving Palestine, Taiwan, Israel, Rhodesia (now Zimbabwe), the Baltic states, and many of the ex-Yugoslav states. However, the clearest example is the former German Democratic Republic (GDR), which used the Olympic movement to great effect as a vehicle for its campaign as an independent country seeking recognition by major diplomatic powers (Strenk, 1980; Hoberman, 1986; Hill, 1996). At the end of the Second World War, Germany was divided among the four main occupying powers. While French, American, and British zones were permitted to combine to form the Federal Republic of Germany (West Germany), the Soviet Union refused to allow the zone it controlled to join and, instead, installed a government under the control of the East German Communist Party which proceeded to seek recognition as an independent country – the GDR. Sport, and membership in major international sports organisations including the Olympic movement, was one of the main elements of the strategy to extend diplomatic recognition beyond the small circle of Communist states.

Sport provided a foreign policy instrument that was both innovative and, without doubt, highly effective. At the heart of the strategy was the assumption that participating in international sports events, 'the GDR' gradually established a perception of *de facto* independence, enhanced by membership in international sports federations and eventually leading to *de jure* recognition and, ultimately, membership in the United Nations. During the 1950s, the GDR hosted a number of sporting events to which foreign teams and athletes were invited and it also participated in a number of 'international' events usually held in sympathetic Communist countries. Once the GDR's international sporting profile had been established, it applied for membership of a number of international federations and the IOC, with the powerful sponsorship of the Soviet Union and its allies. Although the IOC resisted the GDR's request for membership for much of the 1950s and 1960s, it eventually conceded the East German demand in 1968. Ironically, it was at the 1972 Munich Olympic Games that the GDR was allowed to participate as the second German team.

The decision by the IOC to waive its rule of 'one country-one team' was due, in part, to its interpretation of the attitude of key western European and North American governments which was slowly but steadily becoming more accepting of an independent GDR. The IOC decision was also influenced by its concern not to lose its leadership role among the international federations, which had shown an increasing willingness to recognise East Germany. Finally, the IOC and the main Olympic federations were also influenced by the high standard of the East German athletes and were increasingly concerned that these athletes might be lost to international competition through the organisation of rival competitions. The success of the GDR in achieving sporting recognition was due largely to the diplomatic power of its allies, particularly the Soviet Union, but was also due to the sporting strength of the East Germans. Powerful allies and a desired resource (sporting strength) was a highly effective combination.

If international sport and the Olympic movement can be used as opportunities for a country to promote its claim to diplomatic recognition, they can also be used to attempt to isolate a country and undermine its claims to legitimacy. Israel has had repeated problems over the last 50 years in participating in the IOC-recognised Mediterranean Games and Asian Games due to opposition from Muslim states. Rhodesia was the target of similar attempts to exclude it from the Olympic Games, due to its domestic policies which excluded the non-White population from a share of political power. Perhaps best known of all was the protracted campaign, during the 1970s and 1980s, by many African countries to achieve the expulsion of South Africa from the Olympic movement and indeed from all international sport because of its policy of Apartheid, which denied civil and political rights to non-White ethnic groups. South Africa's participation in international sport was a major issue for a number of international federations and also the Commonwealth Games Federation, but it was the Olympic Games that provided the primary focus for the campaign to isolate South Africa from international sport (Booth, 1998).

The anti-Apartheid campaign is closely associated with the period of de-colonialisation in sub-Saharan Africa in the 1950s and 1960s, which created a large number of new states. Membership in the Olympic movement provided not only an opportunity to establish a sense of national identity but, also, an opportunity to campaign on a global stage on the defining issue in post-colonial Africa. Apartheid provided an issue on which Black African states could take a lead while the Olympic movement provided a high-profile international forum which could be used as a stepping stone to other, more diplomatically significant, forums such as the United Nations (Booth, 1998; Ramsamy, 1984).

The formal banning of mixed-race teams by the South African government in 1960 led to the threat from the IOC that South Africa would be excluded from the 1964 Olympic Games. In 1962, the South African Non-Racial Olympic Committee was formed by South African opponents of Apartheid and it lobbied the IOC to expel South Africa from the Olympic movement. Although South Africa was eventually excluded from the 1964 Games, but not expelled from the Olympic movement, the issue returned during the years prior to the 1968 Games. Partly in anticipation of the renewal of the dispute, in 1966, 32 African states established the Supreme Council for Sport in Africa (SCSA), which aimed to achieve the expulsion of South Africa from all international sports federations and from the Olympic movement. Despite the refusal of the South African government to compromise, the IOC persisted in attempting to find a solution which would satisfy the SCSA and also enable South Africa to retain its Olympic membership. In doing so, the IOC seriously misread the changing realities of international politics and soon found itself mired in an increasingly bitter dispute that involved the major powers outside the African continent.

After receiving assurances from the South African national Olympic committee that it would send a multi-racial team to the Mexico City Games, the IOC refused to consider expulsion, only to find that the South African government had overridden the commitment made by its NOC. Despite a threat of a boycott of the 1968 Games from SCSA's 32 members, the IOC appeared determined to maintain its policy on South African membership. Crucial to the eventual outcome was the position of the Soviet Union which had to decide "whether Olympic gold was more important than third world prestige" (Lapchick, 1977, p. 64). Early in 1968, the Soviet Union finally decided to support the SCSA boycott largely because of its concern that the People's Republic of China might exploit its participation in the Games and challenge its leadership of the Communist bloc and consequently its influence within the Third World. Faced with opposition from one of the major Olympic sports powers, the IOC had little choice but to withdraw the invitation to South Africa to attend the Mexico City Games. Expulsion followed soon after in 1970, prompted in part by the recent decision of the United Nations to urge all countries to sever sporting links with South Africa.

The South African case provides insight not only into the attitude of the major powers to international sport, but also into the ability of the IOC to act independently on major international issues. As was the case with Cold War boycotts, participation in the Olympic Games has generally been of secondary importance to the pursuit of other aims in international relations. Essentially, the Olympic movement and Olympic Games were resources to be exploited in the pursuit of broader diplomatic goals. Whether the IOC should be treated as an independent political actor is debatable. On the one hand, there are those (Kidd, 1988) who point to the vulnerability of the IOC to political pressure from the major powers and power blocs, and the ability of those power blocs to exploit the values of Olympism. On the other, it can be argued that the IOC maintained its opposition to the expulsion of South Africa in the face of significant pressure from both the African and Communist blocs, and only altered its policy when the United Nations gave unequivocal support to an international sporting boycott against South Africa.

National and City Promotion

Even before the advent of live broadcasting of the Olympic Games, and the demonstration by Los Angeles that hosting the Games need not be a major financial liability, there were examples of bids to host the Games that were motivated by a desire to make political capital for cities/regions in relation to their national government or the wider international community. The 1992 Games held in Barcelona were underpinned by the intense rivalry between Catalonia (the region in which Barcelona is located) and the central government. The Games were an opportunity not only to regenerate and promote the city of Barcelona, but also for the region to assert its identity and its distinctiveness in relation to Madrid (Hargreaves & Ferrando, 1997). In a similar fashion, the hosting of the Games in 1976 by Montreal was inextricably linked to the growing separatist movement in Quebec and the debate over the future of Canada.

There are also a number of examples of host countries viewing the Games as an opportunity to re-establish themselves in the international diplomatic community, such as Munich in 1972 and Tokyo in 1964. The hosting of the Games was powerfully symbolic of Germany's and Japan's re-admission to the international community after the Second World War. More recently, the hosting of the 1988 Olympic Games by Korea was not only an opportunity to draw attention to its rapidly expanding industrial economy, but also an assertion of its status as an independent state following the bitter conflict with North Korea and its historic rivalry with Japan. Finally, the award of the 2008 Games to China provided an opportunity for the Chinese government not only to 'showcase' its rapid modernisation and industrialisation, but also to demonstrate its status as a regional and global power.

THE INTERNATIONAL OLYMPIC COMMITTEE: A POLITICAL TOOL, A POLITICAL ACTOR, OR A POLITICAL ARENA?

At times it would appear that the IOC has struggled, not always successfully, to avoid being manipulated by powerful, global political actors. During the Cold War, the Soviet Union, with the support of its allies, systematically sought to manipulate the decisions of the IOC to further its objectives, most notably in pursuit of diplomatic recognition for East Germany and as a means of establishing Soviet leadership among Third World and non-aligned countries. However, there is a need for caution in highlighting attempts by Communist bloc countries to use the IOC as a political instrument as this tends to assume that the IOC is a politically neutral body without a political culture and political objectives of its own.

Indeed, the IOC is an international organisation, which consistently invokes Olympism as a highly politicised ideology. From its earliest years through to the present day, the IOC administrative functioning has essentially reproduced western notions of the nation state and nationalism; during the years of the Cold War, the Committee was deeply sceptical of the motives of the Communist bloc, but far less so of those of the western powers; and during and since the period of rapid de-colonialisation, in the 1960s and 1970s, it was patronising and manipulative, especially in relation to the states in the sub-Saharan region. Therefore, the record of the IOC as an independent political actor must be contextualised within this mix of interests and values. As mentioned above in relation to the pressure placed on the IOC to expel South Africa, the Committee successfully resisted the collective weight of the Communist bloc and the African states for a number of years and only expelled South Africa when the United Nations issued a formal directive. Similarly, the Committee refused the demand from Tanzania and 14 other states that New Zealand be excluded from the 1976 Olympics because of its continuing sporting contact with South Africa. This reluctant stance led 30 nations to boycott the Montreal Games. The capacity of the IOC to maintain its resistance to pressure was boosted by the fact that none of the boycotting countries was a significant 'sports power' and, also, the Communist bloc had refused to add its weight to the campaign (due mainly to the fact that the Soviet Union had recently been awarded the right to host the Games in 1980).

However, while there are examples of the IOC resisting external pressure, there are also examples of its inability to impose its authority on host governments. For example, at the 1976 Olympic Games, the IOC failed to persuade the Canadian host government to allow the Taiwanese athletes entry to the country, despite a clear commitment by the government that all accredited athletes would be granted entry visas. The Canadian government's decision to support Chinese claims to Taiwan was a more important political consideration than the possibility of offending the IOC. Moreover, this example illustrates the obvious point that as the date for the opening of the Games draws near, the less influence the IOC has over the actions of the host government. The scale, complexity, and immense financial ramifications of the Games result in the IOC becoming increasingly reliant on the goodwill and co-operation of the host authorities.

The evidence suggests that the capacity of the IOC to act as an independent political actor is highly variable and that, on many issues, the IOC is tightly constrained by the network of resource dependencies within which it works. However, before being tempted to criticise the IOC for its lack of operational capacity or its equivocation in the pursuit of values of Olympism, as reflected in the *Olympic Charter*, one should acknowledge the complex international political environment within which the IOC operates. Few, if any, international organisations can operate consistently in line with their founding values and mission. Organisations, such as Greenpeace, Oxfam, the Red Cross, and Médecins Sans Frontières, which have strongly stated guiding principles, have greater independence from governments than the IOC and also greater opportunity to withdraw co-operation, and are consequently inappropriate comparators for the IOC. More realistic comparators would be the United Nations and its agencies such as UNESCO and the World Health Organisation, which are much more deeply embedded in a network of relationships with powerful governments. The question to ask, thus, is not whether the IOC has been consistent and steadfast in its pursuit of the values in the *Olympic Charter* but, rather, whether the IOC has satisfactorily balanced its commitment to Olympic values with the pragmatism needed to operate effectively in a contemporary international political community that is inclined to treat sport and the Olympic Games as exploitable resources.

In recent years, excepting the adverse atmosphere of suspicion in the post-scandal years, it is possible to argue that the climate within which the IOC operates has become less turbulent and less hostile. First, over the last 20 years or so, the wealth of the Olympic movement has increased dramatically, making it less dependent on the financial resources and goodwill of host governments, though perhaps more dependent on the television companies and commercial sponsors that provide the bulk of its income. Second, the status of the Games has also risen as indicated by the fact that the number of countries bidding to host the Games has increased steadily since 1980 (Preuss, 2000). Third, the popularity of the boycott as an instrument of pressure has markedly declined partly because the political benefits of being present at the Games are considered generally to outweigh the leverage that a boycott threat offers.

Although the major global political issues in international relations, such as the Cold War superpower rivalry, Apartheid, and problems in the Middle East, have either been resolved or are dealt with largely in other arenas, it is possible to argue that the Olympics is still an important arena for a number of issues which, while not dominating the foreign policy agendas of governments, are of major global significance and include issues such as gender equity and environmentalism. As regards gender equity, the role of the IOC is best described as being that of a moderately enthusiastic latecomer. In 1972, there were only three women in decision-making positions within the

Olympic movement – about 1% of the total (Rich, 2004). While, during the 1970s and 1980s, there was a marked increase in the number of events open to women as participants in the Olympic Games, there was not a similar increase in women's involvement in decision making. Although there had been some debate on the role of women in the Olympic movement since the late 1960s, change was very slow in arriving. For example, of the 64 new members of the IOC, appointed between 1981 and 1994, only five were women. However, from the mid-1990s, the IOC adopted a much more pro-active approach to women's involvement, partly as a result of the steady lobbying of the small number of women who were either members of the IOC or in senior positions within international federations, and partly as a result of lobbying designed to promote the objectives of equity and inclusion encapsulated in the Brighton Declaration (British Sports Council, 1994). The endorsement of the Brighton Declaration by over 200 governments and international sports organisations by 1998 was, in part, due to the added momentum given to the objective of equity by the IOC which, in 1995, required NOCs to ensure that 10% of all decision-making positions were filled by women by 2005. A similar requirement was made of the international federations and other sports organisations that belonged to the Olympic movement. To support its decisions, the IOC invested in information seminars, promotional activity and monitoring, and evaluation research. While the IOC has not been in the vanguard of the gender equity movement, it gave a strong lead to the international sporting community and continues to support actively the implementation of its policy on targets.

The embrace of environmentalism by the IOC has been equally late as that of gender equity, but also equally significant. The widely publicised environmental damage that accompanied the Albertville Winter Olympic Games in 1992 was a catalyst for examining the impact of the ever-expanding Olympic Games on the local environment. Cantelon and Letters (2000, p. 300) note, with reference to Albertville, that "construction was on a scale that would result in irrevocable transformation of the natural environment and the subsequent destruction of the existing ecosystem". The coincidence of the Albertville Games with the growing global debate on the environment (e.g., the United Nations Earth Summit held in Rio de Janeiro in 1992) made it difficult for the IOC to ignore the issue. However, as Cantelon and Letters make clear "the IOC had little understanding how it might be an effective and proactive environmental watchdog" (2000, p. 302). Fortuitously, the next Winter Games were scheduled for Lillehammer and Norway provided the IOC with a model for hosting an environmentally sensitive Games. As Cantelon and Letters suggest, "To its credit, the IOC put in motion its significant transnational muscle (economic and political) to build upon the local success in Norway" (2000, p. 304). In 1997, the IOC published a set of environmental guidelines for future-bidding cities and noted that "environmental considerations and compulsory ecological studies have been included in the process for evaluating cities applying to host the Olympic Games" (IOC, 1997, p. 75). Although the current policy is not without its critics (see Lenskyj, 1998), the issue of the environmental impact of mega sports events, such as the Olympics is considerably more prominent due to the lead given by the IOC.

THE IOC AND GOOD GOVERNANCE

The generally positive assessment of the IOC's current policy and practice on matters of corporate leadership and governance in the areas of gender equity and environmental policy might lead one to conclude that the Olympic movement in general, and the IOC in particular, are models of good governance in international sport. While it would be churlish not to acknowledge and applaud the areas of policy where the IOC has embraced current standards of good governance, the Committee has been heavily criticised in recent years for its secrecy and on occasions for its corrupt practices.

For a number of years there have been a small number of critics who have expressed scepticism at the substance that rested behind beguiling phrases, such as the 'Olympic family' and the 'Olympic movement' and the mystical conceptualisation of Olympism as a secular religion. Hoberman (1986) referred to the 'amoral universalism' of the 'Olympic movement' which led the IOC regularly to turn a blind eye to any inconvenient political events, especially the repression of political dissent in host countries which might interfere with the global ambitions of the IOC and President Samaranch. Simson and Jennings (1992) endorsed Hoberman's critique and painted a picture of a deeply corrupt international sport industry with the IOC at its heart. In less dramatic terms, Hill (1996) also expressed similar concern at the dangers of the 'gigantism' of the Games and questioned whether the 'checks and balances' that should be a feature of sound corporate governance – transparency, openness to external audit, and accountability to stakeholders for example – were sufficiently embedded in the management processes of the Olympic movement. In a prescient warning Hill noted that, "As with other unelected bodies which have acquired great power, the IOC's most priceless asset is its integrity" (1996, p. 81).

The challenge to the integrity of the IOC was not long in coming. In 1998, details began to emerge in the media, confirmed by IOC member Marc Hodler, of substantial corruption in the award of the 2002 Winter Games to Salt Lake City involving the payment of inducements to a number of IOC members and their relatives (see Chapter 11). Somewhat reluctantly, the IOC agreed to initiate an internal inquiry, which was rapidly overtaken by a series of external investigations including those by the US Justice Department and the US Congress. The IOC's internal inquiry recommended the expulsion of six members (three had already resigned and one died) and further investigation of four more. Under continuing pressure from external investigations, the IOC established a reform Commission which reported to the IOC session in 1999. The Commission made 50 recommendations, the most important of which concerned the composition of the IOC, the role of IOC members in host city selection, and the accountability and transparency of IOC decision making. With respect to the composition of the IOC, the changes that were made were modest: some alteration to the size of the Committee with a guaranteed 15 seats for recent and current athletes and mandatory retirement at age 70 for new members. Perhaps the biggest change was to limit the role of IOC members in visiting prospective host cities and stricter guidelines on the receipt of gifts. However, the recommendations designed to achieve greater accountability and transparency largely affected internal processes of accountability and did little to facilitate accountability and transparency in relation to the public.

CONCLUSION

The recent reforms of the operation of the IOC go some way towards overcoming the dominant perception of the IOC as a self-absorbed and self-satisfied body and creating a somewhat open, accountable, and ethical organisation that is capable of promoting the idealism of the *Olympic Charter*. However, criticism of the IOC must be tempered by an acknowledgement of the turbulent recent past of the organisation where, on many occasions, it was treated by a wide range of countries as an instrument, albeit a valuable instrument, for the pursuit of non-sporting diplomatic objectives. It is quite understandable that the IOC should display scepticism towards the calls for 'good governance' from countries that, until very recently, were highly exploitive of Olympism, manipulative of IOC decision-making processes, and grossly hypocritical in their attitudes towards doping. Although it is appropriate that we should expect the highest standards of probity from the

IOC, we should not lose sight of the challenging environment within which the Olympic movement has operated over the last 50 years. The fact that the IOC and the Olympic Games have been centrally involved in so many of the major international political issues of the last two generations is testament to the extent to which the Olympics is both a diplomatic resource and also a major diplomatic arena.

REFERENCES

Atkinson, M., & Young, K. (2003). Terror games: Media treatment of security issues at the 2002 Winter Olympic Games. *OLYMPIKA: The International Journal of Olympic Studies, XI,* 53–78.

Booth, D. (1998). *The race game: Sport and politics in South Africa.* London: Frank Cass.

British Sports Council. (1994). *Brighton declaration on women and sport.* London: Sports Council.

Caldwell, G. (1982). International sport and national identity. *International Social Science Journal, 34*(92), 172–183.

Cantelon, H., & Letters, M. (2000). The making of the IOC environmental policy as the third dimension of the Olympic movement. *International Review for the Sociology of Sport, 35*(3), 294–308.

Guttmann, A. (1984). *The Games must go on: Avery Brundage and the Olympic movement.* New York: University of Columbia Press.

Guttmann, A. (1992). *The Olympics: A history of the modern Games.* Urbana, IL: University of Illinois Press.

Hargreaves, J., & Ferrando, M. G. (1997). Public opinion, national integration and national identity in Spain: The case of the Barcelona Olympic Games. *Nations and Nationalism, 3*(1), 65–88.

Hill, C. R. (1996). *Olympic politics.* Manchester: Manchester University Press.

Hoberman, J. (1986). *The Olympic crisis: Sport, politics and the moral order.* New Rochelle, NY: Aristide D Caratzas.

International Olympic Committee (IOC). (1991). *The Olympic Charter.* Lausanne, Switzerland: IOC.

International Olympic Committee (IOC). (1997). *Manual on sport and the environment.* Lausanne, Switzerland: IOC.

International Olympic Committee (IOC). (2004). *Marketing report.* Lausanne, Switzerland: IOC.

Kanin, D. (1980). The Olympic boycott in diplomatic context. *Journal of Sport and Social Issues, 4*(1), 1–24.

Kidd, B. (1988). The campaign against sport in South Africa. *International Journal, XLIII*(Autumn), 643–663.

Lapchick, R. E. (1977). Apartheid sport: South Africa's use of sport in its foreign policy. *Journal of Sport and Social Issues, 1*(1), 55–79.

Lenskyj, H. (1998). Sport and corporate environmentalism: The case of the Sydney 2000 Olympics. *International Review for the Sociology of Sport, 33*(4), 341–354.

Preuss, H. (2000). *Economics of the Olympic Games: Hosting the Games 1972–2000*. Petersham, NSW: Walla Walla Press.

Ramsamy, S. (1984). Apartheid, boycotts and the games. In: A. Tomlinson & G. Whannel (Eds), *Five ring circus: Money, power and politics at the Olympic Games* (pp. 44–52). London, UK: Pluto Press.

Real, M. (1986). *Global ritual: Olympic media coverage and international understanding*. Unpublished paper. University of Calgary, AB.

Rich, E. (2004). *"But we are gender neutral": Organisational discourse and the emergence of a gender target policy in Olympic governance*. School of Sport and Exercise Sciences Working Paper, Loughborough University, UK.

Simson, V., & Jennings, A. (1992). *The lords of the rings*. Toronto: Stoddart.

Strenk, A. (1980). Diplomats in tracksuits: The role of sport in the German Democratic Republic. *The Journal of Sport and Social Issues, 4*(1), 34–45.

Chapter 8

'ANOTHER WORLD IS POSSIBLE': RECAPTURING ALTERNATIVE OLYMPIC HISTORIES, IMAGINING DIFFERENT GAMES

Bruce Kidd

The modern Olympic Games presents itself as a universal, trans-historical, and apolitical international sports festival, based on the ancient Games at Olympia and revived in the late nineteenth century by Pierre de Coubertin. The claim to timelessness was most recently evident in the build-up and conduct of the 2004 Games in Athens, with the reproduction and distribution of classical images in the graphics and souvenirs of those Games, the dramatic use of classical Greek mythologies and sculpture in the opening ceremonies, and the staging of the men's and women's shot put events in the excavated stadium at Olympia. The International Olympic Committee (IOC) has always claimed a classical ancestry, privileging Greece with the very first Games, in Athens in 1896, giving the Greek delegation the right to enter the stadium first (since 1928), linking the Games to Olympia through the Torch Relay (since 1936), and commemorating Greek culture through the official Olympic Anthem, the 1896 composition by Spyros Samaras and Kostis Palamas (since 1960). In co-operation with the Hellenic Olympic Committee (HOC), the IOC has proselytised athletes, sports leaders, physical educators, and journalists about its classical associations at the International Olympic Academy in Olympia, established in 1961. During the last

Global Olympics: Historical and Sociological Studies of the Modern Games
Research in the Sociology of Sport, Volume 3, 143–158

decade, as the IOC has stepped up its peace initiatives, it has persuaded the United Nations General Assembly to call upon member states to ensure the safe passage and participation of athletes at the Games, in resolutions that explicitly refer to the ancient Olympic truce. The IOC and HOC often squabble over the proper ownership of the legacy of antiquity, especially during the Olympic Torch Relay and the sessions of the International Olympic Academy, but they solidly proclaim the continuity of ancient and modern and the ideology of apolitical sport. As a trans-historical cultural celebration, or so goes their argument, the Games should stand above the politics of the day. The argument is further strengthened by the 'Celebrate Humanity' advertisements that the IOC has strategically placed all over the world in the recent past.

These claims are rarely challenged. In fact, they actively discourage critical inquiry. If sport was always essentially the same, they imply, how could things ever be any different? Yet such claims not only distort history, but contribute to the mystification of the power relations inherent in the ancient and modern games and the marginalisation or even obliteration of the more egalitarian approaches to physical activity that have been taken, realised, and enjoyed by different groups and societies in the past. They discourage the exploration and discussion of alternate directions within the Olympic Movement today.

I am a proud supporter of the Olympic Movement. I believe that the Olympic Movement has made a significant progressive contribution to the world historical project. But I also believe that it cannot fulfill its mission as a humanitarian 'change agent' if it continues to cling to an essentialist mystification of its own history, which obliterates the ambitions and achievements of other movements. This only serves to keep a narrow, decision-making elite in place and reduce the canvass of possibilities. We must unpack Olympic history, as Herbert Gutman suggests, to "transform historical givens into historical contingencies, enabling us to see the structures in which we live and the inequality people experience as only one among many other possible experiences, and freeing people for creative and critical thought" (Abelove, Blackmar, Dimock, & Schneer, 1983, p. 203).

This paper is a modest contribution to that end. I will begin by deconstructing the trans-historical myth of the Olympic Games, arguing that the differences between ancient and modern far outweigh the similarities and that, despite their remarkable cultural contributions, the ancient Games legitimised systems of power that kept most people in conditions of brutal slavery. I will then examine five attempts by those excluded from the Coubertin Olympic Games to realise sport for themselves – the Women's

World Games, the Workers' Olympics, the Games of the Emerging Forces, the Paralympics, and the Gay Games – to show that other approaches to the Olympics and international sport have been attempted, but that the IOC has fought fiercely to preserve its monopoly over the modern Games and the naturalisation of Olympic history. I will conclude by discussing some of the alternatives that should be explored today, and the prospects for change within and without the Olympic Movement.

Pierre de Coubertin did not revive the ancient Olympic Games, as he liked to claim, but appropriated the mantle of antiquity for a thoroughly modern project. He was neither the first, nor the only person to do so. During the eighteenth and nineteenth centuries, there were cultural interventions and competitions referred to as 'Olympics' in England, France, Sweden, Canada, Germany, and Greece, all of which sought to recruit the cache of the classical tradition to distinctly modern purposes (Guttmann, 2002). The heirs to the French revolution held *jeux Olympiques* on the Champs de Mars in Paris in 1796, for example, to affirm *l'egalité* of the new order. All citizens were eligible to compete – all citizens who were male, that is. The first Montreal Olympics were held in 1844, in an effort to display the athletic manliness of the growing Anglo-Canadian merchant elite. De Coubertin's interest in the classical tradition came late in his intellectual development. His initial purpose was to contribute to the regeneration and *revanche* of France after its humiliating defeat in the Franco-Prussian War. Believing that the youth of France was physically weak and morally degenerate, he lobbied for increased physical education in the schools. After a tour of Germany, England, the United States, and Canada, he came to believe that the games curricula of the all-male British upper-class schools provided the best means for providing that physical education. The importance of men's intercollegiate sports in the leading universities of the United States and Canada seemed to confirm that conclusion. De Coubertin's reading of the games tradition was heavily influenced by the Christian socialist Thomas Hughes, through the pages of Hughes' best-selling *Tom Brown's School Days*, and he began to adorn sport with educational attributes (MacAloon, 1981). At the same time, he drew upon the humanitarian internationalism that developed in response to what Robertson (1992) has called the 'take-off phase of globalization', during which organisations like the International Red Cross and the Boy Scouts were created, a global language (*Esperanto*) was invented, global prizes (e.g., Nobel Prizes) were initiated, and cities held world's fairs. Although he started his journey in order to improve the fitness of French youth, he came to see the value of sport from an increasingly internationalist perspective. It was only in 1890, when he visited

Dr. W. P. Brookes, the founder of the Wenlock Olympic Games in England, did de Coubertin come to see modern Olympics as the vehicle for the international athletic humanism that he was increasingly advocating. Brookes had long sought to create international Olympic Games. It was a time of growing European fascination with the classical world in the wake of the archeological exploration of sites such as Olympia. A model of the stadium, temples, and statuary at Olympia at the height of its popularity in the second century C.E. was on display at the Paris World's Fair of 1890. Grafting his ideas about sport and education to the Olympics of antiquity proved a genius stroke of public relations for de Coubertin. It is unlikely that his Games would have survived the difficulties and challenges of their first century without that protective mantle. The claims to continuity took attention away from the narrow upper-class, patriarchal, and Eurocentric base of his support and the 'amoral universalism' with which he pursued governments and corporations (Hoberman, 1986). They gave his Games an affirmation of history that helped drown out the almost constant squabbling.

Yet, the classical Olympics were only one form of physical activity practised by humans 2500 years ago. Moreover, many of the claims about the links between ancient and modern Olympics are, in fact, myth. The ancient Games were part of Greek religious ceremonies, and only open to male competitors and spectators, on pain of death to any married woman who dared to defy the patriarchal ban. Today's ideals of sportsmanship and fair play would have been laughable in the ancient Games, for example. The popular combative events were conducted with little concern for safety or fairness. There was no equivalent to modern weight categories to balance size and strength. Bouts were essentially fights-to-the-finish, and the best athletes tried to psyche out their opponents so that there was no competition at all. The intrinsic value of participation, the pursuit of personal bests and records, and the congratulations of opponents – all familiar values and rituals in the modern Games – would have been meaningless to them. Winning was the only goal.

Another example of misappropriation is the so-called 'Olympic truce'. The IOC often suggested that the ancient Olympic truce stopped war, a noble enough objective, but nothing could be further from the truth. The ancient Greeks did not believe that the Games could end military conflict. The truce was designed merely to prevent wars from disrupting the Games. In fact, the ancient Games developed *out of* war games. Long before the first formal Olympics, boxing and wrestling matches, chariot and foot-racing, jumping, discus, and javelin throwing were an integral part of Greek military training and campaigning. As Homer put it, athletics was preparation for war, and war, preparation for athletics. These activities were essential to the creation of state societies based upon slavery and patriarchy. Most men and almost all women during the classical Greek era were slaves. Even in democratic Athens, 40–50% of the population were slaves. The Olympic Games, in which only free males could compete, strengthened and celebrated this system of power. Even after athletics became specialised and lost their direct connection to military campaigning, the Olympics continued to symbolise the harsh class and gender power arrangements in the classical Greek world. It is ironic that the uncritical linking of ancient and modern Games has been used to justify the claim that sport stands above politics when the ancients were quite candid about it. The rulers of city states lavished wealth upon local champions because their own prestige was enhanced by reflected glory. Moreover, the uncritical equation of ancient and modern distorts our understanding of both Olympic traditions and the societies that elaborated them. As the classical scholars Finlay and Pleket (1976) argue:

> ...what we choose to think about sport in the modern world, in sum, has to be worked out and defended from modern values and modern conditions. Harking back to the ancient Greek Olympics has produced both bad history and bad arguments. It might be right or wrong to forbid Olympic athletes to profit financially from their medals (as one example) but the answer will not be found in the northeastern corner of the Peleponnese, and surely not when what happened there two thousand years ago is distorted and perverted to fit one or another modern ideology (p. 132; see also Elias, 1974, p. 94).

Today, representatives of all classes, both genders, and virtually every religion and national community in the world compete in the modern Olympics (albeit with varying degrees of success). It is difficult to contemplate a time when that was not so. But, for most of their history, the de Coubertin Games were far from inclusive or universal. Women, the working classes, and those from most of the developing world were excluded by explicit prohibitions, the economic barriers created by the amateur code, and the strictures of colonialism and, in other cases, alienated by the ideologies of *Citius, Altius, Fortius*, nation-state competition, and corporate celebration. Alongside the familiar history of the de Coubertin movement is a much less well known history of struggles for integration, resistance, and alternatives. It is essential that we revisit that history.

THE WOMEN'S OLYMPICS

Women have always had to force their way into sport and the Olympic Games. Modern sports were developed and elaborated entirely in male-exclusive organisations, explicitly for the cultivation and celebration of masculinity. Most of the early organisers and athletes held the Victorian prejudice that women's participation in sport was against the laws of nature, and actively discouraged them with prohibitions, ridicule, and the 'moral physiology' that vigorous physical activity would undermine maternal health. At the same time, the overwhelming majority of women were prevented from participation because of the endless demands of household, reproductive, agricultural, and industrial labour. Nevertheless, in most western countries, girls and women took up sports for themselves. In the early twentieth century, when physical educators and others began to appreciate the benefits of physical activity for women and physical education for girls was introduced into schools, even greater numbers became interested. They competed wherever they could and, by the end of World War I, excelled in virtually every sport that was played. In most western countries, they had to provide opportunities for themselves, in female-only organisations, led and financed by women, often the athletes themselves. They faced hostile, at best patronising, attention in the mass media. Nevertheless, they persevered and, in many countries, gradually attracted a sizable following (Kidd, 1996).

Although women have competed in the modern Olympic Games since 1900, they did so only on a provisional basis, on the invitation of local organising committees, until 1912, when they were granted official status, and a handful of archery, skating, gymnastics, and swimming events were added to the women's programme. However, women were only begrudgingly accepted into the Games by Coubertin, the IOC, and the amateur bodies which governed sports in most developed countries. In response, in the flush of woman's suffrage in many countries, the Fédération Sportive Féminine International (FSFI), led by Alice Milliat of France, began separate Women's Olympic Games (Leigh & Bonin, 1977). The first Women's Olympic Games, exclusively a track and field competition, were held in Paris in 1922 to considerable international interest and acclaim. A second Women's Olympics, held in Gotenberg, Sweden in 1926 evoked comparisons to the Olympic Games held in 1912. The growing prestige of women's track and field forced the International Amateur Athletic Federation (IAAF) to enter into negotiations with the FSFI. The FSFI agreed to change the name of its competition to the Women's World Games, in exchange for 10 events for women at the 1928 Olympic Games and gender parity on the IOC. But the IOC and IAAF did not honour their part of the bargain. Only five events for women were ultimately granted at the 1928 Games and the IOC membership was left a male domain. While 24 of 46 competing nations sent women's teams to Amsterdam, the English Women's Amateur Athletic

Association, arguably the strongest female track and field nation at the time, boycotted those Games in protest (Leigh & Bonin, 1977). The FSFI persisted, staging Women's World Games in 1930 in Prague, with the addition of several sports to the programme, and in 1934 in London. It continued to agitate for more events for women on the IOC's program and female representation on the IOC. By 1935, Milliat argued that if women did not receive full and equal representation at the IOC's Games, the FSFI should stage a completely separate Olympic Games for women (Kidd, 1996). To counter her threat, the IAAF took control over women's athletics, the cornerstone of the Women's World Games. The world-wide depression, the rise of fascism in Europe, and the consolidation of the sport media complex in North America, with its strong links to advertisers seeking male audiences, had already seriously weakened the womens' sports movement. The IAAF's success in gaining control over women's track and field was the final blow. The FSFI collapsed. The 1934 Women's World Games were the last to be held.

As a consequence, women's sport at the international level was left in the hands of men, who restricted the development of women's opportunities for generations. For example, while the FSFI encouraged women to race over 800 metres and further, the IOC removed the women's 800 metres from the track and field programme after 1928, disturbed that several competitors had raced themselves into the appearance of 'unladylike' fatigue. The IOC did not reinstate the 800 metres event until 1960. In 1924, 1928, 1932, and 1936, the FSFI staged a world basketball championship for women at the same time in the same city as the IOC's Games (as well as staging a basketball championship at its own games) in hopes of putting that popular women's sport on the IOC's programme. The IOC did not put women's basketball on its programme until 1976.

The routing of the FSFI also removed the possibility that women could develop opportunities for themselves in ways that reflected their particular concerns and needs, and might have encouraged progressive changes in men's sports as well. One of the defining features of the FSFI (and other women's sports bodies in the interwar years, such as the WAAA and the Women's Amateur Athletic Federation of Canada) was its concern for the health and well-being of participants, concerns that held little interest for their male counterparts. The feminist sports leaders openly disdained the often harmful 'culture of risk' so characteristic of men's sport. They required competitors in events such as the shot put, javelin, and discus to throw with both hands (sequentially, with total distance counting for the places) in an effort to develop muscular symmetry. With the demise of the FSFI and national federations like it, women were left with very few institutions and forums, let alone a collective voice, to advance a feminist vision in sports. While female participation continues to grow, it does so almost everywhere under male leadership. Today, the idea of gender parity on the IOC and the IFs remains a distant dream. Nevertheless, new generations of sportswomen continue to demand their own voices.

THE WORKERS' OLYMPICS

The Workers' Olympics developed out of the workers' sport movement, which first emerged in the 1890s in Germany. The workers' sport movement sprung, in part, out of the ambition of socialist parties and trade unions to create a proud, sustaining, class-conscious workers' culture, in part as a cover for otherwise illegal socialist political activity (Kidd, 1996). But it also was prompted by the exclusionary policies and practices of the amateur sporting bodies upon which Coubertin relied to organise his games. The amateur code either excluded the working classes through explicit prohibition (as in rowing) or discouraged them with sanctions against training expenses, living stipends, and financial prizes. In response, trade unions and socialist parties in Europe, Canada, the US, Australia, and Japan established sports clubs and then sports federations to provide opportunities for their members directly and to agitate for public recreation. They sought reduced working hours, paid statutory and annual holidays, and public health insurance, and against discrimination in sport and recreation. The goal was to give all working people the opportunity to participate in healthy physical activity in a way that celebrated the strengths and ambitions of the working class and realised a liberating alternative to the chauvinistic, commercial, competitive exclusivity of 'bourgeois sport'.The Socialist Workers' Sports International, which came to be known as the Lucerne Sport International (LSI), was formed in 1913. When the International Socialist Movement split into warring Socialist and Communist camps following the creation of the Soviet Union, the communists walked out of the LSI and formed the Red Sport International. By 1930, the two internationals each claimed a membership of 4 million. Each had their own multi-sport international festival, with the LSI staging winter and summer Workers' Olympics every 6 years, the RSI Spartakiads every quadrennial (Riordan, 1984).

The Workers' Olympics were probably the most inclusive international games ever held. The first International Workers' Games were held in Prague in 1921. The first Workers' Olympics were staged in 1925 in Frankfurt, with representatives from 19 countries, and over 150,000 in attendance.

There were also winter games in Schreiberhau, Germany. The second Workers' Olympics in 1931 in Vienna attracted over 80,000 worker-athletes from 26 countries and more than 250,000 spectators (Riordan, 1984). By contrast, the 1932 Olympic Games in Los Angeles had only 1,048 athletes. While the programme of the Workers' Olympics resembled that of the Coubertin Games, there were important differences. The Workers' Olympics were open to all, regardless of ability. While the medals were hotly contested by highly trained athletes, the majority were recreational participants. Most competed for their sports clubs, and national teams were discouraged in the interests of international working-class solidarity. Women's participation was enthusiastically encouraged. In all, 25,000 women took part in Vienna, compared to a mere 107 in the IOC's Games a year later in Los Angeles. The programme included a children's sport festival, friendly matches, dramatic performances, and mass exercises, in addition to the Olympic championships. Here, too, a much more egalitarian vision of sport was realised and celebrated.

Vienna represented the height of the Workers' Olympics, but this popularity brought increasing pressure from the amateur organisations and western governments to repress it. The Spartakiads had a similar character, although heavy-handed in their ideological support of the Soviet Union. With the Nazi repression of trade unions and workers' sports clubs in Germany, the LSI and RSI combined to stage a People's Olympic Games in Barcelona in 1936. Planned as a protest against the IOC's decision to keep their Games in Germany, the People's Games had to be cancelled when Franco began the uprising known as the Spanish Civil War on the morning of the opening ceremonies. The Workers' Olympics were held for the last time in 1937 in Antwerp. Plans for the 1943 Games in Helsinki were disrupted by the Second World War (Kidd, 1996).

The workers' sport movement survives to this day in a few countries, notably Belgium, Finland, and Italy, but only as a shadow of its former self. In other countries, most clubs were destroyed and their leaders killed or dispersed by Nazism and the Second World War. After the war, the Soviet Union and its satellite states turned to high performance sport to 'beat the Capitalists at their own game' and joined up with the Coubertin Olympics but, in doing so, turned their back on the proud, inclusive traditions of workers' sport. Although Olympic enthusiasts around the world can 'cite chapter and verse' of the Coubertin Olympic history, the remarkable experiment of the Workers' Olympics and the Spartakiads has been largely forgotten. It may well be that the spirit of the workers' sports movement is still pursued by the 'sport for all' movement, and expressed in the various international charters that promise sport as a right. But with the demise of the workers' sports movement, the world lost a passionate, creative voice for genuine opportunity to all, and a network of organisations that were prepared to enter local and national politics to win it.

THE GAMES OF THE NEW EMERGING FORCES (GANEFO)

The Workers' Olympics were not the only movement to recruit sport to a political project that sought to overturn the hierarchies of the modern world. Following the Second World War, the countries of southeast Asia struggled for independence from their colonial rulers. Believing that sport among Asians could foster nation-building and a spirit of Asian unity, regional political leaders created the Asian Games. The first Asian Games were held in New Delhi in 1951 and they were continued in 1954, 1958, and 1962. But, when Indonesia barred athletes from Taiwan and Israel from participation in the 1962 Asian Games in Jakarta, the IOC promptly suspended Indonesia from the Olympic Movement. The IOC's decision, which seemed to parrot US foreign policy, galvanised the desire for an anti-imperialist political movement that would advance the interests of Third-World countries. To give symbolic expression to such an alliance, Indonesian president Soekarno established the Games of New Emerging Forces to unify Asian, African, Latin American, and Socialist countries and to "shake the world balance of power and weaken the economic domination of the world by industrialised countries" (Sie, 1978, p. 289). The ambition was much greater than the Asian Games. The GANEFO Games were to set the stage for a political conference of the developing nations that would result in the establishment of a United Nations style organisation for the developing world. The first Games of the New Emerging Forces were held in Jakarta in 1963, with both western sports and games indigenous to Asia. A prominent participant was the People's Republic of China, which at the time did not compete in the IOC's Games. While the IOC threatened to ban any team that participated in Jakarta from its own Games in Tokyo, 48 countries participated, including Japan. Japan's participation, as well as the threat of an Arab boycott of the 1964 Olympic Games, forced the IOC to soften its condemnation of GANEFO participants. The IOC rescinded its suspension of Indonesia (Sie, 1978).

The conference of the New Emerging Forces never took place. The concerted opposition of first-world countries and the CIA-assisted overthrow of

Soekarno in 1965 ensured that the Conference of the New Emerging Forces was not held. While Chinese sports officials kept the idea of an alternative developing world games alive during the 1960s and early 1970s, the GANEFO Games were never held again. Third-World Olympic Committees gravitated back to the Olympic Movement, once more subject to the domination of western IOC members. In 1976, when the inflammatory New Zealand rugby tour of South Africa was being debated by the IOC, the 45 African NOCs had only seven African IOC members to speak for their interests, and two of them were white defenders of Apartheid, one from South Africa. With little chance to make their numbers felt, 29 African nations left Montreal in protest and the idea of third-world, anti-imperialist games, was raised again. But that revolt lost steam when the IOC was persuaded by the IAAF and FIFA, where every country had one vote and the developing countries as a block had considerably more power than on the IOC, to embrace the anti-Apartheid campaign. In 1978, China joined the IOC, ending once-and-for-all the possibility of third-world games. Perhaps it was not the most effective solution to the tremendous inequalities in the global economy and international sports, but the GANEFO Games helped place the issue of third-world participation, in terms that third-world leaders could shape, clearly on the international agenda. In condemning the GANEFO experiment so forcefully, the IOC exposed again how narrow was its claim to universality and how fiercely it will fight to control it.

THE PARALYMPIC AND GAY GAMES

The experiences of two contemporary movements to broaden the base of international sport, the Paralympic and Gay Games, reveal a similar pattern, although in different ways. The Paralympic Games began as the Stoke Mandeville Games, held in Aylesbury, England in 1948. Created by Sir Ludwig Guttman, for patients with spinal cord injuries, the Games continued in England in 1952 and 1956. Guttman aspired to stage Games for wheelchair athletes, alongside the Olympic Games, ultimately hoping to incorporate events for wheelchair athletes into mainstream sport competitions (Doll-Tepper, 1998). In 1960, in Rome, the first Paralympic Games were held following the Coubertin Olympic Games. The Paralympic Games expanded to include athletes with sensory, mental, as well as physical handicaps. By 1988, in Seoul, Paralympic events were held during the official Olympic programme, and Olympic organising committees have been expected to ensure full accessibility for participants and spectators. In 2000, the President of the International Paralympic Committee was appointed to the IOC.

The Paralympic Movement has been a tremendous force for progressive change. Most of all, it has helped transform the very way that most people think about *ability*, dramatically reinforcing legislative and other changes that give protection and opportunity to those once cast aside as *disabled*. As part of its strategy to 'normalise' sports for persons with disabilities, it has consciously adopted the ethos of the de Coubertin Movement, with an emphasis upon elite sports participation, including a pre-occupation with advancing technology. Yet with this strategy comes considerable risks. Unlike the Special Olympics, which provide affirming participation and recreation for the mentally challenged, the emphasis is upon performance and competition, with little attention to rights-based opportunity. To date, despite such strong links of mutual endorsement and integration, the IOC maintains a clear differentiation between the able-bodied and Paralympic competition and accomplishment, even to the point of denying those Paralympic athletes who would compete during the Olympic Games in Athens a chance to participate in the Olympic Opening Ceremonies. Moreover, the trend of classification seems to be shifting from an athlete-centred to a corporate approach (Howe, 2004, p. 164).

The Gay Games provide another heart-warming example of how the transitionally abused and marginalised have won sports opportunities for themselves, in ways that powerfully affirm their aspirations to justice and a better life. The Games were founded in 1982 by Tom Waddell, an American Olympic decathlete. Critical of what he felt was the sexism, racism, nationalism, heterosexism, and elitism of the de Coubertin Games, Waddell wanted to establish a sports environment characterised by inclusion. In particular, he wanted to create a visible affirming event for lesbians, gays, bi-sexuals, transgendered, and queers (Krane & Waldron, 2000). His first thought was to name his event the Gay Olympics, but the United States Olympic Committee threatened a law suit, and he re-named it the Gay Games. The first and second Gay Games were held in San Francisco in 1982 and 1986, respectively. Participation increased from 1,350 athletes to 3,500 athletes, and the second Gay Games included a 'Procession of the Arts', which included conferences, concerts, films, and plays, and other forms of artistic expression. The third Gay Games held in Vancouver, Canada in 1990 vaulted the Games to world-class status. In total 7,500 athletes from 39 countries participated in the sporting events, and over 2,000 people participated in the cultural events. National and international records set by participating athletes were recognised, for the first time, by international sports governing bodies. Although Waddell died in 1987, the creation of the Federation of the Gay Games (FGG), an elected 55 member board, ensures that Gay Games continues. In 1994, the Gay Games, held in New York City, drew 10,000 athletes from 40 countries and 250,000 spectators. The FGG has created an Outreach programme designed to increase participation for under-represented groups. The Outreach programmes implemented for the 1998 Amsterdam Gay Games resulted in sponsorship for 238 non-Western participants, and an increase in women's participation from 35% to 42%. In recognition of the need to include fewer athletic participants, or those suffering from illness, chess, bridge, and darts have been added to the program (Symons, 2002). The 2002 Games were held in Sydney. Unfortunately, a schism has developed in the movement, and in 2006 competing events will be held in Chicago (7th Gay Games) and Montreal (1st World Outgames).

Despite this remarkable example of inclusion, however, the official Olympic Movement has remained silent about the Gay Games. It refuses to address the challenges of homophobia in sport. While the *Olympic Charter* (p. 9) prohibits "any form of discrimination with regard to a country or a person on grounds of race, religion, politics, gender or otherwise," there continues to be a deep chill against LGBTQ in the Coubertin Olympic communities.

IMAGINING OTHER POSSIBILITIES

The de Coubertin Olympic Games are an important part of world culture. The Games reach billions of people throughout the world and they serve as a focal point for much celebration and inspiration. However, the IOC's claims to historical continuity and universality are highly ideological, 'partial' in both senses of that word. In the first place, as the case studies explored in this paper demonstrate, they present an incomplete version of humanity's attempts to interact through sports and culture, even in our own times; secondly, the history it does celebrate is partisan to western, Capitalist, masculinist, and heterosexual interests. Over and over again, in the face of concerted efforts by the marginalised and excluded – women, the working class, third-world nations, persons with disabilities, and LBGTQ – to take up the torch of international sport, the de Coubertin Olympic Movement turned a deaf ear or, even worse, tried to suppress or isolate them. At best, it maneuvered to incorporate them as participants, while maintaining its narrow focus on high-performance sport and its decision-making power and control, like the runner who takes the lead only to slow down the pace. To be sure, the IOC's hegemony has been enormously enabled by the larger economic and social transformations of the last century, especially the seeming triumph of Capitalism and the growing monopolies achieved in the mass media, which have helped co-opt or silence the oppositional movements, while forcing the de Coubertin Olympic Movement to become more open and inclusive. Yet the doctrine of Olympism, as others have written in this volume, shields the lack of ethical grounding of the Olympic Movement. While Olympism provides hope for the potential of the Games, and can be used to prompt the IOC to action, it has yet to be proactively promoted by the IOC. It undervalues the rich diversity in humanity by requiring all aspirations to physical culture to conform to its singular definition.

This history highlights the tremendous power and command that the de Coubertin Olympic Movement has achieved. But it also suggests that, as long as the Movement continues to be led by a narrowly recruited, male-dominated governing body and responds only rhetorically to the aspirations for healthy physical activity among the diverse populations of the world, alternatives will always be expressed, and pressures develop for change. As the governance reforms introduced in 2000 in response to the crisis of legitimacy created by the simultaneous doping and bribery scandals lose their momentum, and the Olympic Movement in practice becomes even more closely allied with high-performance corporate sport, to the neglect or marginalisation of sport for all, openings for other possibilities will become apparent. It may well be, as public and voluntary institutions around the world seek to revitalise opportunities for broadly based physical activity, and to employ sport and physical activity for the purposes of broadly based social development – not competitive sports – that new alliances will be created to break or at least bracket the IOC's current monopoly over world sport. The decision by athlete activist Johann Koss, a former Olympic champion speedskater from Norway, and those other former Olympic athletes who have pioneered humanitarian sport assistance to break away from the IOC – to leave Olympic Aid for the Right to Play – may foreshadow such a new alternative, as has the United Nations' adoption of 2005 as the International Year of Sport and Physical Education. Certainly the fledgling international development through sport movement is growing by leaps and bounds. Other possible sources of alternative movements include the international campaign against exploitative labour in the production of Olympic uniforms and sports equipment ('Fair Play for the Olympics') and the revitalisation of indigenous sports in some of the poorest countries of the globe. The brazen suggestion in the title of this paper that 'another world is possible' in sport is drawn from the slogan of the World Social Forum, formed as an alternative to the elite World Economic Forum and the agenda of globalising capitalism. If alternative movements in sport are to succeed, they must be linked to the broader struggles of the subordinate and marginalised groups around the world represented today in the World Social Forum and other such interventions.

On the other hand, perhaps the hegemony of the IOC over the Olympic Games is secure enough now that it can move away from a fierce 'survival' instinct and toward a proactive role in the betterment of the world for all citizens. This was an important aspect of de Coubertin's vision and, despite all of the success of the Games, it still needs to be realised. In the meantime, alternatives to the Games, like the Gay Games, should continue to challenge the hegemony of the Olympic Movement and remind us that this model of sport is not for everyone. Faster, higher, stronger, is just one option.

REFERENCES

Abelove, H., Blackmar, B., Dimock, P., & Schneer, J. (1983). Herbert Gutman. In: *Visions of history*. Manchester: Manchester University Press.

Doll-Tepper, G. (1998). Similarities and differences of the Olympic and paralympic movement. In: R. Naul (Ed.), *ICSSPE, Physical activity and active lifestyle of children and youth* (pp. 12–18). Germany: Verlag Karl Hoffman.

Elias, N. (1974). The genesis of sport as a sociological problem. In: E. Dunning (Ed.), *Sport: Readings from a sociological perspective* (pp. 88–115). Toronto: University of Toronto Press.

Finlay, M. I., & Pleket, H. W. (1976). *The Olympic Games: The first thousand years*. Toronto: Clarke, Irwin and Co.

Guttmann, A. (2002). *The Olympics: A history of the Modern Games* (2nd ed.). Champaign, IL: University of Illinois Press.

Hoberman, J. (1986). *The Olympic crisis: Sport, politics and the moral order*. New Rochelle, NY: Caratzas Publishing.

Howe, P. D. (2004). *Ethnographies of injury and risk*. London: Routledge.

International Olympic Committee. (2004). *Olympic Charter*. Lausanne: International Olympic Committee.

Kidd, B. (1996). *The struggle for Canadian sport*. Toronto: University of Toronto Press.

Krane, V., & Waldron, J. (2000). The Gay Games: Creating our own Sports Culture. In: K. Schaffer & S. Smith (Eds), *The Olympics at the millenium: Power, politics, and the Games* (pp. 147–164). United States: Rutgers University Press.

Leigh, M. H., & Bonin, T. M. (1977). The pioneering role of Madame Alice Milliat and the FSFI in establishing international track and field competition for women. *Journal of Sport History, 4*(1), 72–83.

MacAloon, J. (1981). *This great symbol: Pierre de Coubertin and the origins of the modern Olympic Games*. Chicago: University of Chicago Press.

Riordan, J. (1984). The Workers' Olympics. In: A. Tomlinson & G. Whannel (Eds), *Five-ring circus: Money, power and politics at the Olympic Games* (pp. 98–112). Great Britain: Pluto Press.

Robertson, R. (1992). *Globalization, social theory and global culture.* London: Sage.

Sie, S. (1978). Sports and politics: The case of the Asian Games and the GANEFO. In: B. Lowe, D. Kanin & A. Strenk (Eds), *Sport and international relations* (pp. 279–296). Champaign, IL: Stipes.

Symons, C. (2002). The Gay Games and community. In: D. Hemphill & C. Symons (Eds), *Gender, sexuality and sport: A dangerous mix* (pp. 100–114). New South Wales: Walla Walla Press.

Part II

THE OLYMPIC GAMES:
CONTEMPORARY ISSUES AND
CONTROVERSIES

Chapter 9

THE FIVE RINGS AND THE SMALL SCREEN: TELEVISION, SPONSORSHIP, AND NEW MEDIA IN THE OLYMPIC MOVEMENT

Garry Whannel

The impact of television on the world, whether considered from the perspective of politics, economics, or culture, has been profound. In just 50 years, television grew from a nascent technological innovation to a globally ubiquitous and culturally central medium of information and entertainment. It is not merely a new technology, but a facilitator of new ways of seeing, re-composer of space and time, and transformer of social and political relations.

Today, the very taken-for-granted nature of globalised live pictures, rolling news, and the constant recycling of the past as captured in video clips serves only to obscure the depth of television's impact. The dynamic force of television began to become striking in the 1960s, prompting Marshall McLuhan's comment that we were living in "a global village" and Andy Warhol's prescient prediction that "in the future everyone will be famous for fifteen minutes". In 1968, an angry crowd of demonstrators at the Democratic Convention in Chicago, subjected to brutal attacks by the police, responded by chanting "the whole world is watching".

Precisely what they were watching, though, depended on what the cameras were pointing at. The dramatic 'Black Power' salute at the 1968 Mexico

Global Olympics: Historical and Sociological Studies of the Modern Games
Research in the Sociology of Sport, Volume 3, 161–177
Copyright © 2005 by Elsevier Ltd.
All rights of reproduction in any form reserved

City Olympics, offered in protest against racism by US sprinters John Carlos and Tommie Smith, provided an image that went around the world and became a key icon in most subsequent video reconstructions of the 1960s. Just a few weeks earlier, hundreds of demonstrators were shot by the Mexican police, with a relative absence of media attention that was, in retrospect, disturbing. Few things could have demonstrated more clearly the vital role that news management and impression management would play in future Olympic Games, nor presage the era to come, in which a televised Olympics offered a stage for symbolic political contestation.

Major live sport events transmitted around the world have become a key element in broadcast schedules. Within a television landscape where much is recorded, safe, and predictable, only news and sport offer uncertainty, risk and 'liveness', and a powerful sense of being there as it happens. Yet, television does far more than merely relay major sport events to us. Instead, it radically re-constructs them, combining live and recorded 'feeds' from venue and studio, adding replay, slow-motion, montage, commentary, and discussion. A technologically seamless entertainment presentation has, in turn, so transformed our expectations that the experience of being a live spectator can seem somewhat devalued and, increasingly, event organisers feel the need to provide giant screens to add the elements of replay and slow motion, to satisfy our needs. Television, in short, has transformed the nature of the live *spectacle*. Events that do not work well or attract audiences on television (such as shooting and modern pentathlon) are in slow decline, while sports that suit the conventions and constraints of the small (or, recently, not so small) screen (such as gymnastics and figure skating) have thrived. Constant pressure is exerted upon the International Olympic Committee (IOC) to add potentially 'telegenic' sports, such as beach volleyball, to the roster of events.

The globalisation of television has, in turn, prompted the professionalisation, commercialisation, and spectacularisation of sport. In particular, sport agents, sponsorship brokers, and sporting goods manufacturers have capitalised on new lucrative markets. The association of sport with youth, health, and dynamic activity has given it a key role in 'transmitting the cool' and in promoting the brand and the logo (Klein, 1999; Boyle, 2003; Quart, 2003). Soccer's Manchester United and baseball's New York Yankees collaborate on marketing to exploit the global potential of their image. Real Madrid's signing of Manchester United and England star David Beckham was driven partly by its economic strategy to promote the Real Madrid brand in the Far East where, since the 2002 World Cup, David Beckham has assumed 'superstar' status.

The celebrity-studded glamour of major sports events has attracted so much attention from the corporate elite that up to a third of tickets for such events are taken up by corporate hospitality, sponsors, their guests, and other privileged insiders. Yet, in a sense, what happens in the stadium is only as important as its televisual representation. Indeed, the recent suggestion by the IOC that the main stadium no longer needs to be gigantic, amounts to a tacit recognition that the important audience is the television one, and that the live audience is, in effect, a form of 'set dressing' for television, ensuring the atmosphere of the spectacle.

The transformation of the Olympic Games by television and sponsorship has shaped the agenda for a critical analysis of Olympism. All the key topics of discussion – commercialisation and corporate capitalism, politicisation, gigantism and corruption, spectacle and representation, equal rights for women, race and racism, and disability – require also an engagement with the economics of broadcasting and the politics of representation.

HISTORY, TECHNOLOGY, AND AUDIENCE

1896–1928

The Olympics were revived in the same period of the late nineteenth century in which a modern mass communication system began to develop. The combination of photography, wireless telegraphy, a reading public, and entrepreneurial investment gave birth to the modern popular press. Wireless technology was about to spawn broadcast radio. The first cinemas emerged in the closing years of the century and, until television, cinema newsreels were the only way, other than presence at the event, that people could observe sport performance. Commercial companies sold photographs of the 1912 Olympic Games. The first radio broadcast of an Olympic Games took place in Paris in 1924. Newsreel footage was used to resolve the finishing order in the 100 m for the first time in 1932 (*Olympic Games Museum: The Virtual Olympic Games Museum* – http://www.olympic-museum.de).

1936–1964

The television era began in Berlin in 1936, with pictures of some events being relayed to local Berlin cinemas, while newsreel film travelled abroad via the rather ponderous airships. But the first real broadcasting of an Olympic

Games did not occur until the London Olympics of 1948, the world's first large-scale multi-sport outside broadcast. Pictures could only be received within 20 miles of Alexandra Palace in north London, and there were only around 20,000 sets in existence. The audience may have been tiny but the Games provided a huge boost to the technological development of television, helping to kick-start *BBC Sport*, which became the benchmark for professionalism, later to be augmented by the 'show business' ethic of *ABC Sport* from the 1960s. Even 12 years later in 1960, television was still a young medium, and the Rome Olympics were the first to take advantage of the 'Eurovision link' to broadcast live around Europe.

1968–1984

By 1968, the establishment of communication satellites was well under way; television was beginning to spread beyond the developed world. The establishment of the Olympic Games as a global television event gave it enormous potential as a platform for symbolic political acts. The 'Black Power' salutes in Mexico City in 1968, the seizing of Israeli athletes as hostages by a militant Palestinian group in Munich in 1972, and the sequence of boycotts that marked the Games between 1976 and 1984 provide three very different instances of the exploitation of this opportunity (Tomlinson & Whannel, 1984).

1984–1996

By the early 1980s, the Olympics were seen by many as an expensive and risky liability. The only bidders to stage the 1984 Olympic Games were Los Angeles and Teheran. The withdrawal of the Teheran bid following the overthrow of the Shah of Iran in 1979 left Los Angeles as the only option. As the people of Los Angeles had voted not to fund the Games, there was greater pressure on the organising committee to exploit commercial opportunity. The alliance of Horst Dassler and João Havelange in reshaping FIFA and the World Cup in the early 1980s had already revealed the untapped potential of sponsorship. In developing a sponsorship strategy based on exclusive sponsorships in limited product categories, Peter Ueberroth, the head of the Los Angeles Organising Committee, helped establish and prove the viability of a new Games template for commercial success (Ueberroth, 1985).

The apparent success of the Los Angeles Games in generating a 'surplus'[1] encouraged far more vigorous bidding for future games. The IOC Session of 1986, which chose the 1992 Olympic site, was attended by 1,000 journalists and 50 camera crews, and the 13 bidding cities for the Summer and Winter Games may have spent as much as US$200 m between them. The early 1980s represent a watershed in the history of the Olympic movement, during which the IOC took a series of highly significant decisions, including splitting the Summer and Winter Games into different years, and developing the The Olympic Programme (TOP) sponsorship programme.

The IOC became the paradox at the heart of the Games. In most individual sports, the old, traditional, amateur paternalistic governing bodies have been forced to reshape themselves, ceding some of their power and privilege to the demands of the modern market-driven enterprise culture. The IOC has managed to ride and control this commercial leviathan with great success, while retaining its basic form as an aristocratic gentleman's club; as such, it is beyond regulation. It remains non-accountable to any other body apart from the law. Its members remain unaccountable, being seen, in pompous fashion, not as delegates from their countries, but as 'ambassadors' *to their nations* from the IOC. The nearest equivalent is perhaps the Papacy and Vatican City. The power comes with a price tag: the huge sums of money involved have brought corruption and, in the late 1990s, the IOC found itself engulfed by a series of scandals which forced the resignation of several members and the exposure of corrupt practices among bidding cities (see Chapter 11; Simson & Jennings, 1992; Jennings, 1996; Lenskyj, 2000).

It is no surprise, then, that in recent Games the key importance of image and impression have been ever more striking. In 1988, Seoul could boast superb facilities, but the IOC became upset by the widespread appearance of empty seats and, in some latter events, large numbers of school children were even bussed in to provide the full stadia that television requires. The success of Barcelona in harmonising the image of the Games and the city was, perhaps, epitomised by the memorable glimpses of the city that appeared momentarily as the athletes plunged from the high board in the diving events. Atlanta, by contrast, gave the impression of being rather cheap, tawdry, and uninspired, while Sydney was seen as surpassing the success of Barcelona. Of course, in any Olympic Games there are thousands of unique experiences and countless impressions. Two, however, are central to being regarded as a success – the individual experience of IOC members in the city and, crucially, the way that the event appears on global television. Of course, equally as significant, then, are the ways in which it is written into history by journalists. By the late 1990s, the Internet had clearly begun to rival television as a medium of social and cultural exchange. In 1996 in Atlanta, the first Olympic Games website received 189 million 'hits'. Just 2 years later, the Nagano website received 634 million 'hits', while in 2000 the Sydney website received a staggering 11.3 billion 'hits' (Moragas, 1999). The implications of the Internet–Olympic interface are discussed in the final section.

THE ECONOMIC TRANSFORMATION OF A CULTURAL FORM

The explosive growth of television sport from the mid-1960s has inevitably had a transformative impact on the culture of Olympism, specifically, in three main forms. First, competitive bidding for the television rights between the major networks of USA moved the IOC from genteel poverty to grand luxury. Second, the heightened visibility of the Olympic Games, the fitness boom of the 1970s, and the ruthless competitiveness of the sport and leisure goods industry combined to make the Olympic Games an attractive proposition for sponsorship. Third, in becoming the global event par excellence, not to say *sans pareil*, the Olympic Games offered one of the first, and still one of the few opportunities, for global marketing and global visibility.

Television USA Takes Over

From the early 1960s, when Olympic television rights first began to command significant sums of money, it gradually became clear that, with the US being the most affluent television market, and having three major commercial networks which would compete for those rights, US television money would become the predominant income stream for the Olympic Games. The pattern from 1960 to 1988 was one of continuing and spectacular growth (Table 1). During this period, the Olympic Games became the 'stake' in an intense battle between the US networks. The potential for huge audiences, even during the day and late at night, and usually during the slack summer season, helped attract additional advertising revenue. By the 1980s, the escalation in rights payments was in danger of outstripping the level of advertising revenue. In particular, when ABC's determination to retain its 'Olympic Network' tag led them to bid $309 m for the 1988 Winter

Table 1. US network payments for Olympic television rights in US$ million.

	Summer	Winter	Both
1960	0.39	0.05	0.44
1964	1.5	0.59	2.09
1968	4.5	2.5	7
1972	7.5	6.4	13.9
1976	25	10	35
1980	87	15.5	102.5
1984	225	91.5	316.5
1988	300	309	609

Source: Whannel (1992, p. 171).

Olympics, it was widely recognised in the television industry, and not least at ABC, that the payment was too high and could not be recouped in advertising revenue. Despite this danger, the continuing enthusiasm for winning the Olympics among US networks highlights another benefit for them: the Olympics provide an excellent platform on which to promote future television schedules (Billings, Eastman, & Newton, 1998).

The huge payments from the networks led many analysts, including the present author, to suggest that they were in a position to influence the choice of site. Clearly, the networks, and also the sponsors, and agencies such as International Sports and Leisure (ISL) (established and owned during the first half of the 1980s by Adidas boss Horst Dassler) have been in a position to exert pressure and make their views known. However, from the perspective of the 21st century, the evidence that American television, with all of its money, can induce the IOC to choose a particular site is not totally persuasive. Only four of the last 16 Games have been in sites particularly favourable for American television, and three of the last six have been in positively poor sites. To over-simplify somewhat: Europe is not very good; Asia and Australasia probably worse; but anywhere 2–3 hours west of New York time is perfect, as afternoon events can be shown during the evening peak time on the east coast of the USA, the most lucrative advertising region. However, only west coast USA and Canada fits this criterion – which makes a Seattle or Vancouver bid a good bet. Nothing in South America is later than New York. A South American city is better than Europe for US television. The success of the Vancouver bid for the 2010 Winter Games is perhaps notable in this regard.

Is there evidence, then, that site choice affects the size of the rights payment? The summer fees have risen fairly steadily since 1990. Sydney's fees, despite the poor time zone for US television, rose disproportionately. The fee dropped for Albertville and Lillehammer, which were both poor for US television, but then rose sharply for Nagano, which is, in actual fact, in an even worse time zone. In short, it has to be acknowledged that the evidence of an undue influence of the USA television networks is not totally convincing. Other factors – the state of the bidding war, and the state of the economy at the time of the bid – are also important. For example, the Calgary fee was inflated by a well-managed auction of rights, and by the 'macho' determination of ABC to remain the network of the Olympics. In fact, the over-extension of ABC brought its dominance to an end. Fees may have been kept down by the state of the economy in the late 1980s and early 1990s – this would have affected fees for Games between 1992 and 1998. Separating the Summer and Winter Games has made it easier for US networks to bid large sums, as the burden of two Games comes in separate years, with a better chance of recouping the cost in advertising revenue. The networks have had to come to terms with, and devise strategies for, the inconvenient timing of events. NBC has, on occasion, endeavoured to time-shift coverage of the Games under the rubric of 'plausibly live' coverage, with some degree of success, and Olympic television broadcasts have begun to show signs of attempting to address and win a female audience (Toohey, 1997; Andrews, 1998).

The growing proportion of TV revenue that comes from non-US sources, predicted by IOC member Richard Pound in 1986, has contributed to a reduction in the power of the US networks. Indeed, the really dramatic shift took place between the fees for Moscow in 1980 and Atlanta in 1996. Over this period, the proportion of television rights fees provided by the rest of the world rose from 15% to 49%, and in the Summer Games since, the rest of the world share has been between 47% and 49%. The IOC had already decided by the early 1980s that it had developed a dangerous over-dependence on revenue from American television, and that the revenues obtained from the rest of the world would have to rise. The crisis at ABC that overbidding for Calgary brought about had clearly acted as a 'wake-up call' (Table 2).

Following the 1988 Olympic Games, two shifts were clear. First, the Olympic Games had moved from an era in which they were associated with political protests and boycotts, and economic problems, into an era in which they were perceived as part of economic success and building city image. Second, the IOC had assumed a much greater degree of central control over

Table 2. Worldwide Olympic broadcast revenues in US$ million.

	Summer	Winter	Total
1980	101	21	122
1984	287	103	390
1988	403	325	728
1992	636	292	928
1994/1996	935	353	1288
1998/2000	1332	513	1845
2002/2004	1498	738	2236
2006/2008	894	832	1726[a]

Source: http://www.olympic.org/uk/organisation/facts/revenue/broadcoast_uk.asp.
[a]Not all deals have been finalised, which probably accounts for the lower total figure.

the key negotiations regarding television revenue and sponsorship (Larson & Park, 1993). When the television rights negotiations for the 2012 games are complete, it is possible that the rest of the world may provide more than 50% of the television revenue for the first time. So, it seems unlikely that the US Networks could have a major influence on site choice now, if they ever did. Indeed the willingness of NBC to conclude deals for the 2012 Olympic Games 2 years in advance of the choice of site would seem to suggest that the choice of site is no longer seen as a crucial element in determining the value of the rights.[2]

Sponsorship and the Lessons of 1984

Apart from attempting to increase the revenue from the rest of the world, the IOC also decided to increase the level of sponsorship revenue through a process of centralisation and rationalisation. This strategy was prompted by worries about over dependence on US television, but promoted behind the scenes by Adidas boss, Horst Dassler, who had already worked with FIFA President João Havelange to transform the sponsorship revenue of the World Cup (Wilson, 1988; Aris, 1990; Whannel, 1992; Sugden & Tomlinson, 1998).

For the 'private' Games of 1984, Peter Ueberroth had shown how establishing a limited number of product categories and guaranteeing exclusive sponsorships in each category could, by triggering bidding wars between rivals such as Coke and Pepsi, Kodak and Fuji, maximise sponsorship revenue (Reich, 1986; Ueberroth, 1985). Dassler's new sponsorship agency, ISL was hired, controversially without public tender, to establish the TOP programme, which involved persuading the National Olympic Committees (NOCs) to relinquish their own local rights in the key product areas, in order that the IOC could market the Games to sponsors centrally. The introduction of limited product categories with sponsor exclusivity meant that, by 1992, there were just 12 TOP sponsors, but they brought in between $10 m and $20 m each (Barney, Wenn, & Martyn, 2002).

Half of the total revenue of the Olympic movement still comes from television, but now 40% comes from sponsorship, while a mere 8% comes from ticket sales, giving a clue to the importance of the spectator in the scheme of things. It is worth noting that at the Olympic Games, like other major events, a large proportion of tickets are distributed to the 'Olympic family', sponsors, corporate hospitality, and the media. In some major sport events, less than 70% of tickets have been available to the general public. In general terms, the IOC retains 8% of this revenue, and the remainder is shared out between the NOCs, the International Federations (IFs), and the Organising Committees (OCOGs).

Global Audience, Global Markets

There is a major paradox at the heart of Olympic marketing. Normally, advertisers and sponsors are primarily interested in gaining television exposure. But the IOC permits no arena advertising (apart from the trademarks of equipment suppliers). The only other major sporting event to bar advertising is the Wimbledon Tennis Championships. In this way, sponsors do not get television space and are, instead, buying into association with the world's most recognisable symbol – the five Olympic rings, a symbol that connotes world excellence. The only way that corporations can gain television exposure is to buy advertising separately. The paradox lies in the impression of being 'above' commerce produced by a 'clean' stadium that contributes significantly to the aura of uniqueness of the Games and hence enhances their marketability.

Despite these enormous revenues, the IOC still does not cover the cost of its own spectacle. Host cities have to invest massive funds, often in the form of infrastructural support, which are not always included on the balance sheet. In Sydney, for example, only approximately 65% of expenses were covered by revenue. Staging an Olympic Games can, of course, result in capital investment in facilities that will benefit the city for many decades. It can also result in investment in facilities and infrastructure that do not fit the strategic long-term needs of a city. Such important issues suggest a need for comprehensive and accurate value-for-money audits of the Olympic legacy in Olympic cities.

In recent years, the IOC has, like FIFA, also developed the strategy of selling rights years in advance. Deals for 2012 were secured long before the venue was known. Whose interests are at stake here? If one sells in advance, either one feels that the price may be less favourable, or the deals will become more complex, or at the least there is price uncertainty ahead. Conversely, if one buys the rights ahead, one must worry either that the price will rise, or that some other factor will intervene. In this case, both sides are worried about the future of the Internet and specifically of real-time video streaming. Clearly, on a technological level, this could provide a new mode of consuming the Olympics. Television has a lot to lose in potential advertising revenue. But, it is less easy to see from where the Internet income stream might arise. The current IOC commitment to free-at-point-of-access viewing prevents the IOC from exploiting pay-per-view channels, whether broadcast or via the Internet (although breaking up the rights package, and changing its own rules, are both possible options). In this way, one senses a caution on both sides about the uncertain future of new media and convergent technologies and a desire to consolidate now.

The long-term broadcast rights strategy developed by the IOC has now secured television rights deals until 2012. The IOC (http://www.olympic.org/) has commented that:

> ...as a result, future organising committees (and even to a certain extent, future bid cities) will be able to plan firm budgets much earlier, ensuring a more stable staging of the Olympic Games. Deals have been signed with broadcasters who have prior experience in televising the Games, thus ensuring the broadcast coverage and best possible production quality for viewers.

The use, twice, of the word 'ensuring' is striking – there certainly seems to be a substantial degree of 'insurance' involved in this perspective.

Given the uncertainties about the media future, it is not surprising that the major US networks were keen to secure television rights for future Olympic Games, nor was it remarkable that the IOC was keen to arrange such a deal. Between 1984 and 2008, broadcasting revenues were more than US$10 billion (http://www.olympic.org/). In June 2003, NBC, together with its parent company, General Electric (GE), concluded a deal for the Winter Olympics of 2010 and the Summer Games of 2012 worth US$2.201 billion in total, including a commitment by GE to the TOP sponsorship programme.

NBC will pay US$820 m for the 2010 Winter Olympics and US$1.181 billion for the 2012 Summer Games. GE agreed to a sponsorship arrangement of a minimum of US$160 m and a maximum of US$200 m. The deal means that NBC will be broadcasting the next five Olympics, totalling 13 that have been broadcast by NBC, and signals their complete eclipse of ABC as the 'Olympic network' (IOC Press Release June 6, 2003).

A columnist from the *Washington Post* argued that the bid was a "risky but potentially rewarding go-for-broke attempt by a network to hold on to mass viewership events in an era when cable broadcasters are eroding network clout", but also pointed out that NBC would utilise its own cable networks – MSBNC, CNBC and Bravo – to broadcast Olympic events, reaching as wide an audience as possible and maximising advertising dollars. After the IOC announced that it was expecting a sponsorship dimension to the deal, it was the commitment of G. E. that helped secure the deal for NBC (*Washington Post*, June 7, 2003).

Deals such as these that have been struck underline the enormous commercial value of the Olympic Games and the power of the IOC – how many other organisations can successfully sell, for 1 billion dollars, a product not due to be delivered for 9 years, when even the host city is unknown? Indeed, the closing of the deals highlights the manner in which the Games have become a recognisable, routinised, and ritualised form of spectacle, in which stars, narratives, and national identities are all delivered for audience identification (Tomlinson, 1996, 1999; Hall & Hodges, 1997; Roche, 2000; Wilson & Sinclair, 2000). Top sport stars now are the point of intersection between the global spectacle of the Olympic Games and the celebrity-dominated media culture, and star image has become a promotional tool. The issue of sport actuality as intellectual property poses a contradiction – the IOC is selling the images of performance – but the performers receive nothing for this. How long will they be content with this situation? During an era in which top sport stars have agents to oversee their interests, intellectual property and image rights could become the site of a legal challenge to the current structure of Olympic finance.

Because the IOC is selling *exclusive* television rights, the news access rules are now framed very carefully to prevent other competing channels from providing *too much* Olympic footage. Olympic material can only be used as part of a regularly scheduled daily news programme; Olympic 'special' programmes are not permitted. Apart from all-news networks, Olympic material may appear in no more than three programmes per day. The amount of Olympic material used in any one programme cannot exceed a total of 2 mins., and no more than 30 seconds of any particular event. Programmes in which Olympic material appears must be separated by at least 3 hours, except in rolling news channels, which are restricted to 6 mins. per day. Non-rights holders can only broadcast parts of an event for 48 hours after the day of the event.

THE INTERNET: THREAT OR OPPORTUNITY?

Fears have been expressed that the huge television revenues received by the IOC could be jeopardised in a future where any spectator with a digital camera or 3G (third generation) phone could relay live pictures onto 'the net'. The first IOC response to the emergence of the Internet was to treat it with great suspicion and to keep it at arms-length. According to IOC regulations (2003), Olympic material "may not be transmitted or communicated via the internet or any other interactive media or electronic medium without the express prior written approval of the IOC". Website journalists have been refused accreditation, and companies hired to police the net, and protect the Olympics trademark. NetResult's Copyright Control Services will police the web for any sites that show illegal broadcasts or use Olympic trademarks without permission. The Beijing Organising Committee has already set up a legal section to protect Olympic property rights (IOC, 2003). IOC media policy is coming under pressure from two directions. On the one hand, media de-regulation and the rapid growth of new media and digitalisation threaten to undermine the cosy, television-dependent finances of the Olympic movement. On the other hand, the European Union regulatory framework poses a threat to the IOC's cautious and protectionist stance towards new media.

The caution of the IOC is prompted by significant skepticism about the ability of digitised new media to challenge the ability of broadcast television to raise revenue. The European Union competition watchdog has suggested that the IOC may be breaking European competition laws by not offering any rights to new media and mobile phone providers. The European Union wants the Olympics to help boost new communications services via Internet and mobile telephone networks, and especially to help kick-start the market for the new 3G phones (*Guardian Unlimited*, February 20, 2003). The IOC has granted limited Internet broadcast rights to Swiss TV rights holder, Television Suisse Romande, in an experiment, largely designed as an attempt to establish how (if at all) such broadcasts can be limited geographically (*Wired News*, February 8, 2002). Awareness of both the threat and the opportunity of the Internet is edging the IOC towards a strategy of consolidating and securing its existing sources of revenue, while exploring with caution the possibilities of incorporating limited Internet deals into the rights packages. Meanwhile, according to the Association of National Olympic Committees of Africa (ANOCA) Secretary General Tommy Sithole, most people in African countries do not even get to see the Games on television, as the TV rights have been too expensive for most states (*Daily Nation*, June 14, 2001).

The Olympic movement continues to embody and encapsulate many of the tensions and contradictions that characterise a globalised economy and a post-modern culture. Few are untouched by the spectacle of the Olympic Games, yet the gulf between rich and poor seems as wide as ever. Despite new regulations and codes of practice framing the lobbying process and declarations that the bidding race would be closely policed, the five bidding cities for 2012 (New York, Moscow, Madrid, Paris, and London) spent large sums on their campaigns. The fostering of a bidding race featuring so many major cities provides incalculable free publicity to the Olympic movement.

Despite the growth of new media, television will continue to be the primary means by which the Olympic Games commands worldwide attention. The intense focus on the Olympic Games is an instance of a phenomenon I have termed *vortextuality* – a process through which major events temporarily dominate the news and discussion agenda to such an extent that it becomes hard for social commentators to avoid addressing the event (see Whannel, 2002). The next Olympic Games in 2008 will dominate the sports sections of the press and, on occasion, the front pages. Special supplements will be produced, both as preview and as post-mortem. Magazines will run Olympic-oriented features, and radio phone-ins will discuss Olympic themes. Even those columnists disinterested in sport will feel impelled to comment. This process is likely to be all the more intense since it will represent the first major world-sport event to be held in China. Our fascination with China as an emergent political and economic force, the transitional nature of China's political and economic systems, the dynamism of its economy, the human rights issues and the legacy of Tianneman Square will, together, provide a distinctive political dimension to the journalistic interest.

None of this would happen with this intensity, however, without television coverage. Major live sport is perfectly placed to exploit the technical ability of television to relay top quality live pictures around the world. This ability to assemble a global audience is precisely the reason that both journalists and corporate sponsors are so keen to be involved with the Games. In this context, then, it is not surprising that, despite the rapid growth of the new media, the IOC and NBC television have been happy to conclude long-term deals to continue the close relationship between the Olympic movement and American television.

On July 6th, 2005 the IOC, unexpectedly awarded the 2012 Games to London. Given the very rapid pace of technological development associated with digitalisation and the accelerated spread of Internet access around the world, the new media will, by this time, be a far more significant element in the Olympic media-scape. Certainly, in the field of access to Olympic-related information, the Internet will be a prime source. No mode of analysis is more prone to risible error than futurology, especially in the study of everyday life and social practice. In a world in which risk, uncertainty, and fear have become significant components in our collective imaginings, it is not easy to be sure how geo-politics may shift, or in what ways climate change may intervene in our reactions to grandiose spectacles between now and 2012. Internationalist organisations like the United Nations are not currently in a powerful position in relation to the power of the USA or the rising power of China. In this context, it may well be that the Olympic Games, as a global television spectacle, could assume even greater importance as a symbol of internationalism, constituting one of the few prominent forms through which, albeit in peculiarly contradictory ways, concepts of collective global commonality can be marked.

NOTES

1. The IOC dislikes the use of the word 'profit'. In fact, as always in Olympic Games, even in Los Angeles, the financial success depends heavily on infrastructural support from the city (transport, security, cleaning, communications, etc.), which rarely appear clearly as items in the balance sheet.
2. For studies of the power of US TV, see Spence (1988), Wilson (1988), Jackson and McPhail (1989), O'Neil (1989), Real (1989) and, for studies of sport and the media, see Moragas, Rivenburgh and Larson (1996), and Rowe (1996, 1999).

REFERENCES

Andrews, D. (1998). Feminizing Olympic reality. *International Review for the Sociology of Sport, 33*(1), 5–18.

Aris, S. (1990). *Sportsbiz: Inside the sports business*. London: Hutchinson.

Barney, R. K., Wenn, S. R., & Martyn, S. G. (2002). *Selling the five rings: The IOC and the rise of Olympic commercialism*. Salt Lake City: The University of Utah Press.

Billings, A. C., Eastman, S. T., & Newton, G. D. (1998). Atlanta revisited: Prime-time pro-
    motion in the 1996 Summer Olympics. *Journal of Sport and Social Issues, 22*(1), 65–78.
Boyle, D. (2003). *Authenticity: Brands, fakes, spin and the lust for real life.* London: Flamingo.
Hall, C. M., & Hodges, J. (1997). The politics of place and identity in the Sydney 2000
    Olympics: Sharing the spirit of corporatism. In: M. Roche (Ed.), *Sport, popular culture
    and identity.* Oxford: Meyer and Meyer.
International Olympic Committee, Television Access Rules Applicable to the 2004 Athens
    Olympic Games, 2003.
Jackson, R., & McPhail, T. (Eds) (1989). *The Olympic movement and the mass media.* Calgary,
    Alberta, Canada: Hurford Enterprises.
Jennings, A. (1996). *The new lords of the rings.* London: Pocket.
Klein, N. (1999). *No logo.* London: Flamingo.
Larson, J., & Park, H. (1993). *Global television and the politics of the Seoul Olympics.* Boulder,
    CO: Westview.
Lenskyj, H. (2000). *Inside the Olympic industry: Power, politics and activism.* New York: State
    University of New York Press.
Moragas, M. de. (1999). The Olympic movement and the information society. *Television in
    the Olympic Games: The new era,* International Symposium, Lausanne: International
    Olympic Committee.
Moragas, M. de., Rivenburgh, N. K., & Larson, J. F. (Eds) (1996). *Television in the Olympics.*
    London: John Libbey.
O'Neil, T. (1989). *The game behind the game: High stakes, high pressure in TV sports.*
    New York: Harper and Row.
Quart, A. (2003). *Branded: The buying and selling of teenagers.* London: Arrow.
Real, M. (1989). *Super media.* London: Sage.
Reich, K. (1986). *Making it happen: Peter Ueberroth and the 1984 Olympics.* Santa Barbara,
    CA: Capra.
Roche, M. (2000). *Mega-events and modernity: Olympics and expos in the growth of global
    culture.* London: Routledge.
Rowe, D. (1996). The global love-match: Sport and television. *Media Culture and Society, 18*(4),
    565–582.
Rowe, D. (1999). *Sport, culture and the media: The unruly trinity.* Buckingham, UK: Open
    University Press.
Simson, V., & Jennings, A. (1992). *The lords of the rings: Money, power and drugs in the modern
    Olympics.* London: Simon and Schuster.
Spence, J. (1988). *Up close and personal.* New York: Atheneum.
Sugden, J., & Tomlinson, A. (Eds) (1998). *FIFA and the contest for world football: Who rules the
    people's game?* London: Polity.
Tomlinson, A. (1996). Olympic spectacle: Opening ceremonies and some paradoxes of globali-
    sation. *Media Culture and Society, 18*(4), 583–602.
Tomlinson, A. (1999). Staging the spectacle: Reflections on Olympic and World Cup ceremo-
    nies. *Soundings* (Vol. 13). London: Lawrence and Wishart.
Tomlinson, A., & Whannel, G. (Eds) (1984). *Five ring circus.* London: Pluto.
Toohey, K. (1997). Australian television, gender and the Olympic games. *International Review
    for the Sociology of Sport, 32*(1), 19–30.
Ueberroth, P. (1985). *Made in America.* New York: William Morrow.

Whannel, G. (1992). *Fields in vision: Television sport and cultural transformation.* London: Routledge.
Whannel, G. (2002). *Media sport stars, masculinities and moralities.* London: Routledge.
Wilson, H., Sinclair, J. (2000). *The Olympics: Media, myth, madness.* Special issue of Media International Australia, 97, Nathan, Queensland, Australia: Australian Key Centre for Cultural and Media Policy, Griffiths University.
Wilson, N. (1988). *The sports business.* London: Piatkus.

Chapter 10

THE COMMERCIALISATION OF THE OLYMPICS: CITIES, CORPORATIONS, AND THE OLYMPIC COMMODITY

Alan Tomlinson

The Olympics have become such a high-profile global phenomenon that it attracts some of the world's most prominent cities to bid for the prize of hosting the Summer Games in particular. In part to capitalise on the enhanced marketing opportunities presented by this unusual demand, the International Olympic Committee (IOC) separated the Summer and the Winter Games after the Barcelona Summer Games and the Albertville Winter Games of 1992. This decision had been taken in 1986, in the wake of the euphoria of the profile and the profitability of the 1984 Los Angeles Olympics and, no doubt, as a way of giving better value to those companies signing up to be preferred partners in the IOC's new sponsorship programmes. The bidding process and the marketing strategy of the IOC might seem to be separate but, as the IOC has exploited its products in increasingly successfully ways in the two decades since the pivotal Los Angeles Games, it has become clearer that the processes are two dimensions of a single development – the intensifying commercialisation and commodification of the Olympic product.

The spectre of commerce was conspicuous in its absence at the first Olympic Games staged after the Second World War. The President of the

Global Olympics: Historical and Sociological Studies of the Modern Games
Research in the Sociology of Sport, Volume 3, 179–200

IOC (1952–1972), Avery Brundage, was a right-wing businessman from the USA, but he opposed with a messianic vehemence any moves to develop the Olympics on a more commercialised footing. Even at the time of his retirement (at the Munich Olympics in 1972), Brundage was still declaring that the IOC "should have nothing to do with money" (Barney, Wenn, & Martyn, 2002, p. 100). Stepping down as President, he observed that arguments over the distribution of money were destructive, threatening to "fracture the Olympic Movement" (p. 275).

The modern Olympics was, from its inception, vulnerable to the influence of commercial forces. Speaking at the University of Lausanne in 1928, de Coubertin even opposed the escalation in size and costs in the construction of Olympic stadiums: "Almost all the stadiums built in recent years are the result of local and, too often, commercial interests, not Olympic interests at all" (de Coubertin, 2000, p. 184). The idealistic founder of the Olympics spoke against "athletics as a show", implying that commercially based, large-scale events would corrupt the amateur spirit. Drawing upon promotional budgets and generating large crowds to justify the investment in the event, he argued, "these oversized showcases are the source of the corruption at the root of the evil" (p. 184).

Yet, de Coubertin himself knew that his project needed to attract sponsors, and he was not averse to accepting some forms of commercial support. His publication, *Olympic Review*, the IOC's official bulletin, sported a full-page advertisement from a Parisian sporting goods manufacturer in the January, 1901 issue. Further, alcohol helped him fund the October, 1902 issue, when the French brandy-maker, Benedictine, paid for a comparable advertising spread (Barney et al., 2002, p. 29). In 1924 in Paris, the Olympic stadium was bedecked in advertisements for Ovalmaltine, Dubonnet, Cinzano, and many other commercial product labels, and the French Organizing Committee published a 320-page guide to the Games containing advertisements on 256 of its pages, including ones for sporting goods and specialist alcoholic brands (Barney et al., 2002, p. 28). But the IOC was innocent and naïve in terms of the commercial exploitation of its product which, of course in a pre-television age, was hardly a global brand. This left the Olympics open to exploitation by bodies with a more basic commercial rationale. Barney et al. (2002, pp. 31–49) document in meticulous detail the case that alerted the IOC to the dangers of leaving its coveted name, and symbols, unprotected: Helms' Olympic Bread.

Paul H. Helms, head of Helms Bakeries of Los Angeles, founded in 1931, was a well-placed businessman who secured a contract from the Los Angeles Organizing Committee to supply bakery goods for the Olympic Village at the 1932 Olympic Games. But he also registered the marks of the Olympics in all states of the USA, for his own exclusive use. These included the five-ring symbol, the Olympic motto, and the word 'Olympic' itself (Barney et al., 2002, p. 33). Neither the IOC nor any other body had ever attempted to register ownership of these marks. Carl Diem, manager of Germany's Olympic team in Los Angeles, recommended Helms as the supplier for the Berlin Games of 1936. In 1948, Helms was the supplier in London. From 1938, the President of the United States Olympic Committee, Avery Brundage, did all he could to prevent Helms from continuing with his branding, but to little avail, as the visionary baker had watertight legal rights to what nobody else had sought to claim in law. Helms himself gave up his rights, in 1950, and his generosity allowed the IOC to defend its products from commercial exploitation and, when the media potential of the event became clearer, to exploit its products more fully for its own financial interests.

It is illuminating that entrepreneurial operators from outside the IOC were the ones to see the potential of the commercialisation process. In the decades-later phase of this story, it was the German shoe manufacturer Horst Dassler, of Adidas, setting up his company International Sports Leisure Marketing (ISL), who revolutionised Olympic finances. Faced with an almost complete dependency on television sponsorship for IOC revenues, the new President (1980–2003), Juan Antonio Samaranch, learned quickly from the model of sponsorship established by FIFA President, João Havelange (Sugden & Tomlinson, 1998). In 1982–1983, ISL and the IOC established a partnership aimed at the world-wide marketing of the Games, a lucrative enterprise for Dassler's company that gave ISL global domination of arguably the world's two biggest sports events (Simson & Jennings, 1992, pp. 99–110; Tomlinson, 2004a). This was the beginning of TOP (The Olympic Programme), a marketing model that is still in place (now known as The Olympic Partners) at the IOC, with the marketing deals established by and within the IOC itself since the mid-1980s. Before organising committees realised this potent combination of sponsorship and television revenues, host nations had to pay for hosting the Games. In the pre-television era, ticket sales comprised the primary source of revenue but could never completely offset the costs of hosting. Certainly, the performances of nations at the Olympics had become matters of international interest during the pre-World War II era, but the arrival of the Soviets in 1952, a direct and broad challenge to the athletic supremacy of the United States, brought new symbolic value to the Games. The Cold War brought heightened interest in such competition and in the medal count and, also, both pressures and opportunities for host cities. Satellite television provided the medium and the prospect of financial support.

This overview of the rivalries at the apex of Olympic performance is both a political narrative and an economic one. Developing competitive sport became a political necessity for the world's two dominant superpowers. Of course, there were costs. The key funding factor in the case of the two superpower rivals was the form of subsidy that the countries and appropriate institutions could provide, in light of Brundage's iron-fisted rule over amateur regulations. One English journalist, Larry Montague of the *Manchester Guardian*, observing the athletics contests at the 1952 Games, calculated that in a straight 'head-to-head' "the Americans...would just about have beaten the rest of the world in running, jumping and throwing" (Brown, 1952, p. 143). Montague offered astute commentary on the basis of this US performance:

> They owe their supremacy not only to their numbers, their brilliant individuals, and their sports scholarships at universities, but to their intense competition at home and their way of life, in which everyone desires to do everything better and quicker than anyone else; they do not see any limits to their achievement and as a result there are none (Montague, in Brown, 1952, p. 143).

It was a powerful blend: An intense individualism spliced with national patriotic spirit, and institutionalised support in the university athletic system, funded by a combination of private and public sources. If any kind of reliable economic analysis could have been undertaken of the costs of such accomplishments in the middle of the twentieth century, it would surely have confirmed that the rising profile of the Olympics was premised on massive economic subsidies, on ways of funding the so-called amateurs who were, in every respect, full-time athletes and potential tools of state ideology. In the Soviet Union, vaguely defined professional roles and positions, in state-sponsored organisations and the military, provided an equivalent way to harness resources towards not-so-amateur athletes.

In the strictly amateur era, athletes did not receive rewards for their achievements in any way comparable to the sponsored athlete of the future. The magnificent American athlete Jesse Owens – whose four records achieved in 1936 were still intact after the 1952 Helsinki Games – was the son of a sharecropper, and hailed on his homecoming as a hero and a national and global celebrity in tickertape parades down New York City's Broadway, and in Cleveland. But his celebrity status earned him virtually nothing, and he had to take a modestly remunerated job (earning a reported

$130 per month) as a playground instructor, as well as turning to running against horses, dogs, and motorcycles to supplement his income. Endorsing a failed cleaning business, he found no financial security until moving into a public relations role and providing speeches on religion, patriotism, and marketing for corporate sponsors (Wallechinsky, 2000, p. 7). In this era, most Olympic champions had to look elsewhere for lucrative income, not all with the success of the 'five gold-medal' man (from 1924 to 1928), Johnny Weismuller, who was spotted in a photograph for his BVD Underwear Company employer and, instead of competing in the first Los Angeles Olympics, went on to his film debut in 1932 in *Tarzan, the Ape Man*, and 11 more Tarzan films over the next 16 years (Wallechinsky, 2000, p. 696). Harold Sakata, the 1948 silver medalist in light heavyweight weightlifting, became better known and better off as the sinister, frightening 'Oddjob' in the James Bond movie, *Goldfinger* (Wallechinsky, 2000, p. 847). Much to the chagrin of the self-proclaimed amateur watchdog, Avery Brundage, there was a kind of hidden economy underpinning the early Olympics, a mix of state subsidy, amateur commitment, and opportunistic self-promotion. For the athlete, this provided, particularly in market economies of the West, very little in the way of professional or financial security.

As the Cold War consolidated the status of the Olympics as a form of global cultural politics, a more explicit economic logic emerged with the realisation that Olympic events could be staged for world-wide media constituencies and an international television audience. The commercial potential of sport and sporting events was recognised for the entrepreneurial gold rush that it could become. New breeds of entrepreneur, marketing (mostly)-men, and media agents and agencies changed the basic economics of mediated competitive sport (Tomlinson, 2004a). The Los Angeles Games of 1984 was a watershed for this, and the Olympic sponsorship scheme emerged co-terminously with Los Angeles's rewriting of the economic framework for staging an Olympics (Tomlinson, 2004b, pp. 147–148). North American capital came to dominate the macro-economics of the Olympics (Tomlinson, 2004b, p. 160).

In the build-up to the 1984 Los Angeles Olympics, widespread and intense debate centred upon the torch relay. As this pinnacle of Cold War Games warmed up the citizenry of the USA for its patriotic response, nationalistic fervour intensified as athletes, volunteers, and celebrities jostled for an opportunity to carry the Olympic torch. But not all Olympians were equally enthused. This torch relay was unique in the extent to which it commercialised an Olympic ritual. In this respect, the IOC offers its idealised, but purely mythological, conception of the genesis and signifi-cance of the torch:

> The Olympic torch is a symbol taken from the ancient Olympic Games, during which a holy torch burned continuously on the altar of Zeus. Fire is thought to be purifying in most cultures. The Olympic torch is carried along a relay from Olympia to the host city, proclaiming the celebration of the world's greatest sporting festival. As it travels, it carries a spirit of peace and harmony, triggering a huge celebration in which the whole world participates. It is a strong symbol of the international dimension of the Games (IOC, 2000, p. 38).

In its rewriting of the rules of staging the Games, though, the Los Angeles Olympics Organizing Committee (LAOOC) ensured that it did not replicate the financial difficulties experienced by the organising committee of Mon-treal in 1976, which had accumulated colossal debts to be paid by the citizens of the city and the province of Québec for decades to come. In Los Angeles, everything was for sale. This included any components of Olympic symbolism that could be peddled to the public via corporate sponsors – not always for the profit of the Games organisers, but never-theless a commodification of the ritualistic elements of the Games. President of the LAOOC, Peter Ueberroth, costed the privilege of carrying the torch at $3,000 per kilometer, to be donated to a charity of the participant's choice, not to go towards LAOOC costs. Although this plan was initially opposed by Ueberroth's "entire senior management" (Reich, 1986, p. 43), Ueberroth himself was insistent that a 3-month relay, involving 3,350 people across the country, raising 10 million dollars for individually chosen char-ities and causes, would be incomparable pre-event marketing, while ap-pealing to the American volunteering spirit (Ueberroth, 1985, pp. 189–191). The LAOOC boss then had to persuade IOC personnel, including President Juan Antonio Samaranch and his top executives, that selling the flame was not a "commercialization of the relay", as no money would go to the or-ganising committee or the athletes. Ueberroth recalls that not all interested parties were so easily persuaded: "The Greeks weren't as understand-ing…The Greek IOC members, Nikos Filaretos and Nikolaos Nissiotis, objected, claiming we were commercializing the flame" (Ueberroth, 1985, p. 192).

Ueberroth had done his homework and his lobbying, however, and with Samaranch pleading his case, the Greeks were placated by the LAOOC's provision of finances for the Greek 500 m relay from Olympia to Athens, and the contribution of uniforms, shoes, torches, and flags. And finally, to ensure that the organising committee was not diverted from the main event, a sponsor was found to fund the organisation of the marathon event, communications giant AT&T. Each division – AT&T itself, Pacific Bell, AT&T Directory Services, AT&T Long Lines Division Western Electric Company – signed sponsorship deals. All costs were covered – maintenance, manpower, transport, and a squad of runners to run across landscapes where no $3,000 per kilometer runner could be found. For this, AT&T received the status of 'official sponsor,' had national and international exposure in the build-up to and the staging of the Games, and claimed the best hotel rooms in town, reserved by the organising committee, and blocks of tickets for the best events. The selling of the torch relay was framed as a community initiative, mobilising thousands of volunteers, and raising almost $11 million. For AT&T, though, it was first and foremost a commercial proposition.

There is nothing pure and fixed about Olympic rituals and symbols, once operationalised beyond the annals of official IOC rhetoric. The torch relay, itself, was first staged in 1936, for the Nazi Olympics in Berlin. But the selling of the torch, the sponsoring of the relay, was unambiguous testimony to an unbridled commercialisation on which the Olympics would then be based. After the so-called 'Hamburger Olympics' of Los Angeles in 1984 (Gruneau, 1984), at which McDonald's paid for the upgrade of the swimming/diving facility, the mini-mart giant '7–11' paid for the velodrome, and in the time of an IOC leadership that, from the early 1980s onwards, targeted hugely increased sponsorship strategies, the Games became a prize for cities lured by the successes of 1984 and the reported profits of the privatised Games. Los Angeles wrote a new script for the economics of the Olympics. The LAOOC's official record is unequivocal on this:

> It was noted that for past Games, the top sources of funds had been direct government subsidies, receipts from lotteries and Olympic commemorative coin programs, and then television rights sales, ticket sales and the sale of sponsorships. Direct government subsidies were unavailable to the LAOOC, and lotteries were then illegal in the state of California...the planning focused on sources in the private sector: television revenues, sponsorships and ticket sales (Perelman, 1985, p. 116).

The audited results (March 1985) of the event showed the astounding success of this commercial strategy. Broadcasting rights generated (all in US dollars) $286,794,000; ticket sales, $139,929,000; sponsorship and licencing, $126,733,000; the coin programme, $35,985,000; interest income, $76,319,000; and other sources such as non-monetary contributions, revenue from ticket-handling charges and accommodations, $102,884,000. Operating expenses were $398,394,000; payments for venue and facility use, $97,389,000; and expenses to the IOC, $50,145,000. The accounts made joyful reading to sports entrepreneurs and elated politicians: no huge

infrastructural costs, a willing and costless army of volunteers that elim-
inated significant labour costs. The outcome was a reported surplus of
US$222,716,000. The United States Olympic Committee received 40% of
this whopping "excess of revenues over expenses" (Perelman, 1985, p. 119).
Twenty per cent went to national governing bodies of sports in the USA.
The rest went to the Los Angeles Organizing Committee Amateur Athletic
Foundation for sport promotion and development.

The LA model looked irresistible, and significantly changed the fortunes
and the futures of the IOC and its product. Cities, corporations, and consumers became primary partners, as the commercial logic of the Olympics
produced a formula for the event's continuing profile and escalation in a
post-Cold War world. It was not a simple or watertight economic model,
and government subsidies were certainly drawn upon for future Games in
Seoul, Barcelona, Atlanta, Sydney, and Athens. But the central characteristic of the model was the commercialisation of the event, a ruthless commodification of the product, only possible in a wholesale abandonment of
the amateur principle and ethos underpinning earlier Games, alongside a
recognition that just as the Games themselves were fully exploited for their
commercial potential, athletes themselves could make the most of their
individual market potential. A selectively descriptive portrayal of the main
partners in this calculus shows the extent of this transformation in the
political economy of the Games over the two decades following LA's
'Hamburger Olympics'. Cities are not selected on the basis of any core
Olympian value but, rather, as appropriate settings for the consumer
bonanza that the Games have now become. Official Olympic sponsors uni-
versalise contemporary Olympism as a form of global consumerism (Roche,
2000, pp. 26–27).

CITIES

In the early summer of 2004, nine cities still hoped to be awarded the prize
of the rights to host the Summer Olympic Games of 2012. These were
Havana, Istanbul, Leipzig, London, Madrid, Moscow, New York, Paris,
and Rio de Janeiro. In Lausanne, in May 2004, four of these cities were
eliminated: Havana, Istanbul, Leipzig, and Rio. The remaining cities comprised a litany of first-world metropolitan centres in Europe, and their
nearest and highest-profile North American neighbour. It is interesting to
see how the losing and surviving cities represented their candidature to the
international public in that year before the IOC voted to decide upon the

winner. In this section, I consider web-based representations constructed by the bidders (for the specific websites, see the list of sources at the end of the chapter).

First, let us consider the losers. Havana did not bother. Evidence and support for the Cuban enterprise was scarce. Istanbul, by contrast, clarified its motivation through extensive 25-page documentation stating: "Istanbul has a two-fold motivation for hosting the Olympic Games. One is the desire to benefit from the exceptionally enriching experience of Games organization. The other is the impelling drive to inspire a more profound conception of Olympism as a universal value" (p. 5). "The meeting of continents" was its headline, the title of its bid, evoking a vision of international peacemaker, a catalyst for harmony and reconciliation. Leipzig was more modest, perhaps acknowledging with a mix of pragmatics, realism, and disappointment that it was not really in the frame of competition with the other bidding cities. Its December 2003 Newsletter showed Muhammad Ali visiting the city, mentioned agreements on anti-doping, and gave little space to talking up the city's "compact concept" for staging the Games. The importance of such an event to the revitalisation of the city and the region's economy was also highlighted, but there was a lack of overall vision, and a half-hearted mention of the launch of the new logo. But there was little dynamism in Leipzig's tone. Its elimination several months later should have come as no surprise.

Rio had a clearer message: "In 2012, we will bring our passion to the world...ONE VILLAGE, ONE CITY, ONE WORLD". Why Rio? Because it is a city that "loves everything to do with the Games", and "in Rio, the Games will be held within the limits of the host city for the first time in history. Four strategic regions will hold all the facilities required for the event". Typical promotional rhetoric aside, the latest bid to land the Olympics for South America was destined for failure. Its candidature was not helped by the strong likelihood that the world's football governing body, FIFA, was likely to grant the 2014 men's soccer World Cup to Brazil. Sponsors would hardly favour locating the two biggest sporting events in the world in one economically volatile South American country within two years. Without question, Olympic/IOC and World Cup/FIFA politics are inexorably interlinked, with overlapping membership of decision-making bodies, complementary interests in the global sports calendar, and sponsor interests to protect in the global marketplace. The four eliminated candidate cities might have desperately needed economic and related benefits more than any of the other five, but the Olympics is not about social need. It is about position, and the consolidation of position. So the purportedly most idealistic and universalised of sports events in the world, after its diversion to Beijing in 2008, would revert to one of the metropolitan giants – in Europe, all national capitals – of the West.

These 'giants' were not slow in putting themselves forward. London's website brochure fronted the British Prime Minister, Tony Blair, writing of "practical benefits for the capital and the country". As if the parochialism of the failed bid by the English Football Association to secure the 2006 men's World Cup had taught the English/British no lessons, Blair concentrated on local benefits: memories and champions for the country, a "healthier and fitter population". The Games "would drive the environmentally-friendly regeneration and rejuvenation of East London, give a huge boost for tourism across the UK and provide thousands of new opportunities for work and volunteering". Here, Blair perpetuated some of the core Olympic myths regarding projected positive effects, for tourism may decline during an Olympics and any post-Olympic increase in tourism is rarely sustained. Perhaps only Barcelona has been a serious exception to this trend (Kennett & Moragas, 2006). But this did not stop the bid boosters in their tracks. Craig Reedie, Chairman of the British Olympic Association and IOC member, called the decision to make the London bid "the most significant development in British sport in generations". Tessa Jowell, the Secretary of State for Media, Culture and Sport, claimed that a London Games would revitalise the east of the city, and "inspire and enthuse a generation of young people". The Mayor of London, reconciled former outcast and scourge of the Labour government, Ken Livingstone, hailed the bid: "Revitalizing London's East End and showcasing the capital's rich cultural diversity are at the heart of the bid for London 2012. I have no higher priority". He also referred to the 300 languages spoken in London's schools, a nod towards cosmopolitanism.

But the bid promoters were very inward-looking. Barbara Cassani, Chairman of the bid, summarised this perspective: "The entire UK would benefit from the huge sporting, cultural, business, tourism and volunteering opportunities that come from hosting the Games. We would have the chance to show the country, and ourselves, at our best". There was not much wooing of the IOC here, little in any way of greetings to the international community. London survived the cut in May, 2004, but was behind Paris and Madrid in the IOC ratings, and not far ahead of New York and Moscow. Cassani was immediately sidelined and Lord (Sebastian) Coe elevated to the front position of the bid. There was much work to do for the Conservative peer and Olympic 'double gold' medallist. However commercialised the whole bidding process had become, Lord Coe had much to do to galvanise the bid in ways that would assuage the IOC adjudicators who had put London in only third place because of its rusty transport infrastructure and, though not explicitly stated, arrogant mode of self-presentation. This was achieved in London's stunning triumph at the IOC vote in Singapore on July 6, 2005.

Prominent on Madrid's website was the line-up of "Collaborating Companies" – "A shared dream thanks to the support of companies...Madrid's Olympic project is supported by the most important Spanish companies. These companies believe in and are financially committed to our project". The companies were then classified in platinum (13 companies), gold (33 companies), silver (12 companies), and bronze (24 companies) categories. Moscow appealed to culture, tradition, and history, and the widespread popular support of Muscovites and other Russians, pledging levels of support of 90% and 89% respectively in favour of Moscow's candidature for the Games.

New York's documentation was a version of OCOG's (Organizing Committee for the Olympic Games) well-developed preliminary bid document first produced in the summer of 2001. In 2003 US dollars, the projected NYC 2012 OCOG total revenue was estimated at $1,834,000,000. Ticket sales, at $813 million, were the highest single source, followed by income from local and national sponsors and suppliers ($687 million). Licencing and merchandising were predicted at $95 million, Paralympic revenues $69 million, and miscellaneous revenues $170 million. All of this was to be in addition to IOC contributions from both its select list of sponsors, and IOC-negotiated television rights. These latter had been projected, in 2000, at $764 million and $179 million, respectively (New York 2012, 2001, pp. 95–96). In 2003, New York declared its motivation to be based in New Yorkers' "deep need to channel their energies, spirit, and resources to express solidarity with the world...the Games will be remembered for bringing to life the force of the Olympic Movement in a city that, like the Games itself, celebrates the power of dreams and the triumph of the human spirit". To bring to life the Games itself would, though, be the job of accountants, economists, and financiers, media and commercial partners, more than speechmakers or apologists for the Olympic ideal. The New York bidders were explicit about this from the start of the city's candidature. After the attacks on the United States in September, 2001, the rhetoric of renewal and international solidarity could be amplified still further, but this could not conceal the stark economics of planning underlying the financial infrastructure and commercial realities necessary to the hosting and staging of an Olympic Games.

CORPORATIONS

The IOC had in place for 2000–2004 its 'fifth generation' of The Olympic Partners (TOP) sponsorship scheme with its corporate clients. Its 10 sponsors/partners were: Coca-Cola, John Hancock, Kodak, McDonald's, Panasonic, Samsung, Sema, *Sports Illustrated*, Visa, and Xerox. The first cycle of the scheme, TOP I (Calgary/Seoul 1998), generated (all in US dollars) $95 million, from nine partners. TOP II (1992 Albertville/Barcelona) generated $175 million from 12 partners. Ten partners generated $350 million for TOP III (1994 Lillehammer/1996 Atlanta). In TOP IV (1998 Nagano/2000 Sydney), $500 million was generated by 11 partners. For TOP V, the IOC forecast that the scheme would generate "in excess of $600 million in financial and technical support to the organizing committees of the Olympic Games and the Olympic Teams" (IOC Press Release, 6 June 2000).

The ways in which these companies use their status as sponsors vary but, for the four-year cycle, all buy a universally recognisable badge, and the guarantee of inestimable media coverage and profile during the Olympic event itself. This section critically appraises the sponsors' use of the Olympic association in their websites (for the particular web addresses, see the list of sources at the end of the chapter). Coca-Cola's initial emphasis is on its historical pedigree, referencing its unbroken sponsoring of the Games since 1928, and its extension of this partnership already through to 2008, and the importance of "the Olympic spirit of unity and competition...to you, our consumers": "The Olympic Games are truly global events that provide an opportunity to bond with our consumers all over the world through activities and promotions they appreciate and understand". These included selecting 2,500 torchbearers, from among "local citizens", to carry the Olympic flame on its route to the Salt Lake City site in 2002 – people "who had demonstrated courage, dedication, passion or a deep concern for others". Coca-Cola also congratulated itself on its own initiatives: "We've also created original popular activities at the Games themselves, like the Pin Trading Center, where people can trade pins with other fans from all over the world, and Coca-Cola Radio, which gives popular DJs a chance to share the excitement of the Olympic Games with their home town fans". Coca-Cola spoke for itself, its global brand name needing no further logo as it reports its Olympic connection. John Hancock (Financial Services), though, used the Olympic rings on its home page, stating proudly its status as "World IOC sponsor", secured in 1993 and sustained until at least 2008. The company initiated its sport sponsorships in backing the Boston Marathon in 1985, and also sponsors Major League Baseball and ice-dancing.

The company's reasons for sponsoring the Olympics are unambiguously clear:

> Why would the Financial Services giant want to get into sports marketing? Just ask John Hancock's Vice President of Corporate Communications, Steve Burgay. "At John Hancock we believe that the Olympic Games are the one event that allows the world to see so much patriotism, tolerance, selfless sacrifice, individual excellence and plain old virtue crowded into two short weeks", he says. "To the athletes, they are the culmination of a lifetime's hard work. To the host cities, they are the highest possible expression of local pride. When you think of the Olympics, you think of winning".

And, of course, to the commercial sponsor, these are marketing opportunities that cannot be missed:

> "The Olympic Games also provide a unique international marketing platform", Burgay continues. "John Hancock's Olympic Marketing programs, which include matching internationally renowned athletes with hometown clinics, help to strengthen existing client relationships and give Hancock an edge in new client prospecting. More than anybody else, the athletes are the face of the Games. These people really do embody the Olympic ideals.

The metaphor is Hancock's own: Olympic sponsorship as a form of gold digging.

Kodak boasts its historical pedigree, claiming sponsorship of the Olympic Games for 106 years, and now running "the biggest photo lab in the world", and its world-wide sponsor status, heading its sites with the five Olympic rings. Eschewing any broad rhetoric, Kodak presents itself as a technological provider and host to the professionals, the photographers, and the broadcasters at the Games.

Fast-food giant McDonald's freely expresses its Olympic statistics like a badge of corporate honour. In the Olympic Village and Main Media Center at Salt Lake City, the company had a captive market. In the village, 52,695 'guests' were served, of whom 53% were athletes. At the centre, the Snack Station and Restaurant snared 53,588 'customers'. The Big Mac was the "top seller in the village, along with McDonald's World Famous Fries". And research is quoted on the benefits to athletes, for whom the McDonald['s] presence provides the "familiar taste of home". A specialist nutrition consultant, Jacqueline Berning, PhD, RD assured us of the benefits of a McDonald's diet: "I work with swimmers who are calorie-burning machines. They're thrilled when I show them how they can enjoy McDonald's as part of their diets". A Director of Nutrition at the Cooper Clinic in Dallas, Georgia Kostas tells us that "Olympic athletes need 'real-life' food that they enjoy. It's great McDonald's will help meet this need at the Olympic Games". No doubt the company was thrilled to find experts willing to peddle such pseudo-science; unfortunately the site did not have space, it seems, for corroborative lists of scientific sources. On its Olympic site McDonald's also provided information about its charity work and listed the company personnel who had competed in or officiated in the Olympics. Further, one could learn of gold awards made to company personnel committed and dedicated enough to compete in the Big Mac Builder's competition to find the crew that could build the fastest and best 'Big Mac'. Burger builder or basketball selector alike, these were hailed as equal in the 'McFamily of Olympians'. Even IOC first Vice President and marketing committee chair, Richard (Dick) W. Pound, entered into the 'Mcrhetoric': "The McDonald's brand exemplifies 'best-in class'. It's an experience that people have in common around the world. We're very pleased that McDonald's commitment to Olympic Athletes world-wide will not only continue, but grow in strength as one of our leading supporters through 2004".

Panasonic devoted nothing to the Olympics on its main site but, in its global sponsorship section, browsers were directed to several links. These included a brief history of the Games from 1984–2002, its period of sponsorship, with a particular emphasis upon the exploits and achievements of Japanese athletes and competitors; a backstage look at the technologies used and developed for the Olympics; advertisements in the form of both still and moving images; and souvenirs. The five rings of the Olympic logo were prominent, but the self-representation was subdued, restrained, and technical in comparison to some of the other sponsors' sites.

Korean telecommunications giant, Samsung, took a much more direct approach, detailing the company's global market aspirations. Il-Hyung Chang, Senior Vice President, Corporate Communication Team, recalled the company's debut as an Olympic sponsor at the 1998 Winter Olympics in Nagano, Japan, when "Samsung was among the last in the row of companies. Today, only five years later, numbers show we are the third in the world among telecommunications companies". In 2001, Samsung's fourth place was based on a 7.1% market share, in 2002 a 9.8% market share secured a third place, and estimations for 2003 pointed to a 12% plus market share. Vice President of the company, Eric Kim, claimed a direct causal relationship between the rising global profile of the company and its status as an Olympic sponsor: "The Olympic Games is a universal event, attract[s] the interest of the whole world and reflect[s] the ideals of sports that appeal to most people. We have been participating in Olympic projects lately, with very beneficial results for our company". Samsung's sponsorship of Athens 2004 comprised three main axes: sponsoring the torch relay, along with Coca-Cola; creating a 'Samsung Olympic Rendezvous' in the heart of the athletes' village; and providing 22,000 mobile phones to athletes, officials, the media, IOC members and volunteers. "At the heart of sports is fair play, a virtue that SAMSUNG esteems as a key corporate belief" the opening/home page of the site declared, indicating, too, that it is "driven by the corporate belief to promote peace and happiness through sports and its ability to unify regardless of race, gender, religion or geography..."

The sponsor, Sema, presented itself as SchlumbergerSema, world-wide IT partner of the IOC. It boasted of securing "the world's largest-ever IT contract for four games and eight years", from Salt Lake City in 2002, Athens (2004), Turin (2006), and Beijing (2008). Sema summarised its accomplishments at previous Games, and established its strategy for "ramping up for Athens". This way, a self-confident, assertive website emphasised jobs well done and progressive technological achievements. The 300 Schlumberger people at the Salt Lake Games, it reported, "managed a vast IT system that relayed information in real time to the participants, audiences and media. The same team provided IT-enabled accreditations to the 89,000 athletes, officials, sponsors, and media representatives to enable the safe and secure movement between the 79 events held across 10 sporting and 30 non-competition venues". Estimates of numbers of users of SchlumbergerSema services in Athens in 2004 approached a quarter of a million people (involving the administration of 200,000 accreditations), active in more than 80 facilities.

Compared to these technological profiles, *Sports Illustrated* offered little in the way of self-promotion of its TOP status. Its home page contained no reference to the Olympics, and even trails to 'more sports' and 'Olympics' led to very little information or promotion. The Olympics appeared to be a minor emphasis for the sponsor, in comparison to US-specific sports. The magazine did not offer any direct service during the Games, but by definition obviously raised its Olympic profile in the build-up to and during the event itself. VISA, on the other hand, accepted exclusive product placement, "installing a network of cash machines and hundreds of payment terminals at the Olympic venues" – offering VISA cardholders general help and information, and multi-lingual emergency services as well as sponsoring a VISA Olympians Reunion Centre, "where past and present Olympic athletes can meet and chat". The Olympic Games was an ideal marketing opportunity for the credit-card company, "a magical combination of sport and culture that brings together people from round the world". VISA noted the IOC's observation that its sponsorship enabled the competing nations to take part, by supporting National Olympic Committees. Without such sponsors, only 30 of the 200 competing nations could get to the Games, VISA was told.

Xerox, 'The Document Company', made much of its Olympic status. It located its Olympic role within a broader social and cultural history, from its first involvement as sponsor, when it used just five plain-paper copiers at the 1964 Tokyo Games. The first post-'9/11' Games are recalled by Chairman and Chief Executive Officer, Anne M. Mulcahy, as a special case. Not only was her own carrying of the torch for a leg a personal "unforgettable experience," the company's sponsorship of these particular Games was of especial significance:

> In 2002 Olympic sponsorship was about pride: pride in country, pride in people, pride in community and businesses. It was about working together as a team to support an event that unites the world... In Athens, the Olympic Flame will again unite people in the shared experience of celebration and achievement and, as the Olympic Summer Games return home to Greece, we will celebrate a history of admirable resolve in the face of adversity... Our presence in Athens demonstrates our continued commitment to our people, our technology and our customers.

In this 40th year of its Olympic sponsorship, Xerox combined its own mission statement with an interventionist and harmonising global role. Olympic-style rhetoric was blended with company interests, as the Team Xerox Olympian Program, established in 1990, continued to spread "the Olympic message to thousands at charity events, fund-raisers, schools and training clinics. Our specially selected Olympic team has inspired and motivated us in a variety of corporate events for our customers and ourselves". Xerox provided the fullest and most gushing elision of Olympic values with corporate values. The following two extracts speak for themselves:

> Hope, dreams, friendship, inspiration, joy in effort. These are just a few of the emotions the Olympic Summer Games evoke in people throughout the world. Xerox shares and embraces the values, spirit and teamwork that distinguish the Olympics as a vital event in our global society. We hope that you will join us in Athens as we come together in these challenging yet hopeful times in a show of unity, brotherhood and pride that elevates the human spirit.

> Championing innovation – doing what's never been done before – is what the Olympic Summer Games are all about. Like Olympic athletes, we at Xerox are Champions of Innovation. And like Olympic athletes, we marshal every resource to aggressively seek and deliver creative, groundbreaking and powerful results for our most important audience, our customers.

The IOC may not have repeated the marketing innovation of 1924, when advertisements appeared in the stadium but, despite the purity of the stadium, the commercial message saturates the Olympics. At any Olympic park, the sponsors are prominent, foregrounding their services and products. As consumers, not just spectators and fans, the Olympic audiences and crowds are pushed into not just the rhetoric of the official sponsors and suppliers, but towards the consumption of those sponsors' goods and products. Corporations speak to potential consumers in their self-promotional rhetoric, and they want to be situated in the appropriate location to achieve their marketing goals. The IOC also recognises that the major sponsors want luxury for their money, such as the best hotels in the most desirable city locations, and the block bookings of seats for the most sought-after events.

CONCLUSION: COMMERCIALISM, COMMODITIES, AND THE GAMES

Unlike many other sporting events, such as Formula 1 motor racing or the football World Cup, the organisational leadership of the Olympics has sought to keep the commercial imagery of the event under some control. The Olympic Stadium is not permitted to have perimeter boards, and the IOC has traditionally used the word "clean" in its instructions and criteria for bidding cities. Cities must comply with this: for instance, "NYC 2012 recognizes the importance of clean venues to a successful Olympic Games. Accordingly, NYCOG will reach agreements with all venues to ensure that no commercial signage will appear, in accordance with Rule 61 of the Olympic Charter" (New York 2012, 2001, p.119). In the televised version, there appears to be a purity about the Olympic setting, and the five-ring logo has pride of place in the venues. But athletes, of course, wear clothes, and these carry logos; and in the milieu of the surrounding Olympic environment, the sponsors have a heavy presence. Olympic parks and the streets around venues are orgies of consumption, sites of commercial advertising and selling. It is a brilliant conjuring or marketing trick by which the IOC, in the post-1984 era of naked professionalism and blatant commercialism, has preserved a presentational gloss of idealism and universalism. The cities are in it for reconstruction and global positioning, chasing world-wide markets; the corporations are in it for global profile and unprecedented levels and scales of television exposure; the consumers are in it for a mixture of motives, some as sports enthusiasts or idealists, others for the party atmosphere or the feel of being close to something big. But, whatever the drive behind the commitment to the event of these different players, the commercialisation of the Olympics has turned it into a global commodity. The Olympics has a

fascinating claim to speak for international ideals, for the value of tran-
scending difference in friendly competition. But it is *as a commodity* that the
scale of the media and market penetration, and extraordinary longevity and
sustained profile of the phenomenon, must be understood.

There are different definitions of, and levels of thinking about, commodity. It initially referred to a quality or condition of things relating to the
"desires or needs of men", the quality of being commodious or convenient
(*Oxford English Dictionary*, 1971, p. 482). As economics and markets re-
constitute social and cultural boundaries and definitions of needs and desires, the notion of commodity can come to mean, as in everyday economic
life, simply a product in the marketplace, an item of purchase: "an article or
raw material that can be bought and sold, esp. a product as opposed to a
service" (*Oxford English Reference Dictionary*, 1996, p. 291). The modern
Olympics, generally, have always been commodified, in that entrance fees
were set and products were put on display (i.e., the events themselves). But
these were modest levels of circulation, based upon non-profit-making and
'break-even' budgets. To really grasp the escalating scale of the commercialisation and commodification of the Olympic Games entails a recognition
of the more complex nature of the commodity form as it is generated in
contemporary global sport(s).

And for this, there is another level on which the commodity can be con-
ceptualised, drawing upon critical analyses of the fundamental economic
dynamic of market capitalist societies as provided by Marx in *Capital*
(Marx, 1996), and as developed in Braverman's (1974) neo-Marxist exploration of the expansion of the market. For Marx, "the commodity appears,
at first sight, a very trivial thing, and easily understood. Its analysis shows
that it is, in reality, a very queer thing, abounding in metaphysical subtleties
and theological niceties (1996, p. 81)". But, as far as the commodity's "value
in use" is concerned, Marx sees "nothing religious about it..." (p. 81). Marx
takes the simple example of wood. We alter the meaning of wood by making
a table out of it, and without doubt the wood that makes up the table
"continues to be that common, everyday thing, wood" (p. 82). But it becomes something wholly different:

> ...so soon as it steps forth as a commodity, it is changed into something transcendent...
> The mystical character of commodities does not originate...in their use value...
> A commodity is therefore a mysterious thing...a definite social relation between
> men...assumes in their eyes, the fantastic form of a relation between things (pp. 82–83).

It is to the "mist-enveloped regions of the religious world" (p. 83) that
Marx then reverts to account for these features of the commodity form, and

to his famous formulation of the fetishism of commodities, talking of the "mystery, magic and necromancy" (p. 87) of the commodity form and relation. This evokes the notion of ritualistic worship, the commodity relation as adulation and not just equal exchange. Watching the sporting competition of the Olympic event is in this sense not just an exchange – money for a ticket for an event, or payment for the televisual means to watch the event – but a confirmation of the more mysterious meanings that the commodity exchange embodies. As wood becomes more than wood the minute that you walk into the furniture store, so physical performance transcends mere sporting competition as you enter the stadium or turn on your television set. As a table buyer, you buy in to the consumption meanings of the lifestyle programmers and marketing gurus; as a sport spectator, you affirm the meanings of the commodity prioritised by the event managers, sport ideologues and idealists and funding partners. This is where sponsorship is as far removed from philanthropy as it is possible to conceive or imagine. You enter the 'Olympic Park' and immediately are implicated in the fantastical relationship between you and the transcendent bought object – the sports experience. It is a particular experience that you are purchasing, a specific set of values that you are upholding: the remarkable blend of universal idealism and supranational corporatism that has sustained the ideological and economic infrastructure of the modern Summer Olympics.

Braverman (1974) has commented: "How capitalism transformed all of society into a gigantic marketplace is a process that has been little investigated, although it is one of the keys to all recent social history" (p. 271). Supra-national cultural phenomena such as the Olympics, driven by mixtures of political, economic, and social forces, have had their part to play in such a transformation. A certain genre of writing on the Olympics, a kind of topical reminiscence, reveals a simpler form of social and cultural product before the Olympics became such a global and mediated consumer-cultural product. Christopher Brasher (1964) could see the Games as "vast", but felt in touch with "the horde of journalists" flooding in from the 15 different venues, and could even claim to "see a tenth of what goes on" (pp. 41–42). A specialist political focus (Ali, 1976) could address the African issue in purely political and cultural terms. In this less-developed Olympic context and setting, perspectives could still be credibly produced as if the Olympics was a festival of individual human achievement (Benagh, 1976). And involved professionals could predict from their commentary box and diaries and memoirs that "the 'hard core' of the Olympics will never change" (Bateman, 1968, p. 70), centred as it was and remains on the track races and the marathon. But the escalation and commodification of the Games have transformed them first and foremost into a celebration of global consumerism alongside any persisting celebration of the triumph of the human spirit or the political system. 'Celebrate humanity' has been a message from the IOC in the early years of the century (Giardina & Metz, 2001), and it has referred in its web publicity to the 'priceless moments' such as when "the sweet smile of a 17-year-old Russian girl named Olga taught us that our differences weren't as great as they seemed". But, (former Olympic gymnast) Olga Korbut has to share the stage here with the *real* partners, as we are reminded that these moments are "made possible, in part, with the help of our World-wide Corporate Partners":

> Not only do these companies understand the importance of the Olympic Movement, but they have provided food, shelter, training facilities and more to the world's athletes. We thank them for their dedication and ask the world to return the favour by supporting the companies that advance the spirit of the Olympics (http://www.olympic.org/uk/news/media_centre/pressrelease, accessed 1/28/04).

Michael R. Payne, IOC Marketing Director since moving to the IOC from ISL in 1989, wrote here, after the Sydney Games, that "new and innovative programmes" by the sponsors had enhanced spectators' experiences and that "the marketing programmes were presented with a new focus on promoting and enhancing the Olympic spirit, in a commercially controlled, ambush-free environment". The sponsors, he suggested, had enhanced the experiences of the spectators themselves – a direct part of the Olympic experience, he claimed, writing as if the corporations had always been part of the so-called Olympic spirit. Make no mistake, the world-wide partners know the markets into which they want to reach, and what kind of consumerist universalism in what kind of city they want to promote. In this context, it is no small wonder that in the summer of 2005 only cities such as London, Madrid, Moscow, New York and Paris remained standing as Olympic contenders.

ACKNOWLEDGEMENTS

I am grateful to the editors of this book for their stoic patience in awaiting delivery of this chapter, and for their pithy and perspicacious comments in response to the initial draft: and to Paul Gilchrist, research assistant in the Chelsea School, University of Brighton, for generating the web sources/documents that form the basis of the central two sections of the chapter.

REFERENCES

Ali, R. (1976). *Africa at the Olympics.* London: Africa Books.

Barney, R. K., Wenn, S. R., & Martyn, S. G. (2002). *Selling the five rings: The International Olympic Committee and the rise of Olympic commercialism.* Salt Lake City: The University of Utah Press.

Bateman, R. (1968). *The book of the Olympic Games.* London: Stanley Paul.

Benagh, J. (1976). *Incredible Olympic feats.* New York: McGraw –Hill.

Brasher, C. (1964). *Tokyo 1964 – a diary of the xvIIIth Olympiad.* London: Stanley Paul.

Braverman, H. (1974). *Labour and monopoly capital – the degradation of work in the twentieth century.* New York and London: Monthly Review Press.

Brown, I. (1952). *The bedside 'Guardian' – A Selection by Ivor Brown from the 'Manchester Guardian' 1951–952.* London: Collins.

de Coubertin, P. (2000). *Pierre de Coubertin 1863–1937: Olympism, selected writings.* Editing director Norbert Müller, Lausanne: International Olympic Committee.

Giardina, M. D., & Metz, J. L. (2001). Celebrating humanity: Olympic marketing and the homogenization of multiculturalism. *International Journal of Sports Marketing & Sponsorship, 3*(2), 203–223.

Gruneau, R. (1984). Commercialism and the modern Olympics. In: A. Tomlinson & G. Whannel (Eds), *Five-ring circus – money, power and politics at the Olympic Games* (pp. 1–15). London: Pluto Press.

International Olympic Committee (IOC). (2000). *The Olympic Games – Fundamentals and ceremonies.* Lausanne: International Olympic Committee (For the Media).

Kennett, C., & Moragas, M. (2006). Barcelona and its legacy. In: A. Tomlinson & C. J. Young (Eds), *National identity and global sports events – Culture, politics and spectacle in the Olympics and the Football World Cup* (pp. 177–195). Albany, NY: State University of New York Press.

Marx, K. (1996). *Capital, Vol. I – Karl Marx/Frederick Engels collected works Volume 35.* London: Lawrence and Wishart.

New York 2012. (2001). *New York City 2012.* New York: New York Bid.

Oxford English Dictionary. (1971). *The compact edition of the Oxford English Dictionary – complete text reproduced micrographically* (Vol. 1 (A–O)). Oxford: Oxford University Press.

Oxford English Reference Dictionary. (1996). In: J. Pearsall & B. Trumble (Eds) *Oxford English Reference Dictionary* (2nd ed.). Oxford: Oxford University Press.

Perelman, R. B. (1985). *Olympic retrospective – The Games of Los Angeles.* Los Angeles: Los Angeles Olympic Organizing Committee.

Reich, K. (1986). *Making it Happen – Peter Ueberroth and the 1984 Olympics.* Santa Barbara, CA: Capra Press.

Roche, M. (2000). *Mega-events and modernity: Olympics and expos in the growth of global culture.* London: Routledge.

Simson, V., & Jennings, A. (1992). *The lords of the rings: Power, money and drugs in the modern Olympics.* London: Simon & Schuster.

Sugden, J., & Tomlinson, A. (1998). *FIFA and the contest for world football: Who rules the peoples' game?* Cambridge: Polity Press.

Tomlinson, A. (2004a). The making of the global sports economy: ISL, Adidas and the rise of the corporate player in world sport. In: M. Silk, D. Andrews & C. L. Cole (Eds), *Sport and corporate nationalisms* (pp. 35–65). Oxford: Berg.
Tomlinson, A. (2004b). The disneyfication of the Olympics? Theme parks, and freak shows of the body'. In: J. Bale & M. K. Christensen (Eds), *Post-Olympism? Questioning sport in the twenty-first century* (pp. 147–163). Oxford: Berg.
Ueberroth, P., (with Levin, R., and Quinn, A.). (1985). *Made in America – His own story.* New York: William Morrow and Company, Inc.
Wallechinsky, D. (2000). *The complete book of the Olympics.* London: Aurum Press.

Olympic Bidding City Websites consulted, accessed on 13 January 2004 unless otherwise noted [cited in section on cities, see p. 188].

Olympist – The Meeting of Continents, Istanbul 2012 Applicant City.
Leipzig 2012 Newsletter, Issue 12/2003.
London 2012 – A vision for the Olympic Games and Paralympic Games.
http://www.madrid2012.es/Modelo05.asp?CodPag=Patrocinadores, accessed on 30/01/2004.
Moscow 2012 official website.
NYC 2012 – La Candidature de New York pour les Jeux Olympiques – New York City Olympic Bid.
http://www.parisjo2012.fr/eng/index.html, accessed on 30/01/2004.
http://www.rio2012.org.br/ingles/index.html, accessed on 30/01/2004.

Olympic Sponsor Websites consulted [cited in section on corporations, see p. 192].

http://www2.coca–cola.com/citizenship/olympics.html, accessed 1/30/04
http://www.jhancock.com/company/sponsor/olympics.html, accessed 1/29/04
http://www.olympic.org/uk/games/slc2002/kodak/index_uk.asp, accessed 1/28/04
http://www.mcdonalds.com/usa/sports/olympic/sponsor.html, accessed 1/30/04
http://www.panasonic.co.jp/global/top.html, accessed 1/29/04
http://www.samsung.com/About SAMSUNG/SportsSponsorship/index.htm, accessed 1/28/04
http://www.sema.com/olympics/index.htm, accessed 1/28/04
http://www.sportsillustrated.cnn.com/2004/olympics/01/07/2004.index, accessed 1/29/04
http://www.viseu.com/iusevisa/olympics.html, accessed 1/28/04
http://www.ebusiness.xerox.com/olympics, accessed 1/29/04

Chapter 11

LOBBYING ORGIES: OLYMPIC CITY BIDS IN THE POST-LOS ANGELES ERA

Douglas Booth

> Volunteers [from the Georgia Amateur Athletic Foundation] were told that lobbying for
> the votes of IOC members was intensely competitive and that each member should be
> approached on a targeted basis. We believe the GAAF volunteers converted that advice
> into an aggressive strategy to market Atlanta to members one by one and do anything
> within reasonable bounds to cultivate winning relationships.
> (Report to the United States Congress on Atlanta's bid for the 1996 olympic games[1];
> Bell, 1999, p. 5.)

Late in 1998, allegations that members of the International Olympic Com-
mittee (IOC) had accepted bribes from cities aspiring to host olympic games
fuelled a major scandal. The IOC, the United States Olympic Committee
(USOC), the Salt Lake City Organising Committee for the Olympic Games
(SLOCOG), the United States Justice Department, the United States House
of Representatives, and the Sydney Organising Committee for the Olympic
Games all conducted inquiries (Barney, Wenn, & Martyn, 2002, pp. 267–268;
IOC, 1999a, b; Martyn, 2003; Mitchell, 1999; Sheridan, 1999; SLOCOG
Board of Ethics, 1999). However, by trying to pinpoint the wrongdoings of
individual IOC members and the principals of candidate cities, the inquiries
ignored the context and roots of the corruption. In the decade after the Los
Angeles games of 1984, during which time the IOC awarded the summer
olympics of 1992, 1996, and 2000, and the winter games of 1992, 1994, 1998,
and 2002 (Table 1), a coterie of ambitious and self-serving senior members,

Global Olympics: Historical and Sociological Studies of the Modern Games
Research in the Sociology of Sport, Volume 3, 201–225
Copyright © 2005 by Elsevier Ltd.

Table 1. Summer and Winter Olympic Cities: Candidates and Hosts, 1976–2012.

Awarded	Games	Candidates	Host
1970	1976 (S)	Los Angeles, Montreal, Moscow	Montreal
	1976 (W)	Denver, Innsbruck, Sion, Tampere/Are, Vancouver	Innsbruck
1974	1980 (S)	Los Angeles, Moscow	Moscow
	1980 (W)	Chamonix-Mont Blanc,[a] Lake Placid, Vancouver-Garibaldi[a,b]	Lake Placid
1978	1984 (S)	Los Angeles, Tehran[a]	Los Angeles
	1984 (W)	Falun/Göteburg, Sapporo, Sarajevo	Sarajevo
1982	1988 (S)	Nagoya, Seoul	Seoul
	1988 (W)	Calgary, Falun, Cortina d'Ampezzo	Calgary
1986	1992 (S)	Amsterdam, Barcelona, Birmingham, Brisbane, Paris	Barcelona
	1992 (W)	Albertville, Anchorage, Berchtesgaden, Cortina D'Ampezzo, Falun, Lillehammer, Sofia	Albertville
1988	1994 (W)	Anchorage, Lillehammer, Östersund/Are, Sofia	Lillehammer
1989	1996 (S)	Athens, Atlanta, Belgrade, Manchester, Melbourne, Toronto	Atlanta
1991	1998 (W)	Aoste, Jaca, Nagano, Östersund, Salt Lake City	Nagano
1993	2000 (S)	Beijing, Berlin, Brasilia,[a] Istanbul, Manchester, Milan,[a] Sydney, Tashkent[a]	Sydney
1995	2002 (W)	Östersund, Quebec, Salt Lake City, Sion	Salt Lake City
1997[c]	2004 (S)	Athens (f), Buenos Aires (f), Cape Town (f), Istanbul, Lille, Rio de Janiero, Rome (f), San Juan, Seville, Stockholm (f), St Petersburg	Athens
1999	2006 (W)	Heksinki, Klagenfurt, Poprad-Tatry, Sion, Torino, Zakopane	Torino
2001	2008 (S)	Bangkok, Beijing (f), Cairo, Havana, Istanbul (f), Kuala Lumpur, Osaka (f), Paris (f), Seville, Toronto (f)	Beijing
2003[c]	2010 (W)	Andorra la Vella, Bern,[a] Harbin, Jace, Pyeong Chang (f), Salzburg (f), Sarajevo, Vancouver (f)	Vancouver
2005	2012 (S)	Havana, Istanbul, Leipzig, London (f), Madrid (f), Moscow (f), New York (f), Paris (f), Rio de Janeiro	London

Sources: IOC website www.ioc.org and personal correspondence with Wayne Wilson (Amateur Athletic Foundation of Los Angeles).
[a]Withdrew before final vote.
[b]The Lake Placid Official Report also lists Banff, Oslo, and Garmisch-Partenkirchen as early withdrawals.
[c]From 1997 (S) and 2003 (W) the IOC adopted a two-phase selection process. In the first phase, the Evaluations Commission assesses and reports on all bidding cities and a Selection College subsequently selects finalists (f). In the second phase, IOC members visit finalists and then vote.

under the tutelage of President Juan Antonio Samaranch, disingenuously orchestrated 'orgies' of lobbying among candidate cities. Their objectives were to raise the IOC's international standing as well as enhance their personal political power and influence. Lamely claiming that the IOC awarded the games solely on the basis of technical information forwarded by candidate cities, and wilfully failing to regulate or police the bidding process, this group cultivated an environment in which potential hosts mobilised scores of volunteers, professionals, local business interests, and government leaders to flatter, indulge, and pamper IOC members with ceremonies, titles, honorary degrees, private audiences with royals and heads of state, soirees, and gifts. The lobbying orgies bestowed new status on the 90-odd members of the IOC, transforming many former invisible, nondescript, and inconsequential sports administrators into international dignitaries, luminaries, and power brokers; some members exploited their newfound positions to prey on candidate cities and improve their personal lots as well as those of their families.

This chapter contains two substantive sections. The first examines the Los Angeles games of 1984 as a turning point that predisposed lobbying orgies. The second section dissects the lobbying orgies themselves. It looks at the relationships between the principal members of candidate-city bidding teams and the IOC in three phases. In the *preparatory phase*, principals compiled information on IOC members and ingratiated themselves with the olympic family; in the *influence phase*, they deployed various forms of power to win IOC members' votes; in the *final phase*, they responded to winning, or in most cases failing to win, hosting rights. The second section also analyses the reactions of IOC members in each phase of the lobbying orgies. The post-Los Angeles era was a unique historical conjuncture in olympic history, but the IOC's abrogation of its ethical responsibilities in this period has many precedents which collectively lead to damning conclusions about the structure, ideology, and composition of the Committee.

Analysts have long attributed the IOC's choice of olympic host cities to raw politics. Much of the support for Beijing's bid to host the 2000 games, for example, was said to derive from IOC members who saw the Chinese as their ideological representatives, or who wanted to repay long-standing military and economic aid (Gordon, 1994, p. 430). Similarly, Birmingham's poor showing in the race for the 1992 games has been attributed to a loathing of British Prime Minister Margaret Thatcher. An advocate for the unpopular boycott of the Moscow games in 1980, Thatcher refused to support the widely sanctioned boycott of apartheid South Africa, thus precipitating a 32-nation boycott of the 1986 Commonwealth Games in Edinburgh (Dheensaw, 1994, pp. 155–160); in addition, Thatcher allegedly drew the IOC's ire for allowing the Americans to launch bombing raids on Libya from British bases (Hill, 1996, p. 98). Although highly plausible, these accounts, and many like them (e.g., Guttmann, 1992, p. 141; Hill, 1993, pp. 92, 168–169), rest on pure conjecture and speculation. Secret ballots make it virtually impossible to know which cities IOC members vote for and why. As Rod McGeoch, CEO of Sydney's team that won the right to host the 2000 games, warned, "nobody, but nobody, really knows" how members vote. McGeoch learned this lesson early in his tenure when he asked two experienced lobbyists if sub-Sahara Africa voted as a bloc. "Absolutely not", replied the first, adding that "they're all over the place". "Absolutely they do", replied the second (McGeoch, 1994, p. 83). Moreover, members' own accounts of how they voted are notoriously unreliable "since there is a natural propensity to claim afterwards to have voted for the winner" (Hill, 1996, p. 93).

My approach examines the selection of olympic hosts in the post-Los Angeles era as a set of complex interactions between members of the IOC and the principals of candidate cities; political conditions and relationships *and* individual motives and psychological predilections drive these relations. Unlike traditional political studies that largely infer the goals and ambitions of individual members from the IOC's collective interests, this approach looks more closely at the psychological basis of interaction on its own terms. A large body of work conceptualises the IOC as a loose alliance of right-wing and conservative interests whose assorted doctrinal, fraternal, and ideological goals extend far beyond the realm of overseeing an international sports festival (e.g., Guttmann, 1984; Hoberman, 1995; Jennings, 1996, 2000; MacAloon, 1981; Simson & Jennings, 1992). Sugden and Tomlinson's (2003, p. 178) description of the Fédération Internationale de Football Association's 'inner circle' as a hierarchy "steeped in oligarchic and corporate patronage" that "border[s] on... 'oriental despotism'", applies equally to the IOC executive.[2] But it is also critical to look closer at individual rank-and-file members of the IOC, some of whom are fiercely independent. Indeed, the post-Los Angeles era afforded members great latitude in which to forge relationships with candidate cities and these were far more complex than might be inferred from institutional relationships. Journalist Kirk Johnson illustrates this in an evocative description of the relationship that bound Jean-Claude Ganga, the IOC member in Congo, and Tom Welch, a Salt Lake City principal. The two men, Johnson said, "circled one another, sometimes like adversaries or hagglers, sometimes like friends":

> In one letter to Mr. Welch from his home in Brazzaville... Mr. Ganga wrote of the war that was tearing his country apart...and [he] asked that Mr. Welch try to pressure the United States government into a formal condemnation of the killings. [In] another

exchange of letters... Mr. Ganga complained that he couldn't afford to fly to Montreal to attend a wedding, and then after a $4,700 check was sent, wrote back with effusive thanks: "as the saying goes, a friend in need is a friend indeed" (Johnson, 1999).

Interpreting such relationships, particularly those between culturally diverse individuals, requires both a model and careful analysis of the evidence.

The interpretation presented here loosely follows an interactive model of power and influence developed by (Bertram Raven 1992; see also Raven, 1990; Hermann, 1986) and grounded in political psychology. The evidence is more problematic. Much of it comes from active participants and is biased by their perspectives and, in the case of IOC members, mediated by official channels managed by international public relations firms, lawyers, and marketing experts (Martyn, 2003). Other evidence comes from inquiries and newspaper investigations into the 1998–1999 bribery allegations. These are incomplete by virtue of focusing on only a few IOC members and a handful of candidate-city principals, and by their failure to chronicle all of their interactions and the nuances of those interactions. Newspaper accounts insinuated widespread corruption in the IOC, although the different inquiries found that no more than a dozen members had accepted bribes. On the other hand, it is clear that most members welcomed and were receptive to advances from candidate cities. McGeoch identified only "about eight" members, mostly bankers and members of royal families who, in his revealing words, Sydney could not "penetrate" (1994, p. 175); dossiers prepared by Berlin's committee bidding for the 2000 games classified just seven IOC members as "honest" (McGeoch, 1994, p. 160).

THE POST-LOS ANGELES ENVIRONMENT

The appeal of hosting the olympics waxed and waned over the twentieth century. Interest in hosting steadily built from early in the century with two cities bidding for the 1904 games, three for 1908, four for the cancelled games of 1916, and six for 1924. Interest declined in the 1930s and 1940s, when the IOC aligned itself with fascism, but it returned after World War II with seven and nine cities bidding for the 1952 and 1956 games, respectively. In the 1970s, excessive costs and threats of boycotts put a brake on hosting. But, as Table 1 shows, interest resumed after the 1984 games. Specific factors precipitated this fresh interest, in particular the lure of profit and anti-boycott initiatives. In turn, the IOC manipulated competition among aspirant hosts, and individuals, both within the IOC and candidate cities,

exploited the new environment for personal gain. Out of this mix of circumstance and calculation emerged 'lobbying orgies.'

Profits

Cities have always viewed hosting the olympics as a means to convey positive
international images of themselves and nationalist ideologies. Atlanta, for
example, used the 1996 games to advertise itself as a genuine international
city in the south of the United States (Bell, 1999). In the 1970s, interest in
hosting diminished under two conditions: escalating costs and political boycotts. When the Montreal games in 1976 concluded with an estimated debt
of over C$1 billion (Senn, 1999, p. 164), cities not surprisingly baulked at
hosting (see Table 1). Lord Killanin (Sir Michael Morris), then IOC president, identified the issue when he said that Montreal's financial problems
"undoubtedly frightened potential hosts, who believed that it was no longer
possible to stage the Games at a reasonable cost" (Senn, 1999, p. 172).
   Political boycotts and threats of boycotts compounded the cost factor.
African nations threatened to boycott the 1968 games and African-Americans
threatened the 1968 and 1972 games. The former made good with their
threats at Montreal and, in 1980 and 1984, the United States and its allies and
the Soviet Union and its allies engaged in 'tit-for-tat' boycotts of the Moscow
and Los Angeles games respectively (Guttmann, 1992, pp. 141–159).
   Eight years after Montreal, the Los Angeles games recorded a surplus of
US$232.5 million and alerted cities to the olympics as a potential vehicle for
economic gain as well as a source of prestige (Roche, 2000, p. 152; Preuss,
2000). Salt Lake City, for example, pursued the games as "part of a broad
economic development plan to build a winter tourism industry" that would,
in the words of a former mayor, "jump-start the economy and help bring
jobs and investment" (Johnson, 1999, p. A22). The lure of profit did not
entirely alleviate fears of political boycotts felt by prospective host cities and
commercial sponsors. Although Los Angeles made a profit, with the Soviet
Union and 16 of its allies absent, eradicating boycotts from the political
landscape of the olympics was a priority for the IOC.

Anti-Boycott Initiatives

In 1984 Horst Dassler, President of the transnational sporting goods manufacturer Adidas, implored Samaranch to penalise countries boycotting

future games (Lawrence, 1986, p. 210). While the IOC shied from punishing boycotting nations, it went to extraordinary lengths to coax countries to Seoul (Hill, 1996, pp. 170–173) and Barcelona. One hundred and sixty of the 167 eligible national olympic committees sent teams to Seoul (Albania, Cuba, Ethiopia, Nicaragua, North Korea, and Seychelles boycotted, and apartheid South Africa was banned), and every eligible national olympic committee heeded the IOC's clarion call to Barcelona. The IOC arranged South Africa's (premature) re-admission into the olympic movement in time for the 1992 games (Booth, 1998, pp. 189–191) and even flew in Yugoslav athletes to participate as 'independent olympians' in contravention of United Nations sanctions against the country imposed for military aggression against Croatia and Bosnia-Herzegovina. The financial viability of the olympics was not the IOC's only concern; boycotts damaged the Committee's political credibility, scarred its philosophy of olympism, and undermined the political ambitions of its leader.

Thus, 1984 marked a return to competitive bidding for hosting rights, and a shift in the balance of political power to the IOC. As the sole bidder for the 1984 games, Los Angeles, led by Peter Ueberroth, had proven 'truculent' on a number of issues, most notably with respect to the disbursement of television income; the city unilaterally declared that it would retain the entire proceeds and remit only a portion to the IOC as an act of grace (Hill, 1996, p. 140).[3] Although outraged, in an environment of limited interest in hosting, the IOC had few options for appointing alternative cities. But in an era of heightened interest, the IOC exerted substantially more pressure on both hosts and aspirant host cities, and transformed the way cities conducted their bidding.

The Olympic Family

Hill (1996, p. 189) identifies Barcelona's successful campaign for the 1992 games, conducted between 1984 and 1986, as the template for subsequent lobbying.[4] Acting upon advice from IOC president Samaranch, himself from Barcelona and a one-time city councillor there, the bidding committee invited scores of IOC members to visit the city, ostensibly to observe facilities and preparations. Upon arrival, IOC members were showered with deference, gifts, and attention from the Spanish head of state. Samaranch's immediate objective was a Barcelona games – by publicly shying from open support, Samaranch attempted to preserve the neutrality of his office although he admitted that his heart rested with the Spanish seaport (Hill, 1996, pp. 187–188).

But the haughty president also wanted to catapult into public view the political profile and international standing of his Committee, and how better than by enticing the leaders of the world's largest cities to publicly fawn over IOC members?

After the 1984 games, the IOC emphasised candidate cities cultivating personal relationships with individual IOC members. Salt Lake City principal, Tom Welch, recalls Samaranch advising him to "become personally acquainted with as many IOC members as possible and to become part of the 'Olympic Family'" (SLOCOG Board of Ethics, 1999, p. 10). In the post-Los Angeles era, the term 'olympic family' assumed significance far greater than as a synonym for the members of the olympic movement (i.e., the IOC and its staff, the international federations, and the national olympic committees) which it tended to replace. The family metaphor carried connotations of total dedication to, support for, and trust in, the IOC; it was critical to the escalation of lobbying orgies by changing the way candidate cities perceived and interacted with IOC members.

Long-established rules for interacting with IOC members left candidate cities in no doubt as to which party was dominant. For example, on one visit to Los Angeles, Monique Berlioux, the IOC's Executive Director, insisted:

> that a swimming pool was available, that Evian water was supplied, that there were exquisite flower arrangements, that the room service met her French tastes, that restaurant arrangements were made for the finest eateries, that appointments were not scheduled either early in the morning or late at night, and that her travelling staff received equally impeccable treatment (Peter Ueberroth cited in Hill, 1996, p. 141).

IOC members quickly schooled errant lobbyists in official protocol. Walker Wallace, a lobbyist for a Salt Lake City olympic bid in the 1960s, still remembers the reaction when he put his arm around one IOC member at a cocktail reception and proceeded to talk about the virtues of Wasatch Mountain powder snow. The conversation ended abruptly with a rebuke: "remove your arm from my shoulder" (Johnson, 1999, p. A22). Similarly, Hill (1996, p. 97) observes that the "homespun genuineness" of several Birmingham lobbyists "jarred" on those members "unaccustomed to such cheerfully informal invitations as 'brothers, come and sit down'".

By advising candidate cities to join the olympic family, the IOC compelled bidding cities to "travel to international meetings attended by IOC members, meet with representatives from other cities that had hosted the Olympics, visit IOC members in their own countries, and invite IOC members [to their homes]" (SLOCOG Board of Ethics, 1999, p. 10). And "it quickly became clear that being part of the 'Olympic family' put strong demands on this hospitality, as some IOC members expected to be treated on a lavish scale that included first-class airfare, the finest hotels, meals, gifts, and entertainment, all provided at the bid city's expense" (SLOCOG Board of Ethics, 1999, p. 10; see also Williams, 1999). Welch first met the olympic family in 1989 when he arrived with his Salt Lake City team at an IOC meeting in Puerto Rico to find that:

> ...the Greeks were entertaining on their yacht, with gorgeous hostesses. Atlanta had rented a mansion, shipped in furniture...and called it Atlanta House. Toronto had set up a whole wing out by the pool and was serving breakfasts, lunches and dinners to the IOC. Everyone was giving wonderful gifts – I think there were crystal vases and jewellery. Bid cities each had limousines. We showed up with nothing – on a bus (Johnson, 1999, p. A22).

The competitive nature of lobbying obliged candidates not only to follow suit but also to upstage their rivals with more luxurious gifts and bigger parties at more exotic locations. When the IOC met in Birmingham to select the 1998 winter games host, Salt Lake City put a disposable camera in the 'welcome packages' that it gave to each member; Nagano presented each member with a video camera (SLOCOG Board of Ethics, 1999, p. 11).

Pandering to IOC members was the perfect recipe for lobbying orgies. Analysing its defeat by Nagano for the 1998 olympics, Salt Lake City bidders decided to "focus on winning the 'hearts' of... IOC members by developing personal friendships with them and their families" (SLOCOG Board of Ethics, 1999, p. 12). The bid committee thus reorganised itself and set out to establish and maintain "long term, vote influencing relationships with IOC members" and "other key people of the Olympic Family", that is, "those who could influence an IOC member's vote" (SLOCOG Board of Ethics, 1999, pp. 12–13). Salt Lake City's strategy was not unique. Atlanta and Sydney strategists also pursued long-term relationships with individual IOC members under the lobbying slogans 'let's be friends'.

Personal Ambitions

The IOC and candidate cities are agents with their own goals and decision-making abilities. But they also comprise individuals with divergent interests and ambitions that warrant appropriate consideration before one develops a complete picture of the lobbying orgies. The post-Los Angeles environment generated enormous opportunities for individuals to pursue personal ambitions and agendas; their actions and behaviours directly and indirectly fuelled the lobbying orgies. Samaranch, for example, constantly pressed candidate cities to arrange meetings between him and heads of government and state (e.g., Hill, 1996, p. 144). And candidate cities usually obliged, eager to caress the overweening ego of a sports administrator who sought the status of a world political leader (e.g., Jennings, 1996, pp. 250–263).

The vanguards of bidding committees typically comprise non-sporting interests from the transport, construction, hotel and tourist industries, the financial and public sectors, and the commercial media (Booth & Tatz, 1994, p. 8; SLOCOG Board of Ethics, 1999, p. 13). While profit clearly motivates these individuals, analysts must be wary of simply reading their behaviour from their economic positions. For example, John Coates, the President of the Australian Olympic Committee (AOC) and key strategist for the Brisbane, Melbourne, and Sydney bids, saw hosting as a means to financially secure olympic sport in Australia against the funding whims of federal governments. "You don't ever have political independence, true independence, unless you are financially secure", Coates once warned, referring to government pressure exerted on Australian athletes to boycott the 1980 Moscow games (Crombie, 1996, p. 41). After Sydney won the 2000 games, Coates established a special Sports Commission within the Sydney Organising Committee for the Olympic Games – of which he was a senior vice-president – as a vehicle to control all policies pertaining to hosting the games. Under the terms of its contract with the IOC, the AOC would have received 90 per cent of the profits from the 2000 games. Of course, there was no guarantee that Sydney would return a profit, which Coates knew only too well. The Sports Commission thus sold the AOC's profit rights to an extraordinarily gullible New South Wales government for Aus$100 million, to be paid from the government's share of television rights (Crombie, 1999, pp. 85–87). And like Robert Helmick, President of the USOC and an IOC member from 1985 to 1991, who accepted "hundreds of thousands of dollars in consultancy fees from companies wanting to do business with the Olympic movement" (Jennings, 1996, p. 76),[5] Coates had no qualms about using his position for self-enrichment. Chris Davidson, a director of the Melbourne bid, recalls his outrage at the fees Coates charged for advice: "I was disappointed when someone so entrenched in the Olympic movement and supposed to be imbued with the Olympic spirit would even consider charging us for a very valid bid to get the Olympic games" (Crombie, 1996, p. 42; 1999, p. 89). Coates' largesse to IOC members embodied the lobbying orgies.

Thus a unique juxtaposition of circumstances, conditions, and personalities combined after the Los Angeles games to predispose lobbying orgies. And, once in train, they escalated into an unstoppable process.

THE LOBBYING ORGIES: A DISSECTION

Unprecedented levels of preparations by candidate cities, the deployment of new forms of power, and continual assessments and reassessments of strategy, interactions, and relationships, especially after the IOC selected host cities, characterised the lobbying orgies. The following section analyses each of these three phases in turn.

Preparations

No city has ever won the right to host an olympic games without exhaustive preparations. But, in the context of joining the olympic family and establishing personal relationships with IOC members, preparations assumed an entirely new meaning. Acquiring personal information about IOC members was essential in the post-Los Angeles era and, to this end, candidate cities compiled dossiers describing IOC members' personal characteristics, foibles, likes, dislikes, preferences, indifferences, interests, and concerns. Gathering such information was a smart move by lobbyists who were vulnerable to committing *faux pas* or unknowingly offending or humiliating IOC members (McGeoch, 1994, pp. 160–161, 248–249).

Information contained in dossiers was largely innocuous, trivial, and mundane. Dossiers prepared by one key Sydney strategist, Phil Coles – who, ironically, was a member of the IOC – and his partner Patricia Rosenbrock (Rosenbrock, 1999; see also *Sydney Morning Herald*, 1999b), reported, for example, that Anton Geesink (Netherlands) "loves…the opportunity for group 'sing-a-longs'", that Thomas Bach (Germany) is a "tennis nut", and that Hamzah Bin Haji Abu Samah (Malaysia) and Nat Indrapana (Thailand) both liked "*very* hot chilli" with their food. But, in the quest for competitive advantages over their rivals, candidates probed deeper into the preferences of IOC members. Berlin even investigated their sexual preferences (*Financial Review*, 1992). Rosenbrock (1999) alerted Sydney's campaigners to several dubious characters: René Essomba (Cameroon) is "quite devious" and should not be relied on "at all", Lamine Kieta (Malawi) is "more than prepared to take advantage of any expense allowance" and is "not to be trusted", and Mario Vázquez Raña (Mexico) is "interested only in his own benefits and power". However, her reports were far from all negative. She described Fernando Bello (Portugal), Fidel Mendoza Carrasquilla (Colombia), Vladimir Cernusak (Czechoslovakia), Carlos Ferrer (Spain), Carol Ann Letheren (Canada), and Anani Matthia (Togo) as either "honest" or "very honest", while Major General Henry Adefope (Nigeria) was viewed as "a *gentleman* of his word".

IOC members knew only too well that attempts by candidate cities to befriend them were, first and foremost, political strategies. Not surprisingly, then, they also prepared themselves for advances. A handful, including Syed Wajid Ali (Pakistan) and Faisal Fahd Abdul Aziz (Saudi Arabia), refused to meet candidate-city lobbyists as McGeoch (1994, p. 236) discovered on a visit to Riyadh. Others, however, welcomed advances and some manipulated lobbying. Samaranch was the master manipulator. He kept candidates "panting by letting them believe they were in with a chance" (Jennings, 1996, pp. 200–201). In the race for the 2000 games, he assured Brasilia that it was "splendidly prepared" to host the games. The IOC's Evaluations Commission – which assesses each candidate's technical capacity to host[6] – thought otherwise, reporting that the city lacked adequate facilities and popular support. It recommended Brasilia withdraw (Jennings, 1996, pp. 200–201, 290; McGeoch, 1994, p. 264). During his first official visit to Sydney, Samaranch agreed with questioners that the city was "one of the favourites" but he quickly added that it must "fight to the last minute" (McGeoch, 1994, p. 253).

Another group opportunistically turned advances from candidate cities into lifestyles. Phil Coles visited Salt Lake City four times and accepted hospitality worth more than Aus$60,000. Twice he took Rosenbrock and her two children; they stayed at expensive hotels and enjoyed a recreational programme that included a Super Bowl game in Miami, a National Basketball Association All-Star game, and skiing at an exclusive Utah resort. His Salt Lake City hosts paid for everything (IOC, 1999b, pp. 19–23). "We had an absolutely fabulous time and loved every minute of it", Coles wrote in a thank you letter to one host. "Who could ask for more – warm and friendly people, wonderful hospitality, basketball, skiing, snowmobiling! It was just the greatest fun. One complaint, however, your food is too good and we ate too much" (*Sydney Morning Herald*, 1999a; SLOCOG Board of Ethics, 1999, p. 29). Raven (1992, pp. 225–226) draws a distinction between an agent's preparation of a target before attempting to influence them, and the actual application of power as a means of influence. However, many interactions, such as that between Phil Coles and Salt Lake City, blur this distinction.

Power-Exerting Influence

In the post-Los Angeles era, candidate cities employed four principal forms of power to influence IOC members: information, referent, third party, and reward. Technical information is a non-negotiable form of power: the IOC demands that aspirant hosts demonstrate their technical ability to organise a successful olympics. Bid books are critical tools here. They contain exhaustive details of how candidates plan to conduct the games. Sydney's bid books, which McGeoch called the city's "most important sales document", comprised three volumes, ran to 510 pages, and addressed 23 themes (McGeoch, 1994, pp. 132–134, 191–192, 206). Sydney also seconded experts to give special presentations concerning the cultural programme, environment, industrial relations, health, and security to visiting commissioners. For example, Michael Easson from the New South Wales Labour Council gave assurances that the trade union movement would not disrupt the games (McGeoch, 1994, pp. 206–208).

Candidate cities traditionally relied heavily on information power to win IOC members' votes. The advantage of information as a form of power is that it reduces distrust and engenders cooperation by allowing members the opportunity to consider their positions in private. Indeed, olympic protocol reinforces notions of collaboration and assistance by prohibiting candidates from publicly criticising rivals. McGeoch (1994, p. 220) summed up this cast iron rule when he noted that "comparative advertising – in any of its forms – [is] just not on". Candidates must "subtly point out [their] own strengths and leave it to others to conclude how well you shape up compared to your rivals".

While information receded as the critical form of power in the post-Los Angeles environment, no candidate violated protocol by commenting on the weaknesses of their rivals. Even the relatively outspoken Manchester principal, Bob Scott, agreed that the Greeks "had a moral right" to host the 1996 'centennial games' and refused to publicly discuss Athens' susceptibility to political instability and environmental pollution, or Greek competence.[7] If the IOC decided against Athens, then Manchester was the best of the rest, was as much as Scott proffered (Hill, 1996, p. 103). Protocol, however, did not stop candidate-city principals from plotting and scheming. McGeoch initiated plans for a secret public relations campaign against Beijing, to be conducted from London. The campaign included funding for a human rights group to publicly criticise China and to publish a book on state abuses just before the IOC voted for the 2000 host. But other Sydney principals intervened and terminated McGeoch's plans for fear that public knowledge would "destroy" the city's prospects (McGeoch, 1994, pp. 227–228, 232–233).

Evaluations commissioners continued to closely assess all claims made in bid books in the post Los-Angeles era. McGeoch recalls that on the trip from the city to Sydney Olympic Park, one commissioner timed the journey that the bid books said took 24 mins. On this particular occasion the trip took 22 mins (McGeoch, 1994, p. 208). Yet, for all of the effort and money cities invested in their bid books (Sydney spent Aus$600,000, Melbourne Aus$1million) and in their ritual-laden deliveries (two senior officials personally delivered Sydney's books to the IOC in Lausanne), the technical aspects of bids did not win votes, although they could lose them (Hill, 1996, p. 101; Bell, 1999, p. 4). Sydney, for example, earned the Evaluation Commission's highest plaudits; yet, it only defeated Beijing, which received a less than favourable technical assessment, by the narrowest of margins.

As well as demanding that candidates demonstrate their technical ability to host a successful olympics, the IOC insists that it make obvious its commitment to the games and to olympism. However, the amorphous qualities of the olympics and its philosophy afford candidate cities enormous latitude in this area. Cities seize anything that might bestow credibility on them. In his speech to mark Samaranch's visit to Sydney in 1993, Coates asserted that only Australia and Greece belonged to that supposedly prestigious club whose members had sent teams to every modern games (Gordon, 1994, pp. xxv–xxvi).[8] Similarly, the woolly concept of 'olympism' – which the olympic charter defines as a "philosophy of life...based on the joy found in effort, the educational value of a good example and respect for universal fundamental ethical principles" (IOC, 2003, p. 9) – affords candidate cities any number of opportunities to express their "commitment". In the race for 2000, Manchester and Sydney showed 'commitment' by vowing to privilege athletes and place them at the centre of the pageant (McGeoch, 1994, p. 301), while Beijing – much to the chagrin of its rivals – proposed to propagate olympism by showcasing China's political reforms and thus highlighting the olympics as a "weapon of peace" (Jennings, 1996, pp. 207–208).

During the lobbying orgies, ideological commitments to olympism by candidate cities took second place behind building friendships within the olympic family. Such friendships are a classic example of referent power, the forging of a common "identity or sense of one-ness" (Raven, 1990, p. 503; Raven, 1992, p. 221), and were embodied in visits and gift exchanges. Candidate cities lost no opportunity to meet with IOC members whether at official venues such as IOC congresses, meetings of international federations or world games, or socially in either their or members' countries. Salt Lake City and Sydney assigned key personnel responsibility for meeting IOC members in different corners of the world. Tom Welch covered Africa, David Johnson Europe, and Frank Richards South America for Salt Lake City (SLOCOG Board of Ethics, 1999, pp. 13–14). The Sydney bid committee sent Coles and Rosenbrock to Paris for several months in 1993, during which time they met and hosted some 40 European IOC members. Both cities also engaged professional lobbyists. Sydney paid Gabor Komyathy Aus$180,000 and Mahmoud el-Farnawani Aus$200,000 to lobby IOC members in Eastern Europe, and North Africa and the Middle East respectively (Sheridan, 1999, p. 35); Salt Lake City paid el-Farnawani US$148,260 and Muttaleb Ahmad, Director General of the Olympic Council of Asia, US$62,400 (SLOCOG Board of Ethics, 1999, pp. 22–23). Sydney hosted the General Assembly of International Summer Sport Federations congress in 1991 that attracted five IOC members (Jobling, 2000, p. 267); Manchester hosted an astonishing 14 meetings of international federations during its campaign for the 2000 games (Hill, 1996, p. 111).

The object of bringing IOC members to candidate cities was to show them the local sights and introduce them to local hospitality. In its campaign for the 1998 winter games, Östersund brought 72 IOC members to the city (Jennings, 1996, p. 163); Sydney flew 65 willing IOC members – some were too ill or infirm to travel, some simply disliked travelling and others were too busy (Rosenbock, 1999) – to Australia by 'first class'. They were cleared through customs before the plane 'docked' and transported by limousine to five star accommodation; they dined at the best restaurants, were entertained at the Opera House, and invited to structure their own itineraries (Crosswhite, 1993; Hill, 1996, pp. 102–104).

Gifts, like visits, lubricated the wheels of friendship. It is important to note the ambiguities of gift exchanges within the olympic family (Booth, 1999) and that most gifts were harmless (and usually hideous) mementos such as banners and commemorative medals (Hill, 1996, p. 65). They were intended to simply keep the name of the candidate city at the fore of IOC members' thoughts. As the orgies escalated, however, principals put considerable thought into gifts that became highly personal. After discovering that Flor Isava-Fonseca (Venezuela) liked to read, Sydney invited author Bryce Courtenay to a dinner it held in her honour. Courtenay autographed a copy of his book, *The Power of One*, and "it made an enormous impact" (McGeoch, 1994, p. 202). Some cities gave expensive personal gifts; Salt Lake City presented Samaranch with a limited edition Browning pistol valued at US$9,000 (SLOCOG Board of Ethics, 1999, p. 30). But it is highly unlikely that even a gift of this value would actually secure his vote. Compared to the lavish entertainment and gifts that the Nagano bid committee gave Samaranch – over 3 weeks accommodation in the Imperial suite of the Kokusai Hotel valued at more than US$75,000, a Japanese sword valued at US$16,000 and a painting valued at US$16,000 (Cohen & Longman, 1999) – all others simply paled into insignificance.

In some instances what began as relationships of convenience ended in genuine friendships. Rosenbrock cited nearly a dozen IOC members as 'good' or 'very good friends' including Anton Geesink (Netherlands), Flor Isava-Fonseca, Chiharu Igaya (Japan), Nat Indrapana, Willi Kaltschmitt-Lujan (Guatemala), Carol Ann Letheren, Rampaul Ruhee (Mauritius), Jan Staubo (Norway), Walther Tröger (Germany), and Ching Kuo-Wu (Taiwan). And, as she noted on dossiers prepared for Pirjo Haggmann (Finland) and Chiharu Igaya, friendships do not necessarily translate into votes (Rosenbrock, 1999).

Candidate cities commonly invoked the power of third parties to draw votes. Many cities targeted Samaranch, going to "exceptional efforts to earn his approval" in the belief that he wielded "considerable influence" (Hill, 1996, p. 113). Beijing and Nagano made extraordinarily generous donations to the president's pet project at the time, the olympic museum in Lausanne. The Chinese donated a priceless national treasure, a 2200-year-old terracotta soldier from the Ch'in tomb – "we look upon the IOC as God, their wish is our command", exclaimed Chen Xitong, the chair of the Beijing bid committee (*Sun Herald*, 1993); Yoshiaki Tsutsumi, President of the Japanese Olympic Committee, arranged a US$20 million gift (Sullivan, 1999). Yet, for all of the talk that Samaranch wanted Beijing to host in 2000 (Jennings, 1996, pp. 205–208), there is no concrete evidence that IOC members simply rubber-stamp a president's preference (Gordon, 1994, p. 430). Indeed, an awareness of his limited influence is implicit in Samaranch's advice to Barcelona that it should cultivate as many individual IOC members as possible.

Rewards, more than any other form of power, defined the post-Los Angeles lobbying orgies. The Nagano, successive Salt Lake City, and Sydney bids exemplified the resort to reward power. Paradoxically, Salt Lake City and Sydney employed reward power despite high-quality technical bids. Salt Lake City lost its bid for the 1998 games by four votes to Nagano. Shortly after, the president of a national olympic committee informed Salt Lake that Nagano had paid several IOC members US$100,000 each for their votes. Material rewards thus became essential forms of power for candidate cities; in its next bid, Salt Lake City gave Ganga over US$250,000 worth of goods and services (SLOCOG Board of Ethics, 1999, p. 33). Sydney made extensive use of co-operation agreements with third world countries in which the AOC offered to help develop sporting programmes. These agreements typically provided additional assistance if Sydney won the 2000 games. (On the night before the actual vote, Coates calculated that Sydney was two votes shy of a majority and he offered Charles Mukora [Kenya] and Francis Nyangweso [Uganda], a further US$35,000 over 7 years [Sheridan,

1999, pp. 41–42]). Salt Lake City, too, made payments to Mukora for the Kenyan athletics programme and for his personal use (SLOCOG Board of Ethics, 1999, p. 34).

Material rewards were not the only forms offered by candidate cities. Personal approval (e.g., Raven, 1990, p. 499) and caressing egos were equally popular. In July and August 1993, Sydney took former Prime Minister, Gough Whitlam, on a trek through sub-Saharan Africa to bestow prestige on IOC members and raise their domestic political profiles. Many Africans respected Whitlam; he ordered an Australian boycott of South African sport in 1972 and 13 years later, as Ambassador to UNESCO, he chaired a world conference on apartheid sport (Gordon, 1994, p. 436). (Coates estimated that the African safari won Sydney between four and six votes Gordon, 1994, p. 436). The Sydney bid committee caressed many egos. It held a state reception for Samaranch in the Art Gallery of New South Wales and Prime Minister Paul Keating hosted a special lunch for him at Admiralty House. Officials accredited more journalists to cover Samaranch's visit to Sydney in 1993 than for the President of the United States, George Bush, the previous year (McGeoch, 1994, pp. 249, 251). Sydney's *Daily Telegraph Mirror* effusively welcomed Nat Indrapana (Jobling, 2000, p. 267), the IOC member in the sporting backwater of Indonesia. Others received 'royal treatment'. For example, the manager of the Sydney Opera House delayed the start of one show until three IOC members – who were late – had been seated (McGeoch, 1994, p. 203).

How did IOC members react to these attempts to influence them? Not surprisingly, the responses varied. Some members distinguished between acceptable and unacceptable advances and offers. Vladimir Cernusak and his wife Maria did not buy anything on an escorted shopping trip through Sydney's expensive boutiques; they made all of their purchases, to a total value of 'about $200', in a cheap department store (Rosenbrock, 1999). Andrei Siperco, the son of Alexandu Siperco (Romania) refused an offer of employment in the United States made by Salt Lake City "because I consider that it is not appropriate for me to [capitalise on my position as a relative of an IOC member]" (SLOCOG Board of Ethics, 1999, p. 47).

Others became predators. The best-documented cases are Jean-Claude Ganga, who was popularly known as the "human vacuum cleaner", David Sibandze (Swaziland) who travelled between bidding cities "complaining" about his large mortgage (Johnson, 1999), and Un Yong Kim (Korea) (SLOCOG Board of Ethics, 1999). Kim, and Alexandu Siperco, asked Salt Lake City and Sydney to find employment for children and relatives. Salt Lake City subsequently arranged for Kim's son, Jung Hoon, to work with

Keystone Communications, a telecommunications company. (Jung Hoon did not really want the work and Salt Lake City ended up reimbursing Keystone the US$75,000 salary it paid to the IOC member's son [SLOCOG Board of Ethics, 1999, pp. 19–20]). Sydney found Nick Voinov, Siperco's son-in-law, an engineering position in the New South Wales Rail Authority (Bacon, 1993; McGeoch, 1994, p. 268). Salt Lake City also arranged for Kim's daughter, Hae Jung, to perform twice with the Utah Symphony for which she received US$5,000 (SLOCOG Board of Ethics, 1999, p. 41).[9] Predators particularly sought educational assistance for family and friends. Kim asked Salt Lake City to sponsor a Russian woman, Ekaterina Souk-horado, and the olympic host covered her costs at the University of Utah in 1992–1993 (SLOCOG Board of Ethics, 1999, p. 18). Sibandze and René Essomba approached Salt Lake City for assistance to help their children study in America; the aspirant host paid tuition at the University of Utah, and living expenses, for Sibo Sibandze and Sonia Essomba for 5 and 3 years respectively (SLOCOG Board of Ethics, 1999, pp. 15, 27). In response to a request from Sibandze, Sydney paid fees, worth Aus$7,220, for his daughter, Nomsa, to attend a tertiary education college (Sheridan, 1999, p. 37).

In summary, candidate cities in the post-Los Angeles era continued to employ traditional forms of information and referent power, although the new concept of olympic family transformed the substance of the latter. The real difference between the pre- and post-Los Angeles eras was the intro-duction of third party and, especially, reward power.

Post-Influence Assessments

As Table 1 shows, the majority of cities make only one unsuccessful bid for an olympic games but a number mount multiple campaigns. Thus, while many relationships forged during lobbying are temporary conveniences and fall by the wayside after the vote, others continue. The principals of winning candidate cities frequently become the leaders of organising committees and so maintain close relationships with IOC members, and those of losing cities may regroup for further bids.

Winning candidates typically remain circumspect about what they say in public even after the vote. After Sydney won, some lobbyists confessed that they had found the bidding process offensive and demeaning. Sydney Lord Mayor, Frank Sartor, noted that during the week before the decision we "prostituted ourselves to try to get one more vote", and he referred to the Hotel de Paris in Monaco, where IOC members stayed, as the "Brothel de

Paris" (Age, 1993). Needless to say, when IOC members complained about his language, Sartor protested that he had been misquoted (*Sydney Morning Herald*, 1993b). The fact that the Mayor of the host city must work with the IOC imposes some constraints on public utterances. Interestingly, although the IOC portrays itself as the dominant party in relations with host cities, in reality a "good deal of power" immediately passes to the latter. And that "power grows" over time as the option of staging the games elsewhere becomes less and less feasible (Hill, 1996, p. 241).

Former lobbyists-turned-organisers also have to decide whether to pursue friendships and what pledges to honour. Obviously, some genuine friendships endure while relationships of convenience fade. Of course, some individuals will interpret relationships differently. Francis Nyangweso's partner, Naomi, complained that after Atlanta won the hosting rights, her one-time 'friends' in the city vanished (Roesnbrock, 1999). Salt Lake City continued paying the expenses of three Sudanese athletes training in the United States for the summer games in Atlanta. The winter games candidate brought the athletes to the country in 1995, prior to the vote for the 2002 games, at the request of General Zein El Abdin Ahmed Gadir, the IOC member in Sudan. After winning the hosting rights, Salt Lake City organisers debated whether to continue funding the Sudanese. Tom Wilkinson, Assistant Executive Director of the USOC, won the argument by reminding his colleagues that we "may need Sudan again in the future" and should not "burn [our] bridges" (SLOCOG Board of Ethics, 1999, p. 44; Mitchell, 1999, p. 30).

Some predators positioned themselves to continue exploiting relationships with losing cities that signalled their intentions to rebid. Shortly after Nagano's victory, David Sibandze wrote to Tom Welch to "assure" him that their "friendship...was greater than the results of the IOC vote on the 15 June 1991". Sibandze promised to contact Welch "from time to time" and reported that Sibo has a student visa and "will be joining you in the first week of September" (SLOCOG Board of Ethics, 1999, p. 15).

THE POST-SCANDAL ERA AND THE END OF THE ORGIES

The lobbying orgies were unsustainable. They disenfranchised most candidate cities and contradicted the IOC's own ethical standards espoused in its sacred *Olympic Charter*. Not surprisingly, they drew internal criticism.

Candidate cities lodged early complaints with the IOC that even appeared responsive. In 1992, the IOC restricted members to one visit, of a limited duration, to each candidate city, banned lavish exhibitions, receptions and entertaining, and imposed a limit of US$200 on any gifts given to IOC members. Two years later, the IOC approved the Hodler rules, named after Marc Hodler, an IOC member in Switzerland and outspoken critic of corruption in the olympic movement (Booth, 1999, p. 59). The Hodler rules introduced a two-phase selection procedure (see Table 1, Note c) and reduced the value of gifts to IOC members visiting candidate cities during phase one to US$50 and to US$150 during phase two. While helping to curtail many of the crass and gross excesses of the lobbying orgies before the vote for the 2004 games, the Hodler rules did not eradicate opportunism or predation. Indeed, notwithstanding the new rules, IOC leaders largely disregarded candidate cities' concerns. Toronto, Manchester, Athens, and Melbourne – losing cities in the race for the 1996 games – submitted reports critical of the bidding process to the IOC in 1991. One participant at the meeting where the reports were presented to Samaranch remembered the president's nonchalance as he flicked through the submissions: "At the end he said, "thank you," and it was time for dinner" (Cohen & Longman, 1999; Williams, 1999). IOC Executive Board member Richard Pound (Canada) labelled the Hodler rules mere 'guidelines' for candidate cities wanting to reduce their expenses (SLOCOG Board of Ethics, 1999, p. 28). Certainly the IOC made no effort to police or enforce the 1992 or 1994 rules and, not surprisingly, most candidate cities continued flouting them. Just as McGeoch (1994, p. 101) anticipated, the IOC would allow a "bit of give and take" in its interpretation of the 1992 rules.

In 1999, IOC members voted, by overwhelming majorities, to expel six of their colleagues and to warn nine others (another four members resigned after being named by the *Ad Hoc* Commissions and one died before the Commissions released their recommendations[10]); their actions effectively terminated the lobbying orgies. Some candidate cities will continue to host IOC members in contravention of the amended *Olympic Charter*, and some IOC members will visit candidate cities 'wearing their hats' as athletes or as members of international federations or national olympic committees, but the post-scandal expulsions have removed the most predatory members. (Concomitant reforms have reintroduced more order into the bidding process which will undoubtedly also be assisted by the retirement of President Samaranch.[11])

Why did the lobbying orgies continue for so long? Two explanations are offered here. The lobbying orgies shrouded many IOC members and the principals of candidate cities in an air of unreality. Blinded by the family metaphor, neither could see the impropriety in their own behaviour. Explaining his support for David Sibandze, Coates referred to the pair as members of the olympic family which somehow justified their behaviour: "I am the father of six children and I hope that one day my contribution to the Olympic movement can be acknowledged by one of my kids studying overseas. Isn't this what the Olympic family is all about?" (*Sydney Morning Herald*, 1993a). Ironically, two years after expelling Sibandze, the IOC admitted Coates as a member!

The lobbying orgies also flourished because senior IOC members, notably President Samaranch, saw no need to implement policies and rules to control candidate cities and IOC members, because they tolerated blatant conflicts of interest whereby members (e.g., Phil Coles) could also serve as principals for candidate cities, and because they could not grasp the notion of public accountability. Notwithstanding the exemplary ethical conduct shown by many IOC members, institutional abrogation of ethical responsibility served the IOC's political interests.

To conclude, it is worth commenting that the IOC has a long history of such behaviour as is evident in its embrace of fascism (Krüger & Murray, 2003), its sex-testing of female athletes (Ritchie, 2003), its nonchalance at the Mexican state's violent suppression of student protesters on the eve of the 1968 games (Hoberman, 1986), its fury at the racial protests by Tommie Smith and John Carlos on the victory dais in Mexico City (Hartmann, 2003), and its insensitivity at the deaths of Israeli athletes in 1972 (Reeve, 2000). Thus, whatever conclusions one draws about the post-Los Angeles era as a unique historical conjucture in olympic history, or about individual IOC members (whether as predators, opportunists, manipulators, or ethical decision-makers), it is impossible to ignore the nature and structure of the IOC as a key predisposing factor in the lobbying orgies.

NOTES

1. The olympic movement uses a capital 'O' in *olympics* and *olympism* to, in part, decorate and venerate itself. No laws of grammar justify the capitalisation of either word.
2. A good illustration of absolutism in the IOC in the post-Los Angeles era was the selection of members by President Samaranch who retained "virtually sole say" about who joined the Committee (Hill, 1996, p. 66). For example, Samaranch strongly supported Mario Vázquez Raña (Mexico) who was subsequently elected with only 13 votes; 60 members abstained and 10 voted against including six of the

seven women members (McGeoch, 1994, p. 65; Jennings, 1996, pp. 165–167). Barney et al. (2002, p. 219) cite Raña, the President of the Association of National Olympic Committees, as a "key contributor to [Samaranch's] campaign for IOC presidency".

3. In the end the IOC profited handsomely from television rights negotiated by Los Angeles (Barney et al., 2002, pp. 195–198).

4. Hill (1996, p. 168) identifies Seoul as the first candidate city to use gifts as inducements.

5. The United States and International Olympic Committees launched investigations into Helmick who resigned from both organisations before they reached any decisions (*Sports Letter*, 1999).

6. Commissions assess the characteristics of the candidate city and nation, domestic support for the city's bid, immigration and customs facilities, meteorological conditions, environment protection, security, health, athletes' and media villages, accommodation, transport, competition sites, media facilities, telecommunications, data processing, finances, marketing, and legal issues.

7. Athens eventually won the 2004 games but five months prior to the opening ceremony, preparations were well behind schedule and, in many instances, shambolic (e.g., *New Zealand Herald*, 2004).

8. Britain also claimed membership of this 'club' and Coates' comments drew a sharp rebuke from the British Olympic Association, which was supporting Manchester's candidacy for the 2000 games. At issue was whether Irish athletes who attended the 1904 games represented Britain.

9. Early in 2004, the Executive Board of the IOC suspended Kim following an announcement that he was under investigation in Seoul for bribery and corruption in connection with his leadership of the Korean Olympic Committee and the World Taekwondo Federation (*Age*, 2004). After an investigation, the IOC Ethics Commission subsequently recommended Kim's expulsion. Kim resigned before members voted on the recommendation.

10. Expelled: Agustin Arroyo (Ecuador: 72 for, 16 against, 2 abstentions), Zein El Abdin Ahmed Gadir (Sudan: 86, 4, 0), Jean-Claude Ganga (Congo: 88, 2, 0), Lamine Keita (Mali: 72, 16, 1), Sergio Fantini Santander (Chile: 76, 12, 0), Paul Wallwork (Samoa: 67,19, 2). Warned: Phillip Coles (Australia), Louis Guirandou-N'Diaye (Ivory Coast), Willi Kaltschmitt Lujan (Guatemala), Un Yong Kim (South Korea), Shagdarjav Magvan (Mongolia), Anani Matthia (Togo), Austin Sealy (Barbados), Vitaly Smirnov (Russia), Mohamed Zerguini (Algeria) (IOC, 1999c). Resigned: Bashir Attarabulsi (Libya), Pirjo Haggman (Finland), Charles Mukora (Kenya), David Sibandze (Swaziland). Died: René Essomba (Cameroon).

11. Samaranch will retain some influence as the Honorary President for life and his son, Juan Antonio Samaranch Jr, is also an IOC member.

REFERENCES

Age (1993). No glass empty in 'big Australian crawl.' *Age* (Melbourne), 24 September.
Age (2004). IOC vice president arrested over corruption. *Age* (Melbourne), 28 January.
Bacon, W. (1993). Watchdog's bark muffled. *Reportage*, September.

Barney, R., Wenn, S., & Martyn, S. (2002). *Selling the five rings: The International Olympic Committee and the rise of Olympic commercialism.* Salt Lake City: University of Utah Press.

Bell, G. (1999). Text of Olympic report to Congress. *Atlanta Journal-Constitution,* 17 September.

Booth, D. (1998). *The race game: Sport and politics in South Africa.* London: Frank Cass.

Booth, D. (1999). Gifts of corruption: The gift in the Olympic movement. *OLYMPIKA: The International Journal of Olympic Studies, IX,* 43–68.

Booth, D., & Tatz, C. (1994). 'Swimming with the big boys'?: The politics of Sydney's 2000 Olympic bid. *Sporting Traditions, 11*(1), 3–23.

Cohen, R., & Longman, J. (1999). In reviving Games, Olympic chief set little store in halting abuses. *New York Times,* 7 February.

Crombie, A. (1996). A most unlikely foursome. *Business Review Weekly* (Australia), 2 September, 40–46.

Crombie, A. (1999). Mr Olympics chases his own gold. *Business Review Weekly* (Australia), 16 April, 85–89.

Crosswhite, P. (1993). Personal interview, 3 December.

Dheensaw, C. (1994). *The Commonwealth Games: The first 60 years, 1930–1990.* Sydney: Australian Broadcasting Corporation.

Financial Review (1992). No pain in Spain for the five-star Samaranch gang. *Financial Review* (Australia), 5 August.

Gordon, H. (1994). *Australia and the Olympic Games.* Brisbane: University of Queensland Press.

Guttmann, A. (1984). *The Games must go on: Avery Brundage and the Olympic movement.* New York: Columbia University Press.

Guttmann, A. (1992). *The Olympics: A history of the modern games.* Urbana, IL: University of Illinois Press.

Hartmann, D. (2003). *Race, culture, and the revolt of the black athlete.* Chicago: University of Chicago Press.

Hermann, M. (1986). What is political psychology? In: M. Hermann (Ed.), *Political psychology: Contemporary problems and issues* (pp. 1–10). San Francisco: Jossey–Bass.

Hill, C. (1993). The politics of the Olympic movement. In: L. Alison (Ed.), *The changing politics of sport* (pp. 84–104). Manchester: Manchester University Press.

Hill, C. (1996). *Olympic politics: Athens to Atlanta 1896–1996.* Manchester: Manchester University Press.

Hoberman, J. (1986). *The Olympic crisis: Sport, politics and the moral order.* New Rochelle, NY: Caratzas.

Hoberman, J. (1995). Toward a theory of olympic internationalism. *Journal of Sport History, 22*(1), 1–37.

IOC. (1999a). *Report of the IOC Ad Hoc Commission to investigate the conduct of certain IOC members and to consider possible changes in the procedures for the allocation of the Games of the Olympiad and the Olympic Winter Games.* Lausanne: International Olympic Committee Publisher.

IOC. (1999b). *Second Report of the IOC Ad Hoc Commission to investigate the conduct of certain IOC members and to consider possible changes in the procedures for the allocation of the Games of the Olympiad and the Olympic Winter Games.* Lausanne: International Olympic Committee Publisher.

IOC (1999c). IOC expels six members at 108th session. IOC press release, 17 March.

IOC. (2003). *Olympic charter*. Lausanne: International Olympic Committee.

Jennings, A. (1996). *The new lords of the rings*. London: Pocket Books.

Jennings, A. (2000). *The great Olympic swindle*. London: Simon & Schuster.

Jobling, I. (2000). Bidding for the Olympics: Site selection and Sydney 2000. In: K. Schaffer & S. Smith (Eds), *The Olympics at the millennium* (pp. 258–271). New Brunswick: Rutgers University Press.

Johnson, K. (1999). Tarnished gold. *New York Times*, 11 March, Section A.

Kruger, A., & Murray, W. (2003). *The Nazi Olympics*. Urbana, IL: University of Illinois Press.

Lawrence, G. (1986). In the race for profit: Commercialisation and the Los Angeles Olympics. In: G. Lawrence & D. Rowe (Eds), *Power play: Essays in the sociology of Australian sport* (pp. 204–214). Sydney: Hale & Iremonger.

MacAloon, J. (1981). *This great symbol: Pierre de Coubertin and the origins of the Modern Olympic Games*. Chicago: University of Chicago Press.

Martyn, S. (2003). Putting the Olympic house in order: The Salt Lake City bidding scandal and the IOC's struggle to regain credibility. Paper presented at the annual conference of the North American Society for Sport History, Ohio State University, Columbus, OH, May 23–26.

McGeoch, R. (1994). *The bid: How Australia won the 2000 games*. Melbourne: William Heinemann.

Mitchell, G. (1999). *Report of the United States Olympic Committee's Special Bid Oversight Commission*. Colorado Springs, CO: United States Olympic Committee.

New Zealand Herald (2004). High security plan for games. *New Zealand Herald*, 12 March.

Preuss, H. (2000). *Economics of the Olympic Games: Hosting the Games 1972–2000*. Sydney: Walla Walla Press.

Raven, B. (1990). Political applications of the psychology of interpersonal influence and social power. *Political Psychology, 11*(3), 493–520.

Raven, B. (1992). A power/interaction model of interpersonal influence: French and Raven thirty years later. *Journal of Social Behaviour and Personality, 7*(2), 217–244.

Reeve, S. (2000). *One day in September*. New York: Arcade Publishing.

Ritchie, I. (2003). Sex tested, gender verified: Controlling female sexuality in the age of containment. *Sport History Review, 34*(1), 80–98.

Roche, M. (2000). *Mega-events and modernity: Olympics and expos in the growth of global culture*. London: Routledge.

Rosenbrock, P (1999). Secret high notes. *Sydney Morning Herald*, 18 May.

Senn, A. (1999). *Power, politics, and the Olympic Games*. Champaign, IL: Human Kinetics.

Sheridan, T. (1999). *Review of records of the Sydney Olympics 2000 Bid Ltd by Independent Examiner*. Sydney Organising Committee for the Olympic Games, Sydney, Australia.

Simson, V., & Jennings, A. (1992). *The lords of the rings*. London: Simon & Schuster.

SLOCOG (Salt Lake Organising Committee for the Olympic Winter Games) Board of Ethics. (1999). *Report to the board of trustees*. Salt Lake City, UT: Salt Lake City Organising Committee.

Sports Letter. (1999). Amateur Athletic Foundation of Los Angeles. Paul Ziffren Sports Resource Center. *Sports Letter*, 10 March.

Sugden, J., & Tomlinson, A. (2003). Football and FIFA in the postcolonial world. In: J. Bale & M. Cronin (Eds), *Sport and postcolonialism* (pp. 175–196). Oxford: Berg.

Sullivan, R. (1999). How the Olympics were bought. *Time*, 25 January.

Sun Herald. (1993). $100m bribe to Olympics. *Sun Herald* (Sydney), 14 March.

Sydney Morning Herald. (1993a). How games chief wooed the man who didn't vote. *Sydney Morning Herald,* 30 September.

Sydney Morning Herald. (1993b). Sartor lays IOC concerns to rest. *Sydney Morning Herald,* 30 September.

Sydney Morning Herald. (1999a). Salt Lake's largesse: 'Who could ask for more.' *Sydney Morning Herald,* 27 February.

Sydney Morning Herald. (1999b). Powerful pen: The woman behind the man behind the eight ball. *Sydney Morning Herald,* 6 May.

Williams, P. (1999). The rings of ire. *Financial Review* (Australia), 5 March.

Chapter 12

SYMBOLS WITHOUT SUBSTANCE: ABORIGINAL PEOPLES AND THE ILLUSIONS OF OLYMPIC CEREMONIES

Janice Forsyth and Kevin B. Wamsley

A Canadian television broadcaster described the closing ceremonies of the 1976 Olympic Games in Montreal, Quebec that featured Olympic athletes, young female dancers, and hundreds of performers dressed in bright Native costumes holding hands and dancing around massive, colour-coded teepees arranged to match the five Olympic rings in the following way: "This is probably the greatest show the world has ever seen"! (CBC Television, Sunday 1 August 1976). Performed in similar fashion to the carnival shows of P.T. Barnum's travelling circus of the nineteenth century, the ceremonies of the Olympic Games of the late twentieth century emerged as a cyclical sport spectacle, augmented by satellite television broadcasts and burgeoning organising committee budgets. Indeed, over the course of the last quarter of the twentieth century, the opening and closing ceremonies of the Olympics became a focal point for television and for the lure of corporate sponsorship (Barney, Wenn, & Martyn, 2002). Considering the more than one-hundred-year history of the modern Olympic Games, myriad events, crises, and significant organisational changes, MacAloon's (1996, pp. 32–33) assertion that the ceremonies represent the most stable of Olympic images is an appropriate context in which to discuss the role of Aboriginal peoples in this ritual aspect of the Games.

Global Olympics: Historical and Sociological Studies of the Modern Games
Research in the Sociology of Sport, Volume 3, 227–247
Copyright © 2005 by Elsevier Ltd.

For the most part, the opening and closing programmes of the Games consistently provide the host nation with opportunities to showcase national and regional culture – to represent itself to on-site spectators and the television audience. For the inaugural Games of 1896, for example, the host nation, Greece, juxtaposed ancient ruins and ancient history against modern facilities and modern ideas as part of a broader project of national rejuvenation. In this respect, the 1896 Games were not so different from Athens 2004, where similar juxtapositions could be witnessed. From the post-war rubble of Antwerp in 1920 to Nazi Germany in 1936, from Post-World War II London in 1948 to Sydney in 2000, host countries have consistently utilised the Games' ceremonies to represent versions of their national history, as well as their current social, political, and economic trajectories to the rest of the world. Essentially, host cities and nations have always focused on the projection of favourable images and attempted to display attractive national dimensions and reputations internationally; hosting the Games has never been simply based on the organisation of sporting events alone.

As with other major sport and cultural spectacles, the Olympic Games generally tend to sustain the dominant political orders of host nations. Events and ceremonies *per se* do not challenge existing political orders although, in some cases, they provide venues for resistance and disorder (Wamsley, 2002). As such, the historical relations between groups within host nations – in this case Indigenous and non-Indigenous peoples – are often represented in Olympic ceremonies as harmonious and uncomplicated in order for organising committees to project positive images of the nation abroad.[1] This is particularly true of Games held in countries like Canada, the United States, and Australia where Aboriginal peoples are central to national culture, both past and present, and where historical relations between groups have been tense, complex, and often violent. From the time when they first made their appearance in 1976, Aboriginal peoples have come to play a prominent role in Olympic ceremonies. Indeed, the Olympic ceremonies presented in Montreal (1976), Calgary (1988), Sydney (2000), and Salt Lake City (2002) featured elaborate historical renditions of the perceived relations between colonised Aboriginal peoples and their colonisers, in each case of European origin. In these particular locations, Aboriginal peoples and Indigenous cultural imagery have come to represent, and literally embody, liberal democratic ideals of cultural diversity and respect for differences between people. This did not, however, necessarily provide an accurate depiction of relations between Aboriginals and non-Aboriginals in any of the aforementioned cases.

Recently, Olympic organisers and the political leaders of host nations have claimed that the ceremonies pay homage and offer respect to the first people of the land, and that they support Aboriginal struggles for survival by providing them with a global stage on which to promote the richness and meaning of their cultures. The underlying assumption is that the Olympic Games – and, by extension, its ceremonies – help foster cross-cultural awareness and international understanding. On the contrary, however, the historical evidence demonstrates that these ideologies are strategically invoked by the International Olympic Committee (IOC) to legitimise the Games, as part of a long-term, broader campaign of unabashed self-promotion that ultimately results in obfuscations of often deep-seated conflicts between people. The idea that the ceremonies encourage peace, harmony, and friendship cannot be taken at face value, for there are, in this case, always at least two levels of interaction at work: what Olympic organisers communicate to the public at large about Aboriginal peoples in general and, more specifically, their involvement in the Games and, most importantly, the *actual* relationships that are played out in everyday life.

This chapter examines the historical issues and controversies surrounding Aboriginal participation in Olympic ceremonies. Our analysis is drawn from research on Olympic Games where Aboriginal peoples have played a key role in opening and closing ceremonies – specifically Montreal, Calgary, Sydney, and Salt Lake City. Although Olympic ceremonies did not exist in their current form at the turn of the twentieth century, events at the 1904 Games in St. Louis are also discussed here because they introduce the problematic context in which Aboriginal peoples have been situated at Olympic Games and, more significantly, because of the durability of certain images and themes projected through de Coubertin's festival. Scholars who have researched in this area have selected varied controversies on which to focus their attention. However, as a collective body of research, their work accentuates the difference between the Olympic ideals and lived realities of Aboriginal peoples. In the end, the details differ slightly from Games to Games, but the underlying issues – unequal access to power between Olympic organisers and Aboriginal peoples, and the ostensible celebration of Indigenous culture for only brief periods in host nations – always remain the same.

POWER, POLITICS, AND REPRESENTATION

The inclusion of Aboriginal peoples in Olympic ceremonies in Canada, the United States, and Australia is a recent trend that warrants critical attention.

With the exception of the 1904 Games in St. Louis, there is no record of Aboriginal participation in the opening or closing ceremonies in Los Angeles (1932 or 1984),[2] Lake Placid (1932 or 1980), or the later Games held in Melbourne (1956) or Squaw Valley (1960). How, then, is the appearance of Aboriginal cultures in recent Olympic ceremonies to be interpreted?

Although extensive studies exploring the relationship between Aboriginal issues, international politics, and the Olympic Games are scarce and rather inconclusive, it seems that the emergence of Indigenous peoples as performers in Olympic ceremonies follows two broad trends. First, some Aboriginal peoples throughout the world emerged in the Post-World War II era as skilled political leaders seeking to secure and expand their human rights by drawing on support from international networks and organisations such as the United Nations. Second, at about the same time as minority groups began demanding better treatment at home, nations including Canada, the United States, and Australia adopted policies of multiculturalism with the aim of creating a political environment that publicly embraced cultural diversities and provided visible minorities with opportunities for social and economic improvement – matters which, at times, required political expediency. These trends were intimately connected to a global consumer culture that was deeply fascinated with the exotic *Other*, a residue of long-standing scientific and upper-class social communities enraptured with the study of 'primitive' peoples since the early nineteenth century (Rydell, 1984).

The IOC's interest in promoting multiculturalism was rooted in more practical motives to secure short-term profit and long-term organisational viability, in part by advancing a well-versed and particular ideological rhetoric (Roche, 2002).[3] It is well documented that Juan Antonio Samaranch was searching for a Nobel Peace Prize for his role in the Olympic movement during his long reign as President of the IOC (1980–2001) (Jennings, 1996). In the mid-1990s, he introduced *Agenda 21*, which called for the inclusion of sustainable values in the Olympic movement by strengthening the role and participation of Indigenous populations in the Olympic Games. This plan provided an officially sanctioned space for Aboriginal peoples in Olympic ceremonies as well as the art and cultural festivals associated with the Games. With *Agenda 21*, it was imperative that countries hosting Olympic Games involve Aboriginal peoples in some significant way.[4]

Yet, within the context of the Olympic ceremonies, Aboriginal peoples have little or no control over the narratives that are scripted for them by Olympic organisers, a clear indication of their position within national and, therefore, Olympic hierarchies of influence and control. More often than not, they are left to contend with the professional, business, and civic elites who are generally preoccupied with marketing the Games and preserving the public order. Ceremonies do not typically attract significant media attention until they are broadcast; however, one should not underestimate their importance to the IOC and host cities and their spectator appeal. As MacAloon (1996, p. 33) writes:

> ...no other Olympic event, no other sports festival, no other cultural event, no arts performance, no church, no political movement, no other international organization, including the United Nations, indeed no other anything has ever managed to generate regularly scheduled and predictable performances which command anywhere near the same focused global attention as do the Olympic Ceremonies.

Important distinctions characterise the opening and closing ceremonies, which are commonly referred to as 'spectacles'.[5] MacAloon (1996, pp. 33–34) suggests that, at the opening celebrations, the nations of the world "win autonomous visibility for themselves" and that they are crucial in the politics of international relations where, "together with membership in the United Nations, marching in the Olympic Opening Ceremonies is the *sine qua non* of world recognition as a *bona fide* nation-state". The closing festivities are predominantly celebrations of humankind, focusing on images of friendship and respect, which serve as emotional 'proof' that linguistic and cultural differences between people can be overcome (MacAloon, 1984, p. 253). The sheer size and grandeur of the spectacles, combined with the massive audience, makes them ideal platforms to promote ideological agendas[6] (the IOC notes, for example, that the opening ceremonies in Athens 2004 attracted the television audiences in millions of viewers for the following countries – France: 7.3; United Kingdom: 8.5; Germany: 12.95; Japan: 15.8; and the United States: 56).[7] The politics of difference have had a profound impact on Aboriginal peoples throughout the world, as distorted ideas and images about them have constantly reinforced how much they vary from mainstream societies. When these ideas are placed on the platform of the opening and closing ceremonies at the Olympic Games, they become powerful ideological tools.

THE 1904 ST. LOUIS OLYMPIC GAMES

During the early years of modern Olympic history, very few people knew of the Games (Barney, 1992) and, in the case of Paris 1900, St. Louis 1904, and London 1908, they were, in fact, embedded in several month-long World's Fairs and Expositions. In 1904, the Olympic Games were held in conjunction with a World Exposition celebrating the centennial of the Louisiana

Purchase, a sale of land that opened up the interior of the United States for westward expansion, forcing the removal of thousands of American Indians from their traditional territories. The Exposition emphasised several broad themes, including American expansionist policies at home, imperial successes abroad, technological advancement, and scientific enquiry. Collectively, Fair organisers designed the exhibits to demonstrate the progress of men from primitive savagery to civilisation, the latter represented by the achievements of educated white men. Central to this display were Indigenous peoples who had been brought in from different parts of the American empire to reside in native villages for the duration of the event (Rydell, 1984).

As showcase objects, the utility of the 'tribesmen' rested in their ability to attract tourists to the Exposition, but their presence also served as living proof of American white supremacy (Greenhalgh, 1988). Ethnocentric notions of white superiority endowed the organisers with the authority to claim that the Fair was promoting universal harmony by bringing together diverse groups of people in peaceful co-existence. The so-called 'Anthropology Days' – a 2-day sports competition, for Indigenous peoples drawn from the Exposition exhibits – exemplified these themes (Mallon, 1999, p. 205).

As Chief of Physical Culture for the Louisiana Purchase Exposition, James Edward Sullivan was responsible for directing the Olympic Games. Sullivan, an ardent supporter of amateurism and leading figure in the Amateur Athletic Union, exerted control over all physical exhibits and insisted on calling everything 'Olympic'. This resulted in a multitude of 'official' Olympic events, including the Anthropology Days (Mallon, 1999, p. 12).[8] The subject of physical training was premised on notions of cultural progress that equated material wealth and technological advancement with higher forms of civilisation. Not surprisingly, the greatest glory went to prosperous white men, the so-called 'amateurs'.

Open to Indigenous men only, Anthropology Days were held on August 12 and 13, 1904. Participants included African Pygmies, Argentine Patagonians, Japanese Ainu, Indians from Vancouver Island, several different American Indian and Philippine tribes, as well as Manguianas, four families of tree dwellers, and Eskimos. During the 2-day event, the men competed against one another in events such as spear throwing, modified archery, pole climbing, tug-of-war, and mud wrestling. Event organisers recorded the physical characteristics of the Aboriginal participants and compared their overall results, arbitrarily, to white male athletes. 'Primitive' men could not compete with the civilised, it was argued (Mallon, 1999), even though none of the Indigenous men removed from the Fair exhibits were trained athletes. As it was considered to be a 'scientific' anthropological examination, the organisers provided an Olympic lecture series on physical culture. Thus, the Anthropology Days were organised to coincide with this series so that 'world' experts, all of whom were working in various branches of physical education in the United States, would be able to observe the demonstrations.

As an educational display, the results of events held during Anthropology Days were taken as objective measurements, demonstrating the inferiority of Aboriginal peoples as a race and as a group of men. When the Indigenous men failed to display the expected prowess, organisers criticised them for their poor physical condition. For example, in his estimation of the 100 yards run, Sullivan wrote:

> Lamba, an African Pygmy, ran one hundred yards in 14.6 [seconds]. Now the African Pygmy leads an outdoor life, hunts, runs, swims, jumps and uses the bow and arrow and spear, and if anything, his life might be termed a natural athletic one, but, nevertheless, we find it takes him 14.6 [seconds] to run one hundred yards. Arthur Duffy, or any of our American champion sprinters could easily, in this particular race, have given the African Pygmy forty yards and a beating (Mallon, 1999, p. 206).

Recalling a spontaneous game of 'shinny' that took place between the Pygmies and the Cocopa Indians after a full day of events, Sullivan also remarked:

> [The game] required team work and the uninteresting exhibition showed conclusively the lack of the necessary brain to make the team and its work a success, for they absolutely gave no assistance to each other, and so far as team work was concerned, it was a case of purely individual attempt on the part of the players (Mallon, 1999, p. 209).

In principle, the 1904 Anthropology Days project was designed to be educational and instructive. However, such cavalier comparisons between the athleticism of Indigenous tribesmen and trained white athletes, as a measure of human evolution, served rather to emphasise the cultural differences between them, and to reinforce discriminatory scientific ideas about non-Indigenous superiority, while legitimising the harsh treatment of Indigenous peoples who came under the control of colonising governments (Stanaland, 1981). The ideas and images promoted during the events of 1904 circulated throughout the world and ultimately materialised in various European textbooks, thus shaping people's exposure to the supposed everyday lives of Indigenous peoples (Gøksyr, 1990). In the years to come, Aboriginal athletes such as Tom Longboat (1908) and Jim Thorpe (1912) competed in the de Coubertin Olympics, but Indigenous peoples did not participate in any further side-shows or Games ceremonies until much later in the twentieth century.

THE 1976 MONTREAL SUMMER GAMES

The struggles of the Canadian government over the 'Indian problem' during the twentieth century, including its failed policies of assimilation, the residential school system, and the response of Native leaders to ineffective legislation, led to its more multicultural approach to national events. However, in spite of policies designed to encourage informed understandings of multiculturalism, some Canadians continued to romanticise the development of the Canadian frontier and the capitulation of its 'noble savages' to the civilised Europeans throughout history. At issue here are not the Olympic Games *per se* but, in particular, the use of Native images for the closing ceremonies in Montreal in 1976. For this performance, promoted as a tribute to the Aboriginals of Canada, Olympic officials invited local Aboriginal people to take part in a display that was created for them by non-Aboriginal artists. Despite the complete lack of Aboriginal involvement in the organisational process, approximately 300 Aboriginal peoples from eight different communities participated in the celebration, having consented to share centre stage with approximately 250 non-Aboriginals dressed and painted to look like 'Indians' (COJO, 1978, p. 312).

With memories of the slaughter of passive protesters in the streets of Mexico City (1968) and the massacre of athletes in Munich (1972) looming in the background, the major concern for the Montreal organising committee was "to give the world the best impression of Olympism" (Rousseau, 1975, p. 163). It was imperative that the Games be redeemed from past horrors. Thus, organisers utilised the closing celebration to distinguish the Olympics as a humanising force, capable of bringing diverse groups of people and cultures together in peace, harmony, and friendship (Pappas, 1982, p. 407). The official intent, however, was to convey the idea of multiculturalism with its emphasis on the "emancipation and integration" of the Aboriginal peoples of Canada (Schantz, 1996, p. 138). In order to convey such ideas of multiculturalism and 'oneness', Olympic organisers appropriated a variety of popular Native images and arranged them into a vivid and dramatic display, complete with teepees, tom-toms, feathered headdresses, flags, and buckskin outfits – all coordinated to match the five colours of the Olympic rings. In the final performance, the Native performers marched in arrowhead formation as they entered and paraded around the track, erected five massive teepees in the centre of the stadium, dispensed feathered headbands and beaded necklaces to the athletes and spectators, danced and played the drums – all to the tune of the *La Danse Sauvage* (COJO, 1978, p. 306).

Symbols without Substance235

Although Olympic organisers stated publicly that the ceremony was designed to honour Canada's Aboriginal peoples, they did not consult with the
populations whom they professed to want to honour in the construction of
the programme. From start to finish, the celebration was designed *by* Olympic organisers *for* Aboriginal peoples. To prepare for the show, the Aboriginal participants were bused in for one all-night practice. It was
explained to them that funding for the ceremony was extremely limited and
that the organising committee could not afford to transport them to and
from their communities for regular practices. Since, without practice, the
Aboriginal participants would not know how to move through the ceremony, the organising committee hired a professional Montreal dance troupe
to train and practice for the show (Forsyth, 2002, p. 72). In the end, non-
Aboriginal performers dressed and painted to look like 'Indians' led the
Aboriginal participants through their own commemoration. The 'tribute' to
Aboriginal culture did not fairly represent the average Native Canadian in
the least, nor did it represent the state of relations between Aboriginal and
non-Aboriginal Canadians; further, Aboriginal peoples played no part in
creating, and only a secondary part in participating in, the ceremony.

THE 1988 CALGARY WINTER GAMES

Unlike the organisers for Lake Placid (1932, 1980) and Squaw Valley (1960),
the Calgary planners sought to trade on the images and participation of
Indigenous peoples in ceremonies and cultural events for the Winter Games
of 1988. In its civic promotional strategies, Calgary boosters had always
utilised themes of the western frontier in the long-standing annual celebration of the Calgary Stampede. Olympic organisers, in conjunction with local
politicians and business leaders, decided to juxtapose this nostalgic western
motif with more modern images of an oil-rich, business-friendly city. The
Olympic Games, during the 1980s, had become a vehicle for projecting
images of the modern, world-class city abroad through satellite television
(Wamsley & Heine, 1996a). The idealised images of the west included Mo-
unties, cowboys, and Indians, all part of the traditional histories relayed
about the winning of the frontier. Organisers utilised Aboriginal symbols for
the ceremonies and for Games insignia, and in the Olympic medal designs.
Further, the bid committee paraded a local chief and his wife, dressed in
traditional clothing, in front of IOC members during the final stages of the
bid process at Baden–Baden, where the IOC's decision was announced.

Once the IOC awarded the Games to Calgary in 1981, organisers began planning for the event. During the initial stages of preparing for the opening ceremonies for the Olympics, the Calgary Stampede Board, seemingly oblivious and certainly insensitive to the Calgary region's significantly large Aboriginal population, even suggested including images of an 'Indian attack and wagon-burning'. This idea quickly met general opposition and was soon dropped from ceremony plans (Wamsley & Heine, 1996b, p. 173). The ready use of Aboriginal themes in conjunction with the Calgary Olympics suggested that Aboriginal peoples were an important part of the region's social fabric but, in reality, this relationship was deeply troubled and at best symbolic. While the organisers were counting on Aboriginal imagery to attract visitors and Olympics enthusiasts to Calgary, they ignored issues of concern to the Aboriginal peoples around them, specifically the case of the Lubicon, a small band of Cree situated approximately 400 kms north of the city.

Clearly not opposed to using the Olympic Games for their own ideological purposes, the Lubicon attempted to raise public awareness of the plight of their community through the media attention associated with the lead-up to the 1988 Games. They implored museums worldwide to boycott a planned exhibit, *The Spirit Sings*, a visual arts display featuring Aboriginal artifacts collected from around the world (O'Bonsawin, 2002). The exhibit was co-sponsored by Shell Canada and the federal government and hosted by the Glenbow Museum in Calgary. The Lubicon were protesting several issues: the federal government's ongoing refusal to deliver on a land claim settlement that had been promised to them in 1940; the arbitrary way that the federal government had been removing people from the band list; and, the destruction of their trapping lands by major corporations drilling for oil, a development led by the Shell company (Wamsley, 2004, p. 315).

The outward partnership displayed between the corporate organisers and Aboriginal peoples served as a grim reminder of the weak attempts by Canadians to conceal historically oppressive relations that involved a difficult past and a tension-filled present. Partnership, in this sense, meant drawing on Aboriginal imagery for the benefit of the corporate elite in Calgary, those who had a stake in oil and business development. When the Lubicon tried to bring attention to their issues, they were accused of trying to "spoil Calgary's show" (Wamsley & Heine, 1996a, p. 85).

Observing Shell's sponsorship and involvement, Bernard Ominayak, Chief of the Lubicon Cree, noted: The "irony of using a display of North American Indian artifacts to attract people to the Winter Olympics being organised by interests who are still actively seeking to destroy Indian people seems painfully obvious", and commented that it was hypocritical of the

Glenbow Museum to be celebrating "the richness and continuity of Canada's native cultural traditions" when it was quite likely that, under those conditions, the Lubicon as a people would cease to exist (Wamsley & Heine, 1996b, p. 174). At least one member of the Glenbow sided with the Lubicon. Anthropologist Joan Ryan resigned from the Glenbow programme committee. Troubled by the way the museum was dealing with the Lubicon issue, she contended:

> There has been pressure on the OCO [Calgary Olympic Organizing Committee] from Indian bands since 1985. These groups have attempted to establish a significant role for themselves in the Olympics in which they could plan their own presentations. Instead organisers ignored them, hoping when the time ran out that Indian presentations could fit the stereotyped expectations of the world: feathers, beads and dances – and possibly a wagon burning (Wamsley & Heine, 1996b, p. 174).

Federal government officials and corporate organisers devised strategies to distract public attention away from the rather embarrassing issues raised by the Lubicon. A primary tool was the so-called 'Native Participation Program', which provided funding for a wide array of Aboriginal involvement, including an Aboriginal trade show, an Aboriginal youth conference, and powwow competitions. Aboriginal groups in 'Treaty 7' were involved with many aspects of this additional programming, which had the added effect of dividing Aboriginal support for the Lubicon. Sykes Powderface, liaison for Treaty 7, stated that although they were sympathetic to the Lubicon's issues, they wished to keep politics out of the Games (Wamsley & Heine, 1996b, p. 175). Other Aboriginal groups protested the museum display and demonstrated support for the Lubicon by rallying against the torch relay as it made its way across Canada and through the province of Alberta. In the short term, the ceremonies and cultural programmes projected images of harmony in Canadian society, and the viewing world was treated to a clever display of representational 'Canadiana'. With respect to the long-term, however, there is no evidence to suggest that these Olympic Games had any positive impact on social and political relations between Aboriginals and non-Aboriginals in the city of Calgary, the province of Alberta, or Canada more generally.

THE 2000 SYDNEY SUMMER GAMES

As with the Canadian context, the relationship between Indigenous and non-Indigenous peoples in Australia has been rife with conflict and oppression over long periods of time. To raise international awareness of the treatment of Aboriginal citizens in Australia, the Aboriginal legal service of

New South Wales in 1991 demanded that the IOC reject Sydney's bid to host the Games of 2000 (Morgan, 2003). Once the bid was won, however, Aboriginal leaders encouraged supporters to stage protests in Australia, as opposed to encouraging other nations to boycott the Games. Lenskyj (2002) documents these community-based protests by Aboriginal and non-Aboriginal peoples, drawing attention to the plight of Indigenous peoples and to issues of homelessness and poverty, in light of the massive spending for the Games. Morgan (2003) explained that Aboriginal protests were not as disruptive as organisers feared they might be, stating that, for many Australians, sport was a rather complicated cultural venue within which to launch sustained and aggressive protests. Within the Australian political climate, protest leaders and the movements they represent were often vilified for intruding upon events not popularly viewed as political. Additionally, it was argued, Aboriginal peoples held some ambivalent feelings towards undermining the Olympics and not showing support for Aboriginal athletes. Morgan argued that Sydney organisers were able to diffuse some of the pre-Games tensions by featuring prominent symbols of reconciliation during the ceremonies and by encouraging Aboriginals to be a part of their organisation. As in previous Olympic Games ceremonies, however, *The Festival of the Dreaming*, as it came to be called, was constructed for global audiences, invoking once again the theme of domestic harmony, lack of conflict, reconciliation, and thus clearly misrepresenting Australia's complicated history (Watts, 2004) and its ongoing government policies dealing with land rights, the issue of the 'Stolen Children', and the rates of incarceration of Aboriginal people. Within the ceremonies, Aboriginal peoples were, again, represented as archetypical noble savages, uncivilised, child-like, and primordial, with a closer connection to nature than to the challenges and celebrations of the modern world (Hogan, 2003).

Further complicating these social tensions was the use of the Aboriginal track athlete, Cathy Freeman, in the torch-lighting ceremony to create the illusion of national cohesion (Watts, 2004). In the years leading up to the Games, Freeman's outstanding performances on the track became an issue of some tension over the meaning of her success for Aboriginals and non-Aboriginals alike. While some members of the press likened the ancient presence of Aboriginal peoples in Australia to ancient Greece for ceremonial purposes, others sought to advance Australia's political position using Cathy Freeman's popularity: "Our Cathy carries with her not just the nation's sporting hopes...but its political aspirations" as well (Watts, 2004, p. 156). Freeman's torch-bearing symbolism was invoked by organisers to create a sense of national community for Australians, as much as it projected images of unification abroad. In the end, organisers and the John Howard government had achieved exactly what they set out to accomplish; but, not surprisingly, and once again, the Sydney Games did little to address the social issues facing the Aboriginal peoples of Australia.

THE 2002 SALT LAKE CITY WINTER GAMES

Tourism and respect for cultural diversity were the twin themes most prominent at the 2002 Games in Salt Lake City. To attract visitors to the area, Olympic organisers utilised varieties of Aboriginal imagery in its programmes and advertisements, which suggested a long and collective history to the land (Hogan, 2003). The 'Cultural Olympiad' (a specific and common term applied to the cultural programme that must accompany each Olympic Games) featured art exhibits, storytelling, ceremonial dances, social histories, and showcased present-day lives of Indigenous peoples in the state of Utah. With space at a premium, Native Americans found themselves in competition with each other for room within the programme and for tourists' dollars. The Navajo Nation had successfully negotiated for its own pavilion, setting up various interactive exhibits that promised to "take visitors on an authentic, historic journey into the Navajo culture". The pavilion featured arts and crafts, traditional dances, and performances by Navajo medicine men "who normally decline to participate in such events" (*Deseret News*, 9 February 2001, p. 1). To be included in the official Olympic schedule, Native American producers had to pay their own expenses as well as having their artistic credentials confirmed by a selection committee and then meet Salt Lake Organizing Committee (SLOC) standards for what constituted 'authentic' Native American arts and culture. Despite these restrictions, one reporter for the Native American Indian newspaper *Indian Country* (15 February 2002) wrote that the strong Native American presence in the arts and cultural programme was another positive step towards fostering greater cultural understanding and awareness of Native American issues to the visitors who attended their shows.

The most spectacular displays of Aboriginal culture were reserved for the opening ceremony. Approximately 1 year before the start of the Games, SLOC issued a public call for participants for both the opening and closing ceremonies, and volunteers were directed to fill out applications. The SLOC made it clear in its public pronouncements that preferential treatment would be given to individuals and groups whose talents identified them as "visually exciting" (*Deseret News*, 16 April 2001, p. 1). With Hollywood producer

Don Mishcer as Director of Ceremonies, the show was destined to be a grandiose event. The opening ceremony theme was a celebration of the American west and the cultural diversity it had to offer the world.

Wanting traditional dances from each of the five Native American tribes in Utah to feature in the opening ceremonies, the SLOC had approached each group in 1998 in order to secure their participation (*Indian Country*, 6 December 2000, p. 1). Thus, on the opening night, men and women, both young and old, of the Shoshone, Ute, Paiute, Goshute, and Navajo nations danced into the stadium, dressed in their best regalia, followed by drummers situated on five floating pods colour-coded to match the Olympic rings. Singer–songwriter Robbie Robertson, member of the Six Nations of the Grand River, performed selected pieces from his latest album, which provided an interesting counterpoint to the traditional images and sounds of the multitudes of dancers and drummers before him. Before leaving the stadium, one Chief from each of the five tribes blessed the organisers, athletes, and spectators, each in his own language. American broadcasts neglected to translate these blessings into English, thus obscuring the deep cultural significance imparted by the Chiefs for the world to understand. *Indian Country* journalists reported that the ceremony not only legitimised Native American tribes as nations of people, but also "brought the point home that America puts its best foot forward when it embraces its first peoples, its first societies, cultures, and governments" (*Indian Country*, 15 February 2002, p. 1). For the viewing audience, the ceremony was projected as evidence of the strong relationship Native Americans had allegedly always enjoyed with the US government and of the symbolic role that Indigenous peoples played in promoting American cultural plurality.

Despite such positive messages, it was clear that observers were divided on the western theme. Prominent Native American author, Susan Shown Harjo, criticised the celebration for conforming to well-worn stereotypes and for exploiting Aboriginal cultural images:

> After the Indians had their moment in the spotlight, they danced back into history, making way for miners, cowboys and settlers of all races to do-se-do together (as if that ever happened in that place and time). Only the Indians were missing from the hoedown in Salt Lake. But these are just symbols, you say? Well, yeah. Mega-bucks worth of symbols. Symbology that reaches millions of people around the world and leaves a lasting impression in place of reality (*Indian Country*, 16 February 2002, p. 1).

In these provocative terms, Harjo succinctly drew attention to the financial motivation behind the display, the power derived from the images, and the legacy of the spectacle for Native American life. Judith Lowry, Native American painter, underlined the hypocrisy of parading the tattered

American flag from the bombings of '9/11' around the stadium, noting how it was incorporated as an "assurance that somehow, by bravely going forward with the games, we were reclaiming our world from terrorism. We would like to live with the illusion that we are safe, but for those of Native heritage, this is impossible. The reminders stay with us from generation to generation" (*Indian Country*, 16 February 2002, p. 1).

Needless to say, Native Americans pursued their own agendas for participating in the arts and cultural programmes as well as the opening ceremonies; agendas synonymous with the messages of diversity that SLOC had strategically fostered. The Native American tribes wanted to capitalize on the exposure brought about by the Olympic Games and profit from their 'exotic' appeal by promoting cultural tourism on their reservations, which were beginning to experiment with waves of cultural tourism, and were looking to profit from their 'exotic' appeal – opportunities that they hoped would lead to big business (*Reuters Business Briefing*, 16 January 2002, p. 16). Commenting on the opportunities cultural tourism provided for Native Americans, Ed Hall, Director of Transportation and Tourism for the Bureau of Indian Affairs in Washington, D.C., remarked, "It's the first time one of the key elements of being Native American has been recognised as an asset" (*The Salt Lake Tribune*, 24 September 2001, p. 1). Exactly who the subject was in these remarks remains unclear, but the systemic inequalities with which Native Americans have to contend are clearly evident.

While the images of cultural diversity suited local cultures and traditions at the 2002 Salt Lake City Games, the opening ceremony ultimately represented a narrative celebrating Native colonisation. At the same time, the emphasis on tourism highlighted Native American struggles to develop sustainable economic projects on reserves, while simultaneously reinforcing a way of seeing and understanding Native peoples as objects, whose cultural identities were perceived to be their single greatest resource (Hogan, 2003).

CONCLUSION: THE PRIMORDIAL OLYMPIC DANCE VIA SATELLITE

The ways in which Indigenous peoples have been involved in the ceremonies of the Olympic Games and how their cultures have been represented on this globally televised stage have historically followed distinct patterns. With remarkably few exceptions, Aboriginal peoples have not participated in the construction of the ceremonies in any meaningful way. Contrary to what ideologues tell us about the ceremonies and how they are designed to pay homage to Aboriginal peoples, these spectacles may be understood as messages that Olympic organisers and boosters use to tell the world about what kind of place *they* live in and who *they* are as people. All things considered, the ceremonies are epic tales that professional, business, and civic elites weave about themselves and their place in society. That these evocative displays also appeal to masses of people speaks to the fact that the narratives constructed by Olympic organisers fit a narrow conception of social reality and their place within it. Scholars have demonstrated the various ways that Aboriginal images have been utilised in Olympic ceremonies – to legitimise imperialism, to promote ideas about multiculturalism, to encourage civic boosterism, to attract international investments, to foster tourism and, to invent historical traditions that show an intimate connection to the land through a primordial Aboriginal past (Wamsley & Heine, 1996a; Watts, 2004; Lenskyj, 2002). Paraschak (1995) concludes that images of Aboriginal inclusiveness in major sporting events are simply illusions – they are, from this perspective, *symbols without substance.*

When Aboriginal images highlighting their primordial past, without any connection to their place in contemporary society, are placed on the platform of the opening and closing ceremonies of Olympic Games, they become powerful ideological tools that make it extremely difficult for there to be any meaningful cross-cultural dialogue between Aboriginal and non-Aboriginal peoples. Whether or not Olympic organisers were conscious of their actions, in trying to promote Canada, the United States, and Australia as multicultural countries that respect Aboriginal peoples, by incorporating Aboriginal peoples and Aboriginal imagery into the Games it is nevertheless the case that they reinforced common views of Aboriginal peoples as being rooted in the past and having no place in modern social contexts.

One hundred years have passed since Aboriginal peoples first made their appearance at the Olympic Games, and yet their presence is still marked by colonial attitudes and discourses. Their participation in the ceremonies has been 'updated' since the 1904 Games in St. Louis, a change that has been dramatically influenced by the massive financial outlay and global spectatorship only the Olympics can provide. However, public applause and support for these aspects of the Olympic spectacle are not the result of having gained a deeper respect for Aboriginal lives and traditions but, rather, an emotional response to specific images and ideas that have assumed strong symbolic meaning worldwide. At the ceremonies, spectators and participants are encouraged to identify with the teepees, costumes, and feathered headdresses, and the nationalised narratives that celebrate an

Aboriginal past but negate the existence of Aboriginal peoples in the modern world.

Yet, Aboriginal peoples *do* participate in Olympic events and some find meaning through cultural performances associated with opening and closing ceremonies. Even though the imagery represents an extremely limited vision of Aboriginal lives and cultures, the representation still speaks to an important part of their histories, albeit a part that has been negotiated on unequal terms. While Aboriginal peoples have aimed for acceptance and respect by working within the restricted boundaries provided for them by Olympic organisers, they have also sought to advance notions about what it means to be Aboriginal in contemporary society. Aboriginal peoples have creatively adapted to these cultural confines, finding new ways to express themselves through their cultures and attempting to encourage non-Aboriginal peoples to develop a more rounded, accurate, and respectful understanding of what it means to be Aboriginal in the twentieth century (Moses, 2002; Heaman, 1999).

Some people have taken a more cautious approach to the ceremonies, skeptical of the ideological intent embedded in the rhetoric of the Games and the commercial displays they impart. Certainly, critics have good reason to be concerned. Authors who have examined issues of cultural representation have emphasised the negative impact of processes of cultural appropriation on Aboriginal peoples. For instance, in his book *The White Man's Indian*, Berkhofer (1979) argues that the continued production and reproduction of these images in literature, art, and movies has led to naturalised beliefs about Aboriginal people – that they not only share a homogeneous culture, but that their culture has little meaning in the contemporary context except in the form of colourful commercialised displays for mainstream audiences. As Berkhofer aptly points out, cultural appropriation is about images and representations as much as it is about real people, for while Aboriginal images have translated into huge financial gains for the entertainment industries, they have had a harmful effect on Aboriginal peoples who must constantly struggle with images of themselves as people of "little culture and less language" (Berkhofer, 1979, p. 103). The difference between cultural appropriation and cultural appreciation lies in the power relations between who is viewing and what or who is being viewed. In multicultural societies, it is often difficult to distinguish between the two (Hage, 2000).

Despite optimistic assertions that the Olympic Games are beginning to adopt more democratic practices (Kidd, 1996), there is little evidence to suggest that the IOC or Olympic host-city organising committees are moving in this direction where the representation of Aboriginal peoples are concerned. The IOC has been adept at responding to public calls for reform, developing creative solutions to deal with key issues in sport, while leaving fundamental inequalities alone. Despite calls for public participation in the hosting of Games, neither the IOC nor Olympic organisers have welcomed critical inquiries or sought widespread public input that might slow down the development process, or worse, grind projects to a halt in order to reform major sources of conflict (Lenskyj, 2000). When the IOC and Olympic organisers call for public participation and input and seek out 'partnerships' with locals, they generally select like-minded individuals and groups who will support their ideological agendas, and attempt to silence all the rest (Wamsley, 2002). Moving beyond the hyperbole proclaiming that the Olympics are a celebration of humanity and world peace, the Games are indeed a corporate entity managed by professionals whose interests rarely coincide with grassroot issues and the concerns of marginalised peoples.

NOTES

1. While the authors recognise the different political and historical overtones of the terms 'Native' (American), 'Aboriginal', and 'Indigenous', we utilise them interchangeably in this chapter to refer to the same cultural group.

2. There is, however, one small exception with the 1984 Los Angeles Olympic Games. MacAloon has noted that a group of ethnically diverse Olympians, including one Native American male, carried the US flag into the stadium for the opening ceremony, citing this example as a celebration of American cultural plurality on the west coast (MacAloon, 1992, p. 52).

3. Maurice Roche discusses the political ambitions of the IOC and the role it has attempted to carve out for itself, especially in relation to the United Nations (Roche, 2000, pp. 212–215).

4. See http://multimedia.olympic.org/pdf/en_report_300.pdf to view or download a copy of Agenda 21.

5. Here, we draw on John MacAloon's theory of the spectacle (as opposed to rite, drama, or festival) to discuss the Olympic ceremonies of Montreal, Calgary, Sydney, and Salt Lake City. Organisers for each of these Games arranged excessive pageantry and entertainment to communicate their messages to the world, signs that clearly indicate the spectacle according to MacAloon (1984).

6. MacAloon (1996) explains that Olympic organisers are under tremendous pressure to create evocative displays that speak to local cultures and histories, national identities, and international relations, without offending their viewers. It is a delicate balance and an admittedly delicate task. There is no way to please everyone. While we can appreciate their struggles, we are also cognisant of the tremendous power Olympic organisers possess and the way they wield it in order to achieve their desired ends.

7. Figures reported by the IOC: http://www.olympic.org/uk/organisation/commissions/marketing/full_story_uk.asp?id = 1025.

8. Though designated an Olympic event, Mallon has aptly pointed out that 'Anthropology Days' was not what the Baron Pierre de Coubertin, founder of the modern Olympic Games, had in mind when he established the event. Apparently, the news of Anthropology Days so appalled Coubertin that he vowed the Olympics would never again be hosted as a side-show to a major international fair, although the 1908 Games were loosely associated with one.

REFERENCES

Barney, R. (1992). Born from dilemma: America awakens to the modern Olympic Games, 1901–1903. *OLYMPIKA: The International Journal of Olympic Studies, I*, 92–135.

Barney, R., Wenn, S., & Martyn, S. (2002). *Selling the five rings: The international Olympic committee and the rise of Olympic commercialism*. Salt Lake City, UH: University of Utah Press.

Berkhofer, R. F., Jr. (1979). *The White Man's Indian: Images of the American Indian, from Columbus to the present*. New York: Vintage Books.

CBC Television Broadcast. Sunday 1 August 1976. (Authors' copy).

COJO 76. (1978). *Official Report of Montreal 1976, Games of the XXI Olympiad: Organization* (Vol.1). Ottawa.

Deseret News. (9 February 2001). Navajos unveil big plans for Olympic cultural events. *Olympic Press Reviews* (p. 1). London, ON: International Centre for Olympic Studies.

Deseret News. (16 April 2001). Share your talents with the whole world. Olympic *Press Reviews* (p. 1). London, ON: International Centre for Olympic Studies.

Forsyth, J. (2002). Teepees and Tomahawks: Aboriginal cultural representation at the 1976 Olympic Games. In: K. B. Wamsley, R. K. Barney & S. G. Martyn (Eds), *The global nexus engaged: Past, present, and future interdisciplinary Olympic studies* (pp. 71–75). London, ON: International Centre for Olympic Studies.

Gøksyr, M. (1990). One certainly expected a great deal more from the savages: The Anthropology Days in St. Louis, 1904, and their aftermath. *The International Journal of the History of Sport, 7*(2), 297–306.

Greenhalgh, P. (1988). *Ephemeral vistas: The expositions universelles, great exhibitions and world's fairs, 1851–1939*. New York: St. Martin's Press.

Hage, G. (2000). *White nation: Fantasies of white supremacy in a multicultural society*. New York: Routledge.

Heaman, E. (1999). Making a spectacle: Exhibitions of the first nations. *Inglorious arts of peace: Exhibitions in Canadian society during the nineteenth century*. Toronto, ON: University of Toronto Press.

Hogan, J. (2003). Staging the nation: Gendered and ethnicized discourses of national identity in Olympic opening ceremonies. *Journal of Sport and Social Issues, 27*(2), 100–123.

Indian Country. (6 December 2000). Accessed online: http://www.indiancountry.com/.

Indian Country. (15 February 2002). Accessed online: http://www.indiancountry.com/.

Indian Country. (16 February 2002). Accessed online: http://www.indiancountry.com/.

Jennings, A. (1996). *The new lords of the rings: Olympic corruption and how to buy gold medals*. London: Pocket Books.

Kidd, B. (1996). Montreal 1976: The games of the XXIth Olympiad. In: J. Findling & K. Pelle (Eds), *Historical dictionary of the modern Olympic movement* (pp. 153–160). Westport, CN: Greenwood Press.

Lenskyj, H. (2000). *Inside the Olympic industry: Power, politics, and activism.* Albany, NY: State University of New York Press.

Lenskyj, H. (2002). *The best Olympics ever?: Social impacts of Sydney 2000.* Albany, NY: State University of New York Press.

MacAloon, J. (1984). Olympic Games and the theory of spectacle in modern societies. In: J. MacAloon (Ed.), *Rite, drama, festival, spectacle: Rehearsals toward a theory of cultural performance* (pp. 241–280). Philadelphia: Institute for the Study of Human Issues.

MacAloon, J. (1992). Comparative analysis of the Olympic Ceremonies with special reference to Los Angeles. In: M. Bardaif (Ed.), *Olympic Games: Media and cultural exchanges: The experience of the last four summer Olympic Games* (pp. 35–54). Barcelona: Centre d'Estudis Olimpics i de l'Esport.

MacAloon, J. (1996). Olympic ceremonies as a setting for intercultural exchange. In: M. Spa, J. MacAloon & M. Llines (Eds), *Olympic ceremonies: Historical continuity and cultural exchange* (pp. 29–43). Lausanne: International Olympic Committee.

Mallon, B. (1999). *The 1904 Olympic Games: Results for all competitors in all events, with commentary.* Jefferson, NC: McFarland & Company, Inc.

Morgan, G. (2003). Aboriginal protest and the Sydney Olympic Games. *OLYMPIKA: The International Journal of Olympic Studies, XII,* 23–38.

Moses, L. (2002). Performative traditions in American Indian history. In: P. Deloria & N. Salisbury (Eds), *A companion to American Indian history* (pp. 193–208). Malden, MA: Blackwell Publishers.

O'Bonsawin, C. (2002). *Would it be helpful if we organized a boycott?: The Lubicon Nation's appeal for an international boycott of Calgary 88.* Unpublished Paper.

Pappas, N. (1982). The closing ceremonies of the Olympic Games. *Olympic Review, 7,* 407–408.

Paraschak, V. (1995). Aboriginal inclusiveness in Canadian sporting culture: An image without substance. In: F. van der Merwe (Ed.), *Sport as symbol, symbols in sport* (pp. 347–356). Capetown, South Africa: Academia.

Reuters Business Briefing. (January 6 2002). Olympic Press Reviews (p. 16). London, ON: International Centre for Olympic Studies.

Roche, M. (2000). *Mega-events and modernity: Olympics and expos in the growth of global culture.* London: Routledge.

Rousseau, R. (1975). One year before the games of the XXIst Olympiad. *Olympic Review, 91–92,* 163–165.

Rydell, R. (1984). *All the world's A fair: Vision's of empire at American international expositions, 1876–1916.* Chicago: University of Chicago Press.

Schantz, O. (1996). From Rome (1960) to Montreal (1976). From rite to spectacle. In: M. Spa, J. MacAloon & M. Llines (Eds), *Olympic ceremonies: Historical continuity and cultural exchange* (pp. 131–139). Lausanne: International Olympic Committee.

Stanaland, T. (1981). Pre-Olympic 'Anthropology Days,' 1904: An aborted effort to bridge some cultural gaps. In: A. T. Cheska (Ed.), *Play as context: 1979 Proceedings of the Association for the Anthropological Study of Play* (pp. 101–106). West Point, NY: Leisure Press.

The Salt Lake Tribune. (24 September 2001). Indian tribes hope to capitalize on Olympic exposure. *Olympic Press Reviews* (p. 1). London, ON: International Centre for Olympic Studies.

Wamsley, K. B. (2002). The global sport monopoly: A synopsis of 20th century Olympic politics. *International Journal, LVII*(3), 395–410.

Wamsley, K. B. (2004). Calgary 1988: XVth Olympic Winter Games. In: J. E. Findling & K. D. Pelle (Eds), *Encyclopedia of the modern Olympic movement* (pp. 389–396). Westport, CN: Greenwood Press.

Wamsley, K. B., & Heine, M. K. (1996a). Tradition, modernity, and the construction of civic identity: The Calgary Olympics. *OLYMPIKA: The International Journal of Olympic Studies, V,* 81–90.

Wamsley, K. B., & Heine, M. K. (1996b). Don't mess with the relay – it's bad medicine: Aboriginal culture and the 1988 Winter Olympics. In: R. K. Barney, S. G. Martyn, D. A. Brown & G. H. MacDonald (Eds), *Olympic perspectives* (pp. 173–178). London, ON: International Centre for Olympic Studies.

Watts, I. (2004). *Igniting the nation: Print media representations of Aboriginality in the Sydney 2000 Olympic Games.* Unpublished Master's thesis. The University of Western Ontario, London, ON, Canada.

Chapter 13

OLYMPIC DRUG TESTING: AN INTERPRETIVE HISTORY

John Hoberman

The drug testing of Olympic athletes has developed as a response to widespread doping practices that date from the last decades of the nineteenth century. Pharmacological practices of this kind may be understood as responses to the escalating ambitions of high-performance athletes as they have developed since the revival of the Olympic movement in the 1890s. In this sense, it is useful to regard Olympic sport as "a gigantic biological experiment carried out on the human organism" (Hollmann, 1987) over the past century. The quantifiable results of this "experiment" may be witnessed in the vast body of data on various athletic performances that has accumulated over many years. Analysing these data in relation to what is known about drug use, and especially anabolic steroid doping among elite athletes, allows us to estimate some approximate limits to certain drug-free athletic performances. Indeed, the doping epidemic that has spread through some Olympic sports over the past 40 years indicates that certain limits were reached years ago, and can be extended only by the pharmacological manipulation of human physiology. Doping will be inevitable and common whenever governments, commercial interests, and sports officials demand and reward superhuman performances. The claim made by some sports bureaucrats that doping is practised by a "small subculture of drug-cheaters" (*New York Times*, 7 July 2004) has proven to be false. Despite such claims, as Timothy D. Noakes, M.D., has pointed out:

Global Olympics: Historical and Sociological Studies of the Modern Games
Research in the Sociology of Sport, Volume 3, 249–268
Copyright © 2005 by Elsevier Ltd.
All rights of reproduction in any form reserved

...multiple sources of evidence, including personal testimony and an ever-increasing
incidence of doping scandals, suggest the opposite: that widespread use of performance-
enhancing drugs has fundamentally distorted the upper range of human athletic performance. Unfortunately, a global code of silence has kept the problem hidden from
public view (Noakes, 2004, pp. 847–849).

Until recently, this policy of silence was aided and abetted by the International Olympic Committee (IOC) and its affiliated sports federations
(Hoberman, 2000).

EARLY OLYMPIC DOPING

The first recorded case of doping at an Olympiad dates from the 1904
Games in St. Louis. Suffering (along with many other runners) from heat
exhaustion, an American named T. J. Hicks won the marathon, "but only
after faltering several times, on which occasions he was given injections of
strychnine sulfate and by mouth a total of five eggs (preparation not specified) and several glasses of brandy" (Ryan, 1968, p. 717). This century-old
anecdote from the annals of sports medicine reminds us that the very concept of doping is a cultural construct that evolves over time. Given that
Hicks is reported to have required the services of "four physicians" after his
ordeal, it would appear that administering a stimulant (strychnine) and a
central nervous system depressant (alcohol) to this exhausted athlete was
intended not to boost his performance but, rather, to enable him to complete and survive it. It is most unlikely that those who assisted him construed
their own actions as an illegitimate form of "doping". Indeed, whereas the
doping of horses was forbidden in 1903, the doping of human athletes did
not become a publicly discussed ethical problem until the 1920s, as sport
became a form of mass culture in Europe and the United States (Donohoe &
Johnson, 1986, p. 4; Hoberman, 1992, p. 106). Several decades passed before
the IOC finally began to take cognizance of the doping issue during the
1960s.

The relative insignificance of doping as an ethical problem for Olympic
sport prior to the advent of widespread anabolic steroid doping during the
1960s is evident in how infrequently such practices came to public attention.
During the 1936 Berlin Olympic Games, "it was stated that the Japanese
swimmers were 'pumped full of oxygen' in their dressing rooms, and there
followed a discussion of the possible influence of this practice on athletic
performance" (Ove Bøje, 1939, p. 449). But oxygen doping proved to be no
more than a fad. At the 1952 Oslo Winter Games, "there were reports of

used hypodermic needles and empty ampoules found in the locker rooms and it is likely that there was some stimulant use at the time",[1] presumably involving the amphetamine drugs that had been commercially available since the late 1930s. But amphetamine doping did not become associated with Olympic sport. At the 1956 Melbourne Games, "[d]octors alleged that one competitor...showed spasms characteristic of strychnine poisoning" (Donohoe & Johnson, 1986, p. 5). But, in the absence of Olympic doping controls, there was no way to classify or sanction such an event. In 1957, a brief controversy erupted when a New York doctor suggested that the sub-four-minute milers of that era had used the amphetamine known as Benzedrine (*New York Times*, 6 June 1957). It appeared, he said, that these men had been "turned temporarily into super-athletes by the use of drugs". All of the runners who responded to this charge flatly denied that they had used drugs. The 1956 Olympic champion in the 1500 m run, Ron Delany of Ireland, stated: "The whole idea is absurd and crazy. I have never used drugs to help me run and I don't know of anyone else who has, anywhere in the world. That includes all the four-minute milers. Track and field is an amateur sport – a clean sport" (*The Times* [London], 7 June 1957). This trans-Atlantic controversy lived on for a couple of years in the pages of a medical journal, but was otherwise quickly forgotten (*Journal of the American Medical Association*, 1958, p. 775; Smith & Beecher, 1959).

THE DOPING PROBLEM AND EARLY TESTING

The first highly publicised episode of doping at an Olympiad was the death of the Danish cyclist, Knud Enemark Jensen, during the 100 km road race at the1960 Rome Olympic Games. Although this death (and the collapse of two of his Danish teammates) was originally ascribed to "heat stroke", it turned out that the team trainer had given his riders a stimulant called roniacol for the purpose of promoting circulation of their blood while they competed. Official responses to this tragedy came not from IOC, but from governments. A Danish government source declared that: "As roniacol is given only to elderly people with blood circulation difficulties, it must be considered highly irresponsible that the trainer ordered this remedy under the given circumstances" (*New York Times*, August 29, 1960). This statement looks forward to a report expected, not from the (still non-existent) IOC Medical Commission but, rather, from the Rome Legal Institute of Medicine. Three days after Jensen's death, Rome's Deputy Attorney General announced that an investigation would be carried out because "authorities did not exclude the possibility" that the dead athlete had taken stimulants (*New York Times*, August 30, 1960). Decades before the passage of Italy's strict anti-doping law, an athlete's use of a stimulant could only be classified as common drug abuse. The formal involvement of the Olympic movement in the Jensen case seems to have been limited to its final chapter; the Danish Olympic Committee offered to pay for his funeral.

We may assume that the highly-publicised death of Jensen "did a great deal to convince IOC that it had a doping problem, which would have to be met head-on in future Games" (Barnes, 1980, p. 21). Up to this point, Olympic officials' lack of interest in the doping issue could be explained in part by their fervently-held conviction that Olympic sport was amateur sport. It was widely accepted at this time that doping practices were confined to professional athletes in general, and cyclists in particular, even as occasional revelations of amateur drug use called this assumption into question. As the coach of the French cycling team at the Rome Games remarked: "I'm not surprised to hear Jensen had been drugged. A healthy young athlete does not die from sunstroke. Many pros are drugged, of course, but we don't drug amateurs" (*New York Times*, 30 August 1960). As Ron Delany had put it 3 years earlier, amateur sport was "clean sport". Strict adherence to amateur standards was also the favourite theme of Avery Brundage, President of the IOC from 1952 to 1972, and this preoccupation with unremunerated athletic performance made it that much harder for him to recognise the threat doping posed to Olympic sport. As Guttmann has pointed out:

> Brundage was never as concerned about doping as he was about professionalization. Of course he condemned the athletes who popped pills in order to gain a competitive edge over a more sportsmanlike opponent, but drugs never seemed quite the image of evil that Mammon did (Guttmann, 1983, p. 123).

In retrospect, one notes that Brundage's presidency extended from the last years of the pre-steroid era to the Munich Games at which East German female swimmers began to generate the first accusations of steroid use at an Olympiad. We may assume that the IOC's initial engagement with the doping issue during the 1960s was delayed by the effects of Brundage's forceful personality and, more specifically, by his unwillingness to take the drugs threat more seriously than he did. The 1957 amphetamine controversy had demonstrated that many sports officials were highly sensitive to (though not necessarily well informed about) the drugs issue when it came to public attention. But neither Avery Brundage nor any other IOC voices took part in this public discussion. We should also keep in mind that official thinking about athletic doping during the 1950s was still in an early, and somewhat ambivalent, phase that long preceded the effects of the stigmatising of anabolic steroids that occurred during the 1970s and 1980s.

The establishment of the IOC's first Medical Committee on 21 June 1961, occurred less than a year after the death of Jensen on 26 August 1960 (Todd & Todd, 2000, p. 67). Its four members were Ryotaro Azuma of Japan, Joaquim Ferreira Santos of Brazil, Josef Gruss of Czechoslovakia, and Arthur Porritt of New Zealand, co-founder (with Adolphe Abrahams) of the British Association of Medicine and Sport in 1952 (*The Times* [London], 12 July, 1952, p. 90). The charge from Avery Brundage was to look into the doping issue and establish some recommendations regarding how to proceed. This initiative languished until the IOC met in Tokyo in 1964. Prince Alexandre de Merode of Belgium was later named to replace the deceased Ferreira, and he became the Chairman of the IOC Medical Commission in September 1967 (Todd & Todd, 2000).[2] Although he possessed no scientific or medical credentials, Merode retained the chairmanship of this body until his resignation in May 2000 (he died in 2002).[3] His long term as the head of the Medical Commission was marked by controversy, occasional ridicule, and more rhetoric than progress on the anti-doping front (Hoberman, 2000).

ATHLETES AND DRUG TESTING

The history of Olympic drug testing must include an account of the attitudes of athletes and physicians toward a testing procedure that was intended both as a form of medical surveillance and as a pedagogical strategy. In 1966, or two years before IOC testing began at the Mexico City Games, the IOC Medical Committee stated that "only a long-term education policy stressing the physical and moral aspects" of the doping problem would prevent athletes from doping. Arthur Porritt suggested that athletes be required to sign a pledge that their training had not included the use of drugs. At its May 1967 meeting in Teheran, the IOC embraced this principle by requiring all Olympic athletes to sign a pledge that they would not dope their way to higher performances (Todd & Todd, 2000, p. 68).

The idea that elite athletes can be "educated" away from, or out of, doping practices persists to this day as an optimistic alternative to sheer resignation in the face of widespread drug use by elite athletes. The IOC, the United States Olympic Committee (USOC), the United States Anti-Doping Agency (USADA), the World Anti-Doping Agency (WADA) – all have promoted "educational" initiatives that may be aimed at elite performers or the young people who are presumed to regard top-level athletes as role models.[4] In the 1960s, however, the IOC Medical Committee's nascent interest in promoting an anti-doping pedagogy collided with an attitude among some athletes that held they had a right to use performance-enhancing drugs. For example, though there was "no centralized drug testing at the 1964 Games in Tokyo; some spot-checks were done but many athletes refused to cooperate with the medical commission" (Cowart, 1986, p. 3073). The British doping experts Arnold H. Beckett and David A. Cowan later noted that "many of the sports writers" agreed with the athletes who felt they were entitled to the drugs of their choice: "They complained that the tests were interfering with the rights of individuals. They were not convinced that the tests were fair and gave correct results. They had experience of what was happening on the Continent [in professional cycling] and therefore they had quite legitimate doubts". At this time, "the question was sometimes asked 'why should not the right of choice be allowed to any competitor to use any method of training or even any drug despite possible danger to health or life. If he dies in the attempt to excel is that not his responsibility?'" (Beckett & Cowan, 1979, pp. 185, 186). The persistence of this libertarian approach to athletic pharmacology has bedeviled the anti-doping campaign ever since. The American steroid expert James Wright noted in 1987, for example, that:

> ...some athletes feel they are not violating the letter or spirit of the Olympic code because they think of their steroid use in terms of replacement therapy: 'These are drugs that help the body recover from physical and emotional stress, and if the hormone levels are reduced because of stress, then I suppose the argument could be made that it is a replacement dose' (Cowart, 1987, p. 3025).

Every such blurring of the line between therapy and enhancement results in uncertainty about how doping is to be defined and whether it can be effectively regulated on behalf of ensuring fair competitions. But, perhaps the most neglected aspect of the entire doping conundrum has been how athletes actually feel about illicit drug use, including the moral exemption from anti-doping rules to which, as Wright points out, a significant number of athletes feel entitled.

The mindset of Olympic athletes confronting the temptations presented by doping drugs was addressed on at least two occasions by IOC President Juan Antonio Samaranch during his long term in office (1980–2001). In 1983 he stated: "There are, no doubt, those who cheat, and we know it...the really guilty people are not necessarily the athletes, who are often young and 'innocent'; it is those who encourage them to take drugs" (Todd & Todd, 2000, p. 78). In 1998, responding to that summer's Tour de France doping scandal, Samaranch commented once again that: "The ones to blame are not the athletes but those around them" (Todd & Todd, 2000, p. 106). This somewhat paternalistic view of "young and innocent" athletes' involvement in doping practices correctly situates the athletes (at least by implication) in the company of the trainers and physicians who have often borne responsibility for aiding and abetting their drug use. The problem with this interpretation of the athlete's predicament is that it does not address drug use by athletes who may be neither young nor innocent and who take the initiative to dope themselves. As one American journalist, Bil Gilbert, noted in 1969: "There are probably as many cases of athletes demanding drugs from trainers and physicians as physicians and trainers ordering athletes to take them" (Gilbert, 1969, p. 70). How does one "educate" athletes who, while acting as autonomous adults, choose to dope themselves?

At the 1968 Mexico City Games, reporters asked one American weightlifter about the IOC's new rule against the use of amphetamines. "What ban?" he replied. "Everyone used a new one from West Germany. They couldn't pick it up in the test they were using. When they get a test for that one, we'll find something else. It's like cops and robbers". Years later, the limitations of the now familiar detect-and-punish scenario were noted by Professor Arnold Beckett of the IOC Medical Committee: "After we discovered a test for the anabolic steroids the athletes regrouped and considered what to do. They found testosterone. It's a war, and we are facing a whole new battle" (Donohoe & Johnson, 1986, pp. 62–63). An American decathlete competing in Mexico City estimated that a third of American track-and-field athletes had been using anabolic steroids at their pre-Olympic training camp (Todd & Todd, 2000, p. 69). The Olympic Games, Gilbert wrote, had long "served as an exchange for drugs and drug recipes. This was particularly true in 1968, when everyone's attention was forcibly fixed on drug usage by the new anti-doping regulations and dope-detection tests instituted by the International Olympic Committee" (1969, p. 72).

SPORTS PHYSICIANS AND THE PERFORMANCE AGENDA

The role of physicians in the doping practices of Olympic athletes has been a substantial (and often overlooked) dimension of elite athletic doping

(Hoberman, 2002). "If drug usage in sports is a developing scandal", Gilbert wrote in 1969, "then it is a scandal that involves the medical establishment as well as the sporting one". Two decades later, the Dubin Commission report on the Ben Johnson Olympic doping scandal confirmed this assessment:

> Physicians have played an important role in supplying anabolic steroids and other banned drugs to athletes for performance enhancement. Many athletes who testified at this Inquiry received banned substances from physicians, in some cases together with medical supervision and in other cases without any medical care whatsoever (*Commission of Inquiry into the Use of Drugs and Banned Practices Intended to Increase Athletic Performance*, 1990, p. 385).

In fact, the pro-steroid lobby within the ranks of sports physicians has been active since the 1960s. Such doctors are often motivated by ambitions to keep their nations' athletes internationally competitive. For example, in 1969, Dr. H. Kay Dooley, a physician for the USOC, stated: "I don't think it's possible for a man to compete internationally without using anabolic steroids. All the weight men on the Olympic team [in 1968] had to take steroids. Otherwise they would not have been in the running" (Gilbert, 1969, p. 66).

While such public candour about the practical necessity of doping has virtually disappeared, a subgroup of physicians sympathetic to medically-regulated doping remains active to this day. The most important infiltrator of this kind has been the Italian sports physician Dr. Francesco Conconi, whose doping trial in Ferrera lasted for years until the statute of limitations expired in November 2003. In March 2004, Conconi was pronounced "morally guilty" of erythropoietin (EPO) doping by an Italian judge (*Süddeutsche Zeitung*, 12 March 2004). During the 1990s, Conconi was engaged by the IOC Medical Commission to develop a test for EPO doping, and he headed the medical commission of the International Cycling Union (UCI). He remains to this day Vice Rector of the University of Ferrera (Hoberman, 2000, pp. 251–253). The Conconi case is one example of how vulnerable the IOC Medical Commission and other medical commissions have been to infiltration by people with personal or political agendas of their own. When the Medical Committee added its doping and biochemistry subcommission in 1980, following the Moscow Games, its six members included an East German (Claus Clausnitzer) and a Soviet (Vitaly Semenov).[5] The IOC drug-testing programme has expanded dramatically since its inauguration at the Grenoble Winter and Mexico City Summer Olympic Games in 1968 (Ferstle, 1993, pp. 253–282). At the IOC Congress held in October 1968, just before the opening of the Mexico City Games, IOC

President Avery Brundage stated that, while the IOC would organise the drug testing, the "actual responsibility (for the testing and its legal repercussions) should remain with the international federations, who therefore must give a written agreement" (Todd & Todd, 2000, p. 68). The five major categories of drugs banned at the 1968 Games included "sympathomimetic amines (e.g., amphetamine, ephedrine), CNS stimulants (e.g., strychnine and analeptics), narcotic analgesics (e.g., morphine), anti-depressants (e.g., MAO inhibitors or imipramine), and major tranquilisers (e.g., phenothiazine). Alcohol was also banned in fencing and the shooting events, sports in which competitors look for a steady hand" (Barnes, 1980, p. 22). [6] Of the 86 tests performed at Grenoble, all turned out negative. Similarly, all but one of the 668 tests conducted at Mexico City were negative, with the exception of a Swedish biathlete whose blood alcohol level exceeded the allowed maximum of 40 g/100 ml. This positive test prompted the IOC to revoke the bronze medal won by him and his teammate (Barnes, 1980, p. 22; Donohoe & Johnson, 1986, p. 8). The consumption of alcohol would presumably have calmed his nerves during the shooting stage of his event. The alcohol test had been introduced after an intoxicated shooter was discovered at the 1964 Tokyo Olympics (Donohoe & Johnson, 1986, p. 8).

It is unlikely that these testing results reflected the actual incidence of drug use at the 1968 Games. Anecdotal evidence cited above, including the substitution of one type of amphetamine for another, suggests that these tests were less than wholly effective. In addition, testing for anabolic steroids would certainly have produced many positive results. As Dr. Dooley put it: "All the weight men on the Olympic team had to take steroids to remain competitive". Over the next 30 years, IOC drug testing managed to produce only a miniscule number of doping positives among tens of thousands of Olympic competitors.

IOC TESTING: AMBIVALENCE, POLITICS, AND THE JOHNSON ERA

The first extensive drug testing was carried out at the 1972 Munich Games. (At the 1972 Winter Games in Sapporo, Japan, 211 tests had revealed one case of ephedrine use (Barnes, 1980, p. 22)). At Munich, "two screening procedures were used to detect stimulants, narcotics, and sedatives" (*Commission of Inquiry into the Use of Drugs and Banned Practices Intended to Increase Athletic Performance*, 1990, p. 77). The Munich Games produced seven "positives" among the 2,079 athletes who were tested. In addition, ten urine samples from pentathletes contained chlorrdiazepoxide (Librium), three had diazepam (Valium), and one contained the barbiturate substitute glutethimide (Doriden) (Cowart, 1986, p. 3073). As Donohoe and Johnson (1986) put it:

> These anti-anxiety drugs or minor tranquillisers were not on the banned list, but were clearly being used instead of alcohol to 'steady nerves' during the competitions. Further developments during 1972 included the removal of the major tranquillisers from the banned list, because many doctors were prescribing them to athletes suffering from jet-lag (p. 10).

The IOC first tested for anabolic steroids unofficially at the Munich Games, leading to early public suspicion about the possible steroid doping of East German athletes (Ferstle, 1993, p. 257).

The 1976 Montreal Games marked the first official use of the radio-immunoassay technique for detecting the anabolic steroids that the IOC had added to its banned list in April 1975. This method had been developed in England and was first employed during the Commonwealth Games in Christchurch, New Zealand, in January 1974. In Montreal it was "used as a screening test and those samples which gave an apparent positive result were then carried through for detailed examination" by the more sensitive gas liquid chromatography/mass spectrometry method (Beckett & Cowan, 1979, p. 189). The conventional drug testing comprised 1,800 urine samples, while 275 urine samples were screened for anabolic steroids (Beckett & Cowan, 1979, p. 190). The 11 positive tests included eight for steroids. All of those who tested positive were weightlifters, the exception being a female discus thrower from Poland who also tested positive for steroids (Donohoe & Johnson, 1986, p. 13). Speculation about blood doping, a procedure invented by a Swedish physiologist in 1972, accompanied the victories of the Finnish distance star Lasse Virén in the 5,000 and 10,000 m runs. Public commentary about the upper-body development and deep voices of the East German female swimmers also intensified at these Games (Todd & Todd, 2000, p. 74).

Drug testing at the 1980 Moscow Games did not produce a single "positive". The fraudulence of this result can be seen by pointing to the documented use of anabolic steroids in 1979 and 1980 by two East German male gold-medal winners: Lutz Dombrowski (high jump) and Gerd Wessig (high jump), along with their teammate, Jörg Freimuth, who won a bronze medal in the high jump (Berendonk, 1992, p. 152). The doping regimens of other East German medal winners at Moscow that are documented starting in 1981 include Thomas Munkelt (high hurdles), Udo Beyer (shotput),

Marlies Göhr (100 m), Bärbel Wöckel (200 m), Marita Koch (400 m), and Ilona Slupianek (shotput) (Berendonk, 1992, pp. 151, 158, 171). With the exception of Beyer, who won bronze, all of these athletes won gold medals at Moscow. Behind the scenes at Moscow, the IOC doping expert Manfred Donike was using a new (testosterone/epitestosterone ratio) test to examine athletes' urine samples for exogenous testosterone. The results showed that "20 percent of all athletes tested – males and females – would have failed his new testosterone screen if it were officially administered... The 20 percent figure included sixteen gold medalists" (Todd & Todd, 2000, p. 77). As an American physician commented in 1984: "Once it was common for athletes to take anabolic steroids. Recently, however, to avoid detection, an athlete stopped taking anabolic steroids but increased the intake of testosterone, which has anabolic and androgenic effects. Thus, the athlete passed the testing with little loss of power; there were no positive test results at the 1980 Moscow Olympics when 20% of the athletes probably were using testosterone" (Wallach, 1984, p. 566). In 1982, the IOC added testosterone to its list of banned substances.

The absence of doping "positives" at the Moscow Olympics did not create the controversy that should have followed in the wake of such an improbable result. We may assume that this finding was welcomed by an IOC that at this time preferred disengagement to anti-doping activism. Just before the Moscow Games, Michel Bertrand, a Canadian scientist who had analysed many urine samples during the 1976 Montreal Olympics, expressed optimism regarding the ongoing contest between doping athletes and the laboratory personnel assigned to catch them: "The technologists can develop new tests faster than the athletes and their trainers can develop new doping techniques. In the last 10–12 years of doping control the obvious drugs have been taken care of, and even if "state-of-the-art" doping is going undetected, most athletes are still somewhat protected. The situation is, up to a point, under control" (Barnes, 1980, p. 23). The absence of positive test results at Moscow can only have encouraged such unwarranted optimism.

The 1984 Los Angeles Games produced 12 official doping "positives" among athletes competing in weightlifting, volleyball, and track and field (Catlin et al., 1987, pp. 319–327). Apart from one ephedrine "positive", all of the banned substances were androgens (testosterone or anabolic steroids) (*Agence France-Presse*, 26 August 2004). Several months after the Games it was revealed that seven members of the US cycling team had received exogenous blood transfusions in an attempt to boost endurance by means of blood doping (Cramer, 1985; Klein, 1985; Rostaing & Sullivan, 1985). This scandal prompted no action by either the IOC or the USOC. On 8 January

1985, the day the scandal broke, the USOC issued a statement expressing its pride "that not one US Olympic athlete in Los Angeles failed a drug test, nor embarrassed anyone connected with the Olympic movement or amateur sports" (Rostaing & Sullivan, 1985, p. 10). One of the transfused cyclists, Pat McDonough, a silver medalist in the team-pursuit competition, told reporters: "Nothing illegal was done... In the Olympics, you know that everyone is getting the best medical help. So, if it's not illegal, you get it too" (Todd & Todd, 2000, p. 83). It is now known that an undetermined number of positive test results obtained during the Los Angeles testing operation were never reported by Olympic officials. It remains unclear whether this breakdown in the system was the result of accident or a plot by one or more IOC officials to suppress doping positives that would have tarnished the image of the Games (Todd & Todd, 2000, pp. 101–102).

The doping control operation at the 1988 Seoul Olympic Games will be remembered for the IOC's announcement on 27 September 1988, that the Canadian sprinter Ben Johnson, gold medalist in the 100 m race in a world-record time of 9.79 sec, had tested positive for the anabolic steroid stanozolol. The Ben Johnson scandal alarmed the IOC and prompted the international track-and-field federation (IAAF) to introduce more effective out-of-competition drug testing that prevented athletes from improving on some of the steroid-assisted world records set during the 1980s. The scandal also caused the Canadian government to establish a *Commission of Inquiry into the Use of Drugs and Banned Practices Intended to Increase Athletic Performance* (the Dubin Report). In addition to Ben Johnson, nine other athletes, including five weightlifters, tested positive for stanozolol, propanolol (a beta-blocker), furosemide (a diuretic masking agent), pemoline (a central nervous system stimulant), and caffeine. On 17 November 1988, *The New York Times* reported that:

> At least half of the 9,000 athletes who competed at the Olympics in Seoul used performance-enhancing drugs in training, according to estimates by medical and legal experts as well as traffickers in these drugs. These experts also contend that the drug testing programs of the IOC and other sports associations have had no impact in reducing the use of such drugs (Todd & Todd, 2000, p. 91).

The director of Olympic drug testing at the Seoul Games, Dr. Park Jong Sei, stated that at least 20 athletes not identified as "doped" had tested positive but were not disqualified (Todd & Todd, 2000, p. 92).

The 1992 Barcelona Olympic Games produced five doping "positives", for norephedrine, clenbuterol (a bronchodilator often misidentified as an anabolic steroid), and the stimulants strychnine and mesocarb (*Agence*

France-Presse, 26 August 2004).[7] All three medalists in the shot put competition at Barcelona, two Americans, and a Ukrainian, had tested positive for anabolic steroids or testosterone, had served their suspensions, and were allowed to compete.

Doping controls at the 1996 Atlanta Olympic Games resulted in two anabolic steroid positive test results. Although four athletes from the former Soviet Union tested positive for the stimulant bromantan, the Court of Arbitration for Sport ruled that bromantan did not appear on the official IOC list of banned substances and cleared the athletes of having committed a doping offense. The IOC added this drug to its list shortly thereafter.

The integrity of the IOC drug testing at Atlanta was called into question in November 1996 by Dr. Don Catlin, one of the principal scientists involved in the supervision of the Olympic laboratory at the Atlanta Games. In an interview with the *London Sunday Times*, Catlin stated: "There were several other steroid positives from around the end of the Games which we reported. I can think of no reason why they have not been announced". He also expressed his deep reservations regarding the assignment of Olympic drug testing to SmithKline Beecham, a commercial manufacturer of testosterone products (Hoberman, 2000, pp. 253–254). The partnership between the IOC and the World Anti-Doping Agency that began in 2000 has since eliminated this potential conflict of interest.

Shortly before the Atlanta Games began, the chief medical officer, Dr. John Cantwell, predicted that doping controls would produce 12–15 positive tests among the 10,700 athletes scheduled to take part, or about one-tenth of one percent (*New York Times*, July 6, 1996). In fact, the predicted ratio of positives to participants at Atlanta matched almost exactly the results of IOC drug testing over the period between 1968 and 1996, during which approximately one in every 1,000 athletes tested positive for a banned substance (Shipley, 1999).[8] This tiny ratio calls into question the repeated claims over many years by Juan Antonio Samaranch that the IOC had been waging an effective campaign against doping during his tenure as IOC President. Significant change in IOC policy toward doping had to wait for a dramatic sequence of events that was catalysed by the Tour de France doping scandal of 1998.

ANTI-DOPING

The Tour de France scandal marked the advent of state prosecution of doping offenses on a major scale (Hoberman, 2000, pp. 264–267). The deployment of customs personnel and police officers by the French minister of youth and sport, Marie-Georges Buffet, demonstrated that governmental activism could expose and punish doping by elite athletes with an effectiveness the sports federations were either unable or unwilling to match. As Samaranch watched an Olympic sport descend into disgrace, he apparently decided to pre-empt a similar crisis at future Olympic Games by proposing a revised definition of doping itself.

In July 1998, Samaranch told the Spanish newspaper *El Mundo*: "For me everything that does not injure the health of the athlete is not doping" (*Süddeutsche Zeitung*, 27 July 1998). This candid and heretical remark prompted a storm of criticism from both inside and outside of the IOC. To repair his damaged reputation as an anti-doping crusader, Samaranch announced that the IOC would hold the World Anti-Doping Conference that eventually convened in Lausanne on 2–4 February 1999 (Ferstle, 2000, pp. 275–286). Despite the Olympic bribery scandal that broke in December 1998, this conference led to the creation of the World Anti-Doping Agency that commenced its operations on 13 January 2000.

Doping control at the 2000 Sydney Olympic Games was a collaborative operation between the IOC Medical Commission, which administered the drug testing, and the World Anti-Doping Agency in the role of observer. This was the first time that athletes were subjected to pre-Olympic, out-of-competition testing. Another innovation was the introduction of blood and urine testing for the blood-boosting drug EPO (Corrigan & Kazlauskas, 2000, pp. 312–313). While no EPO "positives" were announced, four athletes tested positive for a masking agent – the diuretic furosemide – four tested positive for various anabolic steroids, and the Romanian gymnast Andreea Raducan tested positive for pseudoephedrine, prompting the suspension of the Romanian team physician Ioachim Oano. Another nine athletes were disqualified from the Sydney Games on the basis of pre-competition tests, 11 more were disqualified for testing results obtained before they reached Sydney, and the Chinese cut 27 athletes from their Olympic team in early September, primarily on the basis of failed drug tests (*Agence France-Presse*, 26 August 2004; ABCNEWS.com, 28 September 2000). In summary, Olympic doping control at Sydney demonstrated an unprecedented resolve on the part of the IOC to pursue and sanction doping athletes. This reform was a direct result of the dramatic events of 1998–1999 and the formation of WADA. "This is the most drug-tested games in history", commented the White House drug policy director, Barry McCaffrey, a prominent critic of the IOC at the 1999 Lausanne meeting: "We have seen national governments taking a new mindset. This is a remarkably changed environment" (*Associated Press*, 15 September 2000).

The 2002 Salt Lake City Winter Olympic Games provided further evidence of the IOC's new-found aggressiveness in pursuing doped athletes. Between the 1968 Grenoble Winter Games and the 1998 Nagano Winter Games, only five athletes had tested positive and been punished; and only one of these athletes, the Soviet cross-country skier Galina Kulakova, had lost a medal (at the 1976 Innsbruck Games) on account of a positive drug test (*Austin American-Statesman*, 10 March 2002). A total of seven athletes tested positive at the 2002 Games.[9] The sensational doping cases of the Salt Lake City Games involved the Russian cross-country skiers Larissa Lazutina and Olga Danilova as well as the Spanish (but formerly German) cross-country skier Johann Mühlegg, all of whom tested positive for darbepoetin (Aranesp), a blood-boosting drug that is related to but much more effective than EPO. Mühlegg's blood values had been tracked by sports scientists for months before the Games (*Süddeutsche Zeitung*, 25 February 2002). Like the Russian skiers, he had fallen into a trap set by the IOC, which had made a point of not announcing the new test. This tactic was protested by Nikolai Durmanov, director of anti-doping policy for the Russian Olympic Committee. "Why", he asked, "was it kept a secret until the last day of the Olympiad"? (*Austin American-Statesman*, 10 March 2002). The nationalistic impulse that prompted this anti-doping official to protest effective testing at an Olympiad is one more reminder of how difficult it has been to assemble an international caste of regulators who might enforce anti-doping rules in a consistent and impartial manner.

Like the two Olympiads that preceded them, the 2004 Athens Olympic Games were preceded by the intense global awareness of doping that resulted from the 1998 Tour de France scandal and the events that followed. In addition, the "designer steroid" (THG – tetrahydrogestrinone) scandal that erupted in the United States in October 2003 compromised the reputations of many Olympic track-and-field athletes, almost all of them American, including the charismatic Olympic gold medalist Marion Jones. The aggressive prosecution of this alleged drug-dealing ring by Federal authorities, including prosecutors, the Federal Bureau of Investigation (FBI), and the Internal Revenue Service (IRS), conferred upon athletic doping a social importance and a sense of urgency that was unprecedented in American life. What is more, there were reports of a connection between the accused drug dealer, Victor Conte, and an unnamed coach in Greece, thereby associating the Balco scandal with the Olympic host country only months before the opening of the Athens Games (*San Jose Mercury News*, 24 March 2003; *Süddeutsche Zeitung*, 18 February 2004).

The first and most spectacular doping scandal to erupt at the Athens Games involved the celebrated Greek sprinters Kostas Kenteris and Ekaterina Thanou. Kenteris, the gold medalist at 200 m at both the Sydney Olympic Games and the 2002 World Championships in Munich, had long been suspected of doping. A day before the opening ceremony of the Athens Games, Kenteris and Thanou missed their scheduled drug tests at the Olympic Village, thereby catalysing a national trauma and a series of investigations that continued for months after the closing ceremonies. Both athletes withdrew from the Games. Yet, even before these Greek icons had missed their tests, five athletes (including two Greeks) had already been banned from the Games for doping offenses. During and after the Olympic competitions, another 20 athletes tested positive for doping drugs or were disqualified for refusing to submit to supplementary testing (*San Diego Union-Tribune*, August 29, 2004; *Süddeutsche Zeitung*, August 30, 2004). More than half of all athletes testing positive at Athens came from the eastern regions of Europe: Russia, Ukraine, Belarus, Moldavia, Hungary, Uzbekistan, and Greece. According to the German doping control officer Helmut Pabst, the out-of-competition drug testing of elite athletes is particularly difficult in this part of the world (*Süddeutsche Zeitung*, 14–15 August 2004).

Doping control at the Athens Games continued the IOC–WADA partnership that had handled the drug-testing operation at Sydney. An important innovation in Athens was the application of the WADA Code to athletes competing in 28 sports, meaning that athletes who violated doping control procedures specified in the Code could be excluded from the Games. It was also announced that blood and urine samples would be frozen for possible future testing (*New York Times*, 30 August 2004). For the first time, blood tests were used to detect human growth hormone (HGH), THG, and artificial blood substitutes (*Süddeutsche Zeitung*, 14–15 August 2004). Whether the possibility of its use deterred some athletes from using this drug remains a matter of speculation.

CONCLUSION

It is appropriate to ask what the more effective pursuit of doping athletes at the Sydney and Athens Games means for the future of Olympic sport. It is widely assumed that the campaign on behalf of drug-free (or manipulation-free) performances is essential to the credibility and, thus, the survival of the

Games. At the same time, however, the anti-doping campaign faces some formidable obstacles. We have seen that the political will to enforce doping control came late to the Olympic movement, and it would be naïve to assume that the global political will that will be required to eliminate doping has been achieved. One need only look at the huge swath of territory between Western Europe and the Urals – and the many doped athletes it continues to produce – to appreciate the sheer geographical dimension of doping control. Post-Athens revelations regarding the systemic doping control failures of the IAAF are one more reminder of how difficult it will be to establish credible doping control on a global scale (*Süddeutsche Zeitung*, 1 September 2004). The possibility of genetically-manipulated athletes has been recognised by the IOC as a grave threat to the future of Olympic sport (Sweeney, 2004).

Persuading political leaders around the world to discourage the sportive nationalism that encourages so much doping behaviour presents another formidable challenge that includes guaranteeing the physical safety of doping control officers. When, for example, two IOC officers went to the Hungarian town of Yak following the Athens Games to collect a urine sample from the disqualified Olympic champion in the hammer throw, Adrian Annus, they were met by an angry mob and were forced to leave the scene (*Frankfurter Allgemeine Zeitung* [FAZ.NET], 29 October 2004). In 1997, a Russian doping control officer was brutally attacked on a Moscow street and lost an eye (*Süddeutsche Zeitung*, 1–2 February 1997). The Greek doping control officer responsible for monitoring Kostas Kenteris and other Greek athletes in 2004 was ostracised, threatened, and eventually asked to be relieved of responsibility for testing his own countrymen (*Der Spiegel*, 23 August 2004). In October 2004, a Greek reporter, Filippos Sirigos, a key witness in the Kenteris scandal was stabbed and beaten with crowbars in an apparent attempt to kill him (*Guardian* [London], October 20, 2004). Such violent incidents make it clear that Olympic doping control involves far more than the laboratory science that devises the tests that detect doping drugs in athletes. It remains to be seen whether a critical mass of these performers can be persuaded to honour the anti-doping pledge that was recited, for the first time, at the 2004 Athens Olympiad.

NOTES

1. See Cowart, 1986: "Ludwig Prokop, professor of sports medicine and director of the Austrian Institute of Sports Medicine in Vienna, reported that his first

encounter with substance abuse was with athletes at the Oslo Winter Olympic Games in 1952. There he found broken ampules and injection syringes in the locker room of speed skaters". Cited in *Commission of Inquiry into the Use of Drugs and Banned Practices Intended to Increase Athletic Performance* (Ottawa: Minister of Supply and Services, 1990), p. 70.

2. On the early history of the IOC Medical Committee and (later) Commission, see Todd and Todd (2000: 67–68).

3. In May 2001, at a conference in Oslo, Norway, I asked the current Chairman of the IOC Medical Commission, Dr. Arne Ljungqvist, whether he had ever suggested to IOC President Juan Antonio Samaranch that Merode should be replaced. Ljungqvist told me that he had, indeed, made such a suggestion, to which Samaranch had replied: "I cannot dismiss a friend". Samaranch's IOC presidency lasted from 1980 to 2001.

4. See, for example, http://www.usantidoping.org/education/youth and http://www.wada-ama.org/en/t3.asp?p = 47473. In September 2000, the head of WADA, Richard Pound, stated: "The World Anti-Doping Agency's mission is to eradicate the use of drugs in sports by a combination of scientific work and education". See Tye (2000).

5. The other members were Arnold Beckett (United Kingdom), Donald Catlin (United States), Manfred Donike (West Germany), and Robert Dugal (Canada). See *Commission of Inquiry into the Use of Drugs and Banned Practices Intended to Increase Athletic Performance* (1990, p. 76).

6. The IOC's list of banned drugs announced in May 1967 included "alcohol, pep pills, cocaine, vasodilators, opiates (opium, morphine, heroin, pethidine, and metathadin), and hashish". See Todd & Todd (2000, p. 68).

7. I assume that the (unknown) term "mesocarde" that appears on this and other lists refer to the stimulant mesocarb.

8. This ratio of approximately one-tenth of one percent during the period 1968–1996 represents 52 doping "positives" found in an athlete population of about 54,000.

9. These athletes were Larissa Lazutina, Olga Danilova, Johann Mühlegg (all darbepoetin); Yulia Pavlovic (speedskater, Belarus, nandrolone), Sandis Prusis (bobsled, Latvia, nandrolone), Natalia Baranova (cross-country skier, Russia, EPO), and Pavle Jovanovic (bobsled, United States, nandrolone).

REFERENCES

Amphetamines, athletes, and performance. *Journal of the American Medical Association,* (October 11, 1958), *168,* 775.
Barnes, L. (1980). Olympic drug testing: Improvements without progress. *The Physician and Sportsmedicine, 6*(June), 21–24.
Beckett, A. H., & Cowan, D. A. (1979). Misuse of drugs in sport. *British Journal of Sports Medicine, 12,* 185–194.
Berendonk, B. (1992). *Doping: Von der Forschung zum Betrug.* Reinbek bei Hamburg: Rowohlt.
Bøje, O. (1939). Doping: A study of the means employed to raise the level of performance in sport. *Bulletin of the Health Organization of the League of Nations, 8,* 449.

Catlin, D. H., Kammerer, R. C., Hatton, C. K., Sekera, M. H., & Merdink, J. L. (1987). Analytical chemistry at the Games of the XXIIIrd Olympiad in Los Angeles, 1984. *Clinical Chemistry, 33*, 319–327.

Commission of Inquiry into the Use of Drugs and Banned Practices Intended to Increase Athletic Performance. (1990). Ottawa: Minister of Supply and Services, Government of Canada.

Corrigan, B., & Kazlauskas, R. (2000). Drug testing at the Sydney Olympics. *Medical Journal of Australia, 173*, 312–313.

Cowart, V. S. (1986). State-of-art drug identification laboratories play increasing role in major athletic events. *Journal of the American Medical Association, 256*(December 12), 3073.

Cowart, V. S. (1987). Study proposes to examine football players, power lifters for possible long-term sequelae from anabolic steroid use in 1970s competition. *Journal of the American Medical Association, 257*(June 12), 3025.

Cramer, R. B. (1985). Olympic cheating: The inside story of illicit doping and the U.S. cycling team. *Rolling Stone*, February 14, pp. 25, 26, 30.

Donohoe, T., & Johnson, N. (1986). *Foul play: Drug abuse in sports.* Oxford: Basil Blackwell.

Ferstle, J. (1993). Evolution and politics of drug testing. In: C. E. Yesalis (Ed.), *Anabolic steroids in sport and exercise* (pp. 253–282). Champaign, IL: Human Kinetics.

Ferstle, J. (2000). World conference on doping in sport. In: W. Wilson & E. Derse (Eds), *Doping in elite sport: The politics of drugs in the Olympic Movement* (pp. 275–286). Champaign, IL: Human Kinetics.

Gilbert, B. (1969). Problems in a turned-on world. *Sports Illustrated*, June 23.

Guttmann, A. (1983). *The Games must go on: Avery Brundage and the Olympic movement.* New York: Columbia University Press.

Hoberman, J. (1992). *Mortal engines: The science of performance and the dehumanization of sport.* New York: Free Press.

Hoberman, J. (2000). How drug testing fails: The politics of doping control. In: W. Wilson & E. Derse (Eds), *Doping in Elite Sport: The Politics of Drugs in the Olympic Movement* (pp. 241–274). Champaign, IL: Human Kinetics.

Hoberman, J. (2002). Sports physicians and the doping crisis in elite sport. *Clinical Journal of Sport Medicine, 12*, 203–208.

Hollmann, W. (1987). Risikofaktoren in der Entwicklung des Hochleistungssports. In: H. Rieckert (Ed.), *Sportmedizin-Kursbestimmung [Deutscher Sportärztekongreß, Kiel, 16–19, Oktober 1986]* (p. 15). Berlin: Springer Verlag.

Klein, H. G. (1985). Blood transfusion and athletics. *New England Journal of Medicine, 312*(March 28), 854–856.

No dopers from 'rich' West have been sent home. San Diego Union-Tribune, August 29, 2004.

Noakes, T. D. (2004). Tainted glory – Doping and athletic performance. *New England Journal of Medicine, 351*(August 26), 847–849.

Rostaing, B., & Sullivan, R. (1985). Triumphs tainted with blood. *Sports Illustrated*, January 21, 12ff.

Ryan, A. J. (1968). A medical history of the Olympic Games. *Journal of the American Medical Association, 205*(September 9), 717.

Shipley, A. (1999). Drug tests, troubling results: IOC's system is plagued by false positives in addition to cheating. *Washington Post*, September 23.

Smith, G. M., & Beecher, H. K. (1959). Amphetamine sulfate and athletic performance. *Journal of the American Medical Association, 170*(May 30), 542–557.

Sweeney, H. L. (2004). Gene doping. *Scientific American, 291*(July), 62–69.

Todd, J., & Todd, T. (2000). Significant events in the history of drug testing and the Olympic Movement, 1960–1999. In: W. Wilson & E. Derse (Eds), *Doping in elite sport: The politics of drugs in the Olympic Movement.* Champaign, IL: Human Kinetics.

Tye, L. (2000). Athletes' doping outpaces testing. *Boston Globe*, September 22.

Wallach, J. (1984). Athletes and steroid drugs. *Journal of the American Medical Association, 252*(July 27), 566.

Chapter 14

POLITICAL VIOLENCE, TERRORISM, AND SECURITY AT THE OLYMPIC GAMES

Michael Atkinson and Kevin Young

Whether the association between the Olympic Games and political violence is understood by members of international sports organisations and the authorities as real, imagined, or uncertain, concerns about terrorism and security at the Games now go hand-in-hand. Although Pierre de Coubertin envisioned that international sports events might help pacify conflict between nation-states, modern Olympic competitions undeniably represent a platform upon which political struggle, military posturing, and ideological warfare may be staged. Surprisingly, however, few sociologists have inspected the ways in which acts of political violence and terrorism may be embedded in sporting spheres like the Olympics (Young, 2000, 2001), or the mediated discourses that emerge around such acts that assist in popular understandings of events and viewpoints.

The Olympic Games typically become entangled with matters of political violence and terrorism along one of two axes. In the first instance, the Games may be targeted as a site for *overt terrorist action or violence*. Politically- or religiously-motivated individuals or organisations might find suitable targets in athletes participating in the Games, spectators attending the events, or selected corporate sponsors of the contests. Equally, the Olympics might become a context for 'spill-over' violence where local military, political, religious, or other conflicts between nations become manifest. Especially in those situations where athletic contests draw sizeable international audiences in geographical

Global Olympics: Historical and Sociological Studies of the Modern Games
Research in the Sociology of Sport, Volume 3, 269–294
Copyright © 2005 by Elsevier Ltd.

settings already embroiled in strife, the Olympics may be utilised as a vehicle for waging politically-charged violence against others, or further engaging conflict between nations (Roche, 2002; Atkinson & Young, 2003).

In the second instance, the Games may be used by political opportunists as a forum for *ideologically* underlining differences between their constituencies and those of others. In this context, terrorist activities may be juxtaposed against the explicit and tacit philosophies underpinning sports contests – whether it be 'innocent' philosophies such as civil liberties and human freedoms or more contrived goals such as nation-building, commercialism, and the hegemonic rule of those with power.

Implementing aspects of the figurational (process) sociological perspective (Elias, 1994; Elias & Dunning, 1986), this chapter explores the socio-cultural relevance of the Games as a potential target of political violence. In figurational terms, the Olympics may be poached by nations as a multi-mediated context for demarcating clear boundaries between globally identified 'established' and 'outsider' nation-states or political groups (Elias & Scotson, 1965; Atkinson & Young, 2003). For Elias and Scotson (1965), 'established' social groups are those deeply entrenched in both the base and superstructural segments of social figurations, and consequently control many of its ideological apparatuses. Conversely, outsider groups are more marginal members of a social figuration, less embedded in power positions and dominated on the basis of their limited statuses and resources (Elias & Scotson, 1965; Dowling, 1986; Hallin, 1986). In the case of the Olympics, it is evident that certain participating nations are positioned within the International Olympic Committee (IOC) as 'established' or 'outsider' parties, and that these positions are further crystallised through incidents of (real or threatened) violence at the Games. Such established–outsider positions within the IOC tend to mirror broader ideological and political antagonisms between nation-states often played out violently in other spheres of international tension. Equally, we uncover how groups may challenge their local or global positions as 'outsiders' through the threat of terrorism at the Games. Episodes of real and perceived threats of violence at selected Olympic Games, then, illustrate how sports cultures become saturated with the politics of security and terrorism, as well as questions of global inclusion.

POLITICAL VIOLENCE AT THE OLYMPIC GAMES

The political swordplay between established and outsider groups involving political violence and/or threats of terrorism at the Olympics dates back over a century. Indeed, the very first Games of the Modern Olympic era, Greece 1896, represented a stage for military tension between the host nation and Turkey. In 1896, a faction of Greeks traveled to Crete to stage a guerilla campaign against the Turkish government. At the same time, another Greek army led by the Greek Prince Constantine invaded the Turkish province of Ioannina. A Turkish military force from Monastir eventually pushed the Greek army back to Thessaly, where it routed a Greek counter-attack and advanced to the Gulf of Volo. The Turks subsequently withdrew in exchange for monetary compensation from Western nations (see Senn, 1999).

During the 1908 Summer Games in London, tensions between established English Protestants and outsider Irish Catholics again threatened the peace. While very few Irish nationalists actually participated in the 1908 Games, worry spread throughout England over an impending Irish 'terrorist' attack in London (Senn, 1999). With ardent support for Irish nationalism from the Irish-American contingent at the Games, members of British parliament and the British Olympic Organizing Committee feared imminent violence among spectators at Olympic facilities (Roche, 2002). The strategic lowering of the American flag to half-mast during the opening ceremonies of the Games and recurrent cries of biased British officiating during Olympic events exacerbated the anxieties of local authorities in London (Guttmann, 2002). While the events themselves unfolded without disruption, the 1908 Games foreshadowed how the Olympics would become increasingly inserted into the politics of global identity, militarism, and terrorism over the course of the century that followed.

For Olympic historians, the 1936 Berlin Games, often referred to as the 'Nazi Games', heightened international concerns about military conflict in high-profile sport spheres (see Chapter 3; Mandell, 1987). Because the outsider Aryan Nazi philosophy eschewed sentiments of equality and cultural inclusion underpinning the Olympic ethos, established members of the IOC, led by the American Avery Brundage, rallied to secure Germany's peaceful involvement in the Games, and its promise that the Games would not be compromised by hostility towards 'outsider' African and Jewish competitors (Bachrach, 2000). American politicians and IOC members were concerned with Nazi Germany's ability to host a peaceful and tolerant Games (although it merits noting that only US IOC member Ernst Jahnke suggested a boycott or at least moving the Games, then was consequently expelled from the IOC before the Games). Against a backdrop of flagrant racism and intolerance during the Games, and established, international sentiment that the German Nazi Party had utilised the Olympics to promote its economic and philosophical hegemony, the 1936 Berlin Games showcased an emerging nation-state characterised by ethnic prejudice, jingoism, and xenophobia (though it should also be acknowledged that America's athletic heroes were warmly welcomed by many German people). The dramatic suturing of Nazi politics into the Berlin Games was chillingly brought to cinematic life in Leni Riefenstahl's daunting film, *Olympia*.

By the time of the 1956 Games in Melbourne, Avery Brundage and other members of the IOC pressed for the cessation of all national hostilities during Olympic tournaments (Roche, 2002). In the summer of 1956, however, just weeks before the Games were to begin, two military conflicts undermined Brundage's quest for peace in Australia. First, the Egyptian seizure of the Suez Canal and subsequent military response by the British, French, and Israelis drew out a series of established and outsider tensions. The Soviet Union, supported by the United States, demanded an immediate withdrawal of occupying forces from Egypt. The British and French armies eventually vacated Egypt, yet five nations still boycotted the Olympic Games in support of the Egyptians (Guttmann, 2002). Only a few days later, the Soviet Union mobilised battalions of tanks and other armoured vehicles to occupy Budapest. Despite the promise of military support from established Western nations, including the United States and England, none arrived, and nearly 200,000 Hungarians were killed or fled to neighbouring Austria (Gosper & Korporaal, 2000). As a result of global military affairs, the 1956 Games were plagued with intense security concerns, and local organisers in Melbourne spent 2 weeks worrying if the malice of the battlefields would flow over to the Olympic events themselves (Gosper & Korporaal, 2000), as indeed, they did in an extremely bloody men's semi-final waterpolo match played between Hungary and the Soviet Union, which was eventually suspended.

Throughout the first half of the twentieth century, then, Olympics Games were consistently affected by broader matters of national aggression, ideological propaganda, and cultural exclusion. Members of the IOC and national organising committees developed international programmes and security systems engineered to protect the Games from 'outsider' terror and conflict. Behind the scenes, boycotts of the Games from both established and outsider nations escalated in number and scope (Senn, 1999). Fears about the Olympics becoming a site for actual aggression against innocent audiences increased, despite the fact that the Olympic events themselves remained free of overt political violence. Games of the latter portion of the twentieth century would, however, bear witness to the disturbingly victimising potential of political violence.

Although the 1968 Summer Games in Mexico have not received intense sociological scrutiny as an instance of political violence, tragic events occurring just 3 weeks prior to the Games had clear political trappings. For more than 6 months prior to the opening ceremonies, groups of over 5,000 middle-class and pro-Marxist university student protesters (from the Universidad Autónoma de México and the Instituto Politécnico Nacional) repeatedly gathered near Olympic venues to express dissent against the Mexican government's massive spending on the Games. According to these students, the Mexican government, led by President Gustavo Ordaz, had squandered over US$140 million on the event that could have been utilised to improve pressing social matters such as education, labour opportunities, and health care programmes for the large Mexican working class (Mabry, 1992). Often perceived as a source of cultural and economic success, the Olympics were envisioned (in this case) by Ordaz's government as a symbolic marker of Mexico's 'arrival' in world sport and, for this reason, any negative sentiment surrounding the Games was suppressed. The 1968 Mexico Summer Games, the first to be held in Latin America and the first to be broadcast live on 'prime-time' Western television, could not be seen to be set against a sea of internal protest and violence. However, following a summer of outburst and hostilities between protesters and police, Ordaz's government sought to quell the student movement outright. Under government support, the Mexican army viciously 'cleared out' student protesters from the Plaza Tlatelolco on 2 October 1968, by firing upon demonstrators with machine guns (Zarkos, 2004). Thirty-two student deaths were officially reported by the Mexican government, with other death counts running as high as 300. Two thousand students were jailed following the protest, and the clearly depleted resistance movement dissipated before the start of the Games themselves (Mabry, 1992).

The Munich Games of 1972 arguably involved the most dramatic instance of established–outsider military violence at the Olympics to date. On 5 September 1972, a politically outsider Palestinian group known as 'Black September' stormed an Olympic village in Munich, fatally shooting Israeli wrestling coach Moshe Weinberg and, later, weightlifter Yossi Romano, and holding others hostage. They demanded the release of approximately 200 Palestinian prisoners held in Israel. Following a 20-hour stand-off at a nearby airfield, and during a failed rescue attempt by the German authorities, 9 further Israeli athletes were killed, along with one German police officer and 5 of the terrorists. The event, commonly referred to as the 'Munich Massacre', led to the withdrawal of several Arab countries from the Games including Egypt, Kuwait, and Syria, all fearing retaliation (Leonard, 1988, p. 378; Iyer, 1996, p. 19; *Calgary Herald*, 7 September 2002, p. A19), and the early departure of Jewish American, seven gold medal winner, Mark Spitz. The Munich tragedy sent shockwaves across established, international sports communities, and seriously undermined the likelihood of peaceful future Games.

However, the Olympiads of the remainder of the 1970s were relatively calm by comparison with Munich. Security arrangements in Innsbruck (1976), Montreal (1976), and Lake Placid (1980) were unprecedented in both scope and material resources employed on-site (Gosper & Korporaal, 2000). Perhaps a result of being held on 'neutral' political grounds (Austria and Canada), or heavily militarised grounds (the United States), an air of tight security and political confidence permeated each of these Games. However, the 1980 Summer Games in Moscow and the 1984 Summer Games in Los Angeles provided further evidence of the perpetual ebb and flow of established–outsider political tensions that have affected respective Games.

The Moscow Games of 1980 followed a 1979 invasion of Afghanistan by the Soviet Union. The IOC's Lord Killanin repeatedly rebuffed US attempts to have the Games moved, and spent considerable time trying to convince American President Jimmy Carter not to boycott, but Carter launched a global campaign to boycott the Games as a gesture of solidarity among established, 'civilised' nations (Senn, 1999). American congressman, Walter Mondale, underlined the importance of a unified political response to the Soviets by austerely asserting, "What is at stake here is no less than the future security of the civilized world" (Guttmann, 2002, p. 213). The American anti-Moscow lobby drew support from a dozen nations, and a widespread drop-out of Olympic participation ensued. Boycotting nations warned others venturing to Moscow that, in the absence of established military superpowers like the United States at the Games, hostile attacks against Westerners could occur. Correspondingly, Soviet news broadcasters and politicians warned of a central intelligence agency's plot to kill Olympic spectators through biological or chemical weapons, or via explosives planted at Olympic sites (Guttmann, 2002). As an outsider response to the American boycott, the Soviets, and 13 other nation-states, subsequently boycotted the 1984 Games in Los Angeles, claiming that they, too, feared for the safety of their athletes in a reciprocally hostile American setting (Hill, 1995).

Throughout the late 1980s and early 1990s, security issues addressed both local protests in host cities and wider global political manoeuvrings. Here, though, established and outsider tensions within cities or host countries were paramount. Members of the Canadian Olympic Association at the Calgary Winter Games of 1988, for example, confronted security issues caused by local protesters concerned with environmental disturbance involved in creating Olympic event sites (Whitson & Macintosh, 1996), alongside numerous and broadly documented protests related to the Aboriginal Lubicon 'land claim' (e.g., *Calgary Herald*, 27 September 1987, p. 1; 12 November 1987, p. B1; 28 November 1987, p. 1; 5 December 1987, p. 1; Wamsley & Heine, 1996a, b). Later that year, the Seoul Summer Games unfolded amid fears of military conflict between North and South Korea. Similarly, in 1992, Spanish organisers of the Barcelona Games were besieged with security issues related to local Basque separatist activities (Bernstein, 2000).

More recently, and accompanied by directly violent outcomes, the 1996 Summer Games in Atlanta highlighted the constantly changing face of violence and terrorism at the Olympics. On 27 July 1996, a pipe bomb exploded near a bandstand in Atlanta's Centennial Olympic Park. Two people were killed and over 100 others injured. Police in Atlanta held in custody 33-year-old security guard, Richard Jewell, in connection with the bombing, but subsequently cleared him as a suspect. Unlike the earlier Munich incident, little further information on the Atlanta case has reached the public, and it remains unclear as to whether the incident is best defined as 'terrorism' at all (Iyer, 1996; Price, 1996). Following the Atlanta bombing, news stories about thwarted attacks at other Olympic Games surfaced. According to Mizell (2002), 'unnamed' terrorists attempted an attack on the 1998 Olympics in Nagano, and the 1988 Games in Seoul (on at least two occasions). Former Police Chief and consultant to the American State Department during the 1984 Los Angeles Games, Bill Rathburn, suggested that the 'Weather Underground', a US-based political extremist group, also planned an unsuccessful attack on the Los Angeles Olympics using plastic explosives (Mizell, 2002).

In light of such real, threatened, and alleged terrorist activities linked to the Olympics, the issue of securing the Games is now paramount in Olympic-bid processes. The mere suggestion or implication that a host city might be politically or militarily vulnerable to a terrorist attack is enough to quash a bid. For example, during the 1997 bid process for the 2004 Summer Games, the Swedish Olympic Committee's proposal suffered a fatal blow following a bomb explosion in Stockholm's main Olympic stadium (*Reuters Press*, 1997). The explosion, to this date unsolved but widely thought to be an act of terrorism, contributed to the failure of Sweden's bid. In Sweden, the 2004 Games subsequently became referred to as the 'Lost Games' (*Reuters Press*, 1997). By contrast, bids for the Olympic Games from Sydney (2000), Salt Lake City (2002), and Athens (2004) were all partially successful because of the intensive security programmes promised by the respective organising committees, and the degree to which their members carefully incorporated the need to secure all aspects of the events from terrorist 'outsiders' as an integral component of their Olympic bid (Michaelis, 2003).

On the basis of this evidence and the historical trajectory of real or threatened violence at the Games, it seems reasonable to expect that the Olympic Games of the current era will continue to face new security obstacles and political challenges. While not wanting to underestimate the effects and importance of other acts of political violence and terrorism around the globe, the events of 11 September 2001 in the United States heavily plot the course of security and terrorism issues at the Olympics in the twenty-first century. New lines between established and outsider nations are now contextually drawn and redrawn at 'post-9/11' Olympic Games.

Perhaps more than ever, the modern-day task of securing the Games interfaces with questions of established and outsider political ideologies, religions, ways of life, and international allegiances. For example, the 2002 Games in Salt Lake City, held less than 5 months after '9/11', involved massive security hurdles. The Games spawned an international effort to (re)affirm global allies in a so-called 'new war on terrorism' (*Associated Press*, 2001). In what follows, discourses of security and terrorism at the Salt Lake Games are unpacked as a small case study to illustrate how established–outsider political axes may be symbolically crystallised at the Olympics, and how terrorist activities (both related and unrelated to the Games) may be configured through the mass media. As has been shown elsewhere (Young, 2000), the media may not *cause* sports-related violence, but their role in it is neither passive nor non-participatory.

MEDIATED TERROR: IDEOLOGICAL OPPORTUNISM IN THE CONTEXT OF THE 2002 SALT LAKE CITY GAMES

As the first major international sports event held following '9/11', the 2002 Winter Games in Salt Lake City pushed security measures to unprecedented levels. This included spending in excess of US$310 million on 'securing' the Games – approximately one-quarter of the overall event budget and the highest amount ever for an Olympic Games. The post-9/11 context of the Salt Lake Games also provided a unique opportunity for the relationship between terror(ism), political ideologies, and sport to be played out in the eyes of the world via the mass media at this time. What follows, then, is a summary of that 'playing out' process; of how themes such as victimisation, fear, patriotism, and national strength were assembled as a type of 'social drama' in selected Western media. More specifically, we demonstrate that segments of the Western media opportunistically framed the 2002 Winter Games as an international summit wherein 'established' and 'outsider' relationships in the 'new war on terrorism' became plainly evident. Furthermore, we show how the process of 'securing' the Games became deftly constructed through the media as a symbolic metaphor for the struggle to 'secure' America and the rest of the 'free' world. While there is a degree of overlap between each of the cultural frames (Goffman, 1974; Lenart & Targ, 1995) we explore, there is sufficient conceptual distinction to deal with each frame individually.

American Military Dominance

The most dominant frame evident in media discourses relating to security at the Salt Lake Games underscored the ability of the United States to defend itself (and its allies) against the threat of terrorism. Taking the Games as a case example of how the restructuring of 'homeland security' was needed to sustain a 'free' way of life in a post-September 11th world, media discourses overwhelmingly pointed to the massive effort undertaken by Americans in securing the Games. Highlighting the extensive co-operation between federal/military, state, municipal, corporate, and private agents, media reports about security at the Games drew attention to the temporarily shaken but re-established 'strength' of American society.

Over 80% of our examined media accounts of security/violence matters characterised Salt Lake City as a 'military state' during the Games. Emphasising the US$310 million spent on protecting the participants (Benton, 2002; Vospeka, 2002), the 16,000 security personnel employed during the Games, the continuous surveillance by F-16 fighter jets and Blackhawk helicopters, the 45 mile 'no fly zone' encircling the city, the integrated efforts of US military/intelligence ground personnel (Federal Bureau of Investigation, Central Intelligence Agency, Bureau of Alcohol, Tobacco and Firearms, United States Marshals, Center for Disease Control, National Guard, Army, and Marines) and their advanced anti-terrorism training, and the expansive list of detection technologies utilised to monitor every person's move during the events of the Games (e.g., biometric scanners, portable X-ray equipment, metal detectors, surveillance cameras, computer monitoring systems, and other identification technologies), the public was reassured that "America would be ready" for any terrorist contingency, "ready for anything" (Stearns & Dunn, 2002, p. B3). When asked about the police/military atmosphere at the Games, American cross-country skier Nina Kemppel noted with confidence, "It's like when

I crawl in bed at night and I have my down comforter. It's that kind of comfortable, fuzzy feeling" (Harasta, 2002, p. C2). In what might be seen as an extraordinarily smug boast of readiness, given the events of '9/11' for which the US authorities were clearly unprepared, Federal Aviation Association spokesperson Mike Fergus commented, "If you violate the restrictions [no fly rule around Salt Lake City] you will be able to tell your children and grand-children you flew formation with the Department of Defense" (*New York Times*, 8 February 2002, p. D3). Robert Flowers, head of the Utah Olympic Public Safety Command, underlined the point less ambiguously, "If you fly in our airspace, we're going to shoot you down" (Reaves, 2002).

Complementing the pre- and post-Olympic emphasis on the capability of the American protection/intelligence community to secure the event, com-ments by senior American government officials including President George W. Bush, Homeland Security Director, Tom Ridge, Attorney General, John Ashcroft, Secretary of Defense, Donald Rumsfeld, and Utah Governor, Michael Leavitt, were utilised by the media to assure audiences around the world that America would continue to be "the safest place in the world" (Benton, 2002; Wilson, 2001a, p. E2) – insisting that people would be so impressed by American security that a case would be made to adopt Salt Lake City as the permanent site for the Winter Olympics (*Toronto Star*, 22 January 2002, p. A9). IOC President, Jacques Rogge, bolstered the in-ternational sports community's confidence in American strength, first by refusing to cancel the Games despite pressure and, second, by publicly commending American security efforts. According to Rogge, "The [Olym-pic] village is the most secure place in the world... from a security point of view, you could not be better protected" (Wilson, 2001a). A common trend across the different media was for stories to be punctuated by statements made by participating athletes and spectators brimming with confidence with respect to US military resources:

- "After the attacks [of September 11, 2001], I thought we should cancel, but now I think we should proceed and not let the terrorists intimidate us" (Lynn Ragner, Olympic spectator, cited in Northfield & Bell, 2001).
- "A lot of people say it will be dangerous, but to me this is going to be the safest place in the world... People who want to scare Americans or the rest of the world are not succeeding. The Olympics are happening and they are going to be a success" (Catriona Le May Doan, Canadian speed skater, cited in Petrie, 2002, p. D4).
- "It's very intense security but it makes you feel safe" (Gail Stern, Olympic spectator, cited in *Associated Press*, 2002a, p. D3).

Selected coverage of 'minor' security incidents arising prior to or during the Games also reinforced the perception of the American state of readiness to defend itself and the international sports community. Reports of approximately two dozen planes receiving military escorts away from Salt Lake City prior to or during the Olympics (*CBS Evening News*, 2002), over 600 bomb or 'suspicious package' scares in the downtown core (Cantera, 2002; Morris News Service, 2002), and one anthrax 'hoax' at a local airport (*BBC News*, 2002) served to underscore the perceived professionalism of American defense personnel in dealing with potentially problematic security situations. Not until the final night of the Games did a security problem become widely publicised, involving, rather less threateningly it must be said, the drunken brawling of over 20 spectators outside a Budweiser beer tent in the Olympic village (*USA Today*, 24 February 2002, p. A7). Referring to the Games as the safest on record, many cited the show of 'force' at the event, and lack of terrorist incidents there, as growing evidence of America's reinvigorated ability to protect its citizens and visiting 'guests' from overseas.

Through the recurrent media framing of Olympic policing as a daunting but achievable task in Salt Lake City, preference was given to the degree to which Americans appeared ideologically or practically 'unphased' by the 11th September attacks. In President George Bush's much-quoted words, "We will show the world we can safeguard the Olympics without sacrificing our American ideals – openness, mobility, diversity, and economic opportunity in the process" (Office of the US and Press Secretary, 2002). In the coverage of the massive display of military strength at the Olympics and America's unwillingness to be "frightened away" (*Houston Chronicle*, 2002, p. A1) from cultural practices like sport by terrorists, the American media emphasised the resiliency of its state. Such was summarised in a special edition of the American television programme *Extra* about terrorism at the Games (entitled 'America Under Siege', September 27, 2001): "many believe cancelling the games would be giving the terrorists exactly what they wanted. A safe and successful winter Olympics will prove they can never defeat America".

In these respects, the media's role in extending established images of America's strength and ability as a global leader was evident in discourses on security and terrorism at the 2002 Winter Olympic Games. As Giroux (2002) observes, media agents are extensions of the international, hegemonic power bloc in this sense, helping to shape public opinion about security, social efficacy, and cultural stability in the face of terrorist violence. While the ability to protect athletes and spectators attending the Games was the

surface issue presented in most media reports, there was an embedded understanding that the Olympics were a test of America's ability to police
political violence within its domestic borders. Describing the threat of terrorism at the Olympics as one 'episode' (Iyengar, 1996) of national security,
the media helped emphasise how the sports process becomes embedded in
terrorist and anti-terrorist discourses.

American Victimisation, Global Resolve

Although media coverage of security at the Salt Lake City Games consistently depicted the United States as a powerful and proud nation, another
dominant media frame emphasised an image of America as a recovering –
and vulnerable – victim of senseless violence. Tapping into the 'natural'
arousal of emotions common in sports events like the Olympics, event organisers and media agents deftly linked surging feelings of victimisation in
the American populace to the feelings regularly stirred by athletic competitions (e.g., excitement, doubt, sorrow, frustration, anger, fear, etc.). In
doing so, athletes and their endeavours became metaphors of the American
people's resolve to combat terrorism directly – individuals who would resolve to 'compete' despite their fear of victimisation at the hands of terrorists. Rather than passively accepting the threat to national security posed
by international terrorists at the Games, the American people's determination to combat victimisation was showcased through their athletes' commitment to the task at hand. By insinuating that the Olympics were an
example of the level of 'new' social cohesion and patriotism spawned by the
'9/11' attacks, the media helped frame the Games as an unyielding response
to violent bullying by 'barbaric' outsider states.

News reports of security at the Olympic Games were replete with sentiment about reinvigorated patriotism in America. In the wake of perceived
terrorist threats to the Games, the media underscored how Americans were
living through a period of anxiety, shock, and suspicion. While confident
but concerned about security, the Salt Lake Olympic Committee (SLOC)
reminded citizens around the world that the United States could be attacked
by rogue outsiders at any time (Foy, 2001, p. G3). Considerable leeway was
given to Americans and their displays of patriotism for this reason at this
time. For instance, in an unprecedented exhibition of patriotism by a host
nation, Americans were granted special permission by the IOC to present
the American flag found in the World Trade Center rubble during the
opening ceremonies. Contrasting the tattered (but still intact) symbol of

American nationalism with the pageantry and celebration of the Games, comments offered in the media likened the resulting imagery to a universal statement of victims' rights:

- Anita DeFrantz, IOC member from the United States suggested, "The Olympic movement around the world has expressed its sympathy for the victims of September 11th in many ways since that tragic day. Showing the flag in this respect is just one more way" (*CNN News*, 2002a).
- "I think it's important that the flag comes in simply because it's a part of each and every American now. It's part of who we are" (Amy Peterson, American speed skater, cited in Lopresti, 2002, p. A1).
- "Fireworks ushered in the entrance of [President] Bush and the World Trade Center flag. Organizers hoped to raise the banner during the opening ceremony, but its frail condition made that impossible... A 12-year-old boy, symbolically known as the Child of Light, was then introduced to the world. The child, representing the ability of the human spirit to overcome life's adversities, will remain a theme throughout the Games" (*Associated Press*, 2002b, p. A1).

Such displays of patriotism were justified by media agents and excused by sports commentators as 'natural' expressions of feelings of defensiveness and fear regarding terrorism in America. Importantly, then, the Salt Lake Games evolved into a context in which acts of American patriotism could be discursively organised as a collective healing opportunity for all victims, or potential victims, of terrorism:

- "For those from elsewhere who pass verdict (on displays of American patriotism), kindly remember this is a different country than it was September 10th. That will show in the next 17 days. It must" (Lopresti, 2002, p. A1).
- "Olympic organizers, more determined than ever to market the meaning, began talking about the Games as a chance for restoring America's hope. There were recollections of the 1980 US hockey team that won its proxy war against the Soviets, who themselves were then at war in Afghanistan. These Games would transcend even politics and patriotism on their way toward therapy. 'This is an important event under any circumstance', Utah Governor Mike Leavitt had said a few weeks after the attacks, 'but fate may have fallen upon this state and city to host an event where the world will come together to heal'" (Gibbs, 2002).

Equally inspiring in stories about the Games were announcements made by athletes and administrators seemingly willing to flout security concerns and threats. Claiming that they simply wanted to 'be there' in a collective show of sympathy and support for Americans, the Games were heralded as a universal statement against terrorism by athletes:

- "It is at this time more important than ever that the Olympic Games in Salt Lake should go ahead. The world needs the message that the Olympics in Salt Lake will send. Athletes want to compete and spectators around the world want to see good triumph over bad" (Sergei Bubka, Russian pole-vaulter, cited in Wilson, 2001b, p. E10).
- "Nobody has expressed the wish not to go to Salt Lake or America. The athletes have prepared themselves [for security risks] and they want to go and compete. If we give in to terrorism, the whole society is lost" (Gunilla Lindberg, IOC board member and head of the Swedish Olympic Committee, cited in *CBC News*, 2001).

In these ways, athletes, as established public spokespersons and international representatives, gave voice to the millions fearful of ongoing security threats. The terror aroused by security concerns during the Games (and rampant through the Western world) became counter-balanced by these 'representative' victims coming forward and striking a symbolic blow against outsider terrorist fear-mongering. Instead of employing a standard media tactic of sending 'video postcards' back from the battlefield as a means of engendering sympathy for victims of war (Dobkin, 1992), 'sound bites' from resolute athletes were utilised to promulgate images and ideologies of victimisation and courage.

Through the collective sympathy directed towards America and its people during the Games, and appreciation offered for the extensive security measures taken to protect those involved, the Olympics also evolved into a context for reaffirming political, cultural, and economic loyalties between nations. Revolving around the need to 'protect' one's friends from similar victimisation, the American media aided in the creation of new, anti-terrorist 'imagined communities' through the Games (Palmer, 2001). Support of American initiatives and abilities to protect the Games (and prevent further victimisation) was emphasised in the media as confirmatory evidence of international alignment with the American anti-terrorist war campaign – tacitly apparent, in and of itself, by the continuance of the Olympics:

- IOC president Jacques Rogge commented, "The Olympic Games are an answer to the present violence and should not be a victim of violence. The Olympic Games in America are the best message of brotherhood, fraternity, and universality. There is no better symbol of the world uniting together around the cause" (Visser, 2001, p. 53).

• Suggesting that the Olympic Games celebrate 'American' ideals, President Bush stated, "We believe that these ideals – liberty and freedom – make it possible for people to live together in peace, and the Olympics give us a chance in the middle of a difficult struggle to celebrate international peace and cooperation... All people appreciate the discipline that produces excellence and the character that creates champions" (Fournier, 2002, p. C1).

Implying that everyone participating in the Games (i.e., IOC members, athletes, foreign fans, and corporate sponsors) sympathised with the US regarding such controversial matters as terrorism, security, and even definitions of freedom, media accounts and documentaries painted international responses to security and the Games with an extremely homogeneous brush. Thus, a master media frame categorising all participants of the Games as potential victims of violence – and as those who should emulate America's lead as a nation of people undeterred by, in President Bush's familiar terms, 'the evildoers' – emerged. In this process, de Coubertin-esque ideals underpinning the Olympic Games became linked with America's resolve to not succumb to the threat of terrorism at the Games – or in any other social venue (Vigh, 2002, p. C10).

Most germane for our argument, media coverage of security in Salt Lake City consistently pointed out that *all* members of democratic states should be prepared for victimisation by terrorists (Janofsky, 2002, p. A16). Insisting that terrorism or the threat of terrorism was a concern for *all* nations, and using the recognised ploy of 'taking the public voice' (Hall, Critcher, Jefferson, Clarke, & Roberts, 1978), the media underlined that 'We' must exist in a condition of emotional readiness for 'real' war. While the Olympic Games were described as a mega-event prime for symbolic terrorist 'statements', the Games were discursively constructed as a contest where members of many nations could potentially be targeted for further attacks. As US Olympic Committee Chief Executive Officer, Lloyd Ward, commented, "There's no question that after September 11th, our view of security in the United States, and I would suggest in the world, must be different" (O'Driscoll, 2002, p. C6). Hence, the support for America offered through the Olympic Games, and concomitant concerns about security 'managed' by the media during the event, helped place individuals from ideologically and culturally diverse nations on a similar emotional 'playing field'. Using the international media as the major channel of communication, and rallying around the recent victim of terrorism (i.e., the host nation), members of the international sports community helped validate Americans' feelings of victimisation, reclaimed patriotism, and ideological cohesion.

Axes of Evil, Axes of Peace

A third frame dominating media accounts of security at the 2002 Winter Games highlighted preferred Western constructions of the terms 'terrorism' and 'terrorist' and underlined the distance between 'established' and 'outsider' groups in this connection. At the forefront in media coverage of security risks at the Games were concerns about the types of individuals who might exploit the event for the purposes of political terror. Engrained within such constructions were dominant understandings of the 'face' of terrorism – at this point in time, notably, al-Qaeda or other fundamentalist Middle Eastern or Asian groups. Here, the Western media seized a critical opportunity, given the timing of the event, to emphasise established ideologies about terrorism and terrorists held within many Western nations. By attaching the Winter Games (held, ostensibly, in the spirit of peace, harmony, and cultural exchange) to the global struggle against forms of political violence like terrorism, the media coverage of the Games played a key role in drawing out international axes and alliances following the tragic events of '9/11'. Importantly, media reports of security at the Games contained clear understandings of the modern alliances (e.g., the US and Great Britain) and their rogue enemies (e.g., the Taliban and al-Qaeda) in the new war on terrorism. In figurational/process-sociological terms, the Olympics transformed into a political summit, demarcating clear boundaries between the globally 'established' and the deviantised 'outsiders'. Through an analysis of media narratives about security at the Games, it is evident that 'established' constructions of terrorism were normalised in Western media commentaries, while outsiders were constructed as potential threats to security and global harmony.

As noted earlier, for Elias and Scotson (1965), 'established' social groups are deeply embedded in both the base and superstructural segments of social figurations, and consequently control many of its ideological state apparatuses such as the media. Established groups have greater access to, but not necessarily outright ownership of, varying institutional opportunities to shape social discourse. In the case of 2002 Winter Olympics, since the United States hosted the Games, the voice of Americans became 'established' there – not explicitly as political leaders, but as members of the host nation. Almost immediately following the declaration that the Games would continue despite mounting security threats following '9/11', for instance, the American and Canadian media repeatedly offered constructions of the Olympics as 'Our Games', describing them as, "A Homeland Winter Olympics: With a Few Guests" (Lopresti, 2002, p. A1). IOC delegates, politicians, and athletes subsequently expressed similar sentiments and consented to the 'Americanisation' of the Games in Salt Lake City around this central theme. Participation in the Olympics at Salt Lake City became interpreted in the media as acceptance within American-led 'established' groups of mutually identified nations united in the fight against terrorism.

Conversely, and also in process-sociological terms, outsider groups are more marginal or excluded members of a social group like the Olympic figuration of nations, less embedded in power positions and dominated on the basis of their limited statuses. Outsiders are excluded from participation in socially influential power structures of a figuration, and their voices or ideologies are mainly silenced in the media (Dowling, 1986; Elias & Scotson, 1965; Hallin, 1986). With regard to media reports of security at the 2002 Games, few 'alternative' or outsider constructions of terrorism were offered in the Western media. In this case, 'outsiders' to the Olympic figuration were broadly conceived of as both renegade political factions like al-Qaeda, military regimes such as the Taliban, or entire nation-states like Iraq or Afghanistan. One of the only dissenting 'established' voices of the Games came from Gerhard Heiberg, a Norwegian IOC member, who commented that, "a country at war cannot organize the Olympic Games" (Wilson, 2001b, p. E10). Heiberg's comments instantly appeared in media around the world, but such was the emerging weight of critical media responses that he later felt forced to apologise for his comments and rescind them.

Perhaps most importantly, with Afghanistan's exclusion from the Winter Olympic Games – on the basis of the ruling Taliban's prohibition against female participation in sport – there would be no main 'opposing' viewpoint about terrorism offered by those described as the main enemies of the American State at the Games. Instead, when such outsider ideologies were reported in the media we examined, they were strategically described by established agents as socially uncivilised or barbarous. For example, members of the IOC such as Jacques Rogge were outspoken in their condemnation of the Taliban and their Olympic participation policies. In his words: "[Afghanistan's reinstatement] will only be possible when there is a stable government in place, and when all the conditions that are put by the IOC are fulfilled" (*New York Times*, 27 November 2001, p. A12). In confirming the image of terrorists (or terrorist nations) as outsiders, other media coverage of Olympic security reported on the threats of violence issued by a collective but rarely explicitly defined 'Them', and how security officials at the Games tactically distributed several thousands of leaflets to spectators identifying 'suspected' terrorists from Middle-Eastern nations as a precautionary measure.

As Kamalipour (2000) suggests, established representations of terrorism at the Games also drew attention, often using racist stereotypes, to the 'cunning', 'surreptitious', and 'underhanded' strategies typically employed by terrorists in waging violence. Describing their predilections for warfare as 'cowardly' (President Bush) and lacking any code of military honour, attention was directed towards how these outsiders did not abide by the standard rules of 'civilised' nations. In news reports, audiences were warned about rogue, foreign terrorists seeking to sully the message of harmony cultivated by the Games. In a description of one particular bomb scare in Salt Lake City, for example, the incident became discursively constructed as a 'sneaky terrorist test' of American security systems (Cantera, 2002, p. G2). In other accounts, and exploiting the newsworthiness of widely documented reports of how persons involved in the terrorist attacks of '9/11' had resided in 'ordinary' American neighbourhoods, citizens were warned that suspected terrorists may be living in isolated areas of *their* communities, hiding until the Games commenced. As such, Americans were encouraged to be vigilant in their own neighbourhoods as a type of informal and volunteer extension of security protections against terrorism (*CNN News*, 2002b).

Finally, with the clever intermingling of the Olympic ideals on questions of humanity with American ideals about the appropriate responses to security and violence at the Winter Games, a consistent 'established' message about terrorism became formed. By substituting 'the American' standpoint on terrorism and defence with the 'Olympic' perspective in the popular media, dominant American ideologies became translated into international sports discourses. Again, the influential views of IOC members like Jacques Rogge were frequently cited in media accounts as evidence of the ideological partnership between America and the rest of the world: "Your nation is overcoming a tragedy, a tragedy that has affected the whole world. We stand united with you in the promotion of our common ideals, and hope for world peace" (Harasta, 2002, p. C2). In these ways, the established American political views on terrorists or 'enemies' of the state became absorbed, regurgitated, and promoted to sports audiences around the world by groups like the IOC.

The purpose of this small case study of terrorist threats and related security issues at the 2002 Winter Olympic Games in Salt Lake City is to illustrate the relationship between sport, the media and forms of political violence originating *away from the playing field*. In the wake of the '9/11' attacks on the United States, the 2002 Olympic Games became inserted into a broader context of social, cultural, and ideological struggle, as indeed, we saw had also been the case with earlier Olympic Games experiencing their own forms of real or threatened political violence. Athletes and spectators at the Games were believed to be targets of terrorism, not only for their ca- pabilities as athletes or for their national, ethnic, or political affiliations, but also for their complicity in a mass public gathering held on American soil that captured, as Olympic events have come to do, colossal global audiences (Roche, 2002). Concern about security at the Olympics closely paralleled American fears about terrorism and the degree to which systems of civil protection could be breached by 'foreign aggressors'. For these reasons, Olympic security issues, reported and debated widely in the Western media, evolved into a metaphor of Western societies' abilities to defend their social institutions, cultural practices, ideological systems, and, of course, citizens from what President Bush called 'the axes of evil'. Stated simply, a safe Games would signal a victory for those committed to fighting terrorism around the world. Such views framed in the popular media were funda- mentally based on notions of *established* and *outsider* relationships.

OLYMPIC FUTURES, SECURITY HORIZONS

We are charged with the task of keeping an ancient promise, a promise as old as the games themselves. We must defend the Olympic torch as a beacon of peaceful coex- istence among peoples everywhere... Together we can, and we must, work closely to ensure that those who wish us harm do not achieve their wicked goals. We must ensure that the contests here [Athens] are decided by athletes in the arena and not terrorists in the streets (US Ambassador Cofer Black, Coordinator for Counter-terrorism – remarks made in a Workshop on Olympic Security, Athens, Greece, 29 September 2003).

Exactly 100 days before the 2004 Summer Olympics opening ceremonies, three bomb blasts outside a suburban police station threatened civil security in Athens (posted on www.worldtribune.com, 1 July). The event followed a string of terrorist bombings across continental Europe that started in 2001, including a spate of car bombings in Istanbul in 2003, and the bombing of four commuter trains involving the deaths of over 100 people in Madrid on 11 March 2004 (Geiger, 2004), as well as numerous terrorist bombings elsewhere (such as the nightclub bombing of 12 October 2002 in the town of Kuta on the Indonesian island of Bali, which killed 202 people and injured a further 209 and is considered the deadliest act of terrorism in Indonesian history (http://en.wikipedia.org/wiki/2002_Bali_terrorist_bombing). The Athens bombings occurred just one week following an announcement that, in an unprecedented demonstration of the economic impact or terrorism, the IOC had purchased a US$200 million insurance policy for the 2004 Summer Games (Wilson, 2004). Although the May 2004 bombings in Athens caused no fatalities or serious injury among Greek civilians, the explosions galvanised fears regarding an 'imminent' terrorist episode at the Games.

Security at the 2004 Summer Games (dubbed by some Olympic critics as the 'Armed Camp Games' – Spencer 2004) dominated in pre-Olympic discourses. The sheer financial and personnel commitment made to the Games was highlighted in media accounts, as news reports documented the US$1.5 billion dollars devoted to securing the Greek Games, and the 70,000 security agents posted at facilities across Greece (Chang, 2003; Shipley & Whitlock, 2004). News stories consistently emphasised the considerable NATO military involvement in the Games, missile defence systems covering Greek airspace as a part of 'Operation Active Endeavour' (initiated in the Mediterranean following 11 September 2001), and the scores of counter-terrorism experts informing city and Olympic officials in Athens (Murphy, 2003).

The international mobilisation of an Olympic security brigade for the Athens Games was staggering. Led by American counter-terror experts, CIA officials and the American-based Science Applications International Corporation, the 'Olympic Advisory Group' comprised of political delegates from established 'allies' including Australia, France, Germany, Israel, Spain, Britain, and the United States spent the bulk of 2003–2004 allaying anxieties about terrorist problems in Athens (Chang, 2003). One of the group's toughest tasks was to quell threats of a boycott or withdrawal from the Games (ironically, by the United States, Australia, and Israel) following widely publicised 'failures' during security tests at Olympic facilities (Spencer, 2004; Vistica, 2004). Although threats to security were mentioned widely in the media, there is little empirical evidence to suggest that they were considered seriously by Olympic sponsors, athletes, or spectators.

Fears regarding security at the Athens Games represented a sobering reality for supporters of the Olympics. Clearly, international sports enthusiasts must accept that the Olympics, or other mega-events, do not occur within a political vacuum. Ultimately, the 2004 Games, like the 1972 Games in Munich, became staged within a global figuration characterised by emerging political tempests and terrorist controversies. Ideological and military lines between nations have been redrawn or recalibrated by the 'new war on [global] terrorism' since 2001, and significantly complicated by events such as the wars in Afghanistan and Iraq, campaigns of genocide in

Rwanda, scandals of abuse on prisoners of war perpetrated by American soldiers, and terrorist bombings across Europe. For this reason and others, the Olympics represent an attractive locus for the expression of political views on wider world events. As the Olympic Games bring together established allies and outsider populaces into the microcosmic 'Olympic village', one must conceive of the Games, in Schaffer and Smith's (2000) terminology, as a potential 'big killing event'.

We must consider how the broader figurational politics of militarism and terrorism might be facilitated by the Olympics, and how local hostilities between established and outsider groups may be brought to international audiences through the Games. From one point of view, the 2002 Salt Lake Winter Games may have lulled Olympic officials into a false sense of security; they were situated in an isolated area within the United States, a region of the world relatively free from intense political turmoil and terrorist violence. Securing the Games proved to be achievable in this context.

The 2004 Athens Games, by contrast, were positioned within a world region beset by political conflict. The budget for securing the 2004 Games was over three times the size of Salt Lake City's budget; and for good reason. Concerns about the terrorist organisation 'November 17' – alleged to have committed in excess of 23 political assassinations since 1975, including US military official Stephen Saunders in 2003 – abounded in pre-Olympic discourses (Murphy, 2003). November 17 has been blamed for the 2002 and 2003 bombings of Olympic sponsor offices in Greece. In February 2004, a terrorist group known as 'Phevos and Athena' (the names of the Olympic mascots for the Athens Games) claimed responsibility for the firebombing of two Greek environment ministry vehicles in Athens (Wilstein, 2004). Only one month later, the Athens-based terrorist group 'Revolutionary Struggle' claimed responsibility for a bomb disarmed outside a Citibank outlet situated blocks away from Olympic facilities (posted on www.tsn.ca, 15 March 2004). Reminders of the 1988 Abu Nidal killing and wounding of 108 passengers on a ferry in the Athens port of Piraeus, the potential presence of Hamas, Hitzbullah, and the Afghani Partiya Karkeren Kurdistan (PKK) were circulated in the media, alongside stories of rabid anti-American sentiment in Greece since the initiation of 'Operation Enduring Freedom' (Gertz, 2003). Equally, warnings about violent anti-World Trade Organization protests in Athens during the Games were being touted as yet another security 'headache' (Murphy, 2003). Such local concerns about protesters' behaviours were partially fuelled by memories of the violent, anti-world trade, anarcho-environmentalist demonstrations in Sydney prior to the 2000 Summer Games (see Lenskyj, 2002).

The problem of securing the Athens (and indeed future) Games was complicated by the geographic and physical infrastructure of the city (and future cities). Global critics of the Athens Games pointed to the notoriously poor security reputation of the Athens international airport, the heavy traffic congestion in the city, the 'floating' population of illegal Muslim immigrants in Greece, the relatively 'porous' borders, and the degree to which the country had been an 'access point' for terrorists seeking entry into Europe (*Associated Press*, 2003). Such criticisms were amplified by the tardy construction of Olympic facilities, limited and haphazardly successful security tests at Olympic facilities, and the US State Department's *Patterns of Global Terrorism Report* of 2002 that pointed to cities like Athens as ripe terrorism targets (Chang, 2003). However, despite these problems, the Games were a security 'success' – save for the disruption of a men's platform diving contest when a Canadian spectator (Ron Bensimhon) wearing a blue tutu, jumped into the Olympic Aquatic Centre pool as a publicity stunt for the online casino www.goldenpalace.com and when an Irish protestor (Cornelius Horan), calling himself the 'Grand Prix Priest', tackled and dragged Brazilian runner Venderlei de Lima into the crowd during the final stages of the men's marathon (Smith, 2004). These were hardly significant events in a security sense, though, predictably, the media cashed in on their newsworthiness, given broader sensitivities to matters of security at the Games.

In terms of the role played by the media in 'constructing' Athens as a security concern, the 2004 Games clearly became co-opted into the discourses regarding terrorism in sport established in Salt Lake City. Much as in 2002, security at the 2004 Games (and the assessment of its effectiveness) was ideologically framed by established American military experts, NATO members, and other globally recognised politicians. The security effort in Athens was decisively led by American political–military agents, backed by NATO at the request of the United States, and aligned with framings of the war in Iraq promulgated in Western media. While both Iraq and Afghanistan are – at the time of writing – allowed to participate in the Olympic Games once again, their representation on international anti-terrorism panels in Athens was extremely thin. Established and outsider concerns about security, terrorism, and violence highlighted during the 2002 Winter Games became involved in the build-up to Athens. Despite the contours and flavours of local political problems in Greece, involving myriad ideological and global realities, the American press effectively re-identified the Athens Games as yet another context of 'Us' versus 'Them' (Oakley, 2003; Vistica, 2004). There is scarce political or sociological reason to believe that these processes of global/political identification will be significantly different at sports mega-events in the near future.

The problems and discourses of political violence, security, and terrorism we have explored in this chapter are not 'Athens anomalies' but, rather, contemporary global realities that the IOC and other international sports organisations must anticipate and manage. With increasing numbers of nations included in the Olympic Games and the massive international audiences the Games procure, established and outsider groups might seek to further exploit the Olympics as a context of military/political struggle. Consequently, staging the Games has become a deeply military exercise, with sites taking on the appearance of occupied camps policed by highly trained officials from established nations. Purists and fans enamoured of the romantic lure of the Games may well continue to argue that the Olympics remain, first and foremost, about the athletes and about pushing back the frontiers of human performance, but it is extremely naïve to argue that the Games are sites for these sorts of meanings alone. As we have shown, the modern history of the Games has hardly unfolded free of tension and conflict. Since the 'terrorist' attacks on the US of September 2001, international sports events like the Olympics have transformed into heavily-protected political summits rather than 'innocent' gatherings promoting global citizenship. Missiles, fighter jets, armed guards, machine guns, razor-wire fences, and electronic scanners have now, unwittingly, also assumed the status of Olympic 'symbols' – they have become common and pervasive fixtures at the ostensibly peaceful Olympic Games. For the foreseeable future, at least, de Coubertin's wish for Olympic peace may be far more of a romanticised dream than a practical reality.

REFERENCES

Associated Press. (2001). Bush to bomb through Olympics. *The New York Times*, 17 November, p. A12.

Associated Press. (2002a). Olympic security unprecedented in history of sport. *The New York Times*, 8 February, p. D2.

Associated Press. (2002b). Winter Olympics open with celebration of US heroes past, present. *The Hamilton Spectator*, 15 February, p. A1.

Associated Press. (2003). Istanbul car bomb spark fears over Olympic security. *TaiPei Times*, 29 November, p. 20.

Atkinson, M., & Young, K. (2003). Terror games: Media treatment of security issues at the 2002 winter Olympic games. *OLYMPIKA, XI*, 53–78.

Bachrach, S. (2000). *The Nazi Olympics: Berlin 1936*. New York: Little, Brown and Company.

BBC News. (2002). Anthrax scare at Salt Lake city. Original air date, 13 February.

Benton, J. (2002). A show of force in the name of security. *The Dallas Morning News*, 9 February, p. D2.

Bernstein, A. (2000). Things you can see from there, you can't see from here. *Journal of Sport and Social Issues*, 24(4), 351–369.

Cantera, K. (2002). Bomb scares could strain games security. *The Salt Lake Tribune*, 2 February, p. A3.

CBC News. (2001). Norwegian official apologizes. Posted on www.cbc.ca, 30 November.

CBS Evening News. (2002). Sky patrol in Salt Lake. Original air date, 11 February.

Chang, A. (2003). Major competition: Athens on high alert as the 2004 summer Olympics approach. *USA Today*, 10 December, p. D9.

CNN News. (2002a). Ridge praises Olympic security in Salt Lake city. Posted on www.cnn.com, 10 January.

CNN News. (2002b). Ground zero star-spangled banner to wave over Olympics. Posted on www.cnn.com, 6 February.

Dobkin, B. (1992). Paper tigers and video postcards: The rhetorical dimensions of narrative form in ABC news coverage of terrorism. *Western Journal of Communication*, 56(2), 143–160.

Dowling, R. (1986). Terrorism in the media: A rhetorical genre. *Journal of Communication*, 36(1), 12–24.

Elias, N. (1994). *The civilising process*. Oxford: Blackwell.

Elias, N., & Dunning, E. (1986). *Quest for excitement: Sport and leisure in the civilizing process*. New York: Basil Blackwell.

Elias, N., & Scotson, J. (1965). *The established and the outsiders*. London: Sage.

Fournier, R. (2002). Bush: Olympics celebrate American ideals. *The Detroit News*, 8 February, p. C1.

Foy, P. (2001). Salt Lake chief envisions tighter security. *The Detroit News*, 30 October, p. B3.

Geiger, A. (2004). Athens security questioned as Olympics loom. *Los Angeles Times*, 11 April, p. 16.

Gertz, B. (2003). Greek spy agency tied to terror group: Athens backed anti-Turkish kurds. *The Washington Times*, 10 September, p. C4.

Gibbs, N. (2002). The winter Olympics: Hope and glory. Posted on www.time.com, 3 February.

Giroux, H. (2002). Terrorism and the fate of democracy after September 11. *Cultural Studies – Critical Methodologies*, 2(1), 9–14.

Goffman, E. (1974). *Frame analysis*. Cambridge, MA: Harvard University Press.

Gosper, K., & Korporaal, G. (2000). *An Olympic life: Melbourne 1956 to Sydney 2000*. St. Leonards, Australia: Allen & Unwin.

Guttmann, A. (2002). *The Olympics: A history of the modern games*. Chicago: University of Chicago Press.

Hall, S., Critcher, C., Jefferson, T., Clarke, J., & Roberts, B. (1978). *Policing the crisis: Mugging, the state and law and order*. London: MacMillan.

Hallin, D. (1986). *The uncensored war: The media and Vietnam*. New York: Oxford University Press.

Harasta, C. (2002). Olympic miracle: Everyone was safe. *The Dallas Morning News*, 25 February, p. C2.

Hill, C. (1995). *Olympic politics*. Manchester: Manchester University Press.

Iyengar, S. (1996). Framing responsibility for political issues. *The Annals of the American Academy of Political and Social Science*, 546, 59–70.

Iyer, P. (1996). Lost magic: Terror at the games. *Time*, 5 August, pp. 14–21.

Janofsky, M. (2002). Security kicks in before the winter games. *The New York Times*, 5 February, p. A16.

Kamalipour, Y. (2000). The TV terrorist: Media images of Middle Easterners. *Global Dialogue*, *2*(4), 89–96.

Lenart, S., & Targ, H. (1995). The media war against Nicaragua. *Peace Review*, *7*(3–4), 347–353.

Lenskyj, H. (2002). *Best games ever? The social impacts of Sydney 2000*. New York: SUNY Press.

Leonard, W. M., II (1988). *A sociological perspective of sport*. New York: MacMillan.

Lopresti, M. (2002). A homeland winter Olympics: With a few guests. *USA Today*, 9 February, p. A1.

Mandell, R. (1987). *The Nazi Olympics*. Urbana, IL: University of Illinois Press.

Michaelis, V. (2003). Security in Athens: $1 billion. *USA Today*, 27 September, p. D2.

Mizell, L. (2002). *Target USA: The inside story of the new terrorist war*. New York: Wiley.

Morris News Service. (2002). Stink bomb scare hits Olympics. *The Savannah Morning News*, 21 February, p. 14.

Murphy, B. (2003). Greek Olympics terror threat concerns FBI. *Hamilton Spectator*, 7 September, p. E2.

Northfield, D., & Bell, T. (2001). Is Salt Lake prepared to protect the masses? *NGW Online News*, posted 19 November.

Oakley, R. (2003). Huge security for Athens Olympics. Aired on *CNN*, 13 September.

O'Driscoll, P. (2002). No major security plans expected. *USA Today*, 29 January, p. C6.

Office of the (United States) Press Secretary. (2002). Preparing for the World: Homeland Security and Winter Olympics. Statement released, 10 January.

Palmer, C. (2001). Outside the imagined community: Basque terrorism, political activism, and the tour de France. *Sociology of Sport Journal*, *18*(2), 143–161.

Petrie, M. (2002). Security tight, spirits high. *Calgary Herald*, 5 February, p. D4.

Price, S. L. (1996). Stained games. *Sports Illustrated*, 5 August, pp. 22–31.

Reaves, J. (2002). Olympic security: How far should it go? Posted on www.time.com, 30 January.

Reuters Press. (1997). Explosion at Swedish stadium blunts Olympic hopes. *Globe and Mail*, 25 August, p. A12.

Roche, M. (2002). The Olympics and global citizenship. *Citizenship Studies*, *6*(2), 165–181.

Schaffer, K., & Smith, S. (2000). *The Olympics at the millennium: Power, politics and the games*. New Brunswick: Rutgers University Press.

Senn, A. (1999). *Power, politics and the Olympic games*. Champaign, IL: Human Kinetics.

Shipley, A., & Whitlock, C. (2004). In Athens it's safety at all costs. *Washington Post*, 12 August, p. A01.

Smith, R. (2004). 1.5 billion for this? *Sports Fan Magazine*, 27 August, p. 1.

Spencer, S. (2004). Armed to the rings: Soldiers outnumber athletes at Athens. *The Toronto Sun*, 8 May, p. 60.

Stearns, J., & Dunn, T. (2002). Salt Lake city ready for anything. *Reno Gazette*, 7 February, p. B3.

Vigh, M. (2002). Feds promise SLC heads up. *The Salt Lake Tribune*, 19 January, p. C10.

Visser, D. (2001). IOC chief satisfied with Salt Lake security. *Globe and Mail*, 28 October, p. 53.

Vistica, G. (2004). Tests find porous security for Athens Olympics. *The Washington Post*, 11 October, p. A11.

Vospeka, R. (2002). Olympic security planners finally relax. *Vancouver Sun*, 25 February, p. H7.

Wamsley, K., & Heine, M. (1996a). Tradition, modernity, and the construction of civic identity: The Calgary Olympics. *OLYMPIKA: The International Journal of Olympic Studies, V*, 81–90.

Wamsley, K., & Heine, M. (1996b). Don't mess with the relay, it's bad medicine: Aboriginal culture and the 1988 winter Olympic games. In: R. Barney, S. Martyn, D. Brown & G. MacDonald (Eds), *Olympic perspectives* (pp. 173–178). London, ON: The International Centre for Olympic Studies.

Whitson, D., & Macintosh, D. (1996). The global circus: International sport, tourism and the marketing of cities. *Journal of Sport and Social Issues, 20*(3), 278–295.

Wilson, S. (2001a). Olympics chief: Games will go on in Salt Lake. *Los Angeles Times*, 21 September, p. E2.

Wilson, S. (2001b). Norwegian official apologizes for Salt Lake stir. *Los Angeles Times*, 24 October, p. E10.

Wilson, S. (2004). IOC deal for cancellation insurance. *USA Today*, 19 April, p. D3.

Wilstein, S. (2004). Olympics looking like a big fat Greek mess: Athens appears to be way behind in preparations. *The Toronto Star*, 2 March, p. E1.

Young, K. (2000). Sport and violence. In: J. Coakley & E. Dunning (Eds), *Handbook of sports studies* (pp. 382–408). London: Sage.

Young, K. (2001). Toward a more inclusive sociology of sports-related violence. Paper presented at the North American Society for the Sociology of Sport, San Antonio, TX, October 31–November 4.

Zarkos, J. (2004). Raising the bar: A man, the flop and the Olympic gold medal. *Sun Valley Guide*, 17 May, p. 28.

ABOUT THE EDITORS
AND CONTRIBUTORS

Michael Atkinson is Assistant Professor of Sociology at McMaster University, Canada. His main teaching and research interests focus on body modification, violence in sport, masculine aesthetics, research methods, and figurational sociology. He has conducted ethnographic research on ticket scalpers, tattoo enthusiasts, and youth subcultures. Michael is author of *Tattooed: The Sociogenesis of a Body Art* (University of Toronto Press 2003), and has published in numerous academic journals including *The Canadian Review of Sociology and Anthropology, Sociology of Sport Journal, Sex Roles, Youth & Society* and *International Review of the Sociology of Sport*. Michael's current ethnographic projects include the study of men's cosmetic surgery, criminal violence in Canadian ice hockey, and cultures of dietary supplement use among male bodybuilders. Michael is a member of the Editorial Boards of *Deviant Behavior* and the *Sociology of Sport Journal*, and was recipient of the Social Sciences and Humanities Research Council of Canada's Aurora Award in 2004.

Douglas Booth is Professor of Sport and Leisure Studies at the University of Waikato, New Zealand. His research interests include the broad area of sport as a form of popular culture (with a particular emphasis on political relationships and processes) and historiography. He is the author of *The Race Game: Sport and Politics in South Africa* (1998), *Australian Beach Cultures: The History of Sun, Sand and Surf* (2001), *The Field: Truth and Fiction in Sport History* (2005) and, with Colin Tatz, *One-Eyed: A View of Australian Sport* (2000). He serves on the Editorial Boards of the *Journal of Sport History, Sport History Review, and The International Journal of the History of Sport*.

Douglas A. Brown is Associate Professor in the Faculty of Kinesiology at the University of Calgary. His research on sport extends across a number of disciplines including archival history, oral history, life history, and auto-ethnography. Questions related to experiences of the body and the culture of movement comprise the foundation of Brown's work. His research has been funded by the Social Sciences and Humanities Research Council of Canada as well as the International Olympic Committee. Brown has published in most of the leading international journals for the history of sport. His most innovative publications include "Fleshing-out Field Notes: Prosaic, Poetic and Picturesque Representations of Canadian Mountaineering, 1906–1940" (*The Journal of Sport History* 2003) and "The Sensual and Intellectual Pleasures of Rowing: Pierre de Coubertin's Ideal for Modern Sport" (*Sport History Review* 1999).

Hart Cantelon is Professor and Chair, Department of Kinesiology and Physical Education at the University of Lethbridge, Canada. Previously, Hart was a faculty member in the School of Physical and Health Education, Queen's University. He was also cross-appointed to the Department of Sociology. He received B.A. (1967), B.P.E. (1969), and M.A. (1972) degrees from the University of Alberta and his Ph.D. (1981) from the University of Birmingham, England. His published work includes joint editorship of *Sport, Culture and the Modern State* (with Richard Gruneau, University of Toronto Press 1982), *Leisure, Sports and Working Class Cultures* (with Robert Hollands, Garamond 1988), and *Not Just A Game* (with Jean Harvey, University of Ottawa Press 1987). The latter was also published in French (*Sport et Pouvoir: Les Enjeux Sociaux au Canada*). Hart's current research interest is the impact that the global economy has upon high performance sport.

Mark Dyreson is Associate Professor of Kinesiology and History at Pennsylvania State University, USA. He serves as the President of the North American Society for Sport History, an Associate Editor for the *International Journal of the History of Sport*, and on the Editorial Boards of the *Journal of Sport History* and *OLYMPIKA: The International Journal of Olympic Studies*. He has written extensively on sport and nationalism, and on sport and the social construction of racial and ethnic identities. He is the author of *Making the American Team: Sport, Culture, and the Olympic Experience* (University of Illinois Press 1998), as well as articles in the *Journal of Contemporary History, Sportwissenschaft*, the *Research Quarterly of Exercise and Sport Science*, the *Journal of Sport History* and numerous other historical journals.

Janice Forsyth is a faculty member of the Physical Education and Recreation Department at the University of Manitoba, Canada. She graduated from the University of Western Ontario, where she studied Canadian (Aboriginal) sport history at the International Centre for Olympic Studies. Her research focuses on how power relations shape Aboriginal sport practices in Canada. Specific areas of interest include Aboriginal participation in Olympic Games, the North American Indigenous Games, the Tom Longboat Awards, and sports and games in Canadian residential schools. In addition to her academic pursuits, she has worked for the Aboriginal Sport Circle (the national body for Aboriginal sport in Canada), Sport Canada, and the Esteem Team (a national role model programme) in sport policy-making, administration, and programme development. She is a member of the Fisher River Cree First Nation (Manitoba).

John Hoberman has been doing research on 'doping' in sport for 20 years. His publications in this field include *Mortal Engines: The Science of Performance and the Dehumanization of Sport* (1992), *Testosterone Dreams: Rejuvenation, Aphrodisia, Doping* (2005), *Doping and Public Policy* (co-edited with Verner Møller 2005), 'The History of Synthetic Testosterone' (with Charles E. Yesalis, *Scientific American* 1995), 'Listening to Steroids' (*Wilson Quarterly* 1995), 'How Drug Testing Fails: The Politics of Doping Control' (in *Doping in Elite Sport: The Politics of Drugs in the Olympic Movement* 2001), and 'Sports Physicians and the Doping Crisis in Elite Sport (*Clinical Journal of Sport Medicine*, 2002). John is Professor of Germanic Studies at the University of Texas at Austin, USA.

Barrie Houlihan is Professor of Sport Policy in the Institute of Sport and Leisure Policy at Loughborough University, UK. His research interests include the domestic and international policy processes for sport. He has a particular interest in sports development, the diplomatic use of sport, and drug abuse by athletes. His most recent books include *Elite Sport Development: Policy Learning and Political Priorities* (with Mick Green, Routledge 2005), *The Politics of Sports Development: Development Of Sport or Development Through Sport?* (with Anita White, Routledge 2002), and *Dying to Win: The Development of Anti-doping Policy* (Strasbourg: Council of Europe Press 2002). In addition to his work as a teacher and researcher, Barrie Houlihan has undertaken consultancy projects for various UK government departments, UK Sport, Sport England, the Council of Europe, and the European Union.

Bruce Kidd is Professor and Dean of the Faculty of Physical Education and Health at the University of Toronto, Canada. His books include *The Political Economy of Sport* (1979), *Athletes Rights in Canada* (1982, with Mary Eberts), *The Struggle for Canadian Sport* (1996), and *From Enforcement and Prevention to Civic Engagement: Research on Community Safety* (2004, co-edited with Jim Phillips). Bruce has been involved in the Olympic Movement throughout his adult life. He has participated in the Games as an athlete (track and field, 1964), journalist (1976), contributor to the arts and culture programmes (1976 and 1988), and accredited social scientist (1988 and 2000). He currently chairs the International Development through Sport Committee of Commonwealth Games Canada, and serves as Vice-Chair of the Sport Dispute Resolution Centre of Canada, created by the Physical Activity and Sport Act of 2003.

Arnd Krüger is Professor of Sport Studies at the George-August University of Göttingen, Germany, and served as Dean of the Social Science Faculty of his university. He is the President of the Lower Saxony Institute for Sport History. He was the founding President of the European College of Sport History, and is an International Fellow of the American Academy of Kinesiology and Physical Education. He is an active writer with over 40 books and 300 scientific articles mainly on sport history, sport management and coaching. His recent works include *The Nazi Olympics* (University of Illinois Press 2003). Arnd received his Ph.D. in Modern and Medieval History from the University of Cologne (1971) and his B.A. from UCLA (1967) where he was on its world-record distance medley team. He also participated for Germany at the 1968 Olympics. Arnd is an avid runner and recently rode his racing bicycle across the Alps.

Gertrud Pfister, a Professor at the University of Copenhagen, Denmark, studied Latin, Physical Education, History, and Sociology in Munich and Regensburg. Gertrud holds a Ph.D. in History from the University of Regensburg (1976), and a Ph.D. in Sociology from the Ruhr-Universität, Bochum (1980). Between 1981 and 2001, she was a Professor of Sport History at the Free University in Berlin and, since 2001, is Professor at the Institute of Exercise and Sport Sciences, University of Copenhagen. Gertrud is President of the International Sociology of Sport Association, and was formerly President of the International Society for the History of Physical Education and Sport (1983–2001). Her other posts have included Vice-President of the German Gymnastic Federation (1996) and Head of the

Scientific Committee of the International Association for Physical Education and Sport for Girls and Women (1993). She has been an invited speaker at numerous international congresses and universities and has published several books and more than 200 scholarly journal articles. Her main area of research is gender and sport.

Alan Tomlinson is Professor of Leisure Studies at the University of Brighton's Chelsea School, UK, where he is Area Leader of Sport and Leisure Cultures, and Head of the Chelsea School Research Centre. He studied humanities and sociology at the University of Kent, and sociology at the Master's and Doctorate level at the University of Sussex, and has written extensively and over a long period on the place of large-scale sports events in contemporary global culture. Professor Tomlinson is a former editor of *Leisure Studies* and edited the *International Review for the Sociology of Sport* from 2000 to 2003/4. He is on the editorial advisory boards of *Sport in History* and *Theory, Culture & Society*.

Cesar R. Torres is an Assistant Professor of Physical Education and Sport at the State University of New York College at Brockport, USA. He received his early professional training in Argentina and obtained his Ph.D. from Pennsylvania State University. He has served on the international Editorial Board of the *International Journal of the History of Sport*. A philosopher and historian of sport, he has written on the relationship between skills and the structure of games as well as the development of Olympism and sport in Latin America. He has published articles in the *Journal of Sport History*, the *International Journal of the History of Sport, OLYMPIKA: The International Journal of Olympic Studies*, and the *Journal of the Philosophy of Sport*. Additionally, he has authored numerous pieces in edited collections.

Kevin B. Wamsley is Associate Dean of the Faculty of Health Sciences at The University of Western Ontario, where he is also Director of the International Centre for Olympic Studies and Associate Professor in the School of Kinesiology. A sport historian, his research interests include gender and politics in the Olympic Games and sport, the state, masculinity, and violence in nineteenth century Canada. He is co-author of *Sport in Canada: A History* (2005) and co-editor of *OLYMPIKA: The International Journal of Olympic Studies*. He has published articles in such journals as *Social History, Policy Options, The International Journal, The Journal of*

Sport History, and *Sport History Review*. He has edited four books on the Olympic Games and one on historical research methodology.

Garry Whannel is Professor of Media Cultures, and Director of the Centre for International Media Analysis in the School of Media Art and Design at the University of Luton, UK. He has been writing and researching on the theme of media and sport for over 20 years and his most recent published work includes *Media Sport Stars, Masculinities and Moralities* (Routledge 2001) and (with John Horne and Alan Tomlinson) *Understanding Sport* (Routledge 1999). Previous books include *Fields in Vision: Television Sport and Cultural Transformation* (Routledge 1992) and *Blowing the Whistle: The Politics of Sport* (Pluto 1983). He also edited *Consumption and Participation: Leisure, Culture and Commerce* (LSA 2000) and has previously co-edited collections on television, leisure cultures, the Olympic Games and the World Cup. His current research interests include the politics of the Olympic bidding process and the growth of commercial sponsorship.

David Young is Professor of Classics at the University of Florida. For many years he taught at the University of California, Santa Barbara, and has held several visiting appointments at both Stanford and Ann Arbor. He has two main areas of research. He is internationally known for his research on the ancient lyric poet Pindar, as well as his work on the Olympic Games. He has given over 100 papers and lectures at major universities and conferences. His books include *Three Odes of Pindar, The Olympic Myth of Greek Amateur Athletics*, and *The Modern Olympics: A Struggle for Revival*. His latest work, an overview of the ancient Games and early years of the modern revival, is *A Brief History of the Olympic Games* (Blackwell 2004).

Kevin Young is Associate Professor of Sociology at the University of Calgary, Canada. He has published on a variety of sports-related topics such as violence, gender, and subcultural identity. His books include *Theory, Sport & Society* (with Jospeh Maguire, Elsevier Press 2002), *Sport and Gender in Canada* (with Phillip White, Oxford University Press 1999), and *Sporting Bodies, Damaged Selves: Sociological Studies of Sports-Related Injury* (Elsevier Press 2004). Kevin has served on the Editorial Boards of several journals, including the *International Review for the Sociology of Sport, Sociology of Sport Journal*, and *Soccer and Society*, as well as on the Executive Board of the North American Society for the Sociology of Sport.

He is currently serving a second 4-year, elected term as Vice-President of the International Sociology of Sport Association. He is an internationally recognised expert on aspects of sports-related violence. His current projects include studies of sport and terrorism, sports violence and the law, and sport and social control.

AUTHOR INDEX

303

SUBJECT INDEX